FOUNDATIONS OF EU FOOD LAW AND POLICY

This book offers not only a fresh perspective on the 'internal' workings of the EFSA, but also a comprehensive view of the institution as seen from the perspective of other European agencies interacting with EFSA. An excellent book on the law, policy, and polity of the EFSA, it is a very timely publication, and one which will remain relevant for many years to come.

Petros C. Mavroidis, European University Institute, Italy and University of Neuchâtel, Switzerland

This book presents a comprehensive review and analysis of the origin, history, and accomplishments of the first decade of the European Food Safety Authority, by an impressive group of experts. It is an essential volume for anyone interested in Food Law.

Peter Barton Hutt, Harvard Law School, USA

This book is a fascinating read for anyone dealing with food law and policy. Its topic represents at the same time a valuable case-study of regulatory and administrative law in action. An impressive team of authors sketches law, procedure, science and multi-level politics surrounding the past decade of food regulation in the EU. The book focuses on national, European and international regulatory cooperation, as well as dealing with topics on the fault line of law, scientific-based risk regulation and political sensitivities. This combination raises a host of questions which will be relevant well beyond the next decade of food regulation and modern public law.

Herwig C.H. Hofmann, University of Luxembourg, Luxembourg

This comprehensive edited volume makes an important contribution to the study and understanding of EU food law and the shaping of food policy with a central focus on the European Food Safety Authority. It contains a unique mixture of in-depth study, practical insights and critical analysis and gives food for thought on future challenges. I strongly recommend this impressive book to all academics and practitioners who study, and work with, EU food law and policy.

Ellen Vos, Maastricht University, The Netherlands

Foundations of EU Food Law and Policy

Ten Years of the European Food Safety Authority

Edited by

ALBERTO ALEMANNO
HEC Paris, France

SIMONE GABBI
European Food Safety Authority, Italy

Routledge
Taylor & Francis Group
LONDON AND NEW YORK

First published 2014 by Ashgate Publishing

2 Park Square, Milton Park, Abingdon, Oxon OX14 4RN
711 Third Avenue, New York, NY 10017, USA

Routledge is an imprint of the Taylor & Francis Group, an informa business

First issued in paperback 2016

British Library Cataloguing in Publication Data
A catalogue record for this book is available from the British Library

The Library of Congress has cataloged the printed edition as follows:
Foundations of EU food law and policy : ten years of the European food safety authority / edited by Alberto Alemanno and Simone Gabbi.
pages cm
Includes bibliographical references and index.
ISBN 978-1-4094-6721-2 (hardback) – ISBN 978-1-4094-6722-9 (ebook) – ISBN 978-1-4094-6723-6 (epub) 1. Food law and legislation--European Union countries. 2. European Food Safety Authority. I. Alemanno, Alberto, editor of compilation. II. Gabbi, Simone, editor of compilation. III. Title: Foundations of European Union food law and policy.
KJE6778.F68 2013
344.2404'232–dc23

2013023964

ISBN 13: 978-1-4094-6721-2 (hbk)
ISBN 13: 978-1-138-27002-2 (pbk)

Contents

List of Figures, Tables and Boxes

Figures

Tables

Boxes

Notes on Contributors

Gabriele Abels
Professor for Political System in Germany and the EU and European Integration, University of Tübingen.

Alberto Alemanno
Jean Monnet Professor of EU Law and Risk Regulation, HEC Paris.
Global Clinical Professor, New York University School of Law.
Scholar at O'Neill Institute for National and Global Health Law, Georgetown University Law Center.

David Byrne
SC, Former European Commissioner for Health and Consumer Protection.

Roberto Ciati
Scientific Relations Director, Barilla G&R Fratelli.

Sue Davies
Which? Consumer Organisation.

Patrick Deboyser
Advisor to the Director General, Health & Consumers Directorate-General, European Commission.

Marion Dreyer
Deputy Scientific Director, Dialogik.

Marine Friant-Perrot
Maître de conférences, Nantes University.

Simone Gabbi
Legal Officer, EFSA.

Amandine Garde
Professor of Law, University of Liverpool.

Catherine Geslain-Lanéelle
Outgoing Executive Director, EFSA.
Director General for agricultural, agri-food and territorial policies in the French Ministry of Agriculture, Food and Forestry.

Luis González Vaqué
Former Advisor at the European Commission and Member of the Groupe de Bruges.

Martijn Groenleer
Assistant Professor of Public Administration, Faculty of Technology, Policy and Management, Delft University of Technology.

Alexander Kobusch
PhD Candidate and Research Assistant at the Institute of Political Science, University of Tübingen.

James Lawless
Trainee solicitor at Arthur Cox Solicitors, Dublin.
PhD Candidate at the UCD School of Law and UCD Institute for Food and Health, University College Dublin.

Ching-Fu Lin
SJD Candidate, Harvard Law School.

Caoimhin MacMaoláin
Lecturer in Law, Trinity College Dublin.

Isidora Maletić
Cleary Gottlieb Steen & Hamilton LLP.
Fellow at the Centre of European Law, King's College London.

Bernd M.J. van der Meulen
Professor of Law and Governance, Wageningen University.

Citlali Pintado
Legal Officer, EFSA.

Sara Poli
Professor of EU Law, University of Pisa.

Ortwin Renn
Professor and Chair of Environmental Sociology and Technology Assessment, Stuttgart University; Director, Dialogik.

Sebastián Romero Melchor
Partner, K&L Gates LLP.

Dagmar Roth-Behrendt
Member of the European Parliament.

Raymond O'Rourke
Food and Consumer Lawyer, Ireland.

Vittorio Silano
Former Chair of EFSA's Scientific Committee.

Alessandro Spina
Legal Officer, European Medicines Agency.
Adjunct Professor of Administrative Law, Università Statale Milano.

Rozita Spirovska Vaskoska
Student in the MSc Programme Food Safety, Wageningen University.

Stephanie Tai
Associate Professor of Law, University of Wisconsin Law School.

Paola Testori Coggi
Director General, Health & Consumers Directorate-General, European Commission.

Jennifer Träsch
PhD Candidate and Research Assistant at the Institute of Political Science, University of Tübingen.

List of Abbreviations

ADI	Acceptable Daily Intake
AF	Advisory Forum
AGRC	Advisory Group on Risk Communications
ANS	(Scientific Panel on) Food Additives and Nutrient Sources
AR	Average Requirement
ARfD	Acute Reference Dose
BSE	Bovine Spongiform Encephalopathy
CA	Competent Authorities
CAC	Codex Alimentarius Commission
CCPR	Codex Committee on Pesticide Residues
CFSAN	(FDA's) Center for Food Safety and Applied Nutrition
CJD	Creutzfeld-Jacob Disease
CJEU	Court of Justice of the European Union
CVMP	(EMA's) Committee on Veterinary Medicinal Products
DBES	Data Based Export Schemes
Defra	(UK) Department for Environment, Food and Rural Affairs
DG SANCO	Directorate General for Health and Consumers
EASA	European Aviation Safety Agency
EC	European Commission
ECDC	European Centre for Disease Prevention and Control
ECHA	European Chemicals Agency
EDB	Expert Database
EEA	European Environment Agency
EFSA	European Food Safety Authority
EMA	European Medicines Agency
EMCDDA	European Monitoring Centre for Drugs and Drug Addiction
EP	European Parliament
EPA	Environmental Protection Agency
EPPO	European and Mediterranean Plant Protection Agency
ERA	Environmental Risk Assessment
ERI	Emerging Risk Identification
ESCO	EFSA Scientific Cooperation
EU	European Union
EU-OSHA	European Agency for Safety and Health at Work
FAO	Food and Agriculture Organization
FDA	Food and Drug Administration

FEEDAP	Panel on Additives and Products or Substances used in Animal Feed
FP	Framework Programme/Focal Point
GFL	General Food Law
GMO	Genetically Modified Organism
IEP	Information Exchange Platform
IPPC	International Plant Protection Convention
IRGC	International Risk Governance Council
JECFA	Joint FAO/WHO Expert Meeting on Food Additives
JMPR	Joint FAO/WHO Meeting on Pesticide Residues
MEP	Member of the European Parliament
MRL	Maximum Residue Level
MS	Member State
NCD	Non-Communicable Disease
NDA	Nutrition, Dietetic Products and Allergies Panel
NGO	Non-Governmental Organisation
OECD	Organisation for Economic Cooperation and Development
OIE	World Organisation for Animal Health
PAP	Processed Animal Proteins
PMEM	Post Market Environmental Monitoring
PRAS	Pesticides Scientific Panel
PRI	Population Reference Intake
RA	Risk Assessment
RASFF	Rapid Alert System for Food and Feed
SCFCAH	Standing Committee on the Food Chain and Animal Health
SCISTRAT	Science Strategy and Cooperation Directorate
SGC	Steering Group on Cooperation
SPS	Sanitary and Phitosanitary
SSC	Scientific Steering Committee
TEU	Treaty on European Union
TFEU	Treaty on the Functioning of the European Union
WHO	World Health Organization
WTO	World Trade Organization

Foreword

Catherine Geslain-Lanéelle

Those involved in the food crises that hit Europe during the 1990s and early 2000s reflect on this period as one of the most turbulent in the modern history of European food safety. The negative newspaper headlines across Europe at that time reflect public concern over food scares such as dioxins, BSE and GM foods. In Belgium, the government had fallen on the back of the dioxin crisis, the European beef market was close to collapse and relations between Member States were strained. European unity itself was in danger. In hindsight, the events represented a watershed in European food safety, moving from a position where the emphasis was on the effective functioning of the internal market to one in which the protection of public health was paramount. This paradigm shift in philosophy is reflected in the ground-breaking policymaking that immediately ensued which paved the way for institutional reform including the establishment of the European Food Safety Authority and the placing of EU risk management responsibility in the hands of the then newly formed Directorate General for Health & Consumer Protection. The response of the legislators was swift and effective, led by the Commission's White Paper on Food Safety 2000 which argued effectively for the separation of risk assessment and risk management, and later by Regulation (EC) No 178/2002 which laid down the principles of the general food law and put science firmly at the centre of food policy.

Building on the lessons learned from the previous decade, EFSA was founded on the principles of scientific excellence – first and foremost – and independence, transparency and openness. It was deliberately structured to have its own legal identity, distinct from that of the EU institutions. While it can be mandated by a limited number of institutions, including the European Commission, Member States, and the European Parliament, EFSA has the ability to self-task where it considers that an important knowledge or data gap exists. It has used this in a limited manner to ensure that vital knowledge gaps are filled.

Europe can see the fruits of its investment in risk assessment; the *c.*3,000 scientific outputs that EFSA has produced since inception provide a robust evidence base for EU food policy. And while the Union has continued to experience various food emergencies over the past decade, their impact has been contained, in terms of both public health and economic impact. Large strides have been made in crucial public health areas such as the dramatic reductions in Salmonella and BSE cases and reduced exposure to food colours. In evaluating the scientific basis for more than 3,000 health claims on food, our consumers can have greater confidence in the food labels on supermarket shelves. Furthermore, as obesity emerges as the greatest public health challenge of our time, EFSA is making its mark; its advice on nutrient intakes provides an important evidence base to underpin nutrition policies, the setting of diet-related public health targets and the development of consumer information and education programmes on healthy diets.

EFSA was also given the remit of independent communication to the public; when one considers that the Authority was established on the back of a deficit in public trust, this remains a crucially important aspect of its mission. Since the turn of the century it is no exaggeration to say that there has been a sea change in public communication on the measures taken to protect citizens and, in the new governance model for food safety, transparency is a prerequisite. EFSA uses a variety of mechanisms to ensure that its scientific decision-making is accessible to all: webcasting of Management Board meetings, publication of the minutes of plenary meetings on EFSA's website, open access to declarations of interest, public access to EFSA's ongoing mandates, public consultations on key documents and consultative workshops are all part of the mix that ensures we use every available opportunity to support this core organisational value.

Independence should not be confused with isolation; in reality European cooperation in the field of food safety has been transformed over the past decade, underpinned by the strong platform provided by the Founding Regulation. With many national food safety agencies established around the same time as EFSA and based on similar principles, the risk of duplication of effort existed. Moreover, Europe has a finite supply of scientific expertise in risk assessment and budgets are understandably tight. Consequently, this has required effective planning and sharing of work programmes with Member States, an activity that has been greatly facilitated by the Advisory Forum network, EFSA's bridge to the national food safety agencies. And EFSA has invested heavily in scientific cooperation; in recent years, the Authority has increasingly funded preparatory work for its scientific opinions in Member State institutions. In 2005, €1 m was available for such scientific cooperation under Article 36 of EFSA's Founding Regulation whereas in 2012 the corresponding value is over €9 m.

In the globalised trade environment that characterises the Union today, it is also vital that EFSA's voice is heard in the international risk assessment arena. This ensures we have access to the data to deal with the risks associated with the globalised food chain, bearing in mind that the food sector is the EU's most important economic sector and that the EU is the biggest global trading bloc in foodstuffs and ingredients. Many of the food products on European tables originate from countries with standards that differ widely from those of the Union and it is important to be vigilant to hazards. The Union Rapid Alert System for Food and Feed (RASFF) remains a key tool to counter any threats and is a key information source in EFSA's identification of emerging risks. Some of the notifications in the RASFF system result in urgent requests for advice to EFSA and every year we deal with a small but significant number of such requests that can result in reprioritisation of workloads. Such was the case in 2011 when the outbreak of

Shiga-toxin producing *Escherichia coli* (STEC), serotype O104:H4 meant that we had to focus our attention on providing both scientific advice and, for the first time, technical assistance, working alongside our German counterparts to trace the source of the outbreak.

Europe has moved on since EFSA was established: globalisation has continued unabated, the obesity epidemic is undiminished, the effects of climate change can be seen in the northern movement of crop pests and animal diseases, the age profile of our 500 million citizens continues to increase, and the Union finds itself in challenging economic circumstances. Furthermore, public trust in science continues to be eroded, fuelled by a number of controversies in fields such as climate change and pharmacovigilance, and science itself is increasingly politicised. Like many like-minded public scientific organisations, the independence of EFSA's scientific advice has been called into question and, recognising the importance of public confidence in its work, EFSA has regularly reviewed and strengthened its independence safeguards.

EFSA's operating environment will continue to evolve and it must ensure that it will be prepared to meet the challenges. We have already seen EFSA's work programme progressively change to include more evaluation of regulated products, environmental risk assessments, post-market monitoring of products and assessment of risk-benefit. Changes in the regulatory environment, emerging technologies, socio-demographic shifts, novel communication technologies and even climate change will continue to impact on our work programme and it is important that we prioritise our work to ensure that we can meet the needs of risk managers in the public health area while simultaneously supporting innovation in the Union's agri-food sector. Unsurprisingly, EFSA's *Science Strategy 2012–16* is one of our most important recent strategic documents and it will guide the further development of EFSA's scientific excellence, the evidence base for its risk assessments and the methodologies it uses to assess risks. The availability of adequate risk assessment capacity is a key consideration going forward; the science of risk assessment in relation to food and feed brings together a range of disciplines, including aspects of inter alia toxicology, physiology and biology, and the pool of expertise in Europe is finite. The *Science Strategy 2012–16* recognises the importance of maintaining and building that pool of expertise and outlines the role that EFSA will play in this process, such as training, engagement of seconded experts from Member States, and the creation of risk assessment communities. It also recognises the importance of prioritising requests for scientific advice and EFSA's Scientific Committee is as I write developing a risk ranking project to ensure that our work is aligned with the key public health concerns.

Looking forward, EFSA will be guided by the recommendations of its Management Board of late 2012 which, based on the second external evaluation of the agency, provide robust directions to guide the Authority in the coming years. With the support of its committed staff, stakeholders, partner institutions at national and EU levels, and the 1,000+ experts who contribute voluntarily to its work annually, EFSA will continue to deliver fit-for-purpose advice for Europe's risk managers to ensure that our citizens and our environment enjoy the highest levels of protection.

'Foundations of EU Food Law and Policy' is a timely publication greatly advances our understanding in this complex domain and represents an important addition to the literature available on the subject. It covers many topics that are highly relevant to practitioners and professionals alike and are not adequately addressed elsewhere.

Acknowledgements

We are grateful to the contributors for accepting to offer their personal views on the genesis, evolution and overall nature of EU food law and, in particular, for sharing their own visions of the first ten years of the European Food Safety Authority. This is especially appreciated considering their endless patience in accepting our demanding and multiple remarks on their first submissions and for promptly revising their manuscripts accordingly. A special thanks goes to Catherine Geslain-Lanéelle, outgoing EFSA Executive Director, for her usual support and enthusiasm to personally contribute to this editorial project. We also thank her Chief of Staff, Alberto Spagnolli for his patient assistance along the editorial project. A special thank goes to Peter Barton Hutt (Harvard Law School), one of the founding fathers of food law as an autonomous discipline and a continuous source of inspiration for food law practitioners and thinkers around the world.

We are also grateful to Petros Mavroidis (European University Institute), Ellen Vos (Maastricht University) and Herwig Hofmann (University of Luxembourg) for agreeing to review the manuscript of this volume before its actual publication. All errors and omissions remain the sole responsibility of the co-editors and the individual contributors.

We are also very appreciative of the excellent research assistance, spell-check and copy-editing carried out by Cliff Wirajendi, Scott Lee and Adam Jaffee.

We hope that our volume will accompany and provide a useful source of reference to the increasing number of lawyers, regulatory affairs experts, policymakers, lobbyists, consumer organization representatives and other civil society's organizations, journalists, researchers and academics who populate the fascinating world of food law and policy in Europe and beyond. This book is dedicated to them.

Alberto Alemanno and Simone Gabbi
Paris-Parma, September 2013

Introduction
Foundations of EU Food Law and Policy

Alberto Alemanno

This book revisits and discusses EU food law and policy by bringing together for the first time the viewpoints of academics, policymakers, industry representatives as well as those of food practitioners who are exposed daily to this emerging area of study and practice. It was timed to celebrate the 10-year anniversary of the establishment of the European Food Safety Authority (EFSA). Its broader purpose, however, is to discuss EFSA's future role within the rapidly evolving EU food law regime while at the same identifying new trends of EU food law by focusing on EFSA. Indeed, the Authority and the EU substantive food law regime are, and have always been since their very inception, intertwined to the point that they cannot be unambiguously separated. Hence the methodological choice made in this book to focus on EFSA in order to apprehend the broader, substantive normative framework of EU food law while at the same time discussing substantive EU food law with the aim to better grasp EFSA's rationale and future trajectories.

Genesis

Ten years ago, when both editors of this volume were about to embark on their PhD dissertations, neither EFSA nor EU food law were in existence. Yet they both decided, although unknowingly of one another, to place the cursor of our respective analysis on EU food law and, in particular, on EFSA.[1] This is not to assert our clairvoyance in our choice of dissertation topic nor to claim our individual and collective legitimacy in editing the present volume, but to rather highlight the relative young age of EU food law as an autonomous area of EU law. By now, EU food law has not only acquired its autonomy within EU law and vis-à-vis other disciplines, such as administrative and agricultural law, but – similar to what occurred to food law in general – it also reached a state of maturity, both in the academic world and in the world of practice, with more and more universities offering courses in food law and law firms providing their legal services to the food industry.[2]

---

1 A. Alemanno, *Trade in Food – Regulatory and Judicial Approaches in the EC and the WTO*, Cameron May, 2007; S. Gabbi, *L'Autorità europea per la sicurezza alimentare – Genesi, aspetti problematici e prospettive di riforma*, Giuffrè, 2009.

2 For a useful overview, The Harvard Food Law and Policy Clinic and the Harvard Food Law Society have prepared a Food Law and Policy Career Guide that is available

Scope

The challenge for our volume is not only to account for this process of progressive autonomisation and burgeoning of food law in Europe and beyond, but also to illustrate how this emerging body of law remains today a rapidly evolving discipline, both in the fields of study and practice. The very concept of food law, defined as 'laws, regulations and administrative provisions governing food in general, and food safety in particular, whether at Community or national level',[3] provided by the General Food Regulation (hereinafter, GFR),[4] seems to continuously evolve. In contrast to the original view of food law as a set of food safety rules, the study and practice have moved towards a broader understanding of the discipline. As of today, food law includes, for example, an increasing number of legislative measures pursuing quality objectives,[5] such as the EU quality schemes of geographical indications[6] and organic farming.[7] Similarly, amid the adoption of some ambitious pieces of legislation such as the Nutrition and Health Claims Regulation,[8] the boundaries of EU food law have been significantly extended so as to encompass also nutritional aspects of food. Moreover, in the light of this continuous shift from safety to quality and now to nutritional and lifestyle objectives, it seems to have been increasingly accepted that food law can rely on a set of mechanisms other than those commonly typified as 'command and control'[9] in order to attain such

at http://blogs.law.harvard.edu/foodpolicyinitiative/careers-in-food-law-and-policy/guide/.

3 Article 3 (1) of Regulation 178/2002 of the European Parliament and of the Council of 28 January 2002 laying down the general principles and requirements of food law, establishing the European Food Safety Authority and laying down procedures in matters of food safety [2002] OJ L 31/1.

4 Regulation 178/2002 of the European Parliament and of the Council of 28 January 2002 laying down the general principles and requirements of food law, establishing the EFSA and laying down procedures in matters of food safety [2002] OJ L 31/1.

5 Regulation (EU) No 1151/2012 of the European Parliament and of the Council of 21 November 2012 on quality schemes for agricultural products and foodstuffs (OJ L343, 14.12.2012, p. 1).

6 Council Regulation (EC) No 510/2006 of 20 March 2006 on the protection of geographical indications and designations of origin for agricultural products and foodstuffs (OJ L 93, 31.3.2006, pp. 12–25); Council Regulation (EC) No 509/2006 of 20 March 2006 on agricultural products and foodstuffs as traditional specialities guaranteed (OJ L 93, 31.3.2006, pp. 1–11).

7 Council Regulation (EC) No 834/2007 of 28 June 2007 on organic production and labelling of organic products and repealing Regulation (EEC) No 2092/91 (OJ L 189 of 20.7.2007).

8 Regulation (EC) 1924/2006 of the European Parliament and of the Council of 20 December 2006 on nutrition and health claims made on foods (OJ L 404/9 of 30.12.2006) (hereinafter, the 'Claims Regulation').

9 Command and Control (CAC) can be defined as 'the direct regulation of an industry or activity by legislation that states what is permitted and what is illegal'. This approach differs from other regulatory techniques, e.g. the use of economic incentives, which

objectives.[10] This is certainly the case of the nascent European policy aimed at promoting healthy diets.[11] This policy relies not only on the consumer information paradigm, which aims at empowering consumers in their food choices, but also on the use of other alternative regulatory approaches, such as self-regulation.[12] This effort has recently been tested and operationalised through the creation of a multi-stakeholder platform aimed at the conclusion of voluntary commitments by the industry and the Member States, on issues such as food reformulation, marketing and advertising restrictions.[13] Although not formally falling within the scope of the actual definition of food law as enshrined in the General Food Regulation, these initiatives clearly epitomise today one of the 'new directions in EU Food Law and Policy'. At the same time, Member States are experimenting with new market-based mechanisms at the national level, with countries such a Hungary levying a 'fat tax' on unhealthy products[14] and some timid EU-wide initiatives inspired by behavioural research.[15] It is no surprise that, as a result of the evolution and expansion of the EU food regulatory framework, EFSA has been invested with new responsibilities that were largely borne by national risk assessment bodies, such as for instance the assessment of genetically modified organisms (GMOs) and food additives, while at the same time taking up new roles such as conducting environmental impact assessments in relation to GMOs and, as foreseen in the case of pesticides, to weigh risks and benefits.[16] Moreover, as the EU has progressively addressed the health impact of obesity and diet-related diseases, EFSA's work in

---

frequently includes the use of taxes and subsidies as incentives for compliance. R. Baldwin, M. Cave, M. Lodge, *Understanding Regulation: Theory, Strategy and Practice*, 2nd edn (Oxford: Oxford University Press, 2011).

10 S. Planzer and A. Alemanno, 'Lifestyle Risks: Conceptualizing an Emerging Category of Research', 4(1) *European Journal of Risk Regulation* (2010), pp. 335–7.

11 See Chapter 8, 'From BSE to Obesity – EFSA's Growing Role in the EU's Nutrition Policy', by A. Garde and M. Friant-Perrot.

12 Interinstitutional agreement on better law-making (OJ C 321, 31.12.2003, pp. 1–5).

13 See, e.g., the EU Pledge. This is a voluntary initiative by leading food and beverage companies to change the way they advertise to children. This is a response from industry leaders to calls made by the EU institutions for the food industry to use commercial communications to support parents in making the right diet and lifestyle choices for their children.

14 A. Alemanno, and I. Carreno, 'Fat Taxes in the European Union between Fiscal Austerity and the Fight against Obesity', 4(2) *European Journal of Risk Regulation* (2011), pp. 571–6.

15 A. Alemanno, O. Amir, L. Bovens, A. Burgess, O. Lobel, E. Selinger and K.P. Whyte, 'Nudging Healthy Lifestyles – Informing Regulatory Governance with Behavioural Research', 1(3) *European Journal of Risk Regulation* (2012), pp. 3–46.

16 See Chapter 4, 'The Scientific Governance of EFSA: *Status quo* and Perspectives', by S. Gabbi.

areas related to dietary advice and nutrition has grown and includes today nutrient profiling and dietary reference values as well as nutrition and health claims.

Objectives

By revisiting and discussing the milestones in the history of EFSA – while keeping an eye on the evolution of the underlying EU food regime – this volume presents, from a variety of perspectives, forward-looking views of food leaders and practitioners on the future scientific and regulatory challenges facing the European Union. In particular, by providing a critical assessment of the Agency's activities within its different areas of work, this volume offers readers a set of innovative tools for evaluating policy recommendations and better equips experts and the public to address pressing regulatory issues in this emotive area of law and policy. Despite its celebratory mood, this volume is more about the future than the past of EU food law and policy.

It is in this context that this book and its assessment of the first 10 years of EU food law must not be seen as primarily aimed at praising or criticising the operation of its primary institutional machinery: EFSA. More constructively, it identifies many of the current and future challenges faced by EFSA and its regulatory regime, while at the same time looking at the Authority's first years of operation. It eventually strives to provide some ideas on how such challenges may be successfully addressed in the future.

Structure

We have asked each contributor to tailor his/her contribution so as to offer both a *diachronic perspective* (how EFSA's role has evolved/devolved through time within the broader EU food law and policy) and a *normative perspective* (what EFSA should have done differently) while assessing how EFSA has discharged its mandate.

While it does not seem possible to do justice to the diversity and wealth of comments that the reader will find in the subsequent pages, we will try to briefly identify the major findings of each chapter herewith contained.

This volume proceeds in two main parts: Part I offers the 'view from within' the Authority by focusing on its genesis and is organised along EFSA's dual mandate: scientific advice and scientific communication. Part II gathers instead the 'view from outside' the Authority by providing the perspective of the main EU institutions interacting with EFSA. These include that of the EU Member States, as well as those of its main stakeholders: the industry, the consumers, the food lawyer, the food law professor and, finally, that of other food safety bodies located overseas, such as in the United States, as well as international and global bodies.

Main Findings

The regulation of food involves, as is often the case in the European legal order, a complex interaction of a number of different actors within novel systems of supranational governance that are historically determined, relatively new and continuously evolving. This embraces not only several European institutions, including EFSA, but also local authorities in addition to central institutions of the Member States. As a result, the emerging structure, generally described as a network, involves many layers of responsibility for the development and administration of EU food law. Yet, only 10 years ago, despite the existence of an extensive body of EU legislation, the EU lacked a coherent, principle-based framework capable of ensuring a consistent, scientifically sound and coordinated framework for food safety.

It is against this backdrop that in Chapter 1 one of EFSA's founding fathers, the then Commissioner for Health and Consumer Protection, David Byrne, sets the scene for Part I of the book. He reminds us that EFSA and EU food law found their origins in one of the most difficult moments of EU integration and that, as a result, both respond first and foremost to a political objective: to regain the trust of EU citizens in the safety of the food they eat as well as in those responsible for protecting the public from food safety-related risks. This is the rationale and main driver behind the establishment of EFSA and the laying out of the general principles of EU law. Indeed, while the establishment of EFSA was the most salient innovation introduced by the reform of the EU food regulation, the Authority merely represents one component of an entirely new strategy adopted by the European Union in relation to food safety. Since it stems from the establishment of the Authority itself, the European legislator has opted not solely for a functional separation of the risk management element (the EU Commission and the Member States) from the risk assessment element (EFSA) but also for an institutional separation between these two main components of risk analysis.

The subsequent two sections of Part I focus on EFSA's twofold overall mission: independent scientific advice on all aspects relating to food safety (the Authority as a risk assessor) and communication and dialogue with consumers on food safety and health issues (the Authority as a risk communicator).

The Authority's primary responsibilities are to deliver independent, high-quality and timely scientific advice on risks in the food chain from farm to fork in an integrated manner and to convey those risks in an open manner to all interested parties and the public at large. As the first Chair of EFSA's Scientific Committee, Vittorio Silano had to operationalise the Authority's initial mission by envisioning the governance – and assuring its functioning – of EFSA's scientific production. By leveraging his first-hand experience, Chapter 2 reconstructs the genesis and evolution of EFSA's science strategy by also envisaging some future scenarios. After taking stock of what the Authority has achieved in its first 10 years of existence, the chapter identifies the drivers for progress and change. In particular, it enlists and offers an analysis of the following: the evolving European policy context; the nature and volume of EFSA's workload, the economic context, the prospect of a stable budgetary situation for the duration of the strategy as well as the possibility of EFSA receiving fees for some of its work. In the author's view, the Authority's operating context has evolved considerably over the years, driven by, for example, scientific and technological advancement and the changing legislative framework and, as the organisation has matured, also by its scientific capacity. These evolutions are reflected in EFSA's scientific work programme, characterised in recent years by an emphasis on the evaluation of regulated products, and in particular by a more prominent assessment of environmental risk and risk-benefit and the post-market monitoring of authorised products.

Chapter 3, in turn, provides a pioneering taxonomy of EFSA's outputs aimed at systematising the different scientific products and their workflow within the Authority's services. Citlali Pintado, a Legal Officer at EFSA's Legal and Regulatory Affairs Unit, illustrates the work leading to the definition of EFSA's outputs. She discusses their individual main features as well as the procedural and substantive rules defining their legal status. This is a significant contribution to the important debate regarding the nature of EFSA outputs and their legal status.

The subsequent chapter, written by Simone Gabbi, co-editor of this volume and also Legal Officer at the Authority, delves instead into EFSA's institutional architecture. It provides an analytical, normative and prescriptive evaluation of the overall scientific governance structure of the Authority. The absence in the General Food Regulation of a specific governance model provided EFSA with great discretion to design its operational structure but, at the same time, led the Authority to go through numerous reorganisations since its inception. In the author's view, when compared to the original structure and subsequent transformations, the latest reform is the first to do justice to EFSA's increasing evaluation work in the context of the authorisation procedures of substances, organisms, products or claims, to the benefit of the relevant industries. Yet the same chapter predicts that the actual scientific system, being centred on experts contributing to EFSA's work, is set to reach its structural limits, especially in the light of the progressive centralisation of food and feed authorisation processes at the EU level. While addressing this challenge, EFSA should think creatively and resist the call to choose between pursuing the panel system and internalising its scientific activities. A look at the authorisation procedure for active substances and for setting MRLs for pesticides seems to suggest that EFSA may provide its scientific inputs according to an alternative and more balanced approach. This may consist of entrusting EFSA with a peer review mandate over the scientific evaluations made by the Member States. This lighter scientific involvement of EFSA could strike a reasonable balance between the Panels' limited resources and the need to have EFSA's high expertise brought into the process.

Since EFSA neither runs scientific studies nor possesses labs, but merely reviews the results of tests carried out by other scientific entities, it requires not only a high level of scientific expertise but also some information sharing. These peculiar features of EFSA are closely analysed by Gabriele Abels, Alexander Kobusch and Jennifer Träsch in Chapter 5, which focuses in particular on the relationship between EFSA and national food safety authorities. They portray EFSA as a 'networked agency', mirroring the network architecture between the national and European levels, capable of incorporating national expertise into EU science-making.

Although EFSA's mandate clearly excludes any risk management role, the Authority enjoys some significant authority in those food safety issues marked by urgency and considerable uncertainty. It is against this backdrop that Chapter 6, by James Lawless, explores EFSA's role in 'emergencies', 'crises' as well as vis-à-vis 'emerging risks'. In so doing, it offers an unprecedented legal and empirical examination of each of these notions and of EFSA's related powers. While the differences between these situations are not always clear, the Authority granted to and the role played by EFSA in each of these scenarios seems less dubious. While EFSA's role vis-à-vis emergency risks is limited to proactive information gathering, the Authority is entrusted to play a major part in both emergencies and crisis management situations. In emergencies, the Authority may indeed be called upon to solve ex post disputes between Member States and the Commission over the extent of a cross-border risk, or the adequacy of the chosen risk management measures. Finally, in crisis management, EFSA may also be directly involved not only in the planning of a general strategy for crisis management but also in forming a crisis unit.

In assessing how EFSA discharges its scientific advice mandate, there is no more interesting area to focus upon than that of GMOs. This is not only because of the controversial character of the EU regulatory approach towards biotechnologies, but also because of the frequent criticisms that both Member States and NGOs periodically direct at the Authority. In Chapter 7, Sara Poli offers a detailed and nuanced legal and public policy appraisal of EFSA's role in the evaluation of GMOs. By providing a diachronic survey of EFSA GMO-related activities, this chapter focuses on the most salient actions taken by the Authority and their impact on the efficiency of the EU GMO approval procedures. In the author's view, under the current regulatory framework, EFSA rightly abstains from the discussion on how to integrate socioeconomic factors into the EU authorisation system and should therefore not be blamed for its scientifically plausible stance.

The other sensible, yet more recent, area of work for EFSA is its role in guaranteeing and maximising the nutritional potential of food. Chapter 8, written by Marine Friant-Perrot and Amandine Garde, takes up the challenge of reconstructing and defining the Authority's three main areas of nutrition intervention: (i) the scientific substantiation of health claims, (ii) the establishment of nutrient profiles and (iii) the setting of dietary reference values. While EFSA operates independently and quite transparently also when delivering its scientific advice in the field of nutrition, it encounters – in the authors' view – more difficulties than those it faces when performing other tasks. This seems to be due to the inherent difficulty to distinguish between the analysis of a given food and the reference food model that is used. In other words, being that nutrition expertise is the result of a close interaction between nutrition and social norms, the role that

EFSA is called upon to play in discharging its nutrition mandate nudges it beyond its comfort zone. By referring to the lessons learned from the assessment of the nutrition and health claims as well as the current impasse on nutrition profiles, the chapter builds a case for integrating into EFSA's scientific evaluation system in the nutrition field a socioeconomic approach to be offered by a second circle of experts with relevant experience in social sciences.

The other major task entrusted to the Authority is to convey the risks associated with the food chain. The rationale for this specific competence is that, by disclosing risk in an open and transparent way based on the independent advice of its scientific expert panels, EFSA can help regain public confidence in the way food risks are assessed. Interestingly enough, the Commission, being concerned about losing too much of this prerogative, remains entrusted with the communication of risk management decisions, even though they are based on EFSA's scientific output. As a result, while EFSA's mission includes communication of scientific information on risk, the Commission is responsible for communicating risk management measures. The resulting shared responsibility in relation to food risk communication offers an insightful lens to understand the existing relationship between the Authority and the Commission and, more in general terms, on the overall effectiveness of EU food governance. It is against this backdrop that Raymond O'Rourke offers a critical analysis of EFSA's risk communication mandate by analysing some of the Authority's most salient communication test cases, including the aspartame scare as well as the more recent German e-coli outbreak. In his view, EFSA performed an effective risk communication strategy only in those circumstances, such as in the aspartame case, in which the dynamics of shared competence did not hinder its activity. Instead, the food crises, such as the Irish pork contamination and the e-coli outbreak, showed the inherent limits of a shared system of risk communication, by leaving EFSA 'in a limbo area' between the Commission and the relevant Member State(s). The handling of the recent 'horsemeat scandal' – whose appearance coincided with the publication of this volume – seems to confirm O'Rourke's claim.

In any event, the risk communication mandate entrusted to EFSA has not been conceived as a one-way street boiling down to the Authority's efforts to convey its scientific output directly to the public. The challenge for EFSA when exercising its risk communication competence is more nuanced. On the one hand, the Authority is set to disseminate complex information in a consumer-friendly way in order to become the indispensable port-of-call for the most up-to-date data on food risk. On the other hand, it is also expected to provide more and improved opportunities for the consultation of both industry and civil society actors in relation to the exercise of its scientific tasks. In other words, communication goes both ways. It is precisely in this context that Chapter 10, which closes Part I of the volume, focuses on the role of stakeholder and public involvement in EFSA. Marion Dreyer and Ortwin Renn, the latter being one of the members of EFSA's Advisory Group on Risk Communications, emphasise how the opening up of the scientific advice to non-expert actors represented a true procedural innovation of the EU food safety system. By shifting away from the old expert-dominated risk paradigm, in which the public found little voice, the EU food scientific evaluation system embraced a more inclusive governance model defined as EFSA's 'glass house'. After illustrating the socio-political context and identifying the main drivers behind such a development, the chapter describes and critically analyses EFSA's stakeholder policy and its developing public involvement procedures within the broader framework of risk governance. The authors' view is that despite the significant progress in ensuring EFSA's interaction with stakeholders, the current participatory mechanisms are not designed to capture and deliberate over the wider concerns and expectations of individuals and social groups. It is against this backdrop that they build a case for the establishment – besides the current Advisory Group on Risk Communications – of a 'concern assessment' panel in EFSA made of experts with a background in the social, psychological and economic sciences. This proposal echoes the ideas advanced by Marine Friant-Perrot and Amandine Garde in Chapter 8 in which they call upon the creation of a socioeconomic panel in the area of nutrition evaluation.

The second part of the volume takes the reader outside the Authority thus allowing him/her to look at EFSA through the lenses of other actors. Since EFSA and its broader EU food law regime do not live in a normative vacuum, but are subject to a set of external constraints and interact and affect a multitude of actors, the following chapters broaden our perception of the role played by EFSA within the larger food safety normative framework.

To start with, Chapter 11, by Paola Testori Coggi and Patrick Deboyser, provides the EU Commission's view. As is well known, DG SANCO is the Directorate-General *de tutelle* of the Authority and, as such, it assures the interaction between EFSA and the EU Commission. In this chapter, the authors, who both have been heavily involved in the establishment of EFSA as well as in the drafting of the GFR, offer the Commission's view of the Authority by first reconstructing its genesis and then by comparing the Authority with the other agency under the supervision of DG SANCO: the European Medicines Agency (EMA). They highlight the distinct contexts and missions initially entrusted to these two agencies. Moreover, they detect and underscore some progressive convergence between these two agencies, especially since EMA's mandate has gradually shifted from the free movement imperative to a consumer protection objective.

The subsequent chapter, written by Alessandro Spina, Legal Officer at the EMA, provides the EU agencies' perspective on EFSA's scientific activities. Under the title 'Scientific Expertise and Open Government in the Digital Era: A View from the EU Agencies', this contribution looks at agencies as informational organisations and contextualises them within the open government discourse.[17] It predominantly focuses on the challenges confronting EFSA, but also to EMA and

17 Open government is the governing doctrine that holds that citizens have the right to access the documents and proceedings of the government to allow for effective public oversight. See, e.g., Lathrop, Daniel; Ruma, Laurel (eds), *Open Government: Transparency, Collaboration and Participation in Practice*, O'Reilly Media (February 2010).

several other EU agencies, by the growing demand of access to their data. It is the author's view that the imperative of open government carries the potential to turn EFSA, as well as other EU agencies, from mere providers of technical information to managers of information platforms. In particular, Alessandro argues that open government might have a special significance for EFSA and other EU agencies because it would lead them to engage the public in deliberations and decisions that have a direct and often important consequence on their lives. Agencies should learn from emerging collective crowdsourcing of expertise existing out there and adapt these existing spontaneous models to their institutional setting. Once more, the theme of public participation in EFSA's scientific work resonates throughout this chapter.

Although EFSA has been conceived as the privileged source of food scientific advice in the EU, its output is not binding for the EU institutions and other food actors. In his chapter devoted to the legal status of EFSA's outputs and more in general to the judicial review of EFSA's activities, Caoimhin MacMaoláin takes this atypical feature of the EU food safety decision-making process as a point of departure for his subsequent analysis. He demonstrates that although the Authority can be held to account for its actions, this might occur in limited and well-defined circumstances. After describing in great detail, with the help of the relevant case law, the main avenues to review EFSA's action, the author claims that, despite the limited legal effects stemming from its scientific output, there should be more opportunities to make them more readily subject to the scrutiny of judicial review.

It is time to scrutinise the European Parliament's perspective on EFSA. Chapter 14, written by one of the most attentive and skilled MEPs working on food issues, Dagmar Roth-Behrendt, surveys the past, present and future challenges for EFSA. She predicts that the European Parliament will always remain particularly demanding as regards EFSA's scientific work, by requiring the Authority to ensure scientific independence and the highest sound scientific evidence and transparency. As the shadow of past food safety crises gradually vanishes, this author encourages all EU institutions not to wait for future crises to adopt bold decisions to further improve the overall systems. She inter alia draws attention to the urgent need to introduce mandatory electronic identification of bovines. In the aftermath of the horsemeat scandal her call sounds particularly prescient.

The last but by no means least of the institutional actors and daily interlocutors of the Authority are the EU Member States and their national food authorities. This is due to the fact that scientific cooperation is expressly delineated in the original institutional design of the Authority, as well as in its underlying normative framework. Chapter 15, by Isidora Maletić, explores the relationships existing between Member States and the Authority against the general background offered by EU law. In particular, this chapter studies the dynamics of this interaction by scrutinising several instances in which EFSA's involvement has been of considerable importance from the perspective of national authorities in the context of EU harmonisation. The chapter explores the use of scientific expertise in EU harmonisation and, more particularly, the role played by EFSA within that context from the perspective of the Member States.

As previously discussed, despite its required insular nature, which is needed to protect its scientific mission from external influence, EFSA does not live in a EU institutional 'bubble'. Rather, under the current food regulatory framework, it is confronted on a daily basis with a multitude of external actors, such as industry representatives, consumer organisations, food lawyers and consultants, as well as academics. The following chapters, written by representatives of each of those groups, provide their corresponding perspectives. Thus, Chapter 16, by Roberto Ciati, articulates the viewpoint of the food industry. While welcoming the establishment of a European agency with distinct competence on food safety issues, his chapter aims to identify possible areas for improvement by selectively focusing on two key issues of EFSA's functioning: its independence and transparency as well as its relationship with third parties. We learn that the industry expects EFSA to guarantee a more transparent path and open interaction with all the best experts, including those coming from the industry. This would not only meet the industry's own vested interest in legal certainty but could also provide consumers with clear and science-based opinions. Moreover, the chapter emphasises how, in a world prone to social amplification of risk, EFSA has a special role to play when carrying out its communication task. It is believed that should the Authority succeed in communicating more rapidly and effectively, by leveraging on its combined scientific and communication expertise, it could reduce any potential distortion or alarm to a minimum amongst the general public.

It is Sue Davies, Chief Policy Adviser with consumer champion *Which?*, and later Chair of EFSA's Management Board, who provides us with a public perspective on the work of EFSA and, more broadly, of EU food regulation. Her chapter, by sharing the experience of the author and her organisation throughout the major food crises of the 1990s, both in the UK and the EU, begins by contrasting the original EU regulatory framework for food safety with the one existing in 2013. She observes that while the reasons that have led to the establishment of EFSA and of an autonomous EU food law policy remain valid, one may perceive today – amid the new challenges facing the EU – a progressive departure from the food safety imperative. In the author's view, this trend would be exemplified by a series of recent regulatory failures and missed opportunities. She mentions the initial failure to agree on the revision of the Novel Food Regulation, the lack of agreement on a precautionary-inspired approach towards food from animal cloning as well as current plans to relax controls over the use of processed animal proteins. To address this negative trend, it is suggested to consolidate the achievements attained thus far (swifter response to food crises, better communication and more access to data) by leveraging more on EFSA's self-tasking authority and promoting a more proactive approach to food policy. Her call sounds like a credible and reasonable manifesto for the sort of assertiveness that the Authority should adopt while facing current and future challenges.

Chapter 18, co-authored by Luis González Vaqué, one of the most seasoned and pioneer EU officials working in food law and policy, and Sebastián Romero Melchor, a rising star among EU food lawyers, offers the perspective of those food practitioners exposed to EFSA's work on a daily basis. Not surprisingly, they chose to examine the role played by EFSA within what they call a 'bureaucratic monster': the EU Nutrition and Health Claims Regulation. After exploring the tasks entrusted to the different actors involved with the implementation of this controversial regulation, they identify some of the challenges raised by the daily application of the Permitted List of claims.[18] In so doing, the chapter also offers an insightful analysis of the role that the Court of Justice of the European Union may be expected to play in the interpretation (as well as in the validity)[19] of this controversial regulation. Despite some criticisms of EFSA's handling of the claims dossier, the authors consider the Authority's record as a positive one 'as it evaluated risk without losing sight of the need to ensure the proper functioning of the internal market', but still question EFSA's ability to improve the general public's confidence in the food supply chain. In their view, what could make this happen is a commitment to more effective openness vis-à-vis third parties. It is no surprise that the alleged lack of openness denounced by this chapter echoes the claims made by Roberto Ciati in his chapter discussing the industry's perspective.

It is the food law professor's view, here offered by Bernd van der Meulen and Rozita Spirovska Vaskoska, which closes the section devoted to the stakeholders' perspective of EFSA. This chapter reconstructs the process of autonomisation of food law by contextualising it within the broader debate about the rationale for public authorities' intervention in regulated sectors, such as food. By focusing mainly on the role played by science, this chapter critically discusses the normative relationship existing between scientific expertise, such as it has been entrusted to EFSA, and the broader EU regulatory framework of food safety. In so doing, the chapter provides an analysis of the most salient risk management measures adopted by the Commission and highlights the allegedly limited role played by EFSA. In the author's view, while it is generally understandable under the current regulatory framework that EFSA is not involved in food legislation, the Authority should not be excluded from 'the undisputed domain of its competence': scientific advice for risk management decisions in individual cases. The rule of science would remain as a result too limited in the more current food regulatory framework.

While it is important that EFSA closely cooperates with Member States' authorities and all food stakeholders, there seems to be an increasing awareness that it is equally imperative that the Authority engages and talks to its international counterparts beyond the EU. The following chapters, gathered under Section 3 of

18 Regulation (EU) 432/2012 of 16 May 2012 establishing a list of permitted health claims made on foods, other than those referring to the reduction of disease risk and to children's development and health. [2012] OJ L 136, p. 1.

19 See, e.g., Case T-334/12, *Plantavis and NEM v Commission and EFSA*, pending. See OJ C 311 of 13.10.2012, p. 9.

Part II – *The International Perspective*, aim at providing a systematic and detailed analysis of the external dimension of EFSA's activities and, more broadly, of EU food law.

To fully grasp the main peculiarities and specificity of EFSA's scientific governance, we have asked Stephanie Tai to compare the institutional structures and experiences of EFSA Scientific Panels and their US counterpart, the FDA Food Advisory Committee. Thus, Chapter 20, by focusing in particular on the issue of scientific independence, discusses how the two bodies are structured and constrained along different theoretical conceptions of expertise and, as a result, explains some of the most common misunderstandings occurring across the Atlantic.

Chapter 21, co-authored by Martijn Groenleer and Simone Gabbi, by providing a ground-breaking analysis of EFSA's little known, yet significant, international relations, sets the scene of this section. By blending political science, international relations and legal theory, the authors test whether EFSA has played an active role as a 'policy entrepreneur', making use of the opportunities offered by the EU food law policy within which it acts, in order to gain influence vis-à-vis other food actors. In particular, the Authority's drivers behind its international emergence are functional (i.e. to discharge its scientific duty EFSA needs to have access to the best information available) on the one hand, and strategic (i.e. to impose its scientific authority at the global level) on the other. It is predicted that in the light of the above motivations, EFSA's international involvement will grow even further in parallel to its domestic growth. Indeed, it emerges that overall, despite the limited scope of action allowed by its legal framework, EFSA has – through time – imposed itself on the international scene.

This finding seems to be confirmed, and be further elaborated, by the unprecedented analysis offered by Ching-Fu Lin in Chapter 22 devoted to EFSA's role within global food safety governance. After denouncing the absence of a meta-framework governing the production of food rules at the global level, the author reconstructs the existence of an emerging global food governance framework. It is against this incipient legal context that he tests his claim. In his view, EFSA would at the same time play the role of a participant within that framework, act as a benchmark against which to measure the effectiveness of that framework and finally serve as a model for other jurisdictions. His analysis demonstrates that several features of the EU Authority – that are thoroughly examined throughout the volume – would actually allow it to play, within its underlying regulatory framework, these three roles simultaneously.

While it is true that these conclusions may sound slightly hagiographic in a book entirely dedicated to EFSA and its first 10 years of existence, it is undisputable that, amid the specificity of the EU institutional, political and cultural environment, the context within which the Authority is called upon to operate makes EFSA one of the most original food institutions in existence.

In this volume, our contributing authors often emphasise this specificity. They do so neither to critically promote the EU food law regime as a possible model for other jurisdictions across the world, nor to somehow justify the various flaws they identify in the same system throughout the book.

Rather, our collective attempt is to shed some light, by adopting a contextual analysis, on the inherent complexity behind the unique institutional design, scientific governance and communication mandate characterising EFSA within the broader EU food system.

It is against this backdrop that this volume takes the liberty to formulate several policy recommendations capable of meeting the continuous demand for experimentation and adaption that the EU food regulatory framework constantly calls for.

Our hope is to have succeeded in addressing some of the most frequent criticisms directed at EFSA and its underlying food regulatory regime. The challenge is to differentiate the criticisms based on ill-informed, factual errors and misrepresentation from those that are genuinely well founded and require creative regulatory action.

In general, the wealth of perspectives gathered in this volume seems to demystify some of the common claims portraying the Authority as either 'pro-industry' (e.g. in its scientific assessment of GMOs) or 'anti-industry' (e.g. in its scientific assessment of health claims). *Simul stabunt, simul cadent*, as Latins used to say. The very coexistence of both claims provides the best proof that, as these claims tend to offset one another, EFSA is more than the sum of its parts and that its actions have been fundamentally judicious during its first 10 years of existence.

Overall, the Authority emerges as belonging to a balanced, yet improvable, food legal system that deserves permanent scrutiny, guidance and judgment. That is the expectation of 500 million EU citizens, the daily clients of this very system.

Although predominantly grounded in EU administrative law, this book represents one of the first contextual analyses of a EU agency. As such, it nurtures the ambition to inspire more creative research around the functioning of these archetypally European, yet atypical, creatures and could be applicable to the understanding of other sister agencies.

PART I
EFSA From Within

Section 1 The Genesis
Section 2 Scientific Advice
Section 3 Scientific Communication

Section 1: The Genesis

Chapter 1

The Genesis of EFSA and the First 10 Years of EU Food Law

David Byrne

The President of the EU Commission, Romano Prodi, presented the make-up of the new Commission to the European Parliament on 21 July 1999. During the speech setting out his ambitions for his period in office, he made specific reference to the establishment of an independent food agency. Although there had been repeated calls for such an initiative throughout the 1990s, this was the first expression of a political commitment to do so. In passing, President Prodi referred to the highly regarded FDA in the US as an example.

The political climate at that time was heavily influenced by the many food safety scares around Europe, the most serious being BSE and dioxin. Public confidence in food and in politicians plummeted and governments fell. There was also widespread concern that the competent authorities in some member states were not acting in a fully transparent manner. This was the impetus that led to the demand for a food agency at EU level capable of operating independently, to which the Commission responded.

DG Sanco, the newest Directorate of the Commission, had just been established, for which I had political responsibility as Commissioner for Health and Consumer Protection. A number of additional competences fell under the responsibility of this new Directorate, including food safety and animal health and welfare. Policy development and legal drafting in the area of food law thus became the responsibility of DG Sanco.

A White Paper on Food Safety[1] was quickly drafted and published in January 2000. It was intended as a consultation document in preparation for the anticipated new food law. It set out the broad outlines of what a new framework law should contain, and called for the creation of an independent agency by 2002 – The European Food Authority (EFA). (It is an interesting historical detail that the name was changed to include the word 'Safety' during the legislative process at the suggestion of the late Philip Whitehead MEP, who performed the task of Rapporteur with considerable skill and commitment.)

---

1 European Commission, *White Paper on Food Safety* (COM 719 final, 1999), available at http://ec.europa.eu/dgs/health_consumer/library/pub/pub06_en.pdf.

The key tasks identified in the White Paper[2] were independent scientific advice on the assessment of risk, and a shared responsibility with the Commission for the communication of risk to the public. In stating that 'there must be a clear separation between risk management and risk assessment', it was recommended that the function of risk management should remain with the Commission and the law-making political institutions of the EU. This was an indication that an EU version of the FDA was not intended. In advancing its justification for this decision, the White Paper stated that a transfer of regulatory powers to an independent authority could lead to an unwarranted dilution of democratic accountability.

Although this recommendation caused some small degree of controversy, it is a position I promoted and publicly advocated at that time. I believed that the appetite for risk (the core of risk management), is a legitimate concern of the public, and is best determined by decision-making at the political level by those responsible and accountable to the public, albeit with the advice of the risk assessor.

In further justification of the separation of risk assessment and risk management, the White Paper referred to the legal advice available to the Commission to the effect that the Treaties mandated the Commission to perform the functions of regulation and control and that the delegation of such powers to a regulatory body would require Treaty changes. In any event, the budgetary considerations associated with any such delegation of powers would render such a move quite impractical.

The White Paper[3] also called for an integrated approach, from farm to table, with food operators having primary responsibility for food safety. It pointed to the need for a credible system of traceability and promised monitoring, enforcement procedures and infringement actions. Considerable emphasis was placed on the need to provide scientific advice which was independent, excellent and transparent. A concern of fundamental importance was identified in the statement that 'if consumer confidence is to be regained, the Authority will need not only to act independently of outside pressures but to be accepted as doing so by all parties concerned.' The ideas contained in the White Paper were not only innovative but were also well reasoned. These ideas formed the basis of the General Food Law (Reg. 178/2002)[4] which established EFSA and allowed it to commence its work on time in January 2002.

Many factors influenced the drafting of the General Food Law, not least the issues surrounding the outbreak of the so-called Beef War in October 1999, when France, on the scientific advice of its national food safety agency, announced a ban on the importation of British beef. This advice directly contradicted the

---

2 Ibid.

3 European Commission, *White Paper on Food Safety* (COM 719 final, 1999).

4 Council Regulation (EC) 178/2002 of 28 January 2002 laying down the general principles and requirements of food law, establishing the European Food Safety Authority and laying down procedures in matters of food safety [2002] OJ L31/1, available at http://eur-lex.europa.eu/LexUriServ/LexUriServ.do?uri=OJ:L:2002:031:0001:0024:EN:PDF.

opinion of the Scientific Steering Committee (SSC), whose opinion was relied upon by the Commission in permitting the free circulation of British beef throughout the European Union on the strict conditions of the Date Based Export Scheme (DBES).[5] This ban was a clear breach of EU law and amounted to a significant challenge to the Commission which had entered upon its mandate only two weeks previously.

An appropriate response was demanded. The initiation of infringement proceedings against France was one obvious course of action open to the Commission. However, conscious of the fact that consumer confidence was at stake, I favoured another course by requesting the French authorities to make available their scientific advice to enable the SSC in Brussels make a new evaluation. Within weeks the SSC declared that they found no reason to change their previously expressed scientific opinion on the safety of British beef exported under the DBES. In the interests of transparency I invited members of the SSC to a press conference in order to provide an explanation of their opinion in public. Further discussions ensued between Commission officials and the French administration which reduced the areas of disagreement but failed to reach a satisfactory conclusion. Consequently, it then became necessary for the Commission to institute infringement proceedings against France. Ultimately the CJEU found in the Commission's favour, thereby requiring France to comply with EU law and lift the ban on the importation of British beef.

As France failed to comply, further proceedings were launched pursuant to Article 228[6] seeking the payment of financial penalties to enforce compliance. This resulted in France eventually lifting the ban. However, as the Commission had sought payment of penalties from the date of the prospective order in the Art. 228 proceedings rather than from a date subsequent to the order of the Court in the infringement proceedings, this resulted in no penalties being paid. Nor did the Commission make any claim for payment of a lump sum. Although financial sanctions could have been sought from the earlier date, it had been the practice of the Commission in Art. 228 proceedings not to do so. I requested a review of this practice. It emerged that there was some legal doubt as to whether the Commission could seek the payment of a lump sum and daily penalties. This doubt was quickly resolved in Case C-304/02 *Commission v France*[7] when the Court confirmed that two kinds of financial sanctions (penalty and lump sum) can apply cumulatively for the same infringement, and applied this principle in that case for the first time.

5 Commission Decision (EC) 98/692 of 25 November 1998 amending Decision 98/256/EC as regards certain emergency measures to protect against bovine spongiform encephalopathy [1998] OJ L328, available at http://eur-lex.europa.eu/LexUriServ/LexUriServ.do?uri=CELEX:31998D0692:EN:HTML.

6 Treaty on European Union (Maastricht Treaty) art 228.

7 Case C-304/02 *Commission of the European Communities v French Republic* [2005] ECR I-6263, available at http://eur-lex.europa.eu/LexUriServ/LexUriServ.do?uri=CELEX:62002J0304:EN:HTML.

This decision led to the publication of a Commission Communication on the application of Art. 228 (SEC/2005/1658)[8] in which the Commission announced its change of practice by notifying its intention to include in applications under Art. 228 a request for:

– A penalty by day of delay after the delivery of the Judgement under Art. 228.

And

– A lump sum penalising the continuation of the infringement between the first Judgement on non-compliance and the Judgement delivered under Art. 228.

There is little doubt that such an approach will encourage earlier compliance with orders of the CJEU. Therefore it must be acknowledged that the Beef War led to greater legal certainty. It also led to important improvements in the sometimes turbulent interactions between science, law and politics. It became clear that we needed to put in place dispute resolution mechanisms capable of producing non-confrontational speedy outcomes to resolve such differences in the future. At stake was the confidence of the European consumer.

The ambition expressed in the White Paper that EFSA is to 'become the scientific point of reference for the whole union' was carried through to the General Food Law, where in Art. 22 (2)[9] it states, 'The Authority shall provide scientific advice and scientific and technical support for the Communities' legislation and policies in all fields which have a direct or indirect impact on food and food safety.' Thus the scientific opinions, which are required to be furnished by EFSA, form the scientific basis of Community legislation.

It is further provided in the regulation that on carrying out these tasks, EFSA is required to act 'in close cooperation with the competent bodies in the member states carrying out similar tasks to those of the authority' (Art. 22.7). This consultative process is further reinforced by Art. 30,[10] which establishes a mandatory procedure where EFSA has identified diverging scientific opinions, 'with a view to either resolving the divergence or preparing a joint document clarifying the contentious scientific issues and identifying the relevant uncertainties involved'. Once again, in the interests of transparency, this document must be made public. By this device, the scientists from the bodies concerned, together with EFSA, will either resolve the differences or, at the very least, clarify the uncertainties for the Commission

8 Commission (EC), 'Application of Article 228 of the EC Treaty' (Communication) SEC (2005) 1658 final, available at http://eur-lex.europa.eu/LexUriServ/LexUriServ.do?uri=CELEX:52005SC1658:EN:HTML.

9 Council Regulation (EC) 178/2002 of 28 January 2002 laying down the general principles and requirements of food law, establishing the European Food Safety Authority and laying down procedures in matters of food safety [2002] OJ L31/1.

10 Ibid.

acting as the risk manager. In the event of such uncertainty, the Commission can then have recourse to Art. 7[11] in the specific circumstances where the Precautionary Principle may be invoked.

To further reinforce this network of cooperation and conciliation, an Advisory Forum is established by Art. 27 to form a link between EFSA and the member states. In effect, it is composed of representatives from the national food agencies with a mission to ensure close cooperation between those entities. The Advisory Forum is also conferred with a function in the resolution of diverging scientific opinions in circumstances identified in Art. 30.

For me, the intent and effect of the General Food Law is to create for EFSA a position of scientific pre-eminence in Europe by reliance on the subtle interaction of Arts. 6(3), 22, 30 and 27. It is to be hoped that this approach helps to foster a respectful relationship between scientists by putting in place a mechanism for the achievement of consensus or alternatively an agreement on the precise reason for the divergence or uncertainty. This is done under full transparency in the knowledge that consumer confidence cannot be mandated; it can only be earned. These provisions are designed to achieve that end.

Over the years, EFSA has put in place a number of initiatives, such as the Strategy for Cooperation and Networking between the EU Member States and EFSA, a stakeholder's forum, and the engagement in discussions with similar agencies in other parts of the world, thereby promoting convergence in global scientific risk assessment. These are important developments as they improve the public's understanding of the coherence of scientific evaluation and thereby enhance consumer confidence.

If risk assessment is a core function of EFSA, the commitment to communicating quality science to the risk manager, and ultimately to the consumer, is in the public interest. Communication is an important constituent of risk analysis and a function given to EFSA in Art. 40.[12] The scientist must be courageous in carrying out this function and guard against inappropriate pressure from whatever source, whether it be from public administrations, the food industry, campaigning groups, or politicians advocating ideological viewpoints inconsistent with quality scientific analysis on the available data. In the assessment of risk, scientists can best assist the risk manager by laying out the elements of risk which, put simply, means saying what can happen and what the chances are of it happening. It is then up to the politically accountable risk manager to make the choices in the public interest. Any resulting public debate on the choices made should then be directed to the politician and not the scientist.

This is not to say the work of the EFSA scientists should not be kept under public review to ensure a high level of competence and a clear commitment to independence and transparency as required by Art. 6. The adoption in December 2011 of a new integrated policy on Independence and Scientific Decision-Making

11 Ibid.
12 Ibid.

Processes,[13] which has led to the publication of rules of implementation of the policy in March 2012, is likely to provide a more robust and transparent approach so as to ensure scientific independence and reassure consumer confidence.

The Regulation also provided a further valuable tool of interpretation by including a clear reference to the Precautionary Principle in Art. 7.[14] The Commission published a Communication on this subject in 2000, expressing its opinion on when and how the Precautionary Principle ought to be operated. The Commission's approach was subsequently approved by the Court of First Instance in 2002 in *Pfizer v The Council* (Case T-13/99).[15] The Precautionary Principle provides a risk management tool where harmful effects on health are identified but scientific uncertainty persists. However, it is worth noting that the guidelines set out in the Communication and repeated in Art. 7(2) are quite rigorous, indicating that the Precautionary Principle is not intended to be used as a comfort zone for the risk averse.

Our ambitions for EFSA have been well fulfilled. Since inception, its directors have given good leadership. Whereas some controversies have emerged from time to time, this is to be expected in a new institution carrying out complex tasks in the domain of risk and frequent uncertainty. However, it must be acknowledged, standards of food safety in Europe have considerably improved over the past 10 years and consumers have confidence in the food they eat. For instance, the reduction by half in human cases of salmonella in the EU in the five years to 2009 is largely due to EFSA. This EU agency has made a big impact on the European stage and enjoys significant global influence. EFSA deserves our thanks and the support of the Commission and Parliament in its work. It also deserves our best wishes for the next 10 years.

---

13 European Food Safety Authority; Policy on Independence and Scientific Decision-Making Processes.

14 Council Regulation (EC) 178/2002 of 28 January 2002 laying down the general principles and requirements of food law, establishing the European Food Safety Authority and laying down procedures in matters of food safety [2002] OJ L31/1.

15 Case T-13/99 *Pfizer Animal Health SA v Council of the European Union* [2002] ECR II-3318.

Section 2: Scientific Advice

Chapter 2

EFSA's Science Strategy: Taking Stock and Looking Ahead

Vittorio Silano

Introduction

Considering the importance for the European Institutions of a high-quality independent scientific advice, based on the best scientific knowledge, in order to effectively deal with policy and decision-making issues related to food and feed safety, it is not surprising that different approaches have been put in practice over time to improve its provision at the European level. Before 1997, each one of the competent European Commission's General Directorates used to establish, manage and provide the secretariat for an ad hoc scientific committee covering its area of competence; scientists in each scientific committee were at that time mainly appointed following informal consultations with competent authorities in Member States. Since 1997, eight independent scientific committees charged with the task of providing scientific advice on matters relating to different aspects of human/animal health and food/feed safety and one ad hoc EC Office competent for their management were established under the General Directorate for Consumer Policy and Fishery of the European Commission (EC). In the meantime, the Scientific Steering Committee was also established with the task of facilitating overall coordination of the above-mentioned eight committees and of dealing with truly multidisciplinary issues. The appointment of experts in each committee was carried out through a call for manifestation of interest and subsequent selection among the interested applicants. All the EC Directorates who needed a scientific opinion had to formally ask for the EC Office on scientific advice by providing a clear written mandate. Moreover, since 2002, the European Food Safety Authority (EFSA) was established,[1] with one Scientific Committee and eight Scientific Panels as a new European agency with the task of delivering independent, high-quality and timely scientific advice on issues from farm to fork and to communicate on the risks assessed in an open manner to all interest parties, including the EC, EP, MS and the public at large.

---

1 Council Regulation (EC) 178/2002 of 28 January 2002 laying down the general principles and requirements of food law, establishing the European Food Safety Authority and laying down procedures in matters of food safety [2002] OJ L31/.

Main Achievements of EFSA

Upon its establishment, EFSA's initial priorities were: (i) to put in place its own staff and the Scientific Committee and Scientific Panels (initially 8 and since 2008 10); and (ii) to develop a set of internal procedural rules mainly focused on efficiency, transparency, coherence and optimal approaches to review systematically the quality of the outputs. Such a development has made possible to achieve a much stronger and more effective approach than was possible in the past in the risk assessment and scientific advice activity on a number of different food/feed related areas. Since 2003, EFSA has worked very intensively and published about 3,000 scientific outputs, including:

- 442 outputs for the provision of scientific opinions and advice and risk assessment on public health issues;
- 1,875 outputs for the evaluation of products, substances and claims subject to authorisations by the EC;
- 416 outputs concerning data collection, scientific cooperation and networking;
- 250 outputs supporting publications (e.g. event reports, technical reports and external scientific reports).

These outputs include also a number of highly innovative risk assessment methodologies and related guidance documents produced by the Scientific Committee (see Box 2.1) or the Scientific Panels (see the special issues of the EFSA Journal produced on the occasion of its tenth anniversary) by self-tasking, a new important intervention tool introduced, among many others, by Reg. EC 178/2002.[2]

Box 2.1 Main risk assessment methodologies developed by EFSA's Scientific Committee since inception of EFSA

- Risk assessment of genotoxic and carcinogenic substances (2005 and 2012)
- Identification of emerging risks (2006/2007)
- Qualified presumption of safety of microorganisms (2007)
- Benchmark Dose (BMD) approach in risk assessment (2009)
- Risk/benefit assessment of food (2010)
- 90-day toxicity test on whole food and feed (2011)
- Harmonization of genotoxicity testing strategies (2011)
- Risk assessment of nanomaterials (2009 and 2011)
- Safety evaluation of traditional botanical food supplements and the Compendium (2005, 2007 and 2012)
- Threshold of Toxicological Concern as a risk assessment tool (2012)

2 Ibid.

Moreover, an important added value provided by EFSA has been its success in providing, in accordance with Article 31,[3] scientific assistance and urgent advice to the EC and Member States on public health risks under crisis conditions such as that caused from the occurrence of Shiga-toxin producing *Escherichia coli* in fresh vegetables.

To promote interactions with different stakeholders, EFSA has promoted, in addition to several task forces with specific mandates, the establishment of: (i) Focal Points in all the Member States; (ii) Nine European scientific networks with MS representatives on different subjects (e.g. nanotechnologies and emerging risks); (iii) An 'Information Exchange Platform (IEP)' with MS competent authorities; and (iv) an 'Applications Desk' to improve openness and dialogue with applicant companies. Moreover, a number of ad hoc Meetings and Workshops with selected stakeholder groups have been organised by EFSA to facilitate the discussion of specific issues and a formal Public Consultation mechanism is normally used before the adoption of innovative risk assessment methodologies or of specific opinions. All the comments received in response to public consultations are carefully considered and addressed individually by EFSA. Moreover, EFSA is currently testing a procedure to make possible the participation as "observers" of external experts in the work of the Scientific Committee and Panels.

Moreover, EFSA has also been very successful in establishing a scientific journal, freely accessible on line, to publish according to standard formats all the outputs of EFSA work.

Another success of EFSA has been the ability in promoting effectively the participation of a number of scientific institutions and partners in Member States to EFSA' activities either carrying out preparatory work needed for risk assessment such as: (i) ad hoc data collection from the literature, (ii) developing specific software models, (iii) analysing specific EFSA's outputs and (vi) providing specific statistical support. This approach has contributed remarkably to a number of EFSA's achievements and to the establishment of highly collaborative environment throughout the European Union. The budget devoted to calls concerning EFSA's grants and procurements has been steadily growing between 2008 and 2012 from €5.54 to €9.2 million for a number ranging from 60 to 100 in the different years. The budget proposed for the year 2013 has been further increased up to €10.7 million.

Looking Ahead

The 2012–16 Science Strategy,[4] adopted by EFSA a few months ago, sets out how EFSA aims to further strengthen its scientific work in line with its mission through

3 Article 31 of Council Regulation (EC) 178/2002 of 28 January 2002 laying down the general principles and requirements of food law, establishing the European Food Safety Authority and laying down procedures in matters of food safety [2002] OJ L31/1.

4 European Food and Safety Authority, 'Science Strategy 2012–2016'.

2016. A number of initiatives are highlighted in this document addressing four main objectives:

- ***developing excellence of EFSA's scientific advice*** including the implementation of an Integrated Quality Management System by 2016, the strengthening of the applications help desk and the adoption of more integrated science advice approach across scientific panels;
- ***optimising the use of risk assessment capacity in the EU*** including an increase of EFSA attractiveness for internal staff/external experts through joint training programmes and an increased cooperation with organisations in Member States, EU agencies, international organisations and organisations in third countries;
- ***developing and harmonising methodologies and approaches to assess risks associated with the food/feed chain*** aiming, among others, at standardising at the possible extent the handling of dossiers, investing in an IT template for dossier submission and sharing its view at the occasion of legislation under preparation or revision regarding its potential impact on efficiency and effectiveness of regulatory review processes;
- ***Strengthening the scientific evidence for risk assessment and risk monitoring*** including the organisation of a multi-annual data collection work programme, the strengthening of harmonised food consumption data collection project, monitoring the occurrence of chemicals which are subject to a marketing authorisation (i.e. post-marketing monitoring) and development of an EFSA's database for hazard characterisation in liaison with other European agencies.

The interested reader is invited to consult this important EFSA document available on the EFSA Journal for a more detailed description of the Science Strategy together with the underlying motivations. The remaining part of this chapter focuses on some additional issues that, in my opinion, deserve careful consideration in the future.

An ad hoc Scientific Cooperation Programme between EFSA and MS

As highlighted previously, the scientific cooperation of EFSA with scientific organisations in Member States in the frame of Art. 36[5] has developed significantly and contributed remarkably to a number of EFSA's achievements as well as to the establishment of a highly collaborative environment. However, the current activity is depending largely on the extent of financial resources available each year in the EFSA budget and requires each year a considerable amount of administrative work to allocate a large number of grants and procurements. Moreover, all the

5 Council Regulation (EC) 178/2002.

components of this programme being time-limited, it is very difficult to ensure continuity over time to any of such activities.

It would be very beneficial if, without affecting the positive cooperation framework already in place, a higher continuity could be ensured over time in the collaboration on key activities between EFSA and national Food Safety Agencies or other competent organisations designated by Member States upon request of EFSA. Specific objectives of such a proposal could include, among others, the establishment of more:

- Efficient monitoring systems in selected sectors in order to rapidly identify, through systematic analysis of the open and grey literature, any new information/data which may have an impact on already adopted EFSA's opinions. As a consequence, EFSA's reaction time in reconsidering and/or updating its opinions when needed could be significantly shortened and the possibility of overlooking important information considerably decreased.
- Efficient collection systems of data required at member State level to identify emerging risks related to food and feed and to respond to them. The role of the MS Competent Authorities for food safety in such an undertaking is obviously essential as for a number of emerging risks indicators they are the most reliable source of information.
- Systematic implementation of risk assessment methodologies and of specific models (e.g. for environmental fate) developed by EFSA in different contexts and performance of harmonised dietary surveys or post-marketing surveillance in order to contribute to the evaluation of their wide applicability and usefulness.
- Ad hoc agreements on short-term and medium-term joint work plans to access, when needed, testing facilities in Member States to produce, in special cases, data to fill data gaps or to reduce uncertainties in high-priority risk assessment cases not-related to regulated products.

The establishment of such a more structured and lasting scientific cooperation approach may be beneficial not only for facilitating the achievements of EFSA tasks in the interest of public health, but also for national Food Safety Agencies or other competent organisations designated by Member States as their roles in the frame of a more integrated European system of food safety would be better clarified and recognised. Moreover, this approach would not interfere with the freedom of each National Competent Authority to decide on its action plan that, obviously, has also to reflect national priorities.

EFSA's Scientific Advice on Innovation to Companies in the Food/Feed Sector

The multi-annual experience of the European Medicines Agency (EMA) on provision of scientific advice to pharmaceutical companies has proven to be very helpful to support innovation in the pharmaceutical sector and to reduce the time needed in the European Union to register a new medicinal product. In fact, as it is well known, the largest part of newly authorised medicinal products since EMA existence has gone through such a procedure. In view of such a positive experience, it is suggested that an amendment of the EFSA regulation should be adopted to establish a clear regulatory framework in which also EFSA would be allowed to offer scientific advice on innovation to companies in the food/feed sector. Obviously, it would not be appropriate that such a service of EFSA would be covered by the EFSA regular budget and, as is the case for EMA, ad hoc fees should be applied to cover the costs of scientific advice activities. Moreover, as it happens for EMA, there should be no possible interferences of scientific advice with EFSA risk assessment activities on regulated products. Such a development would not only benefit companies of the food/feed sector increasing their ability to innovate at higher speed while ensuring safety of products, but also the consumers as they are the final target of innovation. Moreover, EFSA could develop through such an activity a much deeper insight about current lines of innovation development in the food/feed sector with a considerable increase of its ability to predict and prevent risks sometimes associated with innovation.

Research Priorities and Science Advice in the Food/Feed Sector

To optimise scientific advice in the food/feed sector it is absolutely essential to stimulate and promote high-quality fundamental, applied and translational research in priority areas. Leadership for developing research strategy is clearly within the EU and MS Bodies in charge for defining priorities, financing research and assessing proposals. As it is well known, currently the most important research fund is the Framework Programme of the Directorate General Research, which is currently running for the seventh time (FP7). A key element for ensuring the success of EFSA mission and the value of its science advice in specific fast developing areas such as nanotechnologies or synthetic biology or to reduce persistent uncertainties preventing quantitative risk assessment in many areas is the availability of new data obtainable only through ad hoc research programmes. These considerations raise the issue of whether the outcomes of the undertaken research programmes are effective and timely in terms of improving the science advice provided by EFSA in specific sectors and of possible approaches to improve the feedback provided to research priorities indicated by EFSA. Obviously, important results could be achieved by developing more interactive mechanisms and procedures to make possible for EFSA explaining the reasoning behind its recommended research priorities and to systematically appraise from the view point of EFSA the outcomes of specific research programmes. One particularly important objective would also be to find out ways to make possible for EFSA to know and make use of at an early stage the research results obtained while preserving their confidentiality.

Chapter 3
A Taxanomy of EFSA's Scientific Outputs

Citlali Pintado[1]

Introduction

Conceived as a regulatory agency of 'assistance'[2] or of 'pre-decision-making',[3] the European Food Safety Authority (hereinafter 'EFSA') has a limited choice of instruments serving the purpose of providing risk managers with the result of its scientific risk assessment. In fact, EFSA has been tasked with providing 'scientific advice and scientific and technical support for the Union's legislation and policies in all fields which have a direct or indirect impact on food and feed safety'.[4]

Since it is not an institution within the meaning of Article 13 of the Treaty on European Union (hereinafter 'TEU'), EFSA is not empowered to propose or adopt measures, of a general nature, applicable *erga omnes*, i.e. to the public at large, in particular food business operators, and legally binding. Indeed, EFSA's outputs do not have a regulatory character and constitute, in their diversity, only instruments of 'soft-law' not having any binding effect.[5] By virtue of Regulation (EC)

---

1 This chapter represents solely the views of its author and cannot be regarded as representing the position, the views or the policy of the European Food Safety Authority or any EU Institution, agency or body.

2 J. Molinier, 'L'élaboration d'un cadre commun aux agences de l'Union', dans *Les agences de l'Union européenne* sous la direction de Joël Molinier, Bruylant, collection droit de l'Union européenne dirigée par Fabrice Picod, 2011, p. 227. See also on this E. Paradis, 'Les agences et organismes divers de l'Union européenne: une appréciation d'ensemble en 2010', in *Les agences de l'Union européenne* sous la direction de Joël Molinier, Bruylant, collection droit de l'Union européenne dirigée par Fabrice Picod, respectivement, 2011, pp. 199–219.

3 Griller and Orator, 'Everything under Control? The 'Way Forward' for European Agencies in the Footsteps of the Meroni doctrine', 35 *European Law Review* 1 (2010), pp. 12–14, cited in M. Chamon, 'EU agencies: Does the 'Meroni' doctrine make sense?, *Maastricht Journal of European and Comparative Law*, 2010, vol. 17, no. 3, p. 285.

4 Article 22(2) of Regulation (EC) No 178/2002 of the European Parliament and of the Council of 28 January 2002 laying down the general principles and requirements of food law, establishing the European Food Safety Authority and laying down procedures in matters of food safety, OJ L 31, 1.2.2002, pp. 1–24, as last amended.

5 Unlike other sister Union agencies, such as the European Chemical Agency (hereinafter 'ECHA'), EFSA is neither entitled to adopt individual decisions binding on third parties, for example for the registration of products, nor to possess a board of appeal for the review of the decisions it takes.

No 178/2002 (hereinafter 'EFSA's Founding Regulation'), EFSA has the task of reinforcing the 'system of scientific and technical support'.[6] In carrying out its role of 'an independent scientific point of reference in risk assessment',[7] EFSA adopts documents producing to a varying degree consensus on scientific technical matters related to its mission. In particular, it gives opinions on contentious scientific issues.

Focusing on the main role of EFSA – which is scientific risk assessment, and for that matter the purpose of the present section of this book – the present contribution will deal with the scientific outputs of EFSA. In so doing, it will exclude an examination of EFSA's role in risk communication as well as of EFSA decisions that might be challengeable under specific legal provisions,[8] such as those adopted in the framework of grants and procurement award procedures or public access to documents.[9]

Since its inception, EFSA has been facing a constant increase in the mandates[10] received, either following requests from the European Commission, or in the framework of the development of sectoral legislation, leading to a steep rise in the production of its documents and of their variety.

A taxonomy of these outputs is hereby proposed in order to highlight the differences between them and stress their singular characteristics and legal status. In general terms, EFSA's scientific outputs are classified according to their terminology in two broad categories by EFSA itself: 'Opinions of Scientific Committee/Scientific Panels' and 'Other Scientific Outputs'.[11] EFSA's scientific

6 Recital (33) of the EFSA's Founding Regulation.

7 Ibid.

8 This excludes outputs produced by EFSA in the field of risk communication, such as event reports or press releases, as well as confirmatory decisions adopted by EFSA in the framework of access to documents requests, and decisions adopted in the framework of the EFSA's contractual relations. Regarding the judicial review of these other outputs, see Chapter 13.

9 Public access to documents is regulated by Regulation (EC) No 1049/2001 of the European Parliament and of the Council of 30 May 2001 regarding public access to European Parliament, Council and Commission documents, applicable to EFSA by reference to Article 41 of EFSA's Founding Regulation.

10 The term 'mandate' designates all requests received by EFSA, to which EFSA attributes a specific number. These requests are those submitted under Article 29 of Regulation (EC) No 178/2002, by the European Commission, Member States or as a self-task (internal mandate), or Article 31. 'Mandate' also covers specific provisions existing in the sectoral legislation requiring EFSA's intervention (either for a Scientific Opinion or for the preparation of a Guidance). When vertical legislation foresees action by EFSA, the European Commission delivers in any case a general 'mandate' to EFSA applicable for all the outputs EFSA produces in the area of the applicable legislation. A number is therefore attributed to this general mandate which is the same for all EFSA's outputs delivered in application of the specific provision concerned.

11 EFSA has made a classification of its scientific outputs with a definition for each one available in its website. See *Definitions of EFSA Scientific Outputs and Supporting Publications* at: http://www.efsa.europa.eu/en/riskassessment/scdocdefinitions.htm.

outputs find their legal basis in the EFSA's Founding Regulation, specifically in Articles 28 to 40 thereof, but also in the sectoral legislation. This chapter provides a full overview of the scientific outputs adopted by EFSA. It discusses their main features and analyses them according to their nature (1) and their effects (2).

The Nature of EFSA's Outputs

As established by the Court of Justice of the European Union, 'the determination of the legal nature of a measure ... does not depend only on its official designation, but should first take into account its object and content'.[12] This section is intended to provide a definition of the outputs, identify their authors, their characteristics, content and deadlines for adoption.

All EFSA's scientific outputs are systematically published on EFSA's website as well as in the EFSA Journal once they have been adopted, in line with EFSA's obligation of transparency resulting from Article 38(1)(b), (c) and (e) of its Founding Regulation. Some draft documents are also published before adoption when they are submitted for public consultation.[13]

Scientific Opinions

A central feature of EFSA's scientific operation is the adoption of Scientific Opinions.[14] A Scientific Opinion can be defined as 'advice provided, following consultation, in answer to a question'.[15]

Scientific Opinions can only be adopted either by the Scientific Committee or a Scientific Panel[16] in accordance with Article 28(1) of EFSA's Founding Regulation.

---

12 Judgment of the Court of 14 December 1962, Joined cases 16/62 and 17/62, *Confédération nationale des producteurs de fruits et légumes and others v Council of the European Economic Community*, [1962] ECR 00901.

13 In this regard, see EFSA's approach on Public Consultations on scientific outputs at: http://www.efsa.europa.eu/en/keydocs/docs/consultationpolicy.pdf.

14 EFSA's Founding Regulation does not provide a specific definition of 'Scientific Opinions', but dedicates a specific provision, in Article 29, to Scientific Opinions, and also shapes the role of EFSA in a consultative-focused form.

15 By reference to national law where this denomination is commonly given to administrative acts adopted by administrative bodies when they carry out consultation tasks. See Gérard Cornu, *Vocabulaire juridique*, definition of 'avis', PUF, 2005, p. 99.

16 Scientific Panels are listed in Article 28(4) of EFSA's Founding Regulation, as amended by Commission Regulation (EC) No 202/2008 of 4 March 2008 amending Regulation (EC) No 178/2002 of the European Parliament and of the Council as regards the number and names of the Scientific Panels of the European Food Safety Authority, OJ L 60, 5.3.2008, p. 17. However, if necessary, the preparatory work of Scientific Opinions can be performed within Working Groups created in the framework of a mandate received by EFSA, or entrusted with specific tasks in relation to draft contributions, in accordance

Scientific Opinions can be identified by their common structure as required by Article 29(2) of EFSA's Founding Regulation: they are accompanied by background information explaining the scientific issue to be addressed and the Union interest.[17] In practice, the majority of requests for Scientific Opinions is submitted by the European Commission although in some cases sectoral legislation foresees specific intervention by EFSA.

Mandates from the European Commission or Member States provide terms of reference together with the mandatory background information. When EFSA is called upon by sectoral legislation to adopt a Scientific Opinion on the scientific assessment of a food, a substance or a health claim, the terms of reference are defined in the applicable legislation and reference to the provision mandating EFSA is made in the Scientific Opinion.[18] Reference to the mandates and the scope of the assessment is made at the very beginning of all Scientific Opinions.

Confidential information received by EFSA for the preparation of a Scientific Opinion, receives special treatment,[19] in particular when the information is provided by food business operators when submitting applications containing commercially sensitive information that, if disclosed, could harm their competitive position. Some sectoral legislation foresees specific provisions in this regard.[20] Similarly, EFSA only publishes raw data collected by Member States to a certain level of aggregation, in accordance with the data owner's authorisations. In this situation, data collection[21] is undertaken by EFSA under a contractual agreement with Member States' national organisations (universities, research institutes, national governmental bodies), which may allow the publication of summarised data, although not the whole raw data provided.[22]

---

with Article 19 of Decision of the EFSA's Management Board concerning the establishment and operations of the Scientific Committee, Scientific Panels and of their Working Groups (hereinafter 'EFSA's Rules of Procedure'), of 15 March 2012, available at: http://www.efsa.europa.eu/en/keydocs/docs/paneloperation.pdf.

17 Article 15(3) of EFSA's Rules of Procedure.

18 For example, Article 16 of Regulation (EC) No 1924/2006 on nutrition and health claims made on foods (Corrigendum of OJ L 12, 18.1.2007, pp. 3–18, as last amended) provides that EFSA is consulted to assess that health claims are substantiated by generally accepted scientific evidence and that EFSA gives its 'opinion' on this, 'including a report describing its assessment of the health claim and stating the reasons for its opinion and the information on which its opinion was based'.

19 Article 39 of EFSA's Founding Regulation.

20 For example, Regulation (EC) No 1829/2003 on genetically modified food and feed (OJ L 268, 18.10.2003, pp. 1–23, as last amended) provides in Article 30 of Regulation (EC) No 1829/2003 that it is the European Commission which determines what information shall be kept confidential. This is not the case for all sectoral legislation, and sometimes it is EFSA that decides, after consultation with the applicant, which information shall be protected.

21 Article 33 of EFSA's Founding Regulation.

22 This is in particular the case for food consumption data that is collected at national level, for example, through surveys made on the local population, which may contain personal data of individuals participating to the surveys.

Finally, the time limit for adoption of a Scientific Opinion varies depending on the mandate and the level of urgency or sensitiveness of the issue. Scientific Opinions requested by the European Commission, Member States or the European Parliament are adopted in a time frame agreed between the requestor and EFSA. When sectoral legislation foresees the need for an EFSA Scientific Opinion, in general, the time allocated to EFSA to deliver its Scientific Opinion is specifically provided for. In principle the time given to EFSA to issue a Scientific Opinion runs from five to nine months.[23]

Statements

A Statement is a document addressing an issue of concern that does not go into the same level of detail and assessment as a Scientific Opinion. Compared to Scientific Opinions, it is a more concise document answering a specific question that requires EFSA's scientific review. Statements can have different purposes, such as answering a request for a fast-track response in order to address an urgent matter, providing a provisional scientific view, addressing a previous risk assessment published by EFSA, reviewing existing literature or updating a refined exposure assessment on the basis of new data.

Statements can be requested either by risk managers or by EFSA as a self-task, also-called an 'internal mandate'. Depending on the request and the level of technicality of the issue to be addressed, Statements can be issued by the Scientific Committee or a Scientific Panel, or by EFSA in its role of 'scientific assistant'.

As far as EFSA Statements are concerned, these Statements imply a scientific or technical work involving the application of well-established scientific or technical principles, which does not require scientific evaluation by the Scientific Committee or a Scientific Panel, in accordance with Article 31 of EFSA's Founding Regulation. In these cases, Statements are prepared in a relatively short time frame.[24]

---

23 See, for example, the deadlines foreseen for EFSA in some sectoral legislations: Regulation (EC) No 1924/2006 on nutrition and health claims made on food (five months), Regulation (EC) No 1829/2003 on GMOs (six months), Regulation (EC) No 1331/2008 establishing a common authorisation procedure for food additives, food enzymes and food flavourings (nine months), Regulation (EC) No 282/2008 on recycled plastic materials and articles intended to come into contact with foods (six months), Regulation (EC) No 1831/2003 on additives for use in animal nutrition (six months).

24 See, for example, European Food Safety Authority; Final review of the Séralini *et al.* (2012a) publication on a 2-year rodent-feeding study with glyphosate formulations and GM maize NK603 as published online on 19 September 2012 in Food and Chemical Toxicology. EFSA Journal 2012; 10(11): 2986. [10 pp.] doi:10.2903/j.efsa.2012.2986. Available at: http://www.efsa.europa.eu/en/efsajournal/doc/2986.pdf. In this case EFSA received the mandate from the European Commission (M-2012–0282) on 26 September 2012. EFSA delivered its final evaluation of the paper by Séralini *et al.* which raised concerns about the potential toxicity of genetically modified (GM) maize NK603 and of a herbicide containing glyphosate on 28 November 2012.

Although EFSA has in this particular context the possibility of using its own staff to undertake the assessment, it always has the possibility of consulting at any time either the Scientific Committee, a Scientific Panel or the competent national organisations that operate in networks in accordance with Article 36 of EFSA's Founding Regulation.[25] EFSA can also create a task force or a working group composed of the scientific staff selected to prepare the Statement and the Chair, Vice-Chair or a Member of the Scientific Committee or of a Scientific Panel competent in the field of the issue to be addressed. In this way, EFSA ensures that the appropriate expertise is used to provide the best advice. The content and publication of EFSA Statements are approved by the Executive Director of EFSA.

Statements prepared by the Scientific Committee or a Scientific Panel are part of the scientific opinion process. These Statements are prepared following a request for the review of a Scientific Opinion when a reassessment is needed in order to take into account new data received either by industry or by Member States, or to update a refined exposure assessment on the basis of the new data.[26] Thus, the Scientific Committee or the Scientific Panel that was previously in charge of the Scientific Opinion is tasked with preparing the Statement. In this way, the process of reassessment is consistent with the previous Scientific Opinion and takes fully account of the new data received.

Guidance

A Guidance is a document pursuing a methodological or procedural purpose, which is aimed at providing advice on the steps to be followed in order to prepare the ground for a satisfactory scientific assessment. Guidance documents are also used to harmonise methodologies and working procedures for the risk assessment within EFSA.

Therefore, the nature of Guidance documents is very different from that of Scientific Opinions or the Statements. Guidance documents are not intended to provide advice on the scientific assessment of a substance, a food or feed product or to reach conclusions on the exposure assessment of a substance. Guidance documents are intended to address practical or methodological indications to applicants or risk assessors (Scientific Committees, Scientific Panels). They are also intended to explain to risk assessors, risk managers and/or applicants

25 See Chapter 5 'Scientific Regulatory Cooperation within the EU: On the Relationship between EFSA and National Food Authorities'.

26 This is mainly the case for the review of food additives. See, for example, the Revised exposure assessment for ethyl lauroyl arginate for the proposed uses as a food additive, available at: http://www.efsa.europa.eu/en/efsajournal/pub/2652.htm. In this case EFSA only reviewed the previous assessment carried out in 2007 using data provided by Member States as well as data received from industry and provided to EFSA by the European Commission. This document was submitted to the ANS Scientific Panel, in charge of food ingredients.

of dossiers submitted for evaluation, the principles of scientific aspects of the procedural issues or assessment practices and approaches. Guidance documents may also explain scientific guiding principles on the best practices for the monitoring, reporting and analysis of data related to food and feed safety and animal or plant health to Member States.[27]

They are either requested by the European Commission, in accordance with Article 31(1) of EFSA's Founding Regulation, or sometimes foreseen in sectoral legislation or self-tasked by EFSA. They can be drafted by the Scientific Committee or a Scientific Panel, or by EFSA in the same composition as for Statements.

Guidance documents of the Scientific Committee[28] or Scientific Panel explain the principles behind EFSA's procedures and approaches to scientific risk assessments to risk assessors (including the Scientific Committee or Scientific Panels), risk managers and/or applicants of dossiers submitted for evaluation. The Scientific Committee initiates such a document or revises Guidance documents, acting in its role of coordinator with the purpose of ensuring 'the consistency of the scientific opinion procedure, in particular with regard to the adoption of working procedures and harmonisation of working methods'.[29]

Guidance documents may also specify the information and data which industry must provide when submitting applications to EFSA for evaluation prior to their authorisation by risk managers.[30] This concerns mainly regulated substances that are submitted for authorisation. In such cases, Guidance documents are aimed at clarifying the requirements for applicants in terms of science and the data they need to submit to EFSA in the framework of the authorisation procedure (technical guidance) or at giving practical information on how to submit an application (administrative guidance). They are generally foreseen in the applicable vertical legislation together with the authorisation procedure.[31]

---

27 Definition of 'EFSA Guidance' provided by EFSA at: http://www.efsa.europa.eu/en/riskassessment/scdocdefinitions.htm.

28 See, for example, Guidance of the Scientific Committee on selected default values to be used by the EFSA Scientific Committee, Scientific Panels and Units in the absence of actual measured data, of 26 May 2009, available at: http://www.efsa.europa.eu/en/efsajournal/pub/2579.htm. See also Guidance of the Scientific Committee on Use of the benchmark dose approach in risk assessment, of 26 May 2009, available at: http://www.efsa.europa.eu/en/efsajournal/pub/1150.htm.

29 Article 28(2) of EFSA's Founding Regulation.

30 See, for example, Guidance of the GMO Panel on the environmental risk assessment of genetically modified plants, of 21 October 2010, available at: http://www.efsa.europa.eu/en/efsajournal/pub/1879.htm.

31 For example, Article 9(2) of Regulation (EC) No 1935/2004 on food contact materials; Regulation (EC) No 1107/2009 on plant protection products, Articles 8(5) (on the peer-review scientific data to submit) and 77; Regulation (EC) No 1925/2006 on nutrition and health claims made on foods, Article 15(5); Regulation (EC) No 1829/2003 on GMOs, Articles 5(8), 11(6), 17(8), 23(6); Regulation (EC) 1831/2003 on feed additives, Article 7(5).

Many Guidance documents are submitted for public consultation in order to ensure that these documents address properly all questions related to the scientific studies and data needed for the risk assessment, and the practical and methodological issues.[32] Therefore, their adoption may take longer than for other outputs and the time limit is more flexible.

Reasoned Opinions

A Reasoned Opinion is a term introduced in Regulation (EC) No 396/2005,[33] and describes the comprehensive scientific evaluation of, and subsequent conclusions from, the consumer exposure assessment and the risk assessment of pesticide residues resulting from the use of pesticides.[34] Reasoned opinions are submitted by EFSA in the framework of the assessment of maximum residue levels for pesticides (hereinafter 'MRLs') which are the upper legal levels of a concentration for pesticide residues in or on food or feed based on good agricultural practices, in order to ensure the lowest possible consumer exposure.[35]

EFSA's Pesticides Unit, in contrast with experts sitting on the Pesticides Scientific Panel (PRAS), is responsible for the risk assessment of MRLs as the work required is the review of existing data.

EFSA has to deliver its reasoned opinion 'as soon as possible and at the latest within three months from the date of receipt of the application'[36] concerning MRLs. This time limit can be extended by 6 months if more detailed evaluations need to be carried out and the clock can be stopped if additional information is requested. However, for the assessment of existing MRLs, EFSA has to submit its reasoned opinion within 12 months from the date of the inclusion or non-inclusion of an active substance in the positive list of Annex I of Directive 91/414/EEC

32 See, for example, the guidance documents covering the principles applied by the NDA Panel in the evaluation of health claims adopted. These documents are also subject to public consultation and sometimes discussed at stakeholder meetings. Reports on the outcome of the public consultations are published and available at: http://www.efsa.europa.eu/en/nda/ndaguidelines.htm.

33 Articles 10, 11, 12, 24 of Regulation (EC) No 396/2005 of the European Parliament and of the Council of 23 February 2005 on maximum residue levels of pesticides in or on food and feed of plant and animal origin and amending Council Directive 91/414/EEC, OJ L 70, 16.3.2005, pp. 1–16, as last amended.

34 Definition provided by EFSA at: http://www.efsa.europa.eu/en/riskassessment/scdocdefinitions.htm.

35 They are produced following receipt of an application (Article 10) for the establishment of temporary MRLs (Article 24) or for the evaluation of existing MRLs (Article 12).

36 Article 11(1) of Regulation (EC) No 396/2005 of the European Parliament and of the Council of 23 February 2005 on maximum residue levels of pesticides in or on food and feed of plant and animal origin and amending Council Directive 91/414/EEC, OJ L 70, 16.3.2005, pp. 1–16, as last amended.

(repealed by Regulation (EC) No 1107/2009),[37] or 12 months from the entry into force of Regulation (EC) No 396/2005.[38]

This category of output is a peculiarity created by vertical legislation and is issued taking the best advantage of EFSA's own scientific staff resources. This sector of Union food law is the only one where the concept of an opinion is used with regard to work undertaken by EFSA's staff.

Conclusions on Pesticides Peer Review

EFSA is mandated by Article 12 of Regulation (EC) No 1107/2009 to prepare these Conclusions.[39] As for Reasoned Opinions, scientists from the EFSA Pesticides Unit and the Member States comprehensively peer review the Draft Assessment Report (DAR), prepared by a Member State *rapporteur* who is the recipient of the application dossier, in order to guarantee the highest possible standards.[40]

EFSA's Conclusions are prepared in the light of current scientific and technical knowledge. An EFSA Conclusion includes details concerning the evaluation procedure, the properties of the active substance concerned and background documents.[41]

EFSA shall deliver its opinion to the European Commission within 120 days of the end of the period provided for the submission of written comments, as foreseen in Article 12(1), last paragraph. This time limit can be extended by 60 days in the event of consultations and by 90 days if additional data is needed from the applicant.[42]

Other Outputs

Apart from the main categories of scientific outputs already analysed, Scientific Opinions, Statements, Guidance documents, Reasoned Opinions and Conclusions, EFSA also prepares reports, such as the Annual Report on pesticide residues (1.6.1.) and Scientific or Technical Reports (1.6.2.).

---

37 Regulation (EC) No 1107/2009 of the European Parliament and of the Council of 21 October 2009 concerning the placing of plant protection products on the market and repealing Council Directives 79/117/EEC and 91/414/EEC, OJ L 309, 24.11.2009, pp. 1–50.

38 Article 12(2) of Regulation (EC) No 396/2005.

39 EFSA definition available at: http://www.efsa.europa.eu/en/riskassessment/scdocdefinitions.htm.

40 See EFSA webpage on pesticides peer review at: http://www.efsa.europa.eu/en/pesticides/pesticidespeerreview.htm. If necessary, discussions between expert scientists from the regulatory authorities of the Member States also take place. Article 12(2) of Regulation (EC) No 1107/2009.

41 See, for example, EFSA Conclusion on the peer review of the pesticide risk assessment for bees for the active substance thiamethoxam, approved on 19 December 2012, EFSA Journal 2013;11(1): 3067. [68 pp.] doi:10.2903/j.efsa.2013.3067. Available at: http://www.efsa.europa.eu/en/efsajournal/pub/3067.htm.

42 Article 12(3) of Regulation (EC) No 1107/2009.

Annual report on pesticide residues Member States are requested to carry out official controls on pesticide residues in order to enforce compliance with Maximum Residue Levels. The results of the controls have to be reported to the Commission, other Member States and EFSA. Once received, EFSA collates and analyses the results of national controls on pesticide residues in food and feed. On the basis of the information received from Member States, EFSA draws up an Annual Report on pesticide residues[43] and renders the Annual Report public together with the comments by the European Commission or Member States.[44]

This Report is prepared by EFSA's Pesticides Unit. Once adopted, EFSA submits the Annual Report to the Commission by the last day of February each year.[45]

Scientific reports and technical reports A Scientific Report of EFSA is a scientific document whose main purpose is, for example, to describe original research results that pertain, for example, to a literature review, statistical data analysis, the compilation of scientific evidence – compilation/collation/ assessment of survey or monitoring results, specifications for the design thereof – or a data collection report.[46]

Scientific Reports can be requested by the European Commission, for example in accordance with Article 21 of Regulation (EC) No 1107/2009, in order to review the approval of active substances in light of new scientific and technical knowledge and monitoring data, or in the framework of other vertical legislation for the purpose of analysing existing data.

They are drafted by EFSA's staff, but in special cases they may be endorsed by the Scientific Committee or the relevant Scientific Panel. It is also possible for EFSA to prepare the report within a task force or an EFSA Working Group composed of members of its own staff together with experts from Member States or bodies with which EFSA collaborates in the framework of Article 36 of its Founding Regulation.[47]

EFSA can also issue a Technical Report at the request of the Commission, on its own initiative or as foreseen in relevant sectoral legislation. A Technical Report is a document that describes the nature, state of the art, progress, or results of a technical process. Requests on these reports are defined in mandates received from

43 Article 32 of Commission Regulation (EC) No 396/2005.

44 Article 32(7) of Commission Regulation (EC) No 396/2005.

45 Article 37(5) of Commission Regulation (EC) No 396/2005. See, for example, the 2009 European Union Report on Pesticide Residues in Food, approved on 26 October 2011, available at: http://www.efsa.europa.eu/en/efsajournal/doc/2430.pdf.

46 See, for example, EFSA's Report prepared by the Dietary and Monitoring Unit, Overview of 2011 European Data Collection of Chemical Occurrence in Food and Feed. Supporting Publications 2012:EN-384. [51 pp.], of 13 December 2012, available at: http://www.efsa.europa.eu/en/efsajournal/doc/3067.pdf.

47 See, for example, EFSA Report on 'Schmallenberg' virus: likely epidemiological scenarios and data needs. Supporting Publications, of 6 February 2012, 2012:EN-241. [31 pp.], available at: http://www.efsa.europa.eu/en/supporting/doc/241e.pdf.

the Commission, internal mandates[48] or internal project mandates approved by the Executive Director.[49]

Effects of EFSA's Outputs

After having carried out an overview of the EFSA's scientific outputs, it is worth analysing their legal effects in order to better understand their significance in the EU legal system. This part will mainly focus on Scientific Opinions, Reasoned Opinions and Statements, as they are mandatory because they are foreseen in the legislation as necessary to build science-based legislation (2.1.). These three kinds of outputs are also those that have the strongest effects in terms of decision-making. Their importance has raised the question of their legal effects and judicial review (2.2.).

Mandatory Character of EFSA's Scientific Opinions, Reasoned Opinions and Statements

Some of EFSA's outputs have a mandatory character resulting from the vertical legislation when the latter makes EFSA's advice an unavoidable step for the preparation of science-based legislation. This is in particular the case for Scientific Opinions required in the framework of authorisation procedures for the marketability of substances or food and feed products.

Thus, many regulations on regulated substances pose the condition to EU risk managers to consult EFSA before adopting a measure with an impact on consumers' safety.[50] In addition, this legislation includes specific provisions entirely dedicated to EFSA's risk assessment and to the procedure that EFSA has to follow to adopt an Opinion.

The mandatory character of taking into account the latest scientific developments in order to adopt harmonised measures within the EU results, first, from Article 114(3) TFEU, which states that 'the Commission, in its proposals envisaged in paragraph 1 concerning health, safety, environmental protection and consumer protection, will take as a base a high level of protection, taking account

---

48 As defined by EFSA, 'Internal Mandates are the internal decisions to allocate scientific tasks in order for EFSA to issue an output within its remit' (self-task).

49 Technical Reports are, as a general rule, prepared by an EFSA Working Group and/or by EFSA scientific staff. The content and publication of a Technical Report are approved by the Executive Director. This is always the case when EFSA's staff drafts scientific outputs.

50 In general, the wording used is as follows 'The Commission, having first consulted the Authority, shall establish … implementing rules' (Article 15(4) of Regulation (EC) No 1924/2006; Article 5(7) of Regulation (EC) No 1829/2003; Article 7(4) of Regulation (EC) No 1831/2003.

in particular of any new development based on scientific facts'.[51] In addition, the mandatory character of scientific and technical assessments for the preparation of Union legislation has been recognised by Union Courts when the formality of consulting the scientific body in charge of the scientific assessment is expressly foreseen in the principal legislation.[52]

Moreover, the mandatory character is strengthened by provisions obliging risk managers to provide justification if they depart from EFSA's opinion.[53]

This mandatory character is also applicable to Reasoned Opinions.[54] The question of whether Statements have a mandatory character mainly depends on the context in which the Statement was requested and delivered by EFSA. When the Statement serves the purpose of reviewing the exposure assessment of an additive, then the European Commission will consider this advice entirely before adopting an implementing act, in consultation of the Standing Committee on Food Chain and Animal Health (SCFCAH), on the authorisation of this additive in the same way as for Scientific Opinions.

The counterpart of this obligation is that the absence of scientific risk assessment in a procedure may invalidate the act subsequently adopted.[55] A failure

51 See D. Gadbin, 'Les nouvelles articulations entre expertise scientifique et décision politique', in *La création de l'Autorité européenne de sécurité des aliments: enjeux et perspectives*, Etudes de l'IREDE coordonnées par Marc Blanquet et Nathalie de Grove-Valdeyron, Presses de l'Université de Toulouse I – Sciences sociales, 2004, pp. 25–52.

52 See, for example, Judgment of the Court of 25 January 1994, Case C-212/91 *Angelopharm v Freie und Hansestadt Hamburg*, [1994] ECR, I-00171, paragraph 39. In this case the Court of Justice of the EU found to be invalid an implementing act refusing the authorisation of a substance on the grounds that the authorisation procedure was vitiated by the 'substantial defect' of not having consulted the Scientific Committee on the substance in question, the consultation of the scientific body being required by the applicable legislation, paragraph 41.

53 See the wording used in much of the vertical legislations: 'Where the draft decision is not in accordance with the opinion of the Authority, the Commission shall provide an explanation for the differences', Articles 7(1) of Regulation (EC) No 1829/2006, 17(1) of Regulation (EC) No 1924/2006, 7(3) of Regulation (EC) No 1331/2008, 9(1) Regulation (EC) No 1831/2003. On this point see S. Krapohl, 'Credible Commitments in Non-Independent Regulatory Agencies: A Comparable Analysis of the European Agencies for Pharmaceuticals and Foodstuffs', *European Law Journal*, 10 (5), p. 532. See also M. Blanquet and N. De Grove-Valdeyron, 'Le recours à des agences de l'Union en réponse aux questions de sécurité', in *Les agences de l'Union européenne*, Bruylant, coll. Droit de l'Union européenne, dirigée par Fabrice Picod, 2011, p. 114.

54 The assessment by EFSA of applications and the evaluation reports is an imperative step in Article 10 of Regulation (EC) No 396/2005. Monitoring (Article 31) and review (Article 12) are also requiring an EFSA assessment prior legal measures are adopted on MRLs for pesticides.

55 See, for example, the invalidity of an act for failure to be based on scientific assessment and the need for the institution receiving the technical advice to verify the 'probative value' of the opinion delivered, Judgment of the Court of First Instance of 11

to consult EFSA as a preliminary step before adoption of Union measures may lead to proceedings for failure to act before the Union Courts, pursuant to Article 265 TFEU, against the European Commission. This holds true also if EFSA fails to provide its scientific advice.[56] In addition, some sectoral legislation foresees the possibility of an administrative review in the event of a decision taken under, or failure to exercise, the powers vested in EFSA.[57] The Commission is, in these circumstances, responsible for ensuring that EFSA withdraws its decision or remedies its failure to act within a given time limit.

Finally, the mandatory characteristic of EFSA's scientific outputs has a limitation. Although these outputs are mandatory, they are not vested with a hierarchical authority within the EU and are not intended to prevail over similar scientific opinions issued by national competent authorities, European Commission's Scientific Committees or other Union agencies. This absence of supremacy of EFSA's outputs over other scientific opinions within the EU is confirmed by Article 30 of EFSA's Founding Regulation, which foresees the possibility of a scientific conflict.[58] Under this provision, divergence between EFSA's scientific opinions and the scientific opinions issued by other bodies carrying out similar tasks leads to the opening of discussions between the divergent bodies in order to resolve the divergence.[59]

Legal Effects and Judicial Review of EFSA's Outputs

The recognition of the mandatory character of EFSA's scientific outputs poses indisputably the question of their effects on third parties and therefore the possibility of their review before the Union Courts.[60]

As far as the effects of EFSA's outputs are concerned, it has to be said that EFSA's Founding Regulation does not foresee the general application of Scientific Opinions, or their direct application. As such, EFSA's scientific outputs do not possess the characteristics of binding legal acts, having a legal basis within

---

September 2002, Case T-13/99 *Pfizer v Council*, [2002] ECR, II-03305, paragraphs 162–9, 198–9. See Chapter 13, C. MacMaoláin, 'EFSA the Respondent: A View from the Court of Justice of the European Union'.

56 Article 265 TFEU explicitly provides that 'this Article shall apply, under the same conditions, to bodies, offices and agencies of the Union which fail to act'.

57 See, for example, Article 19 of Regulation (EC) No 1831/2003 on feed additives, Article 36 of Regulation (EC) No 1829/2003 on GMOs, Article 14 of Regulation (EC) No 1935/2004 on food contact materials, Article 13 of Regulation (EC) No 396/2005 on MRL for pesticides. All these provisions are identical.

58 On this issue, see R. O'Rourke, 'Scientific Conflict, the EFSA and a Common Risk Assessment', *EFFL*, no. 4, 2007, pp. 197–204.

59 See A. Alemanno, 'L'Autorité européenne de sécurité des aliments souffle ses cinq premières bougies: un biland'activités', *Revue du droit de l'Union européenne*, no. 3, 2007, October, pp. 612–18.

60 See Chapter 13.

the Treaties. Scientific Opinions, Statements, Guidance, Reasoned Opinions, Conclusions, Reports fall within the category of legal acts of the EU, along with recommendations, that do not have binding force, in accordance with Article 288, paragraph 5, TFEU. EFSA is required to deliver scientific outputs, on request, to risk managers[61] for the purpose of adopting implementing measures that will take into account the state of play of the most updated scientific assessment. It follows that it can be a priori assumed that EFSA's scientific outputs are not vested with any legal effects. They are necessary for the decision-making process, so as to have science-based decisions at EU level, but cannot as such have direct effects on third parties.

A closer analysis of these effects can be carried out on the basis of the classical determinant characteristics legal acts have. Therefore, we can affirm that EFSA's scientific outputs are not aimed at creating effects *ratione personae* as they are not intended to be of general application and applicable as *erga omnes* acts. Indeed, EFSA's productions are not addressed to individuals, but exclusively to risk managers. In addition, *ratione materiae* EFSA's outputs produce effects only in the field of food law within which they were requested, in the framework of vertical legislation related to food or feed safety but also in relation to other sectors of Union food law. They can also produce effects in the framework of an emergency procedure for the purpose of taking measures to prevent hazards. *Ratione loci*, EFSA's outputs are required for the purpose of building measures for the harmonisation of rules within the Union market. They do not produce effects outside the EU.

Finally, *ratione temporis*, EFSA's outputs do not have an expiry date. Their validity runs until EFSA is requested to undertake a review of its previous assessment, or it does so autonomously.

It follows that EFSA's scientific outputs are not intended to produce effects on third parties and that they are not addressed to food business operators.[62] EFSA makes an objective scientific assessment that is addressed to risk managers[63] who have the final, and legally relevant, responsibility for taking appropriate decisions,

61 See Articles 29 and 31 of EFSA's Founding Regulation. In addition, in the data collection sector of activity, EFSA is also required to forward the result of its work to the European Parliament, the European Commission and Member States, see Article 33(6) of EFSA's Founding Regulation.

62 Some authors, however, consider that EFSA's outputs may produce 'indirect legal effects'; see A. Alemanno, 'The European Food Safety Authority at Five', *EFFL*, no.1, 2008, pp. 19–20.

63 The wording used specifies to whom the EFSA Scientific Opinion is addressed in authorisation procedures: 'The Authority shall forward its opinion to the Commission, the Member States and the applicant' (Article 16(5) of Regulation (EC) No 1924/2006, Article 10(2) of Regulation (EC) No 396/2005, Article 8(5) of Regulation (EC) No 1831/2003, Article 5(2) of Regulation (EC) No 1331/2008, etc.).

taking also into account other factors legitimate to the matter under consideration, including societal, economic, traditional, ethical and environmental factors[64]

In this context, the question of the judicial review of EFSA's scientific outputs does not appear to give rise to any particular difficulties.[65] Indeed, Opinions, Statements, Guidance, Conclusions and Reports are to be defined as instruments of 'soft-law' not having any binding effect whatsoever.[66] This has been confirmed by Union Courts concerning 'opinions' in general.[67] Moreover, the General Court clarified the non-binding character of EFSA's scientific opinions,[68] stating that they are part of a 'preliminary step' in a procedure, and do not therefore qualify as measures against which proceedings for annulment may be brought. Indeed, it is settled case law that only provisional measures, *i.e.* measures which are a step in a procedure, that are the culmination of a special procedure distinct from that which enables the Commission to take a decision on the substance of the case can be challenged.[69]

At this stage, although EFSA's scientific outputs cannot be challenged per se, procedural aspects surrounding the adoption of a scientific output may be raised before Union Courts in order to invalidate a final measure.[70] Thus, for instance, new issues regarding the independence of the Members of the Scientific

64 Recital (19) of EFSA's Founding Regulation.

65 On this matter, see, A. Alemanno and S. Mahieu, 'The European Food Safety Authority before European Courts', *EFFL*, no. 5, 2008, p. 327, and S. Gabbi, 'The European Food Safety Authority: Judicial Review by Community Courts', *European Journal of Consumer Law*, no. 1, 2009, pp. 171–89.

66 See Craig P. and De Búrca, G., *EU Law: Text, Cases and Materials*, 5th edn, Oxford, 2011, pp. 107–108.

67 See Order of the Court of Justice of 17 May 1989, Case 151/88 *Italy v Commission*, [1989] ECR 255, paragraphs 21–2 ; Order of the Court of 13 June 1991, Case C-59/90 *Sunzest Europe and Sunzest Netherlands v Commission of the European Communities*, [1991] ECR I-02917, paragraphs 12–13. On opinions of the European Parliament: Order of the Court of First Instance of 8 June 1998, Case T-148/97 *David T. Keeling v OHIM*, [1998] ECR II-02217, paragraphs 31–4. On opinions delivered upon request by letter see Order of the Court of First Instance of 9 April 2003, Case T-280/02 *Pikaart and Others v Commission*, [2003] ECR II-01621, paragraphs 23, 26, 27. Finally, on scientific opinions, see Order of the Court of First Instance of 2 June 2004, Case T-123/2003, *Pfizer v Commission*, [2004] ECR II-01631, paragraphs 21–3, 26.

68 See, e.g., Order of the General Court of 17 June 2008, in Case T-311/06 *FMC Chemical and Arysta Lifesciences v EFSA*, [2008] ECR II-00088, paragraph 43 ; Case T-312/06 *FMC Chemical / EFSA*, [2008] ECR II-00089, paragraph 43; and Case T-397/06, *Dow AgroSciences v EFSA*, [2008] ECR II-00090, paragraph 40.

69 Judgment of the Court of 11 November 1981, Case 60/81 *IBM v Commission*, [1981] ECR 2639, paragraphs 9–10.

70 Union Courts are not competent to adjudicate on the scientific content and soundness of EFSA's outputs. The role of science has been separated institutionally for the purpose of giving independent advice on which all Union institutions can rely. However, according to the General Court, Union institutions are responsible of assessing the 'probative value of the

Committee or a Scientific Panel adopting a scientific opinion could be brought to the attention of the Union Courts, in the event of conflicts of interests. In addition, the procedure as such within EFSA could also be reviewed by Union Courts in relation, for example, to compliance with deadlines for adopting scientific outputs, or their purpose.[71]

Final Remarks

Going beyond the classification of EFSA's scientific outputs, each single output has a different purpose within the scientific risk assessment and its legislative framework. Although Scientific Opinions, Reasoned Opinions and Statements are clearly aimed at providing advice to risk managers for the purpose of preparing legislation, Conclusions, Guidance documents and Reports fed into the scientific risk assessment as such by providing the state of play in science of existing data or providing practical information for this purpose.

The question also arises as to whether there might be a hierarchy among the different outputs that EFSA issues. It results from the wording of EFSA's Founding Regulation that Scientific Opinions have a stronger and more prominent role than any other output as they serve as a basis for the drafting and adoption of Union measures in the field of food and feed safety and have a dedicated provision in the EFSA's Founding act. This is not the case for Guidance documents and Reports. However, EFSA's Statements would appear to be equivalent to Scientific Opinions when they are aimed at reviewing an exposure assessment that may lead to the amendment of legislation on the authorised levels of a substance within the EU.

Finally, the increasing number of EFSA's staff (approximately 450 staff members) and the capacity of its scientific staff supporting the work of EFSA's Scientific Committee and Scientific Panels could lead to an enhancement of the role of staff vis-à-vis experts. This could be done by taking as a basis the way the EFSA's Pesticides Unit is dealing with the assessment of MRLs for pesticides.

However, this possibility is limited by the state of play of the current legislative framework. In order to enable EFSA to take the full advantage of its own scientific staff, the relevant legislation needs to be more flexible in choosing the way EFSA

opinion delivered'. See Case T-13/00 *Pfizer v Council*, *op. cit.*, paragraph 198 and Gabbi, 'The European Food Safety Authority: Judicial Review by Community Courts', p. 187.

71 One could consider that Union Courts may be requested to review internal procedures and rules adopted by EFSA for its functioning. See for example the indications in this direction by Unions Courts in Case T-70/99 *Alpharma Inc. v Council of the European Union*, [2002] ECR II-03495, paragraphs 180–84; and Joined Cases C-154/04 and C-155/04 *Alliance for Natural Health and Others*, [2005] ECR I-06451, paragraphs 85–8. See Alemanno and Mahieu, 'The European Food Safety Authority before European Courts', pp. 329–30, and Gabbi, 'The European Food Safety Authority: Judicial Review by Community Courts', pp. 187–8.

develops its outputs. This flexibility is also needed regarding the division of labour among staff, contractors, experts and Member States (national organisations interacting with EFSA on the basis of Article 36 cooperation).

It can be concluded from the above that there are many limitations imposed on EFSA to act and to choose an instrument for the delivery of its scientific assessment work. These limitations stem first from the legal framework of its constitution and existence as a 'pre-decision-making agency' of the EU, but also from the sectoral legislation which is always aligned with the general legal framework of EFSA's action. However, in this context, EFSA has shown the ability to produce a great diversity of scientific outputs. The number of scientific outputs has also increased significantly over the past few years, rising from 220 in 2007 to 735 in 2012.

Chapter 4

The Scientific Governance of the European Food Safety Authority: *Status Quo* and Perspectives

Simone Gabbi[1]

Introduction

The European Food Safety Authority was formally established in 2002 with the adoption of Regulation (EC) No 178/2002 (also known as the 'General Food Law').[2] It was, however, in 2003, with the creation of its Scientific Committee and Scientific Panels, that EFSA commenced its scientific operations. More than 12 years have passed by since the European Commission put forward its legislative proposal for what would have become the 'General Food Law'.[3] In the meantime, the Constitutional structure of the European Union has substantially changed:[4] the Union Legislator has updated and revolutionised the body of laws regulating food and feed safety at European level,[5] and from a different perspective the financial and economic crisis has been ravaging the Euro zone and altering the

1 The views expressed here are those of the author and do not necessarily represent, and should not be attributed to, the Authority, or any other institution, body or agency, of the European Union.

2 Regulation (EC) No 178/2002 of the European Parliament and of the Council of 28 January 2002 laying down the general principles and requirements of food law, establishing the European Food Safety Authority and laying down procedures in matters of food safety, OJ L 31, 1.2.2002, pp. 1–24, as last amended.

3 Commission of the European Communities, Proposal for a Regulation of the European Parliament and of the Council laying down the general principles and requirements of food law, establishing the European Food Authority, and laying down procedures in matters of food, COM(2000) 716.

4 With the entry into force of the Treaty on the European Union and Treaty on the Functioning of the European Union on 1 December 2009: see Craig P., 2010, *The Lisbon Treaty: Law, Politics and Treaty Reform*, New York: Oxford University Press; Griller S., and Ziller J. (eds), 2008, *The Lisbon Treaty: EU Constitutionalism without a Constitutional Treaty*? Springer: Vienna.

5 Achieving the ambitious legislative programme set out by the Commission of the European Communities, Commission White Paper on Food Safety, COM(1999) 719. The harmonisation of the Union 'food laws' started, however, much earlier: see Commission of

global geopolitical landscape.[6] Put in simpler terms, it could be easily argued that over the last 10 years the world and political priorities that were valid in 2000 are not the same. It has been shown that procedural credibility is a fundamental property for Union agencies at the post delegation stage.[7] It may therefore be the appropriate time to cast a hard look at the scientific governance of EFSA to verify how it has fared and if it is still the most appropriate design to accomplish the mission attributed to the Authority.

This contribution analyses the structure of the agency and its governing bodies. The analysis will proceed following a hierarchical order. There will be a discussion on the role and core business related functions of EFSA's Management Board. The focus will shift to assess the peculiarities linked to the Executive Director, to move on to the bodies delivering EFSA's scientific outputs. The contribution will highlight the reasons behind certain choices made by the Legislator and confront these with the developments occurred in the meantime to EFSA's operational environment, with the aim of identifying potential patterns for addressing them while ensuring the Authority keeps accomplishing its mission of providing reliable and objective scientific advice on the assessment of risks related to food and feed. The contribution will then conclude by illustrating how resulting problems and their implications are played out.

EFSA's Scientific Governance: Main Features

EFSA's scientific governance is based on four main internal bodies whose existence is required by the General Food Law: a Management Board, an Executive Director and her staff, an Advisory Forum and a scientific apparatus whose minimal composition foresees a Scientific Committee and 10 Scientific Panels.[8]

These bodies build their daily activities on a structure comprising approximately 500 employees and benefiting from the contributions of over 1500 experts from

the European Communities, Completion of the internal market: community legislation on foodstuffs, COM(85) 603 of 6 November 1985.

6 See e.g. Altman, R.C., 2009, Globalization in Retreat – Further Geopolitical Consequences of the Financial Crisis, *Foreign Affairs*, 88(4), 2–14; Germain, R., 2009, Financial Order and World Politics: Crisis, Change and Continuity, *International Affairs*, 85, 669–87; Schmidt, A., Arancibia, P., Kahlon, R., Komoto, N., Myers, J., Munyi, M., Ngororano, T., Omondi, G., Sepaha, P. and Yeojeong, K., 2009, Geopolitics, Global Governance and Crisis Narratives, *IDS Bulletin*, 40, 89–100.

7 Borrás, S., Koutalakis, C. and Wendler, F., 2007, European Agencies and Input Legitimacy: EFSA, EMeA and EPO in the Post-Delegation Phase, *Journal of European Integration*, 29(5), 583–600.

8 Article 24 of Regulation (EC) No 178/2002: *Ex multis v.* Capelli, F., 2002, Qualità e sicurezza dei prodotti agroalimentari nell'Unione europea, *Diritto comunitario e degli scambi internazionali*, 4, 882–3; and Capelli, F., Klaus, B. and Silano, V., 2006, Nuova disciplina del settore alimentare e Autorità europea per la sicurezza alimentare, Milan: Giuffrè.

countries inside and outside the European Union and over 350 national scientific organisations from Union Member States.[9]

EFSA's Management Board

The Management Board is the body responsible for exercising the powers going beyond the daily management of the Authority, ranging from strategic and policy documents to the adoption of EFSA's internal rules. In other words, the Board is a key player in EFSA and sits at the very top of its organigram.

Its composition, the appointment process of its members and more in general the provisions regulating its activities are therefore of significance to comprehend how EFSA discharges its mission and tasks in the Union legal system vis-à-vis other institutions, interested parties and partners.[10]

The Composition and Appointment Procedure of the Management Board

The appointment process of the members is one of the manners in which some control can be exercised by delegating bodies to minimise the losses of power ensuing from the creation of a new institution.[11] Irrespective of the fact that the real willingness of the delegating bodies to use these powers should not be overestimated, it is therefore necessary to understand whether in the case of EFSA the delegators designed a system allowing them to exercise this option.

EFSA's Management Board is composed of 14 members and of a representative of the European Commission.[12] The members of the Board are appointed in their personal capacity following a selection procedure aimed at choosing the most competent and experienced individuals, with no pre-ordinate requirement concerning nationality or geographical representation. In this respect, it may be worth highlighting the first peculiar feature of EFSA's governance, which is the composition of the Board. If one indeed considers the management boards of

---

9 European Food Safety Authority, Press Release on EFSA's commitment to ensuring that Europe's food is safe – 10 years and going from strength to strength, available on EFSA's website at the following address (last visited on 20 July 2012): http://www.efsa.europa.eu/en/press/news/120130g.htm.

10 Craig, P., 2012, *EU Administrative Law*, Oxford: Oxford University Press, at 163.

11 See Thatcher, M., 2002, Regulation after Delegation: Independent Regulatory Agencies in Europe, *Journal of European Public Policy*, 9(6), 956. This notwithstanding, the theoretical availability of certain control methods is not systematically exploited by the delegators. In that respect one could recall the case of the so-called administrative review clause, inserted by the Commission in the first legal acts adopted immediately after the creation of EFSA, but never used ever since: about this point see in more detail, Gabbi, S., 2009. *L'Autorità europea per la sicurezza alimentare. Genesi, aspetti problematici e prospettive di riforma*, Giuffrè: Milan, § 6.2.

12 Article 25(1) of Regulation (EC) No 178/2002.

other regulatory agencies of the Union performing tasks similar to EFSA's,[13] he could identify three general models: one that could be described as that of the 'competent individuals' (i.e. EFSA's); the 'Council' model, where the members of the Board are in fact representatives of each Member State (EASA, ECDC, EEA, EMCDDA and partially ECHA); and the 'Legislators model', where the Commission, the Parliament and the Council all appoint certain members of the Board (EU-OSHA and EMA).[14] The 'Council model' can therefore be considered the norm among Union regulatory agencies, although this means that the members are often chosen on the basis of the principle of representativeness alone, to the detriment of expertise on aspects relevant to their role.[15]

It follows that EFSA's Board can be considered the exception to the rule, for its Board members have to be chosen on the basis of their experience and knowledge in budgetary, financial matters or experience in the sector of competence of the agency.[16] To mitigate an approach that could be considered extreme,[17] the General Food Law prescribes that the selection procedure of candidates for Board membership should balance their experience in areas related to EFSA's core business with the principle

---

13 For the purpose of the present contribution were considered comparable to EFSA's competences those of the European Aviation Safety Agency, the European Centre for Disease prevention and Control, the European Chemicals Agency, the European Environment Agency, the European Medicines Agency, the European Monitoring Centre for Drugs and Drugs Addictions and European Agency for Safety and Health at Work.

14 See for instance Groenleer, M., 2009, *The Autonomy of European Union Agencies*, Delft: Eburon. On European regulatory agencies there is an abundant literature: see e.g. Gerardin, D. et al. (eds), 2006, *Regulation through Agencies in the EU*, Cheltenham: Edward Elgar Publishing. There are, however, several ways of classifying agencies: Joerges, C. and Dehousse, R. (eds), 2002, *Good Governance in Europe's Integrated Market*, Oxford: Oxford University Press; Ekelund, H.M., 2012, Making Sense of the 'Agency Programme' in Post-Lisbon Europe: Mapping European Agencies, *Central European Journal of Public Policy*, 6(1), at 40.

15 Along this line Busuioc, M., 2012, European Agencies and Their Boards: Promises and Pitfalls of Accountability beyond Design, *Journal of European Public Policy*, 19(5), 727. Recently the Common Approach outlined in the Joint Statement, identifies the Council model as the norm between the several options available: point n. 10 of the Common Approach annexed to the Joint Statement of the European Parliament, the Council of the EU, the European Commission on decentralised agencies of 19 July 2012, available online at the following address (last visited on 3 December 2012) http://ec.europa.eu/commission_2010–2014/sefcovic/documents/120719_agencies_common_appr_en.pdf. Before this document, along the same line one could recall Commission of the European Communities, *Draft Interinstitutional Agreement on the Operating Framework for the European Regulatory Agencies (presented by the Commission)*, COM(2005) 59; European Commission, Communication from the Commission, The operating framework for the European Regulatory Agencies, COM(2002) 718 final.

16 See Recital n. 41 of Regulation (EC) No 178/2002 which refers to expertise in management and public administrations.

17 At least taking into account EFSA's nature as a supranational agency of the EU.

of geographical rotation.[18] In addition, the Legislator came up with a second mechanism that could attain the same goal while preserving the autonomy of the newly created agency from the political inputs of Member States. We will examine in the next paragraph how EFSA's Advisory Forum fulfils this role.

Four of the 14 members are required to have their background in 'organisations representing consumers and other interests of the food chain'. Thus far, this concept has been interpreted as legitimating the appointment of representatives of industry associations, consumer organisations and *similia*. Nonetheless, a literal interpretation of the provision and the transcripts of the discussions linked to a defeated amendment[19] support a more narrow interpretation, i.e. that the original intent of the Legislator might have been closer to having professionals with past experience in those organisations than members with still active links sitting in the Board.

The role of the assembly in the appointment process is rather limited, as it echoes the more limited powers the Parliament had before the entry into force of the Treaty of Amsterdam. As a consequence, the Parliament enjoys a mere advisory role, with the Council in a position to appoint certain candidates even against the advice delivered by the assembly.[20] Should the Parliament fail to adopt its opinion in the prescribed period of three months, the Council would be entitled to proceed with the appointment. The role of the European Parliament is therefore quite limited, especially if one considers the powers it enjoys in other regulatory agencies of comparable importance, such as the EMA and the EEA.

Considering the 'constitutional' developments occurred since the adoption of the GFL, it can reasonably be expected that the Parliament will strive to take advantage of the earliest chance to amend the General Food Law to gain a more prominent role in the procedure examined above. If this were to take place, it could be anticipated that candidates with active careers in organisations having an interest in the food chain could be excluded from appointment.

At least this is the consideration that could be drawn from the rejection by the Council, following significant pressure from the European Parliament,[21] of a candidate heading FoodDrinkEurope, the association representing food

---

18 Pursuant to recital n. 41 of the General Food Law the Board 'should be appointed in such a way as to secure the highest standard of competence, a broad range of relevant expertise, for instance in management and in public administration, and the broadest possible geographic distribution within the Union. This should be facilitated by a rotation of the different countries of origin of the members of the Management Board without any post being reserved for nationals of any specific Member State'.

19 I am referring to amendment n. 101 included in the Report A5- 0198/2001 (Rapporteur Phillip Whitehead) according to which the Board should have been composed of 12 members 'included two representatives of consumers and two of food industry'.

20 Committee on Environment, Public Health and Food Safety.

21 See the strong position of the Committee on Environment, Public Health and Food safety of the European Parliament on certain candidates on the shortlist proposed by the European Commission: *EU Food Law Weekly*, No 526 of 30 March 2012.

and drink industry interests in the European Union, in the context of the 2012 appointment process.[22]

The Powers of the Board: Impacting on EFSA's Core Business

The tasks of the Board reflect its main mandate, which can be identified in all the powers going beyond the day to day management of the Authority,[23] from strategic and policy documents to the adoption of EFSA's internal rules.

In agreement with the Common Approach annexed to the Joint Statement on Agencies of the European Union,[24] the Board adopts the decisions appointing and removing the Executive Director, the members of the Scientific Committee and Panels, approving the final budget and other comparable functions, such as the adoption of the Authority's internal regulations. Furthermore, the Board is competent for the approval of the annual activity report of the preceding year[25] and of the work programme of the reference year, as well as to exercise control over the activities of the Authority to ensure they comply with its founding regulation and with the relevant legal framework.

The original proposal of the Commission, aiming at retaining the power to provide a binding opinion on the formulation of the draft work programme of the agency,[26] was changed at the request of the European Parliament, as it would have allegedly compromised the operational autonomy of the Authority. The result has been a balanced provision, where the programme is first drafted by the Executive Director in consultation with the Advisory Forum, and is then adopted by the Board in complete autonomy. The only trace left of the original intention of the Commission is the requirement for the Board to ensure the consistency of the programme with the legislative and political priorities of the European Union.[27] The absence of any requirement to consult with the Commission,

---

22 Keating, D., 2012, Council rejects EFSA nominee [online *EuropeanVoice.com*]. Available at the following address: http://www.europeanvoice.com/article/2012/june/council-rejects-efsa-nominee/74562.aspx (last visited on 29 July 2012).

23 Which according to Article 26 of Regulation (EC) No 178/2002 are assigned to the Executive Director.

24 Point n. 16 of the Common Approach, *supra sub* footnote 14.

25 Which represents a summary of the activities undertaken in the previous year to be approved by 30 March of the following year (Article 25(8) of Regulation (EC) No 178/2002): see by way of example *Annual Report 2011*, available on EFSA's website at the following address: http://ec.europa.eu/governance/docs/comm_agence_en.pdf (last visited on 1 May 2012).

26 The position of the Commission was in line with the indications included in the Communication on regulatory agencies, *sub* footnote 33, page 9. The more recent Common Approach, *sub* footnote 43, point n. 29 is, however, in favour of a less intrusive mandatory consultation of the Commission on the agencies' draft programmes.

27 Article 26(2)(b) of Regulation (EC) No 178/2002. Also Craig, 2012, *EU Administrative Law*, 165 classifies the Regulation establishing EFSA for this aspect in an

although formally respectful of EFSA's autonomy, would have run the risk of relegating the Authority in an ivory tower and possibly resulted in a breach of the principle of efficacy of the European administrative action.

The Board's competence for adopting the work programme and for setting the strategic objectives of the agency can be considered as the most relevant powers from the perspective of its involvement in EFSA's core business activities. A decision of the Board to divert or reassign resources from one sector to another might have far reaching implications on the possibility of developing the area that has been 'sacrificed'.

The second, and last, relevant attribution to the Board concerns the selection of the members Scientific Committee and Scientific Panels. In this case, however, the wording used by the General Food Law appears to be supporting an interpretation which would see the Board as a notary, taking note of the preparatory work undertaken by the Executive Director and its staff, and competent only for the legality and compliance check with EFSA's Founding Regulation and the Authority's internal rules.[28]

The Executive Director

The Executive Director of the EFSA is responsible for exercising all the powers related to the daily management of the agency, from the allocation of its resources to the implementation of the strategic directives and orientations given by the Management Board. EFSA's Executive Director is appointed by the Board among a list of candidates drawn up by the Commission following an open call for expression of interest.[29]

The original proposal of the Commission foresaw that the Director be appointed by the Management Board upon indication of the Commission, which would have proposed a name directly to the Board.[30] The Board's role would have been limited to the validation of the choice made by the Commission. The Parliament managed to get through an amendment aimed at leaving to the Board the power of choosing the appointee from a shortlist prepared by the Commission.[31]

---

intermediate position between those that foresee a substantial influence of the Commission and those that do not even contemplate its consultation.

28 Article 28 of Regulation (EC) No 178/2002.

29 Article 26 of Regulation (EC) No 178/2002.

30 *Proposal for a Regulation of the European Parliament and of the Council laying down the general principles and requirements of food law, establishing the European Food Authority, and laying down procedures in matters of food* COM (2000)716.

31 Amendment n. 107, Report A5–0198/2001, 57. For a more detailed analysis of the legislative process leading to the adoption of these provisions of the General Food Law, see Losavio, C., *Commento agli Artt. 26, 27, Reg. 178/2002,* in *La sicurezza alimentare nell'Unione europea*, above, at 321.

The provision in force prescribes a confirmatory hearing before the Parliament that takes place before the Board appoints the candidate Executive Director. At the time of writing this never resulted in a challenge to the choices made by the Management Board.[32]

In a (maybe not-so) distant future one could anticipate that the Director might be called to the competent Committee of the European Parliament to answer certain regulatory choices[33] and be tested by the members of the Parliament to make him answerable before the parliamentary assembly. At the moment of writing, the practice of holding public and annual hearings of EFSA's Executive Director before the Committee of the European Parliament had indeed been introduced voluntarily by the Authority and other fellow agencies, although this process seems delinked from the appointment or renewal of EFSA's top manager.[34]

Competences of the Executive Director

The Executive Director is a key player in EFSA's governance: she is the legal representative of the Authority, is responsible for the daily management and for all personnel-related matters and is competent for the preparation of the annual work programmes,[35] the internal rules of the Authority, the draft estimates of expenditures,[36] whose formal adoption is left to the Management Board.

Also from the perspective of EFSA's core business the Executive Director is pivotal for the Authority's efficacy. The Authority's top manager is responsible for the implementation of the work programme she prepares for adoption by the Board; for organising the selection of EFSA's scientific experts, ensuring the appropriate administrative and scientific support for its Committee and Panels and providing the responses to requests for scientific and technical assistance.

In other words, it can be concluded that the Executive Director holds the real managerial powers of the Authority, with the Management Board in the position of validating the proposals put forward by her in a sort of *ex ante* verification and legality check. This line of thought would see the possibility for the Board of holding the Executive Director accountable for his actions as a confirmation of the role of arbiter, or guardian of the rules, that the Board would undertake.[37]

---

32 The formal nomination of the second director occurred on 13 April 2006, by '*taking into account the views of the European Parliament*'. Along this line see *Unanimous appointment for Geslain-Lanéelle*, *EU Food Law* n. 253 of 28 April 2006.

33 Craig, *EU Administrative Law*, 177.

34 This regular dialogue could also be interpreted as a mere implementation of the obligation for the Executive Director to develop and maintain contacts with the European Parliament and its competent committees: Article 26(2)(h) of Regulation (EC) no 178/2002.

35 About which see Gabbi, *L'Autorità europea*, Cap. V.

36 Article 26 of Regulation (EC) No 178/2002.

37 Although the willingness of individuals to use their powers in a complex and supranational political context should not be overestimated, research has shown that accountability forums often fail to exercise in practice the formal powers at their disposal:

The Advisory Forum

The Advisory Forum (hereinafter also Forum) is composed by representatives of Member States of the European Union and countries with which the European Union has signed agreements by virtue of which they have adopted and apply Union legislation in the field covered by the General Food Law. The Forum is chaired by the Executive Director and its functions are strictly linked to EFSA's core business: it advises its Chair on how to best ensure the development and maintenance of a cooperative approach between EFSA and the national competent authorities.[38]

EFSA's Advisory Forum has been created to compensate for the absence of a direct representative link between the members of the Management Board and the EU Member States,[39] to improve the efficiency of the European administrative action and the cooperation between the European and national level and ultimately to act as a coordinating hub for EFSA's networking activities.[40] It is widely acknowledged that Union regulatory agencies de facto develop into a networking tool that over the years greatly contribute to the creation of epistemic communities of technocrats[41] or a European multi-level public administration.[42] The existence of an Advisory

Busuioc, 2012, European Agencies and Their Boards; and id., 2010, The Accountability of European Agencies: Legal Provisions and Ongoing Practices. The same finding appears to be applicable also for the accountability forums available towards the agencies, although probably the same could be said about other Institutions: Busuioc, M., 2010, *The Accountability of European Agencies: Legal Provisions and Ongoing Practices*, Delft: Eburon; id., 2010, European Agencies: Pockets of Accountability, in Bobens, M., Curin, D. and Hart, P.'t (eds), *The Real World of Accountability: What Deficit?* Oxford: Oxford University Press, 87–116; Curtin, D., 2009, Holding (quasi) Autonomous EU Administrative Actors to Public Account, *European Law Journal*, 13(4), 523–41; Thatcher, M., 2005, The Third Force? Independent Regulatory Agencies and Elected Politicians, *Europe, Governance: An International Journal of Policy, Administration and Institutions*, 18(3), 347–73.

38 In that regard see also Article 2(1), *Decision*, above.

39 Majone, G., 2003, European Regulatory Agencies: The Dilemma of Delegation of Powers in the European Union, in id., (ed.), *Risk Regulation in the European Union: Between Enlargement and Internationalization*, San Domenico di Fiesole (FI), at 62.

40 Article 27(2) of Regulation (EC) No 178/2002.

41 Waarden, F. Van and Drahos, M., 2002, Courts and (epistemic) Communities in the Convergence of Competition Policies, *Journal of European Public Policy*, 9(6), 913–34.

42 Chiti, E., 2002, Decentralised Integration as a New Model of Joint Exercise of Community Functions: A Legal Analysis of European Agencies, in *ERLP/REDP*, 14(3), autumn, 1267 ss.; id., European Agencies: A Legal Form for Network Management?, in George, A., Machado, P. and Ziller, J., Law and Public Management: Network Management, EUI Working Paper Law No. 2001/13, 23 ss.; Coen, D. and Thatcher, M., 2008, Network Governance and Multi-level Delegation: European Networks of Regulatory Agencies, *Journal of Public Policy*, 28, 49–71; Dehousse, R., 1997, Regulation by Networks in the European Community: The Role of European Agencies, *Journal of European Public Policy*, 4(2), 246–61; Keleman, D.R., 2002, The Politics of 'Eurocratic' Structure and the New European

Forum is therefore to be considered an essential feature of EFSA's governance, which could be disposed of only if the Legislator amended the composition of its Board in the direction of what is the norm for other regulatory agencies.

In 2006, when the then newly appointed Executive Director wanted to enhance EFSA's networking and cooperation strategy with the competent authorities of the Member States, she put at the centre of her action the Advisory Forum.[43]

From a scientific point of view the Forum is required to prevent or at least identify at an early stage potential divergence between scientific opinions of EFSA and of national competent authorities[44] and facilitate a better identification of emerging risks.[45] This is a fundamental task for EFSA as a scientific authority with the mission of being recognised as European point of reference in the risk assessment of food and feed risks: in the absence of a provision granting supremacy to the scientific opinions adopted by the Parma-based agency[46] it is indeed essential that all available tools are in place to facilitate a consensus building process that cannot afford to leave behind Member States' risk assessment bodies.[47] From a managerial perspective, such an exercise contributes to the optimal allocation of human and financial resources to scientific projects, thereby ideally avoiding possible duplications between work programmes of agencies in EU Member States. It could be easily argued that the composition and mission of the Advisory Forum is designed with the plausible objective of achieving a gradual alignment, or even convergence, of the operations of the national agencies active in EFSA's fields of competence. It could be concluded that via the Forum, chaired by EFSA's Executive Director, the Authority is expected to become the place where risk assessment work programmes of the entire Union are discussed and 'coordinated', if not harmonised.

Agencies, *West European Politics*, 25(4), 93–118; Majone, G., 1997, The New European Agencies: Regulation by Information, *Journal of European Public Policy*, 262–75.

43 See EFSA, MB 19.12.2006–6a *Strategy for Cooperation and Networking between the EU Members States and EFSA*, but also the more recent *Interim Review of the Strategy for Cooperation and Networking between EU Member States and EFSA and Technical Report of EFSA on Scientific Cooperation between EFSA and Member States: Taking Stock and Looking Ahead available on EFSA's website at:* http://www.efsa.europa.eu/en/networks.htm. Speech of Catherine Geslain-Lanéelle, Nominee to be the Executive Director of EFSA, given to the ENVI Committee of the European Parliament on 23 February 2006, point n. 3 of her priorities. The speech is available at (last visited on 4 August 2012) http://www.efsa.europa.eu/en/edspeeches/speeches/brussels060223.htm.

44 The identification of a divergence would automatically trigger the ad hoc procedure foreseen in Article 30 of Regulation (EC) No 178/2002.

45 On EFSA's activities re. the identification of emerging risks see Kocharov, A., 2010, EFSA and Identification of Emerging Risks, *European Food and Feed Law Rev.* 3, 144–55.

46 Aside from the peculiar 'mediation procedure' laid down in Article 60 of Regulation (EC) No 178/2002 which indeed assigns a quasi-adjudicatory role to EFSA (through the Commission).

47 Specifically for EFSA: Buonanno, L., Zabloteney, S. and Keefer, R., 2001, Politics versus Science in the Making of a New regulatory Regime for Food in Europe, *EIoP*, 5, n. 12.

In that perspective, at the Forum, the Authority could be expected to exercise some kind of moral suasion towards the agencies and other bodies represented there.[48]

The cooperation between EFSA and national competent authorities is also pursued on a more operational level via the thematic networks of a scientific nature foreseen in the General Food Law.[49] A feature that EFSA shares with its fellow regulatory agencies, these networks are composed of officials of EU Member States' authorities. At the moment of writing, it is difficult to identify an area where EFSA has not created a Network to enhance the level of cooperation with national competent authorities.[50] In parallel, these kinds of operations are also likely on the one hand to reduce the likelihood of opposition to EFSA's scientific activities from a technical perspective, as the daily cooperation between EFSA's officials and their national counterparts can be expected to lead to a feeling of increased ownership; and on the other hand to facilitate the development of a single community in the field of authorities active in the risk assessment of food and feed.[51]

EFSA's Scientific Structure

The internal bodies dealing with EFSA's core scientific activities can be identified in its Scientific Committee, Scientific Panels and their working groups supported by the staff providing the ancillary functions necessary for their performance.

---

48 In the way first pioneered by the European Commission with its DG Competition and the European Competition Network (ECN), composed of the Member States' antitrust authorities: Monti, M., 2004, Competition Policy in a Global Economy, *International Finance*, 7, 495–504; Wilks, S., 2005, Agency Escape: Decentralization or Dominance of the European Commission in the Modernization of Competition Policy? *Governance*, 18, 431–52. This work inter alia questions the assumption that only agencies would be able to develop epistemic communities.

49 Article 36 of Regulation (EC) No 178/2002.

In that respect see also the rules of procedure of Networks: *EFSA, Decision concerning the establishment and operation of European Networks of scientific organisations operating in the fields within the Authority's mission*, available online at the following address (last visited on 18 March 2012) MB 18.03.10 – item 7 doc 6: http://www.efsa.europa.eu/ en/ keydocs/docs/networksoperation.pdf.

50 See by way of example *Technical Report of EFSA on Scientific Cooperation between EFSA and Member States: Taking Stock and Looking Ahead* and MB 19.12.2006–6a *Strategy for cooperation and networking, Strategy for Cooperation and Networking between the EU Member States and EFSA*, available online at the following address (last visited on 18 March 2012): http://www.efsa.europa.eu/en/keydocs/docs/msstrategy.pdf. See Chiti, Decentralised Integration, 1290, and idem, European Agencies: A Legal Form for Network Management?, in George, A., Machado, P. and Ziller, J., 2001, Law and Public Management: Network Management, *EUI Working Paper* Law, 13.

51 There are, however, prerequisites that some suggest should be present for a network to be effective: Majone, G., 2000, The Credibility Crisis of Community Regulation, *Journal of Common Market Studies*, 38(2), 273–98.

The Scientific Committee and the Scientific Panels

The Scientific Committee and the Scientific Panels (hereinafter also simply 'Panels') lay at the heart of EFSA's structure, at the very basis of the decision of establishing an independent scientific risk assessment body. The Scientific Committee and the Panels are indeed the only scientific bodies within EFSA that are responsible for adopting its scientific opinions.[52]

From a diachronic perspective, EFSA's Scientific Panels have been created at the end of 2002 by one of the first decisions of the Authority's newly established Management Board,[53] in order to ensure the appropriate business continuity for the scientific advice provided before EFSA by the Scientific Committees managed by the Commission.[54]

The reform of these Commission scientific committees undertaken in 1997 was performed in accordance with three fundamental principles, i.e. independence, transparency and scientific excellence.[55] The same principles, whose importance was in the meantime confirmed by a seminal ruling of the then Court of First

52 Article 28(1) of Regulation (EC) No. 178/2002 entrusts the power of adopting 'the scientific opinions of the Authority, each within their own spheres of competence' to one scientific committee and 10 scientific panels competent for specific domains.

53 European Food Safety Authority, MB 17.10.2002–3 *adopted Decision concerning the establishment and the operations of the Scientific Committee and panels*.

54 About which see e.g. Gornitzka, Å. and Sverdrup, U., 2008, Who Consults? The Configuration of Expert Groups in the European Union, *West European Politics*, 31(4), 725–50. During 1997, following the internal reorganisation of the Commission linked to the so-called mad cow disease, the Scientific Committee for Foods (SCF) and the Scientific Veterinary Committee (SVC) were moved under the responsibility of DG Industry and DG Agriculture, while others committees linked to consumer protection were reassigned to DG Consumer protection, together with RAPEX, the alert system that facilitates the rapid exchange of information between Member States and the Commission on measures taken to prevent or restrict the marketing or use of products posing a serious risk to the health and safety of consumers (with the exception of food, pharmaceutical and medical devices). For more details on these events see Vos, *Institutional Frameworks*.

55 Substantiated by European Commission, Commission Communication on Consumer Health and Food Safety, COM(97) 183. The introspective analysis of how to best manage scientific expertise did not stop at that as the Commission still manages scientific experts' committees on e.g. on consumer safety (SCCS), health and environmental risks (SCHER) and Emerging and Newly Identified Health Risks (SCENIHR). In that respect see European Commission, Communication of the Commission on the collection and use of expertise by the Commission: Principles and Guidelines 'Improving the knowledge base for better policies' COM(2002)713 of 11 December 2002, 8 and ff. and European Commission, Maximising the contribution of science to European Health Safety, a DG SANCO paper, Brussels, July 2005.

Instance of the European Union (now General Court),[56] were then used as guiding canons for the activity of EFSA's scientific apparatus.[57]

This is certainly not the only characteristic in common between EFSA's Scientific Panels and the Commission's committees. For instance, the Scientific Steering Committee used to be composed of the chairs of the sectoral committees and by eight experts not involved in the other committees,[58] with a choice that is essentially reflected in the composition of EFSA's Scientific Committee.[59] The independence of the members of the committees was ensured by the fact that the Commission,[60] the supranational body pursuing the 'Community method',[61] and not the Member States, was in control of the selection and appointment process, with an approach not too dissimilar from the one chosen for EFSA in its Founding Regulation.[62] At the time this was considered a sufficient guarantee against what was deemed to be the biggest threat to the scientific objectivity of the committees of the newborn Authority: the political pressure coming from Member States to ignore or undervalue a certain risk in the way the UK had done during the mad cow crisis.[63]

Closing this diachronic digression, it is evident how the design of EFSA's scientific apparatus draws largely from the experience gained by the Commission services in managing their internal scientific committees. Comparative studies

---

56 Judgement of the Court of First Instance, of 11 September 2002 in Case T-13/99 *Pfizer Animal Health v. Council* [2002] ECR II-3305.

57 Those principles indeed were to be found in the study which formed the basis for the first reflections on the structure and mandate to be attributed to EFSA: James, P., Kemper, F. and Pascal, G., 1999, *A European Food and Public Health Authority: The Future of Scientific Advice in the EU. A Report Commissioned by the Director General of DG XXIV*, Brussels: European Commission, specifically at 19. See Gabbi, *L'Autorità europea*, § 3.6 and ff.

58 Article 3 (1), Decision of the European Commission N° 97/404/CE, *GUCE* L 169 of 27.6.1997.

59 The only difference indeed lies in the number of the independent experts: eight for the then SSC; six for EFSA's Scientific Committee. See Article 28(3) of Regulation (EC) No 178/2002.

60 See Article 3(4) of the Decision of the European Commission N° 97/404/CE, above, and Article 6 of the Decision of the Commission n. 97/579/CE.

61 Eberlein, B. and Kerwer, D., 2004, New Governance in the European Union: A Theoretical Perspective, *Journal of Common Market Studies*, 42, 121–42; Schäfer, A., 2004, Beyond the Community Method: Why the Open Method of Coordination was Introduced to EU Policy-Making, *European Integration online Papers (EIoP)*, 8(13).

62 See for instance, the way the Authority has regulated in every detail all the procedural arrangements of the selection and appointment procedures of its scientific experts: Decision of the Executive Director concerning the selection of members of the scientific committee, scientific panels and external experts to assist EFSA with its scientific work, above.

63 On the evolution of the concept of independence over time, see Gabbi, S., 2011, Independent Scientific Advice: Comparing Policies on Conflicts of Interest in the EU and the US, *European Journal of Risk Regulation*, 2, 213–17 and Shamoo, A.E. and Resnik, D.B., 2009, *Responsible Conduct of Research*, Oxford: Oxford University Press.

attribute the remaining influence to the model of the French agency created only some time before EFSA.[64]

In the case of EFSA, the powers attributed to the Scientific Committee and to the Panels are firstly of relevance from a functional perspective, with the former responsible for ensuring coherence of the assessment methodologies and work programme of the 10 Panels, and the latter competent for specific matters falling within their specific remits. The Scientific Committee also adopts opinions and other outputs on matters that do not fall under any of the Panels' attributions or regard more than one Panel.[65]

The fields of competence of each Panel are well defined in the General Food Law,[66] and further specified in EFSA's internal rules.[67] Since the Scientific Committee is competent for setting horizontal standards, assessment methodologies and has among its members the chairs of the 'vertical' Panels, it could be regarded as a *primus inter pares*. Nonetheless, affirming the Committee's role and supremacy vis-à-vis the 10 Panels has been an enduring endeavour, as at times has also been acknowledged by those very bodies.[68] In 2012, to support the Scientific Committee in this exercise, EFSA adopted a decision regulating the approach to so-called multi-sectoral opinions.[69] At the time of writing it seems

64 See on this point see Borraz, O., Besancon, J. and Clergeau, C., 2006. Is it Just about Trust? The Partial Reform of French Food Safety System, in Ansell, C. and Vogel, D. (eds), What's the Beef? The Contested Governance of European Food Safety, at 144 and Gabbi, *L'Autorità europea*, at 80.

65 Article 28(2) of Regulation (EC) No. 178/2002.

66 Pursuant to Article 28(4) of Regulation (EC) No. 178/2002, 'The Scientific Panels shall be composed of independent scientific experts. When the Authority is established, the following Scientific Panels shall be set up: (a) the Panel on food additives and nutrient sources added to food; (b) the Panel on additives and products or substances used in animal feed; (c) the Panel on plant protection products and their residues; (d) the Panel on genetically modified organisms; (e) the Panel on dietetic products, nutrition and allergies; (f) the Panel on biological hazards; (g) the Panel on contaminants in the food chain; (h) the Panel on animal health and welfare; (i) the Panel on plant health; (j) the Panel on food contact materials, enzymes, flavourings, and processing aids'.

67 Article 6 of the Decision of the Management Board of the European Food Safety Authority concerning the establishment and operations of the Scientific Committee, Scientific Panels and of their Working Groups, mb 15 03 12, available on EFSA's website at the following address (last visited on 25 July 2012): http://www.efsa.europa.eu/it/keydocs/docs/paneloperation.pdf.

68 European Food Safety Authority, MB 20.6.2006–6 *Plan of Action re. Functioning of Scientific Committee and Panels; EFSA*, MB 29.3.2006–7, *Proposal from the Secretariat on the functioning of the EFSA Scientific Committee and Panels*, and EFSA, MB 29.3.2006–7 Annex, *Issues related to the functioning of the Scientific Committee and Panels*, 2.

69 Decision of the Executive Director of the European Food Safety Authority regarding multisectoral issues, EFSA/2012/LRA/03, available on EFSA's website at the following address (last visited on 14 May 2012): http://www.efsa.europa.eu/en/request%20/docs/edmultisectoral.pdf.

that the coordinating role of the Scientific Committee is more affirmed than ever, with the adoption in the time span of a few months of several key opinions for a coherent approach to the work of the Scientific Panels, such as the opinions on the assessment of mutagenic substances,[70] on the Threshold of Toxicological Concern[71] and on the terminology to be used in risk assessment.[72]

The General Food Law initially foresaw the establishment of eight Scientific Panels[73] and it offered the Commission the possibility of adapting the number and names of the Panels in view of technological and scientific developments[74] upon request of the Authority. A provision of this kind was needed to ensure the appropriate flexibility to EFSA Panel centric scientific structures, so as to avoid the recourse to the considerably more lengthy ordinary legislative procedure.[75]

The first application of this provision has been the creation of a Panel devoted to matters linked to Plant Health. The Panel was created in 2006 at the request of EFSA and following the approval of the proposal for the Commission Regulation.[76] From the wording of the General Food Law it appears that the Commission does not retain any residual discretion for submitting the draft to the Standing Committee

70 EFSA Scientific Committee; Scientific Opinion on the applicability of the Margin of Exposure approach for the safety assessment of impurities which are both genotoxic and carcinogenic in substances added to food/feed. EFSA Journal 2012;10(3):2578. [5 pp.] doi:10.2903/j.efsa.2012.2578. Available online at the following address (last visited on 18 July 2012): www.efsa.europa.eu/efsajournal.

71 EFSA Scientific Committee; Scientific Opinion on Exploring options for providing advice about possible human health risks based on the concept of Threshold of Toxicological Concern (TTC). EFSA Journal 2012; 10(7):2750 [103 pp.] doi:10.2903/j.efsa.2012.2750. Available online at the following address (last visited on 18 July 2012): www. efsa.europa.eu/efsajournal.

72 EFSA Scientific Committee; Scientific Opinion on Risk Assessment Terminology, EFSA Journal 2012; 10(5):2664. [43pp.] doi:10.2903/j.efsa.2012.2664. Available online at the following address (last visited on 18 July 2012): www.efsa.europa.eu/efsajournal.

73 Article 28(4) of Regulation (EC) No 178/2002 (OJ L 31, 1.2.2002) identified a Scientific Panel on food additives, flavourings, processing aids and materials in contact with food; a Panel on additives and products or substances used in animal feed; a Panel on plant health, plant protection products and their residues; a Panel on genetically modified organisms; a Panel on dietetic products, nutrition and allergies; a Panel on biological hazards; a Panel on contaminants in the food chain; and a Panel on animal health and welfare.

74 With the adoption of a Commission regulation via the 'comitology procedure': Article 58(2) of Regulation (EC) No 178/2002, referring to Regulation (EU) n. 182/2011 of the European Parliament and Council of 16 February 2011, laying down the rules and general principles concerning mechanisms for control by Member States of the Commission's exercise of implementing powers, OJ L 55/13 of 28.2.2011.

75 Article 294 of the Treaty on the Functioning of the European Union.

76 Commission Regulation (EC) No 575/2006 of 7 April 2006 amending Regulation (EC) No 178/2002 of the European Parliament and Council as regards the number and names of the permanent Scientific Panels of the European Food Safety Authority, OJ L100/3 of 8 April 2006.

for the Safety of the Food Chain (SCOFCAH), once the request has been made by EFSA.[77] It therefore seems that leaving aside the most formal aspects, in this case the Parma-based agency has a direct regulatory power.[78]

EFSA triggered a second time this procedure for the creation of a Panel devoted to food additives and nutrient sources[79] after the adoption of the so-called 'Food Improvement Package'.[80]

EFSA's Peculiarity – The Composition of EFSA's Scientific Groups

EFSA scientific groups' defining characteristic lies in their composition, which consist of experts who are not employed by the Authority and decide to cooperate with the Parma-based agency on a voluntary basis.[81]

These experts are appointed by the Management Board of the Authority in a personal capacity, and as such cannot present any views other than their own and cannot represent anyone but themselves, employers included. From a diachronic perspective, the rationale that prompted the Legislator to make EFSA's scientific advice dependent on independent experts was to avoid the national bias

77 Article 28(4), second indent of Regulation (EC) No 178/2002.

78 This is not the only case where legal effects are linked to the expression of a request or opinion from EFSA: see for instance Regulation (EC) No 1925/2006 of the European Parliament and of the Council of 20 December 2006 on the addition of vitamins and minerals and of certain other substances to foods, OJ L 404/26 of 30 December 2006, or Directive 2002/46/EC of the European Parliament and of the Council of 10 June 2002 on the approximation of the laws of the Member States relating to food supplements, OJ L 183/57 of 12 July 2002.

79 Commission Regulation (EC) No 202/2008 of 4 March 2008, OJ L 60 of 5 March 2008, 17.

80 Regulation (EC) No 1331/2008 of the European Parliament and of the Council of 16 December 2008 establishing a common authorisation procedure for food additives, food enzymes and food flavourings (Text with EEA relevance), OJ L 354 of 31 December 2008; Regulation (EC) No 1332/2008 of the European Parliament and of the Council of 16 December 2008 on food enzymes and amending Council Directive 83/417/EEC, Council Regulation (EC) No 1493/1999, Directive 2000/13/EC, Council Directive 2001/112/EC and Regulation (EC) No 258/97 (Text with EEA relevance), OJ L 354 of 3 December 2008; and Regulation (EC) No 1333/2008 of the European Parliament and of the Council of 16 December 2008 on food additives (Text with EEA relevance), OJ L 354, 31.12.2008.

81 This characteristic is also shared by EEA and EMCCDA: see respectively Article 10 of Regulation (EC) No 401/2009 of the European Parliament and of the Council of 23 April 2009 on the European Environment Agency and the European Environment Information and Observation Network, OJ L 126 of 2 May 2009, pp. 13–22 and Article 13 of Regulation (EC) No 1920/2006 of the European Parliament and of the Council of 12 December 2006 on the European Monitoring Centre for Drugs and Drug Addiction (recast) OJ L 376 of 27 December 2006, pp. 1–13.

that had allegedly polluted the risk assessment of the 'mad cow' crisis.[82] While this decision grants the experts intellectual freedom and flexibility in terms of professional and scientific behaviour, it is also of complex implementation due to the relative scarcity of 'pure' scientists with no link with national bodies or private interests whatsoever. It is possible to identify additional downsides resulting from this approach in the position of external expert, due to the absence of a salary and of the possibility to rely on the structure provided by their respective employers.

The maximum number of times an expert may serve is specified in EFSA's internal rules, according to which experts cannot serve for more than three mandates in the same Scientific Panel or in the Scientific Committee. As each mandate spans over a three-year time frame, the total number of years an expert may contribute to the same Panel is limited to nine. By adopting this approach, EFSA probably aimed at avoiding that experts remaining on the same Panels for too long would have the possibility of developing an undue influence over their sector of competence. At the same time, the obligation to regularly renew the composition of the Panels is a healthy process which substantially contributes to voiding scientific intellectual entrenchment. This is in line with the Internal Control Standards of the European Commission that set at five years the time limit that an official should spend in a sensitive function, with the possibility of granting waivers in certain conditions.[83] Considering the relative scarcity of scientific experts in the domains of EFSA's interest who are willing to offer their contribution to EFSA, and the fact that the Commission's ICSs are addressed to officials, who enjoy an indefinite time contract of employment with that institution, it can be argued that EFSA's line is proportionate to the peculiar conditions of the members of its scientific bodies.

The way in which the selection of the members of EFSA's scientific groups is performed is another key element to ensure the intellectual objectivity of an institution like the Authority, having as *raison d'être* the very provision of objective scientific advice.[84] It may be challenging to contest that EFSA's procedure for the selection

82 In that regard, see European Parliament, *Report on alleged contraventions or maladministration in the implementation of Community law in relation to BSE, without prejudice to the jurisdiction of the Community and national courts*, Temporary Committee on BSE, Rapporteur, Manuel Medina Ortega. 1997, para. n. 5 available online on the website of the European Parliament at the following address (last visited on 19 March 2012): http://www.europarl.europa.eu/sides/getDoc.do?pubRef=-//EP//TEXT+REPORT+A4-1997-0020+0+DOC+XML+V0//EN.

83 See Communication to the Commission, Revision of the Internal Control Standards and Underlying Framework – Strengthening Control Effectiveness, SEC (2007) 1341 – Appendix I The Revised Internal Control Standards For Effective Management, Internal Control Standard 7.

84 See Jasanoff, S., 2005, Judgment under Siege: The Three-Body Problem of Expert Legitimacy, in *Democratization of Expertise?, Sociology of the Sciences Yearbook*, 24, 209–24; Gabbi, Independent Scientific Advice; Majone, G., 1999, The Regulatory State and its Legitimacy Problems, *West European Politics*, 22(1), 1–24; Shapiro, M., 2004–2005, Deliberative, Independent Technocracy v. Democratic Politics: Will the Globe

of its experts represents a significant progress when compared to the previous state, when the scientific committees were managed by the Commission. The General Food Law prescribes that the experts of the Scientific Committee and Scientific Panels be appointed by the Management Board upon proposal of the Executive Director, following an open call for expression of interest.[85] However, it does not lay down any further step or principle that this procedure should comply with.

The procedure of the selection of members of EFSA's scientific groups is regulated in detail by EFSA's internal rules,[86] which lay down in a very meticulous manner the steps to be followed to select the members of the Authority's scientific groups. According to these rules, the call has to be thoroughly disseminated in the academic and scientific environment via the Advisory Forum and EFSA's partners, such as universities, research institutes, Member States' authorities, international partners and other interested parties.[87] Candidates are confronted with a selection procedure designed to screen the applications on the basis of pre-determined eligibility and selection criteria laid down in the call for expression of interest for membership.[88] Compliance with the rules is ensured by a group of external scientific experts of high calibre not part of, or interested in, the process and by observers from Union Institutions, such as the European Parliament and the Commission.[89] The selection committee prepares a shortlist that is then shared with the Advisory Forum for comments.[90] Given the nature of the Forum, that body's opinions and comments do not bind EFSA. Nonetheless, they may be particularly relevant in identifying possible inconsistencies of the assessments, overrepresentations of certain nationalities or other geographical imbalances.

Echo the E.U.? *Law & Contemp. Probs.*, 68, 341; Shapiro, M., 1997, The Problems of Independent Agencies in the United States and the European Union, *Journal of European Public Policy*, 4(2), 276–91; Thatcher, *Regulation After Delegation*.

85 Which has to be published on the Official Journal of the European Union and on leading scientific publications Article 28 of Regulation (EC) No 178/2002.

86 Decision of the Executive Director of 14 March 2011 concerning the selection of members of the Scientific Committee, Scientific Panels and External Experts to Assist EFSA with its scientific work, available on the website of the Authority (visited on 12 March 2012): http://www.efsa.europa.eu/en/keydocs/docs/expertselection.pdf.

87 See for instance Call for expression of interest addressed to scientific experts interested in EFSA's scientific panels and scientific committee (Parma, Italy), *OJ* C 99 of 31 March 2011.

88 Article 5 of the Decision of the Executive Director concerning the selection of members of the Scientific Committee, Scientific Panels and External Experts, *supra*, footnote 115.

89 Article 6 of the Decision of the Executive Director concerning the selection of members of the Scientific Committee, Scientific Panels and External Experts, *supra*, footnote 115.

90 Article 7(4) of the Decision of the Executive Director concerning the selection of members of the Scientific Committee, Scientific Panels and External Experts, *supra*, footnote 115.

After addressing the comments received by the Forum, the Executive Director validates the shortlist that is then sent to the Management Board for an 'adoption' which in fact seems to be closer to a legality check of the selection procedure as a whole.[91]

The complete and total autonomy of the Authority in the selection procedure and in the management of its scientific experts is also confirmed by EFSA's power to terminate the relationship with its experts at any point in time during the mandate. This may occur, for instance, when the concerned person breaches EFSA's internal rules, with specific reference to those ensuring the independence of EFSA's decision-making processes.[92]

The number of experts who compose the Panels has been set by EFSA at 21 per Panel. This self-imposed limit does not seem to take account of the different workloads assigned to the Panels, which vary considerably depending on the subject matter and on the scope of each Panel's remit.[93] For instance, the Panel on Nutrition, allergies and dietetic foods deals with such a broad range of sensitive topics compared to a more homogeneous Panel such as the one dealing with Plant Health, that it would probably need a higher number of Panel members. A way to ensure a higher flexibility could be the setting of a minimum and maximum number of members, within which the Executive Director would be free to choose the appropriate number of members for each Panel depending on the expected workload and programme of work.[94]

From a legal perspective, the Scientific Committee and Scientific Panels operate on the basis of the collegiality principle, meaning that for the adoption of a scientific output it is sufficient that the majority of the members votes in favour of the document. Nonetheless, EFSA's has often taken pride in highlighting that the vast majority of its opinions are adopted by consensus, i.e. with the support of all the components of the relevant scientific body. This is indeed a significant achievement, for it means that there are no major scientific reasons opposing the conclusions reached. For such an event, the Legislator designed in the General Food Law a clause obliging EFSA to disclose all minority opinions, i.e. any opinion underpinned by a scientific reasoning that would not be supported by the majority of the members of the Panels.[95] This should ensure full transparency of the scientific decision-making process supporting the opinion adopted by the

91 Article 28 of Regulation (EC) No 178/2002.

92 Articles 5 and 23(2), Decision of the Management Board of the European Food Safety Authority concerning the establishment and operations of the Scientific Committee, Scientific Panels and of their Working Groups, above.

93 Article 3(1), Decision of the Management Board of the European Food Safety Authority concerning the establishment and operations of the Scientific Committee, Scientific Panels and of their Working Groups, above.

94 In effect, if an egalitarian approach could have been useful when EFSA was created, could be considered unjustified after 10 years of operation.

95 Article 38(1)(b) of Regulation (EC) No 178/2002.

majority, as a member not sharing the views of his peers would have the opportunity (better, the duty) of identifying supposed errors and inaccuracies to the benefit of the outside world.[96] As with minority views expressed by judges in certain legal systems,[97] a minority opinion of a Panel member might be of great significance for a third party interested in obtaining a comprehensive understanding of a scientific issue. Furthermore, one should not overlook that from a legal standpoint the risk manager is not obliged to follow blindly EFSA's opinions and may decide to take into account other legitimate factors or even other scientific opinions.[98] These could be opinions of other agencies or regulatory bodies or even minority opinions of EFSA's Panels. It should not be impossible to imagine a situation where the Authority publishes an opinion on a contentious scientific matter with the support of a thin majority of the members of the competent Panel and with the specification of one or more minority opinions. Against this background, it could easily be argued that such minority opinion(s) might represent an alternative option for a hard looking risk manager. Be that as it may, thus far EFSA's Scientific Committee and Scientific Panels have not expressed many minority opinions,[99]

96 More critical on the sufficiency of this feature O'Rourke, R., 2007, Scientific Conflict, the EFSA and a Common Risk Assessment, *European Food and Feed Law Rev.*, 4, 197 and ff.

97 The most pertinent (and easiest) example being the Supreme Court of the United States of America and its justices' dissenting opinions: Scalla, A., 1994, The Dissenting Opinion, *Journal of Supreme Court History*, 19, 33–44 and Walker, T.G., Epstein, L. and Dixon, W.J., 1988, On the Mysterious Demise of Consensual Norms in the United States Supreme Court, *The Journal of Politics*, 50, 361–89.

98 See Case T-13/99 *Pfizer Animal Health v. Council*, *supra*, paras 198 and 199.

99 Eleven scientific opinions are available on EFSA's website where at least one minority opinion had been expressed. This is out of a grand total of 2,003 scientific opinions of the Scientific Committee or Scientific Panels. The minority opinions are the following: EFSA Panel on food contact materials, enzymes, flavourings and processing aids (CEF). Scientific Opinion on Bisphenol A: evaluation of a study investigating its neurodevelopmental toxicity, review of recent scientific literature on its toxicity and advice on the Danish risk assessment of Bisphenol A., *EFSA Journal* 2010;8(9): 1829. [110 pp.] doi:10.2903/j.efsa.2010.1829; Scientific Opinion of the Panel on Animal Health and Welfare on a request from European Commission on the overall effects of farming systems on dairy cow welfare and disease, *EFSA Journal* (2009) 1143, 1–38; Scientific Opinion of the Panel on Animal Health and Welfare on a request from the Commission on the risk assessment of the impact of housing, nutrition and feeding, management and genetic selection on behaviour, fear and pain problems in dairy cows, *EFSA Journal* (2009) 1139, 1–68; Scientific Opinion of the Panel on Animal Health and Welfare on a request from the European Commission on animal welfare aspects of husbandry systems for farmed fish: carp, *EFSA Journal* (2008) 843, 1–28; Scientific Opinion of the Panel on Biological Hazards on a request from EFSA on the maintenance of the QPS list of microorganisms intentionally added to food or feed, *EFSA Journal* (2008) 923, 1–48; Scientific Opinion of the Panel on Animal Health and Welfare on a request from the European Commission on Animal Welfare Aspects of Husbandry Systems for Farmed European Eel, *EFSA Journal*

which have never been chosen by a risk manager of the European Union as the scientific reasoning underpinning a risk management measure.

An Element of Flexibility: the Working Groups of the Scientific Committee and Scientific Panels

It has already been discussed how EFSA decided to self-impose the limit of 21 members to all its Scientific Panels. If one combines this aspect with the fact that certain Panels require the most diverse expertise, he would comprehend the reason why the Legislator gave EFSA the possibility of creating Working Groups for the Scientific Committee and each of its Panels.

Working groups are delegated by Panels the responsibility of undertaking preparatory work instrumental to the drafting and finalisation of their scientific opinions.[100] Different from the Scientific Committee and Scientific Panels, which are by law composed of members selected in accordance with the procedure set out analysed in the previous paragraph, the external experts forming the Working Groups may be selected and appointed directly by EFSA on the basis of their expertise. Different than with the composition of the Panels, there is nothing prescribing compliance with a geographical principle and there are no limits to the total number of expert who may be called up to take part in a Working Group. As a consequence, Working Groups are hyper-specialised scientific fora aimed at eviscerating a very specific matter to the benefit of the more generalist Panel of reference. It is therefore understandable that for the composition of the Working Groups the expertise takes the precedence over political or geographical considerations. Once appointed, external experts are subject to the same provisions applicable to the members of the Scientific Committee or Scientific Panels on independence, confidentiality and independence.[101]

(2008) 809, 1–18; Scientific Opinion of the Panel on Animal Health and Animal Welfare on a request from the European Commission on the Animal welfare aspects of husbandry systems for farmed trout, *EFSA Journal* (2008) 796, 1–22; Scientific Opinion of the Panel on Animal Health and Welfare on a request from the European Commission on Animal welfare aspects of husbandry systems for farmed Atlantic salmon, *EFSA Journal* (2008)736, 1–31; Scientific Opinion of the Panel on Animal Health and Welfare on Migratory Birds and their Possible Role in the Spread of Highly Pathogenic Avian Influenza, *EFSA Journal* (2006) 357, 1–46; Scientific Opinion of the Panel on Genetically Modified Organisms (GMO) and the Panel on Biological Hazards (BIOHAZ) on a request from the European Commission on the use of antibiotic resistance genes as marker genes in genetically modified plants, *EFSA Journal* (2009) 1034, 1–81.

100 Article 19 of the Decision of the Management Board of the European Food Safety Authority concerning the establishment and operations of the Scientific Committee, Scientific Panels and of their Working Groups, above.

101 Articles 31–3 of the Decision of the Management Board of the European Food Safety Authority concerning the establishment and operations of the Scientific Committee, Scientific Panels and of their Working Groups, above.

A leaner selection process and the absence of a maximum limit of experts sitting in a Working Group translate in a high degree of flexibility which substantially contributes to an optimisation of the internal workflows of EFSA's scientific bodies. On the other hand, this arrangement presupposes that the profile of the experts selected as members of the Panels has to be different from that of the external experts sitting in the working groups. While Panel members should have a broader (and extended) expertise allowing them to discuss a variety of scientific matters, working group experts should be highly specialised and knowledgeable in the very matter for which the group is created. The high degree of specialisation characterising the Working Groups is also of great help to increase the level of efficacy of the system as a whole, which could otherwise encounter serious limits in terms of the fields of expertise that can be covered by 21 components of the Panel and ultimately in the quality and in the number of outputs that EFSA's scientific bodies would be able to adopt.

EFSA's Staff

The work of EFSA's Scientific Committee and Scientific Panels is supported by a secretariat: this term is used to define EFSA's staff tasked with the duty of ensuring the appropriate administrative and scientific support to its scientific groups.[102]

The staff providing the scientific support needed for the performance of the scientific functions, contrary to the experts cooperating with the Scientific Committee, Scientific Panels and their Working Groups, work as full-time employees with the Authority and are, as such, subject to the regulations applicable to the employees of the European Union.[103] EFSA scientific staff are therefore required to comply with the obligations of independence, impartiality, courtesy and sound administration as laid down in the Staff Regulations,[104] in the Code of good administrative behaviour

---

102 In more detail, Article 8 of the Decision of the Management Board of the European Food Safety Authority concerning the establishment and operations of the Scientific Committee, Scientific Panels and of their Working Groups, above, gives the following ones as tasks of the Scientific Committee 'Ensuring best use of the resources allocated to the Scientific Committee or Scientific Panels and planning to meet priorities and time-limits; Ensuring compliance with internal rules of the Authority such as those regulating the Declarations of interests, transparency et cetera; Exercising vigilance in order to identify at an early stage any potential source of divergence between the scientific opinion of the Scientific Committee or Scientific Panel and those issued by other bodies carrying out similar tasks'.

103 Except certain institutions, bodies and agencies that are still enjoying a privileged status, such as the European Central Bank and the Council of the European Union.

104 Articles 11–26 regulation No 31 (EEC), 11 (EAEC), laying down the Staff Regulations of Officials and the Conditions of Employment of Other Servants of the European Economic Community and the European Atomic Energy Community (OJ P 45 of 14 June 1962, p. 1385).

adopted by EFSA in 2003[105] and as developed by the 'case law' of the Civil Service Tribunal, General Court and European Ombudsman, respectively.

The initial structure of the Authority reflected the centrality granted to Scientific Panels: staff with a scientific background were essentially required to provide support to the Panels. Over the years, however, the development of EFSA's internal structure along the orientations set out in the General Food Law, coupled with legislative developments mainly linked to the sector of plant protection products and managerial efforts aimed at mitigating the structural limits built-in a Panel system, scientific tasks and preparatory work assigned to staff members gained more and more prominence. The scientific units delivering these outputs are tasked with the implementation of the cooperation with the competent authorities of the Member States,[106] or with the side assignments related to the risk assessment function *strictu sensu*, such as data collection[107] or emerging risks identification,[108] although the extent of their effective involvement in the drafting of EFSA's outputs depends extensively on the applicable legal framework.[109]

Conclusions

In the preceding paragraphs this contribution discussed the scientific governance of the EFSA, highlighting the peculiarities of the bodies allowing the Parma-based agency to provide scientific advice and scientific and technical support to the Union risk managers, and identifying some aspects showing a potential for further development. It has shown how the risk assessment process, barely sketched in the principles set out in the General Food Law, has grown into a complex and multilayered system of provisions of different sources, the most relevant of which come from within the Authority.[110]

---

105 European Food Safety Authority, MB 16.09.2003–11 – Adopted, EFSA Code of Good Administrative Behaviour, available online at the following address (last visited on 18 March 2012): http://www.efsa.europa.eu/en/keydocs/docs/admincode.pdf. EFSA's Code matches completely the one issued by the European Ombudsman: about which see Cadeddu, S., 2004, The Proceedings of the European Ombudsman, Law and Contemporary Problems, *The Administrative Law of the European Union*, 68(1), 161 and ff. and Magnette, P., 2011, Between Parliamentary Control and the Rule of Law: The Political Role of the Ombudsman in the European Union, *Journal of European Public Policy*, 10(5), 677–94.

106 Pursuant to Article 36 of Regulation (EC) No 178/2002.

107 In that respect, see in more detail Gabbi, *L'Autorità europea*, § 4.3, 174 and ff.

108 Ibid., § 4.4, 177 and ff.

109 On this point see in detail in this book Pintado, C., Chapter 3.

110 Which for the moment is still not subject to direct judicial review: see Alemanno, A., 2007, L'Autorité européenne de sécurité des aliments souffle ses cinq premières bougies – Un bilan d'activité', *Revue du droit de l'Union européenne*, 3, 610–29; Alemanno, A. and Mahieu, S., 2008, The European Food Safety Authority Before European Courts – Some Reflections on the Judicial Review of EFSA Scientific Opinions and Administrative Acts,

At the moment of writing, EFSA has proved capable of providing an added value to the legal system of the European Union, by furnishing sound scientific advice to the actors taking risk management measures so as to allow them also to act in compliance with international obligations. This has been proven in a number of occasions, from the timely reaction during the E.coli crisis of May 2011 to the processing of thousands of dossiers and applications of health claims and active substances in little more than four years.[111]

The scheme adopted by the European Legislator for EFSA's Scientific Panels starts however to show some limitations, put under the significant pressure exerted by a gradual and steady centralisation at Union level of the risk assessment process of food and feed related risks.

The possibility of creating Working Groups has probably provided the system with the indispensable flexibility needed to achieve the steep increase in number of outputs issued by EFSA: in 2011[112] the Authority adopted 658 scientific outputs, while in 2006 EFSA that number stood at 174.[113] Nonetheless, it is difficult to ignore that even taking into account the flexibility built-in the Panel/Working Group blend, the system centred on experts contributing voluntarily to EFSA's work may sooner or later reach its structural limits, at least in quantitative terms. This may be regarded as particularly pertinent if one considers the gradual and steady centralisation of food and feed authorisation processes at Union level. As a rule, under the GFL this presupposes the systematic involvement of EFSA's Panels with their independent experts and it is accompanied by the prescription of legal deadlines that are often set by the Legislator with scant consideration to the business needs of the risk assessor.[114] On the medium-to-long term, this approach

---

European Food and Feed Law Rev., 3, 320; and Gabbi, *L'Autorità europea*, § 5.3, 244 and ff. and id., 2009, The European Food Safety Authority: Judicial Review by Community Courts, *European Journal of Consumer Law*, 1, 172 and ff.

111 European Food Safety Authority, Annual Activity Report of the European Food Safety Authority for 2011, mb 15 03 12 item 4 doc 3 – Annual Activity Report 2011 – adopted, at 5, available at the following address (last visited on 25 July 2012): http://www.efsa.europa.eu/en/corporate/doc/aar11.pdf. On EFSA's contribution to recent emergencies see in this book Chapter 6.

112 European Food Safety Authority, Annual Activity Report of the European Food Safety Authority for 2011, above, at 3.

113 European Food Safety Authority, Annual Activity Report 2006, MB 27.03.2007–4, at 31, available at the following address (last visited on 25 July 2012): http://www.efsa.europa.eu/en/corporate/doc/aar06.pdf.

114 A clear example of this tendency can be found in Regulation (EC) No 1924/2006 and with particular reference to the time lines in Article 18 thereof. Impact assessments should improve the overall situation by taking into account also the feasibility of the overall regulatory project from a resource perspective. However, these are normally limited to assessing the impact that a legal act or provision may have on the economic or industrial sector, on the society at large, and on the environment, without dedicating much attention to the human or financial resources that are needed to achieve the policy goals set by

might lead to the impossibility for the Panels to accommodate all the requests for evaluation or re-evaluation they may receive from the risk managers, applicants and concerned business operators.

However, there is an alternative approach that is often ignored or overlooked by academics and practitioners alike and that may represent a compromise between the current Panel system and a system relying exclusively on internal staff. The authorisation procedure for active substances and for the setting of Maximum Residue Levels for pesticides foresees a limited involvement of the competent Scientific Panel: this is mainly summoned to develop guidance documents and other complex analysis that require a very high level of expertise, once methodologies and guidance are established. The assessment of the application dossiers by way of contrast is performed by the national competent authorities and it is peer reviewed by EFSA. In the so-called Regulation on Maximum Residue Levels, the Legislator went so far as to explicitly derogate to the General Food Law and state that EFSA opinions on the setting of MRLs may be adopted without the involvement of the Scientific Panel.[115]

Probably this would represent a balanced approach, preserving the limited resources of the Panels for the assessment of the most scientifically complex matters and attributing the daily and (relatively) routine work to EFSA staff, or to the staff of the national competent authorities.[116] Nonetheless, such a system would

---

the Legislator: e.g. Commission Staff Working Document Accompanying document to the Proposal for a Regulation of the European Parliament and of the Council amending Regulation (EC) No 998/2003 laying down the animal health requirements applicable to the non-commercial movement of pet animals, Impact Assessment, SEC(2009) 776 final of 16 June 2009. In any instance, even in those rare cases where this aspect is duly considered by the Commission, it is often forgotten when political compromises are reached in the ordinary legislative procedure. For an analysis of the evolution of impact assessments in the Union legal system see Alemanno, A. and Meuwese, A.C.M., 2012, Impact Assessment of EU Non-Legislative Rulemaking: The Missing Link of 'New' Comitology, *European Law Journal*, 19(1), available at SSRN: http://ssrn.com/abstract=2178128; Radaelli, C.M., 2007, Whither Better Regulation for the Lisbon Agenda? *Journal of European Public Policy*, 14(2), 190–207; Renda, A., 2006, Impact Assessment in the EU, Brussels: Centre for European Policy Studies; and Meuwese, A., 2008, *Impact Assessment in the EU Lawmaking*, Leiden: Kluwer Law International. From a more critical perspective: Baldwin, R., 2005, Is Better Regulation Smarter Regulation? *Public Law*, 485–511. From the Union institutions particularly relevant Commission of the European Communities, *Second Strategic Review of Better Regulation in the European Union*, COM(2008)32 final.

115 Article 44(1) of Regulation (EC) No 396/2005 of the European Parliament and of the Council of 23 February 2005 on maximum residue levels of pesticides in or on food and feed of plant and animal origin and amending Council Directive 91/414/EEC, OJ L 70/1 of 16 March 2005. On this point see in detail in this book Pintado, C., Chapter 3.

116 With an approach not too dissimilar from the one adopted for EMA or for the Food and Drugs Administration of the USA: Cuvillier, A., 2001, The Role of the European Medicines Evaluation Agency in the Harmonisation of Pharmaceutical Legislation, in Goldberg, R. and Lonbay, J. (eds), *Pharmaceutical Medicine, Biotechnology and*

inevitably require a significant investment in terms of financial resources which is hardly conceivable in the climate of economic crisis affecting the European Union for the foreseeable future.[117]

Similarly, this contribution has identified a few changes that could be brought to the design of EFSA's Management Board, although its influence on EFSA's scientific processes is at the time of writing limited to a quasi-notarial role. The next few years will tell us which of these potential novelties, if any, has been opted for by the Legislator for the review of the General Food Law. The hope is that the changes occurred in the meantime to the institutional, political and economic environment will not prompt the Legislator to disregard the lessons learnt during the crisis at the root of the adoption of the GFL.

Probably the major challenges that the future holds for EFSA will be to maintain the high level of excellence achieved in what has gradually become a complex risk analysis system. This against a geopolitical and macroeconomic background characterised by an endless inter-systemic competition which consistently pushes the respective macro areas in a contest for the most business friendly environment, with sanitary and phytosanitary measures often relegated to the corner of technical barriers to trade.

European Law, Cambridge University Press; Alemanno, *Trade in Food*; id., The Evolution of European Food Regulation – Why the European Food Safety Authority is Not a EU-Style FDA?, in Ansell and Vogel, What's the Beef?; Gardener, J.S., 1996, The European Agency for the Evaluation of Medicines and European Regulation of Pharmaceuticals, *ELJ*, 48–82; Gehring, T. and Krapohl, S., 2007, Supranational Regulatory Agencies between Independence and Control: The EMEA and the Authorization of Pharmaceuticals in the European Single Market, *Journal of European Public Policy*, 14(2), 208–26; Healy, E.M. and Kaitin, K.I., 1999, The European Agency for the Evaluation of Medicinal Products, Central Procedure for Procedure for Product Approval, Current Status, *Drug Information Journal*, 33, 969–78; Vos, *Institutional Frameworks*.

117 A number of economists draw a parallel between the situation of the European Union after the 2009 crisis with the one Japan found itself into towards the end of the 90s: see e.g. Kennedy, S. and Miller, R., 2012, Central Banks Commit to Ease as Threat of Lost Decades Rises [online Bloomberg], available online (last visited on 20 July 2012) at http://www.bloomberg.com/news/2012–06–25/central-banks-commit-to-ease-as-threat-of-lost-decades-rises-1-.html.

Chapter 5
Scientific Regulatory Cooperation within the EU: On the Relationship between EFSA and National Food Authorities

Gabriele Abels, Alexander Kobusch and Jennifer Träsch

> Only through close collaboration on scientific activities, through greater dialogue and effective communication and through shared activities the network will be able to enhance the sense of common ownership of its activities and output. Through sharing best practices with the scientific organisations and institutes across Europe, EFSA and the national food authorities will be able to continue to develop their reputation and their standards of scientific excellence.[1]

Introduction

In EFSA's Founding Regulation,[2] the relationship between the European Food Safety Authority (EFSA) and Competent Authorities (CAs) in the Member States is a prominent issue. The requirement for *scientific* cooperation is explicitly delineated in several recitals and articles of this regulation. While cooperation is not a novel issue,[3] the Founding Regulation (often referred to as the General Food Law – GFL) and its interpretation by EFSA adds a new quality.

This emphasis on cooperation is rooted in EFSA's key mission: *risk assessment* (RA). Food-related RA is conducted at EU (EFSA) *and* at national levels (see Chapter 6 in this volume). Given that divergent scientific concepts and methodologies, standards and procedures result in differing RA outcomes, developing a common scientific framework becomes instrumental to avoid the

1 EFSA, 'Strategy for Cooperation and Networking between the EU Member States and EFSA' (MB 19.12.2006, 19 December 2006). All EFSA documents cited can be accessed on EFSA's publication homepage: http://www.efsa.europa.eu/en/publications.htm.

2 Regulation (EC) No. 178/2002 of the European Parliament and of the Council of 28 January 2002 Laying Down the General Principles and Requirements of Food Law, Establishing the European Food Safety Authority and Laying Down Procedures in Matters of Food Safety [2002] OJ L31/1.

3 Council Directive 93/5/EEC of 25 February 1993 On Assistance to the Commission and Cooperation by the Member States in the Scientific Examiniation of Questions Relating to Food [1993] OJ L52/18 already required Member States to cooperate with the Commission's Scientific Committee for Food.

RA dilemma of 'the potential for diverging scientific opinions'.[4] Accordingly, EFSA 'should take on the role of an independent scientific point of reference'.[5] Its key mandate is 'to promote and coordinate the development of uniform risk assessment methodologies in the fields falling within its mission'[6] by more closely involving Member States in scientific procedures,[7] through 'the coordination of activities, the exchange of information, the development and implementation of joint projects, the exchange of expertise and best practices'.[8] Thus, scientific contestation should be minimised by scientific cooperation. Whenever diverging opinions occur, EFSA shall initiate scientific information-sharing and identify potentially contentious scientific issues.[9]

We claim that EFSA is designed as a 'networked agency' simultaneously fostering and depending on cooperation with the Member States. In this chapter we outline EFSA's networking strategies. Networks are specific configurations of *actors* using specific *mechanisms* for interaction. Based on these findings we elaborate some recommendations for the future.[10]

EFSA as a 'Networked Agency' – Conceptual Issues

In the EU, regulatory competencies are divided among authorities at different levels. In the evolving regulatory networks the role of EU agencies grew stronger since the late 1990s.[11] The predominant rational choice argument proclaims that Member States try to solve the credible commitment problem by delegating power to non-majoritarian EU agencies without fully giving up control.[12] Agencies shall promote regulatory efficiency especially in complex and technical sectors.

EU agencies have often lofty tasks, but typically few formal *real* regulatory powers (i.e. decision-making). While formal delegated powers are important, a less legalistic regime perspective calls attention to power via informal institutions and

4 Regulation (EC) 178/2002 recital 44.

5 Ibid., recital 34.

6 Ibid., art. 23b.

7 Ibid., recital 51.

8 Ibid., art. 36 (1).

9 Ibid., art. 30.

10 Methodologically, the chapter is primarily based on an analysis of numerous EFSA documents and policy papers.

11 See for example Giandomenico Majone, *Regulating Europe* (Routledge 1996); Renaud Dehousse, 'Regulation by Networks in the European Community: The Role of European Agencies' (1997) 4 *Journal of European Public Policy*, 24; David Coen and Mark Thatcher, 'Network Governance and Multi-Level Delegation: European Networks of Regulatory Agencies' (2008) 28 *Journal of Public Policy*, 49.

12 For an overview of the debate see Jørgen Grønnegaard Christensen and Vibeke Lehmann Nielsen, 'Administrative Capacity, Structural Choice and the Creation of EU Agencies' (2010) 17 *Journal of European Public Policy*, 176.

dynamic processes involving multilevel, network-based regulation.[13] Combining the analysis of EU agencies with network-oriented approaches is thus particularly fruitful.[14] This literature provides sufficient evidence that EU agencies can be effective and influential even if formal powers are limited. Eberlein and Grande argue that neither national regulators (nationalisation hypothesis) nor EU agencies (Europeanisation hypothesis) take the lead in regulatory networks; they identify a dynamic division of labour between national and EU actors operating via informal institutions and processes (differentiation hypothesis).[15]

We argue that EFSA works as a 'networked agency',[16] not as a European 'super agency' or 'research organisation'[17] priming national scientific expertise. Its main scientific mission can only be fulfilled if it is closely linked to national authorities. Moreover, EFSA is expected to actively operate as a *network manager*. Strong ties to national CAs are a precondition for the effective functioning of EFSA and networking becomes an empowerment tool because it allows EFSA to develop a professional reputation vis-à-vis national CAs due to repeated interactions.[18] This resonates with the concept of a 'transnational agency cluster' in which EU agencies act as a *primus inter pares*;[19] they 'serve as hubs of regulatory networks'.[20]

Information is the key network resource;[21] Majone even speaks of 'regulation by information'.[22] The production of unimpeachable scientific expertise shared by other regulatory bodies, national or international, is vital for building up a credible reputation. The challenge is how to become the scientific point of

---

13 See Burkhard Eberlein and Edgar Grande, 'Beyond Delegation: Transnational Regulatory Regimes and the EU Regulatory State' (2005) 12 *Journal of European Public Policy*, 89.

14 See David Levi-Faur, 'Regulation and Regulatory Governance' in David Levi-Faur (ed.), *Handbook on the Politics of Regulation* (Edward Elgar 2011).

15 See Eberlein and Grande (n 13), 97ff.

16 Ellen Vos, 'Responding to Catastrophe: Towards a New Architecture for EU Food Safety Regulation?' in Charles F. Sabel and Jonathan Zeitlin (eds), *Experimentalist Governance in the European Union: Towards a New Architecture* (Oxford University Press 2010), 157.

17 EFSA, 'Science Strategy 2012–2016' (MB 15.12.2011 – adopted, 15 December 2011), 7, 13. Supremacy over national organisations was neither politically negotiable nor desirable.

18 Majone made this convincing claim as early as 1997. See Giandomenico Majone, 'The New European Agencies: Regulation by Information' (1997) 4 *Journal of European Public Policy*, 262. European agencies could boost their efficiency by building good relations with national CAs.

19 Morten Egeberg and Jarle Trondal, 'National Agencies in the European Administrative Space: Government Driven, Commission Driven or Networked?' (2009) 87 *Public Administration*, 779f.

20 Daniel R. Kelemen, 'The Politics of Eurocracy: Building a New European State?' in Nicolas Jabko and C. Parsons (eds), *With Us or against Us? European Trends in American Perspective* (Oxford University Press 2005), 181.

21 See Eberlein and Grande (n 13), 101.

22 Majone (n 18) 265.

reference. Formally, EFSA enjoys the 'more or less exclusive responsibility'[23] for performing RA at EU level, and the 'monopoly over the collection, structuring, and interpretation of scientific knowledge'[24] in RA. Yet in practice EFSA is embedded in a 'two-tier regulatory framework'[25] and cannot rely solely on formal powers but is highly dependent on national CA's motivation and their capacities to cooperate.[26] In turn, national CAs are obliged to cooperate with EFSA.[27]

In sum, the construction of EFSA as a 'networked agency' was a deliberate choice to embark upon the fundamental epistemological (contested science) and regulatory dilemmas (multilevel system) of RA in the EU context.

The Development of Multilevel Scientific Cooperation

Conceptualising and designing EFSA as 'networked agency' has immediate consequences for EFSA's functioning and management. The Authority cannot rely on political, i.e. regulatory power, but is rather bound to the scientific domain; according to this domain's logic it has to persuade partners by the wide acceptance and 'truth' of its results. Thus, confidence becomes the cornerstone of EFSA's reputation. This is strongly echoed by EFSA's core values independence, scientific excellence, responsiveness, openness and transparency[28]

---

23 Trygve Ugland and Frode Veggeland, 'Experiments in Food Safety Policy Integration in the European Union' (2006) 44 *Journal of Common Market Studies*, 607, 618.

24 Ellen Vos and Frank Wendler, 'Food Safety Regulation at the EU Level' in Ellen Vos and Frank Wendler (eds), *Food Safety Regulation in Europe: A Comparative Institutional Analysis* (Intersentia 2006), 74.

25 Eberlein and Grande (n 13), 11f.

26 This argument should be considered in the light of the intense debate over whether or not to grant regulatory tasks to EFSA. Eventually, the Commission and the Council (i.e. the Member States) opted for the model of an information agency – denying regulatory tasks – fearing to lose their own risk management competencies. See in detail e.g. Alberto Alemanno, *Trade in Food: Regulatory and Judicial Approaches in the EC and the WTO* (Cameron May 2007), 161–8; Alberto Alemanno, 'The European Food Safety Authority at Five' (2008) 1 *European Food and Feed Law Review*, 2; Laurie Buonanno, 'The Creation of the European Food Safety Authority' in Christopher Ansell and David Vogel (eds), *What's the Beef? The Contested Governance of European Food Safety* (MIT Press 2006). This control interest is also reflected in EFSA's design: the scientific panels are mainly composed of scientists based in national CAs and risk assessment institutions, thus EFSA relies on national professional experts. Furthermore, EFSA does not conduct intra-mural research but employs data provided by national institutions (and the industry in the case of authorisations). Consequently, tight relations with these institutions are of vital interest for EFSA which is reflected in the composition of the Advisory Forum and the installation of the Focal Point System.

27 Regulation (EC) 178/2002 art. 22 (8) and (9).

28 Also see ibid., art. 22 (7) and footnote 29.

and becomes more and more obvious in the development of its strategic vision.[29] Simultaneously, EFSA has to maintain the equilibrium between organisational autonomy and dependence on its partners. Its scientific excellence hinges on data produced by others. At first glance EFSA's organisational design thus appears to mismatch its core values.

We argue that successful cooperation relies on three foundations: a strategic vision provided by EFSA as 'manager' of the evolving network (section 3), wider institutional structures fitting the daily work (section 3 and 4) and mechanisms to facilitate and enhance cooperation among the partners (section 5).

Scientific Excellence and Efficiency as Key Objectives for Cooperation

The GFL aims to ensure a high level of consumer protection in the EU *and* the functioning of the Internal Market as well as international trade.[30] As confidence in EFSA's scientific output by all stakeholders – i.e. consumers *and* producers, regulators and national institutions – is paramount to reach both objectives, EFSA puts in its core strategic documents a strong emphasis on confidence.[31]

In what follows we illustrate that two interlocking objectives are at the heart of cooperation: scientific excellence and resource efficiency. *Excellent science* is regarded as the key to build confidence in its work and to fulfil EFSA's legally defined mission.[32] Therefore, it is important to seek the international recognition

---

29 Here the lessons drawn from the BSE crisis – which was also a crisis of confidence – becomes obvious in the spirit of Regulation (EC) 178/2002: 'The confidence of the Community institutions, the general public and interested parties in the Authority is essential. For this reason, it is vital to ensure its independence, high scientific quality, transparency and efficiency' (Recital 40).

30 Regulation (EC) 178/2002 recitals 1–4; art. 1 clearly establishes a link between the GFL and the functioning of the Internal Market. Consequently, EFSA's design also reflects considerations concerning the market: EFSA 'shall contribute to a high level of protection of human life and health … in the context of the operation of the internal market' (ibid., art. 22 (3)). The Regulation thus puts an emphasis on consumer 'confidence' in order to stabilise the market. Also see Klara Kanska, 'Wolves in the Clothing of Sheep? The Case of the European Food Safety Agency' (2004) 29 *European Law Review*, 711, 713.

31 The functioning of the Internal Market formulated as general goal by the GFL is seldom picked up in the rhetoric of EFSA itself as it is in its self-understanding more orientated towards the protection of health. Nevertheless, confidence-building implicitly advances market-orientated goals.

32 Scientific excellence is best measured by international recognition of EFSA's work in the scientific community. Anthony Hardy, Chairman of EFSA's Scientific Committee, underlined this aspect when pointing to the growing importance of the *EFSA Journal* 'that is part of engaging with the scientific community to get the confidence and recognition that its science is up there with other peer reviewed journals' (conference statement at EFSA@10: Ready for the Challenges of Tomorrow, EFSA–DG Sanco high-level conference, 13 November 2012 in Parma. Quote is taken from webcast).

of EFSA's work and to harmonise science and data delivered by various authorities to avoid contestability. First attempts for RA harmonisation already began in 2000 well before EFSA was set up.[33] EFSA has fostered this process which aims at harmonising RA standards across Europe and exchanging data to allow experts to participate more easily in EFSA's work thereby reducing the likelihood of differing scientific opinions and to broaden the base EFSA's science is relying on. Furthermore, EFSA's workload has constantly augmented in the past decade. For the *effective use of scarce resources* a duplication of work by EFSA and national CAs shall be avoided. A well-coordinated work programme of all network partners also allows to raise the efficiency and to identify diverging opinions at an early stage.

The Development of EFSA's Strategy on Cooperation and Networking

The *strategic* cooperation approach was developed fairly late. Following the first external evaluation on EFSA,[34] the Authority's Management Board endorsed the evaluation's recommendations in June 2006 declaring collaboration and networking key priorities for the next five years. The Board explicitly introduced a notion of 'common ownership'[35] of EFSA activities and output provided by and benefiting both EFSA *and* national CAs. Since the first 'Strategy for cooperation and networking between the EU Member States and EFSA'[36] was adopted in December 2006, cooperation activities became more coherent and are today a cornerstone of EFSA's development. The document outlines EFSA's strategic vision:

> A well-functioning network between the EU Member states and EFSA will increase the effectiveness and efficiency of EU risk assessments. The strategy will also help build awareness and recognition of the value of these risk assessments in Europe and beyond.[37]

Henceforth the strategic priorities concentrated on exchange and collection of scientific data; sharing of RA practices; harmonisation of RA methodologies; and

---

33 Vos and Wendler (n 24), 85.

34 The report was issued in December 2005 by Bureau van Dijk Ingénieurs Conseils and Arcadia International EIGG, 'Evaluation of EFSA. Final Report' (EFSA/FIN0105, 5 December 2005) and identified as one of seven priorities the need to strengthen corporation and networking as this was so far 'mainly one way' from EFSA to CAs.

35 EFSA, 'Management Board Conclusions of the External Evaluation of EFSA and Recommendations Arising from the Report' (MB 20.06.2006 – 4 – Adopted, 20 June 2006), 6.

36 The strategy was prepared by a 'AF Working Group on Cooperation and Networking' that took into consideration the external evaluation report, the endorsement by the Management Board and a report issued by a AF 'Working Group on the Input of National Authorities' (AFWG–INA) (see footnote 41).

37 EFSA, 'Strategy for Cooperation' [2006] (n 1), 4.

Table 5.1 EFSA's risk assessment strategy and toolbox

	Risk assessment strategies		
	Exchange of data	Sharing of practices	Harmonisation
Actors	– AF – FP – MS	– AF – Scientific Committee – Scientific Panels – MS	– AF – Scientific Committee
Aim	– Effective scientific cooperation – Access to information	– Stimulate cooperation – Share experiences – Share burden	– Harmonised methodologies – Build trust among agencies
Benefit	– Facilitate participation of CAs in EFSA's work – Information on Member States' work	– Raise profile of EFSA and networks with CAs – Trust between partners – Transfer of knowledge	– Enhanced level of confidence – Common use of methodologies – Trust between partners
Mechanisms (strategy)	– Declaration of Intent – Information Exchange Platform (IEP) – EFSA Extranet – Sharing work plans	– Build on existing cooperation – Workshops & trainings – Study tours – Involvement of new MSs – Database of national experts	– Develop harmonised methodologies –Set priorities for preparatory work – Consider international activities – Priority/pilot projects
Additional mechanisms (interim review)	– Data request by EFSA – Dedicated networks to collect data – EFSA compiles data and issues reports – Standardisation of data collection – Specific databases – Financing of data collection – Grants and contracts – Sharing work plans needs more effort – AFWG on IT tools – More motivation to share information	– Bilateral meetings where expertise diverges – Cooperation influenced by area (legally) – Pilot projects (ESCO) – Steering Group on Cooperation – More strongly involve small and new MSs – Expert Database	– Guidance – Colloquia, workshops and conferences on emerging issues – ESCO WG on harmonisation

Abbreviations: MS = Member States; AF = Advisory Forum; AFWG = Advisory Forum Working Group; CA = Competent Authority; FP = Focal Point.

Source: Compiled by the authors.

promotion of coherent risk communication (see Table 5.1).[38] The ambitious goal is 'a common approach for European Risk Assessment'[39] to be achieved within 10 years by 2016/2017. Scientific excellence must be pursued by mutual benefits in terms of sharing burdens, access to expertise nationally not available, and the efficient use of scarce resources. Ultimately, these elements will promote the overall goal of confidence-building:

> Strengthening cooperation and networking between Member states and EFSA will enhance coherence in risk assessment and communications. This in turn will contribute to increased consumer protection and ultimately, help to build confidence of consumers, stakeholders and all interested parties in the EU food safety system.[40]

EFSA did not introduce new instruments or tasks within this document, rather it bundled all activities related to cooperation, connected them to its core values and gave an outlook what to achieve in a longer term perspective. This vision is important for the orientation of EFSA and its partners and the functions they are to carry out.

Simultaneously, at its Vienna meeting in May 2006 the Advisory Forum (AF) paved the way for a major *structural* innovation that eventually lead to the creation of the Focal Point System which provides the institutional structures to put the strategic vision into work.[41] Eventually, in September 2006, the AF members on behalf of their organisations signed the 'Declaration of intent of Members of the EFSA Advisory Forum concerning enhancement of the exchange of scientific information amongst the Advisory Forum Members and EFSA'. They agreed to expand vertical (with EFSA) and horizontal (among each other) relations via more formalised communication channels concerning exchange of data and information about ongoing work, work plans and new RA initiatives.[42] Each Member State must provide a Focal Point (FP) in one of its organisations allowing for permanent contact with EFSA and facilitating information exchange.

The 2008 Interim Review of the strategy was largely positive. Especially the establishment of FPs was rated very important and half of the survey respondents

---

38 For cooperation in *risk communication* see chapters 9 and 10 in this volume.

39 EFSA, 'Strategy for Cooperation' [2006] (n 1), 3.

40 Ibid 10.

41 As input a report by the Working Group on the Input of National Authorities (AFWG–INA) had been commissioned by the AF in May 2005. See EFSA, 'Recommendations to Enhance the Exchange of Scientific Information in Order to Facilitate and Improve Risk Assessments of Feed and Food, EU Wide' (AF 29.09.2006 – 6b (AF 19.05.2006 – 5 – Revised), 29 September 2006).

42 See EFSA, 'Declaration of Intent of Members of the EFSA Advisory Forum Concerning Enhancement of the Exchange of Scientific Information Amongst the Advisory Forum Members and EFSA' (AF 29.09.2006 – 6a, 29 September 2006). The Focal Point System was operational in 2008.

even called for intensified cooperation. Furthermore, national CAs emphasised the need for further engagement particularly regarding data collection and harmonisation of RA methods.

From Short-Term to Medium- and Long-Term Planning: Boosting Capacities

The 2008 Interim Review also highlighted the exchange of work plans and information on national activities to facilitate mid- and long-term action plans by EFSA and national CAs. The subsequent strategy paper 'Moving ahead from cooperation between EFSA and the Member States to boosting capacity of RA in Europe' pointed out that:

> EFSA and the [Member States] are fully embedded in cooperation activities, exchanging data and information and building scientific activities … EFSA's governance in fact presents a unique model enabling it to be independent while fulfilling its mission to make full use of the cooperation tools provided for it.[43]

For the first time support for the development of national expertise is recognised as a 'vital element of EFSA's capabilities'.[44] It was acknowledged that the organisations represented in the AF are very diverse in their mandates, sizes as well as capabilities; thus, support shall respond to individual needs, and longer-term planning (3–5 years) is required to use resources efficiently. Identifying 'areas of mutual benefit'[45] is important to encourage Member States' cooperation and to boost capacities in European RA. EFSA itself implemented a medium- and long-term planning by linking its cooperation strategy to the (first of its kind) Strategic Plan 2009–13 and the Science Strategy 2012–16, thus starting to integrate cooperation into an overall broader strategy.

Both strategic plans claim to establish EFSA as a globally recognised RA reference point. The Strategic Plan identifies six key areas[46] all involving cooperation with national partners. While the targets and initiatives introduced are not necessarily innovative, their publication in a brochure speaking to the public at large and the explicit benchmarking of targets must be seen as an important step forward. Likewise the Science Strategy 2012–16 advances a coherent approach to

---

43 EFSA, 'Moving Ahead from Cooperation between EFSA and the Member States to Boosting the Capacity of Risk Assessment in Europe' (MB 18.06.2009 item 6 doc 5, 18 June 2009), 4.

44 Ibid., 6.

45 Ibid., 7.

46 (1) An integrated approach to deliver science; (2) providing high-quality and timely evaluations for authorisations; (3) coordination of collection and analysis of data; (4) positioning EFSA at the forefront of RA; (5) reinforcing confidence and trust in EFSA and the EU food system; (6) assuring the effectiveness and efficiency of EFSA. See EFSA, 'Strategic Plan of the European Food Safety Authority for 2009–2013' (18 December 2008).

goals and initiatives introduced earlier.[47] Both documents signal simultaneously continuity and a more coherent and far-reaching strategy.

Yet, cooperation has not reached its full potential. In the latest external evaluation, the Ernst & Young consultants rate the overall system as functioning well, while the cooperation with the Member States could be fostered. An 'unclear sharing of responsibilities, a weak work programme sharing and communication and a limited effectiveness of the Advisory Forum, and … the highly differentiated contribution of [Member States], due to differences in risk assessment capacity'[48] are identified as main obstacles. The report recommends improving the data collection process and the exchange of information and work plans. This shows that, while the structures and instruments needed for cooperation are so far operational, it needs the engagement from EFSA to further promote these instruments and the willingness and capacity of national institutions to use them adequately.

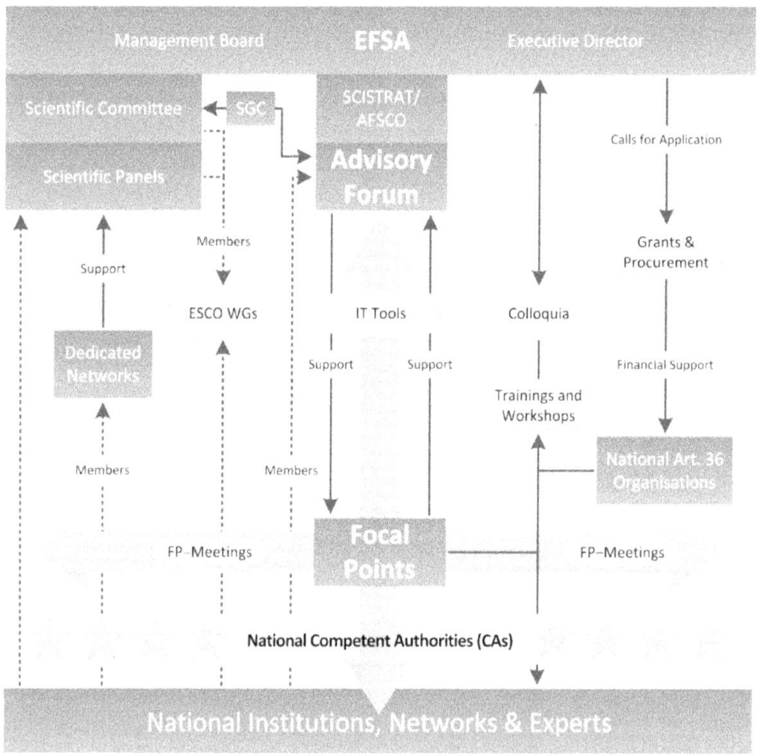

Figure 5.1 Actors in the two-tier Food Safety regime

47 See EFSA, 'Science Strategy 2012–2016' [2011] (n 17).

48 Ernst & Young, 'European Food Safety Authority. External Evaluation of EFSA. Final Report' (6 August 2012), 10.

Actors in the Two-Tiered Regulatory Framework

Networking is clearly at the heart of the new food safety regime. Over the course of time a complex and multilevel organisational architecture evolved consisting of several interconnected networks (see Figure 5.1). Although EFSA acts as a network manager, a two-level system emerges: At *EU level* EFSA's Advisory Forum serves as hub, while for the Member States the Focal Points are the central interface. The AF and the FPs create a vertical channel, with the former developing general strategic guidelines and the latter conducting preparatory work and managing the day-to-day contact to EFSA. Unforeseen by hard law, the FP system becomes increasingly important at the *national level* particularly through informal routines and 'soft' mechanisms.

Actors and Networks at EU Level

EFSA's *Management Board* is competent to take the final decisions concerning the agency's strategic development. All core documents are discussed and adopted by the Board.[49] Nevertheless, in contrast to the *Advisory Forum* as a 'natural place' for developing cooperative strategies, here the Management Board's role is rather limited: usually Member States are instead represented on the management boards of EU agencies – not so in EFSA.[50] Representatives from national CAs are members of EFSA's Advisory Forum and all of EFSA's cooperation activities are centralised within the AF. Systematic inclusion of Member States' representatives (assisted by the national FPs) assures Member States' commitment to cooperation and underlines the notion of common ownership of expertise. Meeting four to five times a year the AF 'shall constitute a mechanism for an exchange of information on potential risks and the pooling of knowledge. It shall ensure close cooperation between the Authority and the competent bodies in the Member States'.[51] Each Member State's member 'represents all the work done on risk assessment … for their respective country'.[52] The AF regularly sets up specific Working Groups to advance and implement the strategy on cooperation. EFSA's *Executive Director*, who chairs the sessions, is advised by the AF and leads the strategic planning and day-to-day business. She is assisted by a Directorate for cooperation first established in 2008. In the course of EFSA's restructuring in 2011, it became the *Science Strategy and Cooperation Directorate* (SCISTRAT) composed of units for the Scientific Committee, the AF and Scientific Cooperation (AFSCO) and Emerging Risks. This restructuring

49 See Regulation (EC) 178/2002 art. 25 (3, 4, 8 and 9).

50 Yet, many of the current Management Board members de facto cover important positions within the national CAs. See also Gabbi (Chapter 4), Testori-Coggi and Deboysier (Chapter 11) and Tai (Chapter 20) in this volume.

51 Regulation (EC) 178/2002 art. 4.

52 EFSA, 'Recommendations to Enhance Exchange' [2006] (n 41) 3.

underlines EFSA's endeavour to integrate previously dispersed units into a more coherent strategic vision. SCISTRAT is responsible for strategic planning of scientific activities and implementation of the Science Strategy. It administrates AF and SC affairs and coordinates cooperation.

EFSA's RA activities mainly rest on the work conducted by the *Scientific Committee* (SC) and in the *Scientific Panels*.[53] Strictly speaking, the *Scientific Panels* and their Working Groups are not part of EFSA's cooperation with the Member States since Panel members are not national delegates, but selected as individual professionals. Nevertheless, many of the *national experts* in the Panels are affiliated with national RA institutions, thus serving as vertical interlinkages disseminating information on EFSA's work in their organisations and vice versa. Some official documents acknowledge this fact as a 'critical aspect of scientific cooperation'.[54]

The *Steering Group on Cooperation* (SGC) comprises members of SC and AF as well as EFSA staff. It interlinks the AF and SC, provides oversight over the implementation of the networking strategy and control over ESCO Working Groups.[55] While ESCO projects are now becoming less important due to more permanent dedicated networks, the future of the SGC is not yet clear. It seems likely that it will address cooperation issues more generally.

The GFL requires that EFSA establishes a network of organisations and ensures its operation,[56] but it does not further specify its form. These so-called *dedicated EFSA networks*, consisting of 'organisations of EU Member States with expertise in the fields covered',[57] are set up on specific topics (e.g. biological hazards) and entrusted with highly specialised remits.[58] Recent attempts seek 'to give the existing cooperation networks a permanent basis enabling enhanced programming and mutually beneficial exchanges'.[59] Network members (usually one per country) are affiliated with national CAs having special expertise in the given field. Additional experts from the Commission, further EU institutions and from outside

53 For further information on the structure, tasks and functioning of the Panels and the SC, see chapters 3 and 4 in this volume.

54 EFSA, 'Interim Review of the Strategy for Cooperation and Networking between EU Member States and EFSA' (5 December 2008) 14; see also EFSA, 'Recommendations to Enhance Exchange' [2006] (n 41), 13.

55 EFSA, 'Technical Report of EFSA on Scientific Cooperation between EFSA and Member States: Taking Stock and Looking Ahead' (11 January 2011), 7.

56 Regulation (EC) 178/2002 art. 23 g.

57 See EFSA, 'Decision Concerning the Establishment and Operations of European Networks of Scientific Organisations Operating in the Fields within the Authority's Mission' (MB 18.03.2010 – item 7 doc 6 – adopted by written procedure, 7 April 2010) art. 2 (3).

58 For an overview of existing networks see EFSA, 'Taking Stock and Looking Ahead' [2011] (n 55), 9f.

59 EFSA, 'Moving Ahead' [2009] (n 43), 7.

the EU may be invited by the AF to participate.[60] Their meetings are held on a regular basis, EFSA provides the Chair and Secretariat. These institutionalised fora coordinate activities, exchange information, best practices and expertise, and initiate joint projects thereby supporting EFSA and the Member States in their RA activities.[61] As 'service providers' they support EFSA's units with expertise on a specific topic, thus collecting information and data.[62] Furthermore, they are vital for RA within the mandatory cooperation procedures laid down in various specific regulations on authorisation processes.[63]

Actors at National Level

Member States and their CAs are participating in various bodies (above all: the AF) and networks. Art. 36 was the GFL's original centrepiece regarding networking with Member States. The so-called *Article 36-network* is an invaluable inventory of national scientific organisations allowing EFSA to outsource specific tasks by grants and procurements. When it turned out that it was insufficient for *managing* networks, national FPs became an alternative. Hence, despite its name we classify the Article 36-network as a mechanism.

The establishment of a *Focal Point System* was a milestone: unforeseen by the GFL, it developed in an incremental fashion based on so-called Focal Point Agreements first signed in 2008 (and renewed ever since by all Member States).[64] The FP System is today a 'key player in cooperation activities in Member states'.[65] FPs owe their unique role to their two-dimensional networking capacities: they *vertically* function as an interface between Member States and the EU acting as 'EFSA's 'ambassadors' in the Member states.'[66] They also contribute to *horizontal* cooperation since they create and maintain national networks of public authorities, stakeholders and science; furthermore, they can be contacted by CAs from other

60 See EFSA, 'Rules of Procedures Concerning the Establishment and Operations of European Networks of Scientific Organisations Operating in the Fields within the Authority's Mission' (MB 18.03.2010 item 7 doc 6, 18 March 2010) art. 3.

61 See EFSA, 'Establishment of European Networks' [2010] (n 57) art. 1 and 4.

62 EFSA documents do not entail instructions on the precise relationship between dedicated networks and Scientific Panels.

63 EFSA, 'Taking Stock and Looking Ahead' [2011] (n 55), 9; see Section 5.1.

64 Norway and Iceland signed FP Agreements for full membership in 2010; Switzerland and Candidate Countries have observer status.

65 EFSA, 'Taking Stock and Looking Ahead' [2011] (n 55), 8. Supporting an initiative of the German Federal Institute for Risk Assessment (BfR) the national FPs prepared country profiles for a 'EU Food Safety Almanac', which provides an overview over CAs and national structures. The authors assisted in the preparation of the profiles. An updated and revised edition was published in 2011. See Federal Institute for Risk Assessment, 'EU Food Safety Almanach' (2011) http://www.bfr.bund.de/cm/364/eu-food-safety-almanac.pdf [accessed: 5 September 2012].

66 Food Safety Authority of Ireland, 'fsainews' (March/April 2008), 1.

Member States. They guarantee the exchange of scientific data and allocate support as well as information about joint projects.[67]

The FPs organise the day-to-day business and prepare dossiers for 'their' AF Member and assist in sharing national working plans and programmes. They coordinate activities of national organisations regarding other networks in the system, e.g. they facilitate information exchange among Article 36 organisations, help enlist new organisations, promote the use of IT tools and organise events and trainings. By so doing, they act as an interface manager between EFSA and national actors. Especially in regard to technical-instrumental issues, FPs evolve into national hubs. In line with the differentiation hypothesis, this development does not jeopardise EFSA's managing powers, but illustrates the division of labour in a multilevel network. Further tasks are 'to facilitate the exchange of scientific information; to support activities under Article 36; to support activities to populate EFSA's Expert Database; and to raise the visibility of EFSA's scientific work, at national level'.[68]

The organisational linkages of Focal Points and their creation differ between Member States. There are no legal requirements regarding FP's organisational design. They are eligible to EFSA financial support in exchange for reporting tasks.[69] National CAs recruit staff specifically for FP activities. In many cases the organisational design of national authorities replicates the bifurcated EFSA model of risk regulation.[70] However, a comparison of organisations represented on the AF with those acting as Focal Points illustrates that in most cases (31 out of 35 FPs plus observers) the AF Member comes from the institution serving as FP.[71] If this is not the case, it becomes an obstacle for the information flow.[72] In some cases (8 out of 35 countries),[73] the AF Member (or its alternate) is simultaneously the FP contact person; where this is not the case, close collaboration between the AF Member and FP is needed.[74]

---

67 EFSA, 'Scientific Cooperation between EFSA and Member States. Taking Stock and Looking Ahead' (2011), 3.

68 EFSA, 'Report. Focal Point Activities 2008' (EFSA/FP/D/2008/026/PUB, 04 December 2008), 6.

69 Ibid., 4.

70 See Gabriele Abels and Alexander Kobusch, 'Regulation of Food Safety in the EU: Changing Patterns of Multi-Level Governance' (Third Biennial Conference'Regulation in the Age of Crises' of the ECPR Standing Group on Regulatory Governance, Dublin, 17–19 June 2010) http://ssrn.com/abstract=2131363 [accessed: 10 December 2012]; e.g. Hungary see Jennifer Träsch, 'From Chaos to Separation – an Update of the Hungarian Food Safety Regulation System' (2011) 2 *European Journal of Risk Regulation*, 560.

71 Exceptions are Italy, Poland, Slovenia and the observer country Montenegro.

72 See EFSA, 'Recommendations to Enhance Exchange' [2006] (n 41), 3.

73 France, Ireland, Lithuania, Malta, Romania, Slovakia, Croatia and the Former Yugoslav Republic of Macedonia.

74 See EFSA, 'Focal Point Activities 2008' [2008] (n 68), 6.

Focal Points closely cooperate with EFSA's AF and Scientific Cooperation Unit (AFSCO) within SCISTRAT. Often FPs host the regular meetings enabling coordination of activities and information exchange on what are mostly very specific, highly technical issues.[75] At the national level, FPs organise events for their national organisations; fellow FPs are often invited to raise their profile and to foster information exchange.

Mechanisms of Cooperation in Scientific Networks

A number of mechanisms for vertical scientific cooperation were developed. It is first of all important to distinguish between networking activities taking place within and beyond the GFL framework and those mandatory based on specific sectoral legislation.

Mandatory Cooperation Based on Specific Food Legislation

Most pieces of EU food law include binding requirements for cooperation between national CAs and EFSA regarding authorisation, thus influencing the nature of cooperation.[76] EFSA is responsible for RA prior to authorisation in the cases of food contact materials, food and feed additives, enzymes and flavourings, GMOs, novel foods, pesticides, health claims and biohazards.[77] Authorisation-related activities have augmented in the last decade from initially 20 per cent to today 2/3 of EFSA's workload.[78]

All authorisation procedures involve national CAs in RA, yet the degree of their formal consultation and their involvement in the RA process varies. In all of the cases mentioned above there is some kind of common procedure 'involving Member States and the Commission'.[79] But it ranges from the submission of applications to the Member States' authorities under the 'Community authorisation' method[80] over the MS supporting EFSA's risk assessment activities and networking through an authorisation list[81] to a joint authorisation with the nomination of a

---

75 See ibid., 6.

76 EFSA, 'Interim Review' [2008] (n 54), 20.

77 For an overview see EFSA, 'Taking Stock and Looking Ahead' [2011] (n 55), 28–47.

78 EFSA, 'Science Strategy 2012–2016' [2011] (n 17), 5.

79 Regulation (EC) No. 1829/2003 of the European Parliament and of the Council of 22 September 2003 On Genetically Modified Food and Feed [2003] OJ L268/1 Recital 5.

80 See Regulation (EC) No. 1935/2004 of the European Parliament and of the Council of 27 October 2004 On Materials and Articles Intended to Come into Contact with Food and Repealing Directives 80/590/EEC and 89/109/EEC [2004] OJ L338/4.

81 See Regulation (EC) No. 1331/2008 of the European Parliament and of the Council of 16 December 2008 Establishing a Common Authorisation Procedure for Food Additives, Food Enzymes and Food Flavourings [2008] OJ L354/1.

rapporteur.[82] Especially the latter shows a specific characteristic with a very high degree of Member State involvement thus being an exceptional case.

Networking Within the General Food Law Framework and Beyond

In contrast to hard law, the implementation of networks within the framework of food safety regulation as laid out in the GFL was done incrementally over time, and they are 'softer' and 'more flexible'. Interacting networks and exchange activities were initiated following EFSA's 2006 networking strategy and the AF's 'Declaration of Intent' involving multiple communication and networking mechanisms as well as IT tools. Especially Focal Points utilise and promote these mechanisms extensively, thus supporting EFSA's role as network manager.

The GFL foregrounds *Article 36 networks*, whose composition and operation are further refined in the Commission Regulation (EC) No. 2230/2004.[83] Given functional limitations and its current status, we interpret this network, despite official nomenclature, as a *mechanism*. The list, first established in December 2006 by EFSA's Management Board, currently includes about 400 organisations from all Member States.[84] EFSA has to facilitate RA cooperation, information exchange, joint projects and dissemination of expertise and best practices between these organisations. A 2008 evaluation highlights its importance for scientific cooperation between EFSA and the Member States.[85]

Enlisted organisations are eligible for grants (2012: 3 Mio. Euro) and procurement issued by EFSA. This often involves scientific cooperation between individual organisations. IT tools for cooperation exist since 2010 and differ from the Article 36 Extranet Workspace;[86] the Article 36 Organizations Database

---

82 See Regulation (EC) No 1107/2009 of the European Parliament and of the Council of 21 October 2009 Concerning the Placing of Plant Protection Products on the Market and Repealing Council Directives 79/117/EEC and 91/414/EEC [2009] OJ L309/1.

83 Commission Regulation (EC) No. 2230/2004 of 23 December 2004 Laying Down Detailed Rules for the Implementation of European Parliament and Council Regulation (EC) No. 178/2002 with Regard to the Network of Organisations Operating in the Fields within the European Food Safety Authority's Mission [2004] OJ L379/64.

84 See EFSA, 'List of Competent Organisations Designated by the Member States Which May Assist the Authority within Its Mission' (15 December 2011).

85 EFSA, 'Review of the Work Carried out under Article 36 and Proposed Contract and Grant Activities for 2009' (5 December 2008), 3.

86 The so-called ART36–NET supports active networking and project management and provides information on open calls as well as projects.

(ART36–DATABASE) and the Internet-based *Information Exchange Platform (IEP)*[87] to the *Expert Database (EDB)*.[88]

EFSA's strategy explicitly allows for joint RA projects as 'front-runners', so-called *ESCO projects*. ESCO Working Groups (WGs) comprise members of the Scientific Panels/Scientific Committee and nominees by Member States. This ensures integration of specific expertise not represented in the Panels. First projects were initiated based on EFSA's right of self-tasking on topics such as botanicals, emerging risks, the Expert Database, folic acid or methodological harmonisation. Proposals for ESCO WGs are developed by the Steering Group on Cooperation and reviewed by the AF and the Scientific Committee. ESCO WG reports are not official EFSA scientific opinions, but are addressed to the Executive Director incorporating recommendations on further initiatives. ESCO projects often include the collection of available data in Member States; yet, their importance will decrease due to the increasing number and prominence of more permanent dedicated networks.

To promote coherent RA approaches, *trainings and workshops* provide an indispensable tool. The 2006 Strategy on Cooperation proposed a training programme for experts. In the 2008 Strategy Review especially the newer Member States requested more training activities.[89] To identify needs, FPs, in cooperation with EFSA's Scientific Cooperation Unit (the predecessor of AFSCO), analysed existing training programmes at the national, EU and international levels.[90] Since trainings on general RA principles are identified as underprovided, EFSA works on a multi-annual training programme filling this gap. A Working Group was set up in 2010 proposing specific courses in its report as of April 2011.[91]

In 2004 EFSA founded the *Scientific Colloquium Series*; 17 events were organised until June 2012 serving as open fora for scientific topics (e.g. emerging

87 Launched in 2008 the IEP is 'considered the best tool to easily share scientific information on topics of high interest for the Member states and ESFA in a timely two-way exchange' (EFSA, 'Focal Point Activities 2008' [2008] (n 68), 8). Since 2009 the platform focuses on RAs requests/outputs, national work plans/strategy papers and country specific information. By the end of 2011 the IEP contained over 1,000 documents. See EFSA, 'Project Report of EFSA. Focal Point Activities 2009' (EFSA/FP/R/2010/058/PUB/FIN, 1 March 2010); EFSA, 'Technical Report of EFSA. Focal Point Activities 2011' (Supporting Publications 2012: EN-268, 9 April 2012), 9.

88 It aims to 'pool information on external scientific experts capable of assisting Member states and EFSA ...; *and to enhance the transparency of the invitation process by which experts participate in EFSA*'s scientific activities' (EFSA, 'Focal Point Activities 2008' [2008] (n 68), 13). Especially EFSA's Scientific Panels and ESCO Working Groups consider the EDB to be a crucial tool. More than 3,500 applications were submitted until the end of 2011. See EFSA, 'Focal Point Activities 2011' [2012] (n 87), 1.

89 EFSA, 'Taking Stock and Looking Ahead' [2011] (n 55), 20.

90 Similarly, the Commission offers training for risk managers and national CAs as part of the 'Better Training for Safer Food' programme.

91 See EFSA, 'Technical Report. Technical Specifications on Training Regarding Principles and Methods of Food Safety Risk Assessment' (14 April 2011).

risks, GMOs or health claims). Topics can be proposed by the Scientific Committee, AF or Scientific Panels and EFSA units. Colloquia may conclude with recommendations directed to EFSA and might be related to ongoing EFSA work or suggest further projects.[92] Overall, Member States consider colloquia useful for exchanging knowledge and identifying future thematic priorities.

Guidance documents serve two purposes: firstly, EFSA working procedures become transparent; secondly, industry, stakeholders' and Member States' organisations are informed about best practices. Guidance documents facilitate the harmonisation of RA; they call for transparency in the RA process by explaining underlying data, methods of analysis and assumptions, and reflecting upon uncertainty. In a questionnaire on GMO risk assessment across Europe, for example, all Member States reported that they rely on EFSA's guidance; many also take into account guidance by OECD, FAO/WHO and Codex Alimentarius. A common request by Member States and experts alike is to expand guidance, to clarify certain key steps and to make the development of guidance more transparent. The Member States are usually consulted on the development.[93] EFSA has published over 80 guidance documents both on procedural and scientific issues. Yet, it seems that the development and use of harmonised guidance is patchy in the different areas within EFSA's remit.

In sum, the dynamic and numerous mechanisms demonstrate EFSA's efforts to creatively implement its mandate beyond the GFL yet within its framework and spirit. As EFSA's vast reporting and evaluation schemes illustrate, it is so far difficult to assess the efficiency of single mechanisms.

Which Way Forward? Conclusions and Suggestions

We have portrayed EFSA as a 'networked agency'. This argument confirms the differentiation hypotheses according to which European and national agencies are highly interdependent and interconnected by a complex division of tasks. The network dynamic, the multitude of actors and the creativeness of introducing new mechanisms are striking. Hence, looking at the GFL and formal powers delegated to EFSA is indeed only a fraction of the much broader picture of 'experimentalist governance' in food safety based on a 'carefully designed architecture of networking between the national and European levels, incorporating national capacities into European science making'.[94]

92 E.g. the establishment of a European Food Consumption Database; see EFSA, 'Taking Stock and Looking Ahead' [2011] (n 55), 20.

93 Member States also often use public consultations, which are addressed to stakeholders, to contribute feedback on e.g. guidance documents or procedural rules. See ibid., 22.

94 Vos (n 16), 171.

Information-sharing is the key in the two-tier framework. For EFSA networking is an empowerment tool: in epistemic networks actors acquire credibility because they provide 'tools' to tackle the fundamental epistemological dilemma and create incentives for information-sharing. The creation of national Focal Points simultaneously enabling vertical and horizontal networking is most important. While some of these networks were legally required by the GFL, others developed – as illustrated in this chapter – much later in response to functional deficits. Overall, this incremental approach is typical for the experimentalist governance style of EU policy – and concurrent policy-making.[95] While FP development was initially an incremental step, over time these actors became increasingly important and part of the more coherent strategy for scientific cooperation between EFSA and the Member States. We recommend *streamlining of relations between EFSA and FPs* in terms of the organisational affiliation of FP members in those Member States where this is so far not the case. As FPs have been established to support AF, it is beneficial for cooperation if national AF members come from those institutions acting as FP. This operational proximity allows for a smooth, fast information flow and for immediate, comprehensive action. Furthermore, *organisational isomorphism* seems to have clear advantages: Member States with a bifurcated model of risk regulation and a RA agency modelled like EFSA (with its panel structure) can facilitate communication and cooperation activities between organisations. Additionally, we suggest *intensive training programmes* for FP staff or directorates responsible for collaborating with EFSA and the relevant persons of the European agency to develop routines and best practices.

The continuous development of a comprehensive cooperation strategy based on 'common ownership' is required; this should include further *incentives also for strengthening mechanisms of horizontal networking* between Member States and their CAs. This could imply a weaker role of EFSA as a network manager, yet may foster the commitment of national CAs. Considering the diversity of national CAs – ranging from full-blown research organisations with scientific staff and resources to smaller CAs lacking fundamental scientific resources – is vital for EFSA as network manager in order to be able to respond to different needs and capabilities of the single network members. Thus, there should be *tailor-made offers working for the benefits for every single member*; given institutional diversity a one-size-fits-all approach is insufficient. Fostering horizontal cooperation, CAs with similar needs can *pool their resources for a common benefit*. This includes a more extensive use of IT tools by national CAs and constantly adapting them to their needs. Obviously IT tools have not reached their full potential: national CAs do not yet upload all available scientific information and work plans (especially RA-related mandates); also some information might be confidential.[96] Language skills might still be a major constraint since even larger CAs sometimes lack resources to translate all relevant

95 See ibid.

96 EFSA, 'Focal Point Activities 2011' [2012] (n 88), 8; See e.g. EFSA, 'Technical Report of EFSA. Focal Point Activities 2010' (23 March 2010), 10.

documents into English. It is thus very important for EFSA to mobilise all CAs to share information via the platforms and crosslink with each other. Especially in the case of new risk assessments and study activities, this is the best way to create synergies and avoid duplication of work.[97] EFSA already tries fostering scientific cooperation with CAs through conferences, workshops and trainings. We propose to *further develop these instruments and create new permanent fora* to conceptualise a European scientific space in the field of food safety.

EFSA's crucial rationale is building up a credible scientific reputation. Thereby consumer confidence in European regulation and the functioning of the internal market are to be improved. By focusing so strongly on *standards of scientific excellence*, it restricts itself to the scientific robustness of its expertise. From a more comprehensive view of risk governance, the exclusive focus on science 'acting as a stabilising mechanism'[98] in risk regulation is disputed, since RA knowledge is inherently contestable for epistemological reasons. EFSA's RA philosophy is rooted in a rational-instrumental paradigm resting on positivist, 'sound science'. Yet, whether contestation of expertise can solely be solved in a scientific manner, is so far an open question in need of being taken up by EFSA and national CAs. In the future *addressing the cognitive bias and developing closer linkages between the* scientific *and the* social *robustness of a RA framework* is a key issue.[99]

EFSA cannot tackle this task by itself, yet it can guide this process by means of scientific colloquia and its right of self-tasking. At the end of the day, policy-makers must decide how they envision future RA and the role of agencies. In this sense, the creation of a science-based agency striving to build up its own identity is linked to – as Waterton and Wynne rightfully argue[100] – much broader questions of identity and the EU political order.

---

97 In their external evaluation report Ernst & Young (n 48) also highlight the necessity for the improvement of data exchange and avoidance of a duplication of work.

98 Julia Black, 'The Role of Risk in Regulatory Processes' in Robert Baldwin, Martin Cave and Martin Lodge (eds), *The Oxford Handbook of Regulation* (Oxford University Press 2010), 316.

99 See Susana Borrás, Charalampos Koutalakis and Frank Wendler, 'European Agencies and Input Legitimacy: EFSA, EMeA and EPO in the Post-Delegation Phase' (2007) 29 *Journal of European Integration*, 58; Marion Dreyer and Ortwin Renn (eds), *Food Safety Governance: Integrating Science, Precaution and Public Involvement* (Springer 2009).

100 See Claire Waterton and Brian Wynne, 'Knowledge and Political Order in the European Environment Agency' in Sheila Jasanoff (ed.), *States of Knowledge: The Co-Production of Science and Social Order* (Routledge 2004).

Chapter 6
EFSA under Pressure: Emerging Risks, Emergencies and Crises

James Lawless

Introduction

As has been well documented in many studies of EU food regulation, the changes brought about by the adoption of Regulation 178/2002 (hereinafter the 'General Food Law' or GFL) were largely a reaction to the high-profile food safety incidents of the 1990s; in particular the UK BSE outbreak and the Belgian dioxin contamination.[1] With this unhappy legacy in mind, the adopters of the General Food Law developed specific provisions aimed at governing such critical situations. Given that urgency and uncertainty are key features of such scenarios, the importance of decisive risk management cannot be overemphasised. Officially, risk management as a role is specifically excluded from EFSA's mandate. Nevertheless, the legislative provisions and institutional arrangements governing 'emerging risks', 'emergencies' and 'crisis management' have created important scope for EFSA. Through a legal and empirical examination, this chapter explores EFSA's role in the regulatory regimes envisaged for these inevitable eventualities.

The Legal and Institutional Context

Emerging Risks, Emergencies and Crisis Management under the General Food Law

Despite the linguistic similarities between them, the terms, 'emerging risks', 'emergencies' and 'crises' are considering as three separate and distinct legal concepts within the General Food Law. While emerging risks (Article 34) are not specifically defined in the General Food Law, they can be said to encompass future risks which require a long-term preventative strategy.[2]

---

1 Knowles, T., Moody, R. and McEachern, M., 'European food scares and their impact on EU food policy' (2007) *British Food Journal*, 109(1), pp. 43–67.

2 Recital 50, Council Regulation (EC) 178/2002 of 1 February 2002 laying down the general principles and requirements of food law, establishing the European Food Safety Authority and laying down procedures in matters of food safety [2002] OJ L31 pp. 1–24.

Emergencies (Articles 53-54), on the other hand, cover the specific situation of an immediate and serious cross-border risk that '*cannot be contained satisfactorily by means of measures taken by the Member State(s) concerned*',[3] thus requiring the Commission to take action. In this way, supranational control should enable '*artificial disparities in the treatment of a serious risk in relation to food or feed*'[4] to be avoided. Emergency situations are frequently accompanied by political conflict with EU Member States, where their actions have been judged by EU risk managers to be inadequate and requiring EU level intervention. The rules on emergencies enable the Commission, in conjunction with Member States, to actively manage a known risk within the Union, which is not being effectively controlled by the Member States. These emergency powers are activated in 'wartime' scenarios.

In turn, crises management (Articles 55-57) is regarded as the task of elaborating contingency plans and procedures at the European level to deal with:

> … the types of situation involving direct or indirect risks to human health deriving from food and feed which are not likely to be prevented, eliminated or reduced to an acceptable level by provisions in place or cannot adequately be managed solely by way of application of Articles 53 and 54 [i.e. emergency procedures].[5]

The provisions on emerging risks and crisis management form a legal architecture within the General Food Law designed to account for those complex instances where scientific uncertainty meets risk volatility at the limits of conventional regulation. This architecture also has consequences for EFSA and the way in which it conducts its work. This mirrors the preoccupation contained in the 2000 *White Paper on Food Safety* for a proactive approach to food risk.[6]

However, the interaction between emerging risks on the one hand and emergencies and crisis management on the other is not totally clear. Depending on the gravity of the emerging risk identified, it may trigger a crisis situation or the need for the adoption of emergency measures. Therefore, as Kocharov has noted, the identification of emerging risks may carry with it serious implications in terms of liability for risk managers and overall issues of credibility and confidence in the EU food and feed safety regime.[7]

It is also important to acknowledge one of the EU's oldest tools for managing urgent cross-border food incidents, the Rapid Alert System for Food and Feed

3 Ibid., Article 53.

4 Ibid., Recital 60.

5 Ibid., Article 55(2).

6 European Commission, White Paper on Food Safety (COM 719 final, 1999).

7 Kocharov, A., 'EFSA and Identification of Emerging Risks' (2010) *European Food and Feed Law Review*, 3, pp. 144–55.

(RASFF).[8] This tool has been a key mechanism for coordinating EU food risks, on the basis of 'regulation through information', for over 30 years. The current legal basis for this communications system is contained in the General Food Law,[9] which requires the existence of a network of Member State, Commission and EFSA 'contact points' obliged to notify each other of '*information relating to the existence of serious direct or indirect risk to human health deriving from food or feed*'.[10] A further subparagraph of Article 50 envisages a role for EFSA within the RASFF network to '*supplement the notification[s] with any scientific or technical information, which will facilitate rapid, appropriate risk management action by the Member States*'.[11] The risk information generated through RASFF notifications is one of the key sources of evidence of a Union-wide food and feed safety issue which may require the activation of many of the regulatory procedures contained under EU food law. Information notified through RASFF has most recently been used as a source of risk indication for EFSA's work on emerging risks.

EFSA and Emerging Risks

Article 23 of the General Food Law establishes that one of the tasks entrusted to EFSA is:

> (f) to undertake action to identify and characterise emerging risks, in the fields within its mission;[12]

Article 34 of the General Food Law goes on to require the following:

> 1. The Authority shall establish monitoring procedures for systematically searching for, collecting, collating and analysing information and data with a view to the identification of emerging risks in the fields within its mission.
>
> 2. Where the Authority has information leading it to suspect an emerging serious risk, it shall request additional information from the Member States, other Community agencies and the Commission. The Member States, the Community

8 Bànàti, D. and Klaus, B. '30 years of the rapid alert system for food and feed' (2010) *European Food and Feed Law Review*, 5, pp. 10–21; Mahy, A. 'Food: Clear-cut Legal Basis for the RASFF: Mere Formalisation or a Concrete Move Forward?' (2012) *European Journal of Risk Regulation*, 1, pp. 72–80.

9 Articles 50–52, Council Regulation (EC) 178/2002 of 1 February 2002 laying down the general principles and requirements of food law, establishing the European Food Safety Authority and laying down procedures in matters of food safety [2002] OJ L31, pp. 1–24.

10 Ibid., Article 50(2).

11 Ibid., Article 50(2).

12 Article 23, Regulation (EC) No 178/2002, OJ L31, 1.2.2002, pp. 1–24.

> agencies concerned and the Commission shall reply as a matter of urgency and forward any relevant information in their possession.
>
> 3. The Authority shall use all the information it receives in the performance of its mission to identify an emerging risk.
>
> 4. The Authority shall forward the evaluation and information collected on emerging risks to the European Parliament, the Commission and the Member States.[13]

Overall, EFSA's principal role in relation to emerging risks is to gather information connected to foreseeable future risks and to pass on serious cases to the EU's risk managers. The central legal concept is the 'identification' of an emerging risk. It should be remembered that identification of a hazard is only one component of the risk assessment process, as per Article 3(11) of the General Food Law. When read together with the provisions of the General Food Law as a whole, it is clear that the identification of an emerging risk does not equate with an official EFSA scientific opinion, i.e. risk assessment. This is further reflected in the fact that the General Food Law does not provide for a specific panel for emerging risks;[14] the allocation of an existing sectoral panel to look at an emerging risk only comes into play if a decision is made, either by the European Commission, European Parliament, Member State(s) or EFSA itself, to pursue a formal scientific opinion on foot of the identification of an emerging risk.[15] In this instance, the panel that is competent to deal with the relevant matter will be assigned the task of elaborating and adopting a scientific opinion.[16]

The task of generating information on emerging risks is foreseen as an iterative function shared by an EFSA/Member States network. This is reflected, for example, in Article 27(4)(d) and envisages the Advisory Forum as a '*mechanism for an exchange of information on potential risks and the pooling of knowledge*',[17] where EFSA or the Member States identify an emerging risk.[18]

---

13 Ibid., Article 34.; the General Food Law's Recital (50) provides a further understanding of the objective of the provisions on emerging risks:

> *Improved identification of emerging risks may in the long term be a major preventive instrument at the disposal of the Member States and the Community in the exercise of its policies. It is therefore necessary to assign to the Authority an anticipatory task of collecting information and exercising vigilance and providing evaluation of and information on emerging risks with a view to their prevention.*

14 Article 28(4), Council Regulation (EC) 178/2002 of 1 February 2002 laying down the general principles and requirements of food law, establishing the European Food Safety Authority and laying down procedures in matters of food safety [2002] OJ L31, pp. 1–24.

15 Ibid., Article 29(1).

16 On this process, see in this book Pintado, Chapter 3, and Gabbi, Chapter 4.

17 Article 27(4), Regulation (EC) No 178/2002, OJ L35, 1.2.2002, pp. 1–24.

18 A similar exhortation to deal with emerging risks via networking between organisations operating in the areas of food and feed safety is found in Article 36(2) of

EFSA and Emergencies

By contrast, and in line with the overall emphasis on establishing a clear divide between risk assessment (EFSA) and risk management (Commission and Member States), the provisions on emergencies do not include a central role for EFSA. Articles 53 and 54 reflect the 'panic room' of EU food crises, where the Commission and the Standing Committee on the Food Chain and Animal Health (SCFCAH) may take an incident in hand where measures taken at Member State level are deemed unsatisfactory.[19] Where these considerable powers are invoked, the value judgement being made by the Commission as to the unsatisfactory nature of national management of a safety issue need not be predicated on an EFSA opinion. In such urgent circumstances, the niceties of the functional separation between risk assessment and risk management may be overridden in the immediate stage; reflecting the exceptions to systematic risk analysis as provided for in Article 6(1)[20] and Article 7 of the GFL on the precautionary principle. The scientific soundness of decisions taken by Member States under emergency provisions can be established *ex post* through the possibility of activating a formal request for EFSA's scientific advice. Here EFSA may play a central role in resolving any conflict between Member States and the Commission over the extent of a cross-border risk or the adequacy of the measures taken to mitigate that risk. Where formal scientific assessments are sought as part of an incident which could potentially involve the invocation of Commission emergency powers, the political significance of EFSA's opinions will come into stark focus.

EFSA and Crisis Management

The GFL provisions on crisis management contain legal requirements to 'plan ahead' for food incidents. Under these requirements a role is envisaged for EFSA in the creation of a general plan for crisis management[21] and through participation in a crisis unit, where one is established by the Commission.[22]

Article 36 provides that where a crisis does arise, a crisis unit is to be established by the Commission on notification of the Member States and EFSA. Article 56(2) goes on to stress the very central role which EFSA should play in any such crisis

---

Regulation (EC) No 178/2002, OJ L35, 1.2.2002, pp. 1–24. On these matters, see Abels, Kobush and Träsch (Chapter 5).

19 Article 53(1), Regulation 178/2002, OJ L35, 1.2.2002, pp. 1–24; Berends, G. and Carreno, I. (2005) 'Safeguards in Food Law – Ensuring Food Scares are Scarce', *European Law Review*, 30(3), pp. 386–405.

20 '*... food law shall be based on risk analysis except where this is not appropriate to the circumstances or the nature of the measure*'.

21 Article 55 Council Regulation (EC) 178/2002 of 1 February 2002 laying down the general principles and requirements of food law, establishing the European Food Safety Authority and laying down procedures in matters of food safety [2002] OJ L31 pp. 1–24.

22 Ibid., Articles 56–7.

unit, in contrast to the usual distance maintained between EFSA risk assessment activity and the work of risk managers.

The crisis management plan and technical arrangements for crisis units was realised in 2004 with the adoption of Commission Decision 2004/478/EC. However, given the detailed extent of food legislation as prescribed by an extensive corpus of EU food law, the capabilities of Member State competent authorities and the Commission's supranational powers, Decision 2004/478/EC considers that such crisis situations would be '*very few in number, not to say exceptional*'.[23]

Somewhat unclearly, Decision 2004/478/EC makes a distinction between classic crises, as defined in Article 55 of the GFL, and situations where a '*risk is potential but could evolve into a serious risk which is unlikely to be prevented, eliminated or reduced by existing provisions or solely by way of application of Article 53 and 54*'.[24] In this latter situation, the establishment of a crisis unit is not deemed necessary. Instead alternative 'adequate provisions' are to be put in place 'to ensure effective management of this type of situation'.[25] Such a scenario, however, echoes the notion of emerging risk and reflects an attempt to ensure some form of risk management for such situations.

It is for the Commission to make the determination as to whether a crisis has come about and it will then request information on the risk from EFSA. A crisis unit will then be set up and will be composed of representatives of the Commission, Member States and EFSA. While the crisis unit is to be '*responsible for gathering and evaluating all the relevant data and identifying the options available for managing the crisis*',[26] Decision 2004/478/EC goes on to stress that '*the crisis unit is not responsible for adopting decisions on the management of risk or for implementing legislation*'.[27] Additionally, the establishment of the crisis unit should in no way substitute or displace the usual procedures relating to conventional EFSA scientific opinions. EFSA should provide the crisis unit with the necessary scientific and technical assistance, as distinct from formal scientific opinions.[28]

23 Paragraph 2.1, Annex, Commission Decision (EC) 2004/478 of 29 April 2004 concerning the adoption of a general plan for food/feed crisis management [2004] OJ L160/98 pp. 60–68.

24 Paragraph 2.2, Annex, Commission Decision (EC) 2004/478 of 29 April 2004 concerning the adoption of a general plan for food/feed crisis management [2004] OJ L160/98 pp. 60–68.

25 Ibid.

26 Ibid., Paragraph 5.2.

27 Ibid., Paragraph 5.2.

28 Ibid., Paragraph 5.3, see Chapter 3.

Institutional Arrangements within EFSA for the Identification of Emerging Risks

The mandate on emerging risks prescribed for EFSA by the General Food Law was organised institutionally during the mid 2000s. Much of the initial work on emerging risk reflects a grappling with the exact nature of the concept provided under the General Food Law. Adding meaning to the relatively limited legislative provision on a non-defined concept seems to have been an understandable challenge.

While the EFSA Scientific Committee gave nominal support for a system to identify emerging risks, it was not until 2006 that a scoping report on the issue was produced for EFSA by the Dutch Food and Consumer Product Safety Authority (VWA) under the outsourcing programme envisaged by the General Food Law.[29] This report (the 'VWA Report') clearly demonstrates the vast potential field of information which EFSA would need to distil in order to develop a useful '*pre-early warning system for the identification of emerging risks*'.[30] The initial task involved the determination of the so-called key 'influential sectors' – the disciplines most linked to the food chain – which focused down on the three areas of agriculture, health and welfare and energy and environment. Within these influential sectors, the VWA report stressed the need to further select indicators which should enable a channelling of pertinent information.[31] Drawing on past cases of emerging risks which turned into major food safety incidents, the report generated a number of examples of failure in identifying emerging risks:

1. late lessons from early warning;
2. gaps in scientific knowledge;
3. necessity for abnormal clinical signs surveillance;
4. fatal coincidence of circumstances, and
5. breakdown in collaboration between scientists, stakeholders and authorities.

The report also noted that the degree of preparedness for emerging risks was of a '*fuzzy character*'.[32] The report advocated the establishment of a special unit within

---

29 Article 36, Council Regulation (EC) 178/2002 of 28 January 2002 laying down the general principles and requirements of food law, establishing the European Food Safety Authority and laying down procedures in matters of food safety [2002] OJ L31/1 pp. 1–24; Commission Regulation (EC) 2230/2004 of 23 December 2004 laying down detailed rules for the implementation of European Parliament and Council Regulation (EC) No 178/2002 with regard to the network of organisations operating in the fields within the European Food Safety Authority's mission [2004] OJ L379 pp. 64–7.

30 VWA, 'Forming a Global System for Identifying Food-related Emerging Risks EMRISK Final' (2006) The Hague, 6 April 2006, available at www.efsa.europa.eu/en/supporting/doc/224r.pdf (last visited 12 November 2012).

31 Ibid., p. 9.

32 VWA, 'Forming a Global System for Identifying Food-related Emerging Risks EMRISK Final' (2006) The Hague, 6 April 2006, available at www.efsa.europa.eu/en/supporting/doc/224r.pdf (last visited 12 November 2012), p. 63.

EFSA for emerging risk activities. In 2006 the Scientific Committee adopted an opinion on the early identification of emerging risks. This initial policy document also acknowledged the vast informational field that would need to be structured and managed in order for EFSA to fulfil its role under Article 34 of the General Food Law.

The Emerging Risk Unit was established for this purpose. Interestingly, the Emerging Risk Unit has also become occupied with what EFSA itself has termed 'crises' and 'emergencies'. However, it is important to stress that, somewhat confusingly, these crises are distinct from the crises and emergencies envisaged under the GFL and Decision 2004/478/EC. Instead, they relate more generally to situations where an urgent response is required by the EU institutions and Member States in situations of significant risk. However, given the linkage between EFSA's role and the potential development or abatement of a crisis or emergency (in the GFL sense), it is worth examining EFSA's internal logic for these scenarios.

By 2007, EFSA's Scientific Committee adopted a so-called 'definition and description' of emerging risks. This text understands an emerging risk as:

> a newly identified hazard to which a significant exposure may occur or from an unexpected new or increased significant exposure and/or susceptibility to a known hazard.[33]

The Scientific Committee's text also attempts to distinguish between emerging risks on the one hand and emergencies and crises on the other. While the distinction is grounded primarily in the fact that emergencies and crises are governed by other legislative provisions of the GFL, they are also contrasted with emerging risks which are not derived from '*risks characterized by a sudden appearance, such as food or feed contamination episodes … or the sudden release of a toxic or radioactive cloud …* [*or*] *… the inadvertent or accidental intake of food or feed that are not in compliance with recognized safety requirements*'.[34] However, as will be examined below, while such high-profile incidents may not fall strictly within the meaning of emerging risks, they are nonetheless 'core business' of the EFSA Emerging Risk Unit, reflecting the close interconnection between emerging risk, emergencies and crises/crises management. Both the Stakeholders' Consultative Group on Emerging Risk (StaCG-ER)[35] and Member

33 EFSA, 'Definition and Description of 'Emerging Risks' within the EFSA's Mandate' (2007) EFSA/SC/415 Final, p. 1, available at www.efsa.europa.eu/en/scdocs/doc/esconemriskdefinition.pdf (last visited 12 November 2012).

34 Ibid., p. 2.

35 The StaCG-ER is linked to the Stakeholder Consultative Platform (SCP) of EFSA which itself was established in 2005. The SCP of EFSA brings together representative of all stages of the food chain, from feed business operators and the food industry to consumers and NGOs. The StaCG-ER was formed in 2011 and is intended to continue its dialogue throughout 2012 and 2013.

States in the Emerging Risks Exchange Network[36] (EREN) have identified some of the problems inherent in the precise meaning of emerging risks, with emphasis being placed on the need for a '*common lexicon of terms*'[37] as well as '*a common language with shared terminology and definition and methodology … able to discriminate between urgent issues (crises) due to known risks and emerging risks*'.[38]

The Scientific Committee's definition and description also highlights nine examples of factors pointing towards the emergence of an ultimate risk:

1. new research indicating previously unknown properties;
2. new trends in disease of an unknown etiology;
3. exotic threats;
4. new analytical and diagnostic results obtained with new methods;
5. conditions likely to lead to consequential events, e.g. major energy blackout, identified lack of safety conditions;
6. unusual agronomic and weather conditions;
7. new plant or animal production methods;
8. unexpected adverse effects on the environment caused by the emission of some pollutant, and
9. outbreaks of infestations associated with climate change or species hybridisation.[39]

Ideas surrounding emerging risk were further elaborated upon by a technical report of the EFSA Scientific Cooperation (ESCO) Working Group on emerging risks[40] which slightly broadens the scope of emerging risks by referring to wider geographical trends beyond agriculture, health and welfare and energy

---

36 The Emerging Risks Exchange Network was established in 2010 and is the principal network for the purposes of exchanging information on emerging risks between EFSA, Member States, the Commission, other EU agencies and international organisations.

37 EFSA, 'Annual Report on the Emerging Risks Exchange Network 2010' (2011), p. 6, available at www.efsa.europa.eu/en/supporting/doc/153e.pdf (last visited 12 November 2012).

38 EFSA, 'Outcome of the Stakeholders' Consultative Group on Emerging Risks submitted to EFSA: Report on Stakeholders' activities in the area of emerging risks' (2011), chapter 5, available at www.efsa.europa.eu/fr/supporting /doc/170e.pdf (last visited 12 November 2012).

39 EFSA, 'Definition and Description of 'Emerging Risks' within the EFSA's Mandate' (2007) EFS /SC/415 Final, p. 1, available at www.efsa.europa.eu/en/scdocs/doc/esconemriskdefinition.pdf (last visited 12 November 2012).

40 The EFSA Management Board encourages the establishment of scientific cooperation on specific projects within networks involving EFSA staff, national experts and panel members which report to the EFSA Executive Director. The work produced by these ESCO projects may then be brought to the attention of EFSA Panels and the EFSA Scientific Committee.

and environment by also encompassing so-called 'megatrends' such as ageing, innovation, migrations and financial crisis.[41]

This wide thematic scope for the identification of emerging risks was subsequently reinforced in 2011 by stakeholders in the StaCG-ER.[42] This group identified five drivers of emerging risk where attention may need to be focused, including:

1. social/economic developments (i.e. ageing population; economic environment causing pressure for cost reductions on food production and purchasing; changes in animal welfare; increased consumption of nutritional/organic foods; impact of 'zero-tolerance' policies);
2. changes in human lifestyle/diet (i.e. new foods and food preparations; immoderate/unbalanced food consumption; decreased human physical activity);
3. operation and functioning of the food and feed chain (i.e. more globalised food supply chain leading to: longer transportation chains; different regulatory controls and standards; issues of food security);
4. technological/analytical developments (i.e. analytical capacities enabling detection of new low levels of contaminants which cannot be adequately risk assessed; new technologies in non-food sectors).[43]

These attempts to expand the categories of factors leading to new emerging risks are all illustrative of the broadness of the task entrusted to EFSA. It includes not merely the classic 'scientific' factors, but also a broad range of economic, social and behavioural issues.

Kocharov places emphasis on the fact that emerging risks are risks currently not regulated by risk management measures. However, that does not appear to be what is reflected in the GFL or the EFSA definition. Emerging risks may well be identified as a result of the re-examination of an issue which is currently exhaustively regulated by legislation, due to the fact that gaps in scientific knowledge have been identified. In this case, existing risk management measures may ultimately be deemed to be insufficient following the identification of new trends or relevant factors. Similarly, changes in susceptibility vis-à-vis a known and regulated risk may lead to the identification of a clear emerging risk requiring, inter alia, legislative change.

---

41 EFSA, 'Report of the EFSA Scientific Cooperation (ESCO) Working Group on Emerging Risk' (2009) 224, 1–33, available at www.efsa.europa.eu/en/efsajournal/doc/224ar.pdf (last visited 12 November 2012).

42 EFSA, 'Outcome of the Stakeholders' Consultative Group on Emerging Risks submitted to EFSA: Report on Stakeholders' activities in the area of emerging risks' (2011) available at www.efsa.europa.eu/fr/supporting /doc/170e.pdf (last visited 12 November 2012).

43 Ibid.

Crisis Management

EFSA has also pursued internal discussion on its role as part of crisis management of various kinds. In its early conceptualisation of crises, the Scientific Committee stated that:

> a crisis is defined as a time when it becomes difficult to appraise, treat and control an emerging event that may have a large impact on the community. It is a specific process which often starts when a triggering event reveals a series of disfunctionings that had not been anticipated or even thought possible.[44]

It should be noted, however, that EFSA has become keenly aware that not all scenarios requiring quick response times equate with a crisis situation as envisaged by Articles 55-57 of the GFL. It appears that the specific word 'crisis' was being used somewhat liberally during the initial stages of EFSA's development.[45] In what have become annual reports termed 'crisis preparedness', EFSA has developed in-house procedures and training to enable it to deliver urgent scientific advice, which will be discussed further below. This is distinctly different from the crisis management role for EFSA as prescribed by Decision 2004/478/EC.[46]

In terms of the administrative arrangements, the Emerging Risk Unit is responsible for matters falling within the crisis management remit of EFSA. While a Permanent Crisis Unit was initially called for within EFSA[47] by the Scientific Committee, it was not created. In effect a Permanent Crisis Unit could easily be considered as somewhat of an oxymoron, and as such was rejected by EFSA.

Emerging Risk, Emergencies and Crisis Management at EFSA – Experiences To-Date

Kocharov has already argued that distinctions are not easily drawn in EU food law between emerging risks, emergencies or crisis conditions.[48] This less than

44 EFSA, 'Advice of the Scientific Committee in relation to EFSA's activities in a crisis' (2003) p. 1, available at www.efsa.europa.eu/en/efsajournal/pub/14r.htm (last visited 12 November 2012).

45 EFSA, 'Annual report on EFSA's food and feed crisis preparedness 2009' (2011), p. 9, available at www.efsa.europa.eu/en/supporting/doc/100e.pdf (last visited 12 November 2012).

46 EFSA, 'EFSA Procedures for responding to urgent advice needs' (2011) available at www.efsa.europa.eu/en/supporting/doc/102e.pdf (last visited 12 November 2012).

47 EFSA, 'Advice of the Scientific Committee in relation to EFSA's activities in a crisis' (2003), p. 4, available at www.efsa.europa.eu/en/efsajournal/pub/14r.htm (last visited 12 November 2012).

48 Kocharov, A., 'EFSA and Identification of Emerging Risks' (2011) *European Food and Feed Law Review*, 3, pp. 144–55.

clear distinction is reflected in the scope of activities which appear to fall within the domain of the Emerging Risk Unit of EFSA. The unit is responsible for developing the sort of 'peace time' studies associated with the monitoring and surveillance of emerging risks, but also manages what has come to be known as 'crisis preparedness and response', procedures frequently linked to emergency, or possible emergency, scenarios.

Piloting Emerging Risks Identification (ERI)

The most recent progress in developing EFSA's emerging risk capacity has come with trials of the emerging risk identification (ERI) process between February 2010 and May 2012. This process has involved not only the systematic processing of potential signs of emerging risks, but also an examination of the usefulness of the data sources feeding the ERI process. Lessons were then drawn from these experiences. During this period over 2200 issues were examined, mainly drawn from RASFF, and evaluated for the purposes of identifying emerging risks.[49]

Perhaps the most significant output of this project has been the ability of EFSA to distinguish with more clarity the nuanced differences between an 'emerging issue' and an 'emerging risk'. Both must potentially satisfy EFSA's definition of an emerging risk, but while an emerging risk proper comes after the ERI process, emerging issues are identified at the beginning of the ERI process.[50] In addition, emerging issues are regarded as information which is limited and preliminary, while the information grounding an actual emerging risk is sufficient to fulfil the requirements of the EFSA definition of emerging risk.[51] In addition, follow-up actions can be identified. The ERI process now follows a clear, stepwise procedure, whereby emerging issues are subject to various levels of filtering, initially by scientific officers, then by monthly roundtable discussions of the EMRISK unit and then by the Emerging Risks Internal Collaboration Group (ERIC),[52] with a potential for ultimate 'self-tasked' risk assessment by an EFSA panel or the EFSA Scientific Committee.[53]

Interestingly, while the EMRISK unit has depended considerably on RASFF as a source of information up to this point, the piloting exercise has cast doubt on its usefulness. Out of the 2200 issues evaluated, EMRISK drew 90 per cent of

49 EFSA, 'Piloting a process for Emerging Risk Identification: Lessons learnt and next steps' (2012), available at www.efsa.europa.eu/en/supporting/doc/310e.pdf (last visited 12 November 2012).

50 Ibid., p. 8.

51 Ibid.

52 ERIC is an internal multidisciplinary task force of EFSA staff members with expertise to support ERI.

53 EFSA, 'Piloting a process for Emerging Risk Identification: Lessons learnt and next steps' (2012), available at www.efsa.europa.eu/en/supporting/doc/310e.pdf (last visited 12 November 2012), p. 11.

them from RASFF. However, none of these actually survived the filtering process to produce follow-up actions.[54] Instead, the most fruitful source of information for substantive ERI came from EFSA Panels or Scientific Panels, EFSA's own networks or scientific literature.[55]

Three issues have been prioritised for action as a consequence of the ERI pilot process: i) aflatoxins in European cereals due to climate change, ii) the consumption of energy drinks and iii) the effect of volatility in food trade and food prices as a key driver of emerging risks.

With regard to aflatoxins, models were developed to account for elevated temperatures over a 100 year period, with the conclusion that an increased likelihood of aflatoxin contamination was expected. The examination of energy drinks was closely linked to current consumption patterns, in particular the trend for such drinks to be consumed by a younger population, often in conjunction with sporting activity or as part of alcohol use. A lack of data was noted as a particularly weak point in the understanding of this issue. In terms of the effects of globalised trade and food price volatility on food safety, EMRISK focused on the possible negative consequences such as '*compromising safety and quality, adulteration, instability in the food chain and adoption of less healthy diets*'.[56]

As part of the filtering process for ERI, EFSA has noted that issues of general risk management, resulting from a lack of compliance with existing regulations, should not be a criteria for identifying emerging risks. However, the depth of some of the issues, such as the effects of global food price volatility, does seem to suggest a role for compliance/behavioural issues as part of ERI.

Dioxins in Pig Meat – Avoidance of Emergency Measures

As previously mentioned, EFSA's scientific opinions can stand at the centre of a potential fracture in Commission/Member State relations over the control of a food incident, leading to the potential adoption of emergency procedures by the European Commission. This fracture became particularly controversial during the 'food scandals' of the 1990s. A chemical contamination of pig meat occurred in Ireland in the winter of 2008 and caused a major international food recall of Irish pork and pork products. The contamination occurred at a feed establishment in which bakery product for animal feed was dried through the use of a direct flame dryer, fuelled with dioxin laden transformer oil. While maximum residue levels (MRLs) for dioxins in foods were breached, the Food Safety Authority of Ireland (FSAI) concluded that consumption of contaminated products would not lead to adverse health effects for consumers. Significantly, this risk assessment was reinforced by EFSA's own

54 Ibid., p. 18.

55 Ibid., p. 33.

56 EFSA, 'Piloting a process for Emerging Risk Identification: Lessons learnt and next steps' (2012), available at www.efsa.europa.eu/en/supporting/doc/310e.pdf (last visited 12 November 2012), p. 11.

scientific opinion which followed shortly afterwards.[57] Crucially, EFSA's opinion that the incident posed no risk to European consumers was grounded on the recall measures already taken by the Irish authorities. This recall included cuts of Irish pork and pork products, but did not include those processed pork products incorporated into composite products. The EFSA opinion, in supporting the FSAI risk assessment, ensured an unambiguous and unanimous scientific opinion on the incident and left little legal scope for dispute among Member States. Therefore, in this case, it seems clear that EFSA accomplished its mission of ensuring consumer's health while also preserving the functioning of the internal market.[58]

The Irish dioxin incident has generally been regarded as a 'well-managed' food incident which avoided the creation of fault-lines and fragmentation among Member States over how to handle risk.[59] EFSA played a crucial role in this respect by reducing the potential for any remaining doubt or diverging risk assessment, albeit in a situation where a major product recall was underway. The incident is a good example of how EFSA speediness and responsiveness helped to avoid crisis and panic in EU food safety regulation.

Crisis Preparedness

As previously mentioned, EFSA's Emerging Risk Unit has also developed an internal policy of crisis preparedness and response.

In 2003, the Scientific Committee advised:

> Not only will the Authority need to be prepared to react to a crisis as identified in the Regulation [General Food Law] it will also need to have in place systems which identify developing potential crisis situations and be able to be proactive in this respect. The Authority should define its ad hoc arrangements and procedures for providing scientific information and communication in order to cope with its responsibility.[60]

However, here again the notions of emerging risks and emerging crises appear as somewhat fused concepts. The advice goes on to note that:

> a crisis is defined as a time when it becomes difficult to appraise, treat and control an emerging event that may have a large impact on the community. It is

57 Casey, D., Lawless, J. and Wall, P., 'A Tale of Two Crises: The Belgian and Irish Dioxin Contamination Incidents' (2010) *British Food Journal*, 112(10), pp. 1077–91.

58 Ibid.

59 Lezaun, J. and Groenleer, M., 'Food Control Emergencies and the Territorialization of the European Union' (2006) *European Integration*, 28(5), pp. 437–55.

60 EFSA, 'Advice of the Scientific Committee in relation to EFSA's activities in a crisis' (2003), AF 11.12.2003, available at www.efsa.europa.eu/en/efsajournal/doc/14r.pdf (last visited on 12 November 2012).

> a specific process which often starts when a triggering event reveals a series of disfunctionings that had not been anticipated or even thought possible.[61]

As previously mentioned, crisis in this context does not carry the same meaning as developed in Commission Decision 2004/478/EC. However, EFSA has demonstrated a clear vision of ensuring its own in-house readiness for various types of crises. The Crisis Preparedness and Response Procedures are designed to '*respond quickly and efficiently to provide scientific and technical support to inform the risk managers and the consumers in Europe on a 'hot issue' and to communicate about its findings, if possible before it develops into a crisis*'.[62] This development of in-house procedures is regarded as a complement to the procedures under Decision 2004/478/EC. Procedures for dealing with urgent requests are contained in the so-called 'Emergency Manual'. The table below shows the urgent requests which EFSA has dealt with in the context of its Crisis Preparedness and Response Procedures.

Table 6.1 Urgent requests to EFSA

Incident	Year
Melamine in food and feed	2007
Dioxins in pork meat	2008
Mineral oil in sunflower oil	2008
Melamine in infant milk and composite foods	2008
4-methylbenzophenone in breakfast cereals	2009
Nicotine in wild mushrooms	2009
Chlormequat in table grapes	2010
Volcanic ash	2010
Shiga-toxin producing *Escherichia coli* (STEC O104:H4)	2011
Schmallenberg virus	2011

The outbreak of E-coli in Germany and in France during 2011 due to contaminated fenugreek seeds imported from Egypt was perhaps the single gravest European food safety incident in the past 10 years. It demonstrates well the Crisis Preparedness and Response Procedures in action. Over the course

61 Ibid.

62 EFSA, 'Annual report on EFSA's food and feed safety crisis preparedness 2009' (2011), available at www.efsa.europa.eu/en/supporting/doc/100e.pdf (last visited 12 November 2012).

of the incident (early May to late July 2011), in addition to the tragic deaths of 53 people, there were more than 3,100 reported cases of bloody diarrhoea and over 850 cases of haemolytic uremic syndrome (HUS).[63] The early stages of the outbreak in Germany were marked by considerable uncertainty over the source of contamination. An early identification of cucumbers from Spain as the source was communicated by German authorities via RASFF but turned out to be inaccurate, causing considerable loss to the Spanish horticulture sector and political tensions between German and Spanish authorities.[64]

EFSA was active at various stages of the incident. On 9 June 2011, EFSA responded to a 6 June request from the European Commission for an assessment of consumer exposure through the consumption of raw vegetables and provided advice on options to mitigate the risks of possible food contamination and human infection. On 24 June France reported the occurrence of an incident which was causing a very similar pattern of bloody diarrhoea in patients; EFSA responded on 29 June with a rapid risk assessment linking the German and French outbreaks through a common vector of fenugreek sprouts and, in response to an urgent request from the Commission, EFSA established a task force to trace back the seeds in question in the EU food supply chain.[65] This task force included EU Commission officials from DG SANCO, EFSA staff and representatives of the European Centre for Disease Prevention and Control (ECDC) as well as the UN Food and Agriculture Organisation and World Health Organization (WHO). This task force reported on 5 July and recommended efforts to forward trace fenugreek seeds throughout the supply chain.

Alemanno has commented that the E-coli outbreak could have been coordinated at a European level so as to ensure greater credibility and cohesion in EU food safety regulation.[66] In particular he has noted the failure on the part of the Commission to establish a crisis unit under Article 56 of the GFL and thereby employ a neutral, clear and EU-wide line of risk communication. The creation of a crisis unit would also have placed EFSA in the 'driving seat' during the incident, rather as a player operating in response to risk managers' requests.

---

63 EFSA, 'E-coli: Rapid Response in a crisis' (2012) – EFSA Features, available www.efsa.europa.eu/eu/press/news/120711.htm (last visited on 12 November 2012).

64 Alemanno, A., 'A More Sophisticated Crisis Response', *European Voice*, 16 June 2011.

65 EFSA, 'Shiga toxin-producing E.coli (STEC) O104:H4 2011 outbreaks in Europe: Taking Stock' (2011), available at www.efsa.europa.eu/en/efsajournal/doc/2390.pdf (last visited on 12 November 2012).

66 Alemanno, A. (2011) 'Europe's E. Coli Outbreak: The EU Food Safety Regime under Stress' (2011) Blog – Penn Program on Regulation, available at https://www.law.upenn.edu/blogs/regblog/2011/06/europes-e-coli-outbreak-the-eu-food-safety-regime-under-stress.html (last visited on 12 April 2013).

Conclusions

This chapter has examined the role of EFSA in those food safety issues marked by urgency and uncertainty and outside the 'usual' core business of scientific opinions as required under sectoral food law. In the area of the emerging risk mandate, EFSA has used the past 10 years to come to terms with the different (and conceptually difficult) nuances of this concept and to put in place the ERI system for data collection and screening. It has identified the risks of being 'swamped' by excessive and meaningless information and put valuable filters in place to make the process of ERI more effective. One significant development in this regard has been the ability to distinguish between emerging issues and emerging risks. As this streamlining of ERI is used in the years to come, EFSA should play an important role in ensuring the next BSE epidemic is avoided or mitigated in a timely way. Greater reliance will need to be placed on picking up the tacit and latent knowledge of tomorrow's risks through academic literature and through EFSA's evolving networks of risk assessors, as described elsewhere in this book by Abels, Kobusch and Träsch[67] and by Gabbi and Groenleer, respectively.[68] EFSA's responsiveness to the volatile nature of European food risk regulation is also reflected in its procedures for crisis preparedness and response which show sensitivity to the urgency generated by food incidents. In particular a strong understanding is evident of the need to provide a credibly speedy and decisive response to requests for information and risk assessment. This is vital in situations where the activation of emergency procedures under the GFL are at stake and meaningful collaboration and proactive assistance it vital in avoiding regulatory breakdown.

67 See Chapter 5.

68 See Chapter 21 on EFSA's International relations.

Chapter 7
Scientific Advice in the GMO Area

Sara Poli

Introduction

One of the most controversial areas of EFSA's activity concerns the genetically modified organisms (GMOs). This is due to the fact that there is a wide spread scepticism on the use of these organisms in the agricultural practices and as food/feed in the EU. This chapter is intended to briefly present the internal organism within EFSA which is responsible for providing scientific opinions in this area and to make a diachronic survey of EFSA's instruments and activity between 2003 and 2012 in the area of GMOs. The Authority's activity will be examined taking into consideration the number of authorisations[1] issued in the referring period and the problems they gave rise to, the opinions released on national restrictive measures vis-à-vis GMOs, the self-tasking activity and the interventions with respect to emergency measures, as enshrined in Article 53 of Regulation (EC) No 178/2002 (the General Food Law, hereafter 'GFL'). The analysis of the documentation mentioned above will be selective. Only the most significant measures adopted by the EFSA for the purpose of exemplifying the legal issues rising out of its activity will be accounted for.[2]

The description of the EFSA's work will be put into the EU institutional context. Special emphasis will be placed on the dialogue between the EFSA and the Commission to address the criticism that Member States (*uti singuli* or within the Council) and NGOs turned to EFSA's initiatives in the area of GMOs. Then, the critical remarks coming from these different actors will be highlighted with the view to evaluate how EFSA responded and what consequences its response had on the efficiency of the EU GMOs approval procedures.

As is known, authorisations to place GMOs on the market may be asked by biotech firms under Article 5 of Regulation (EC) No. 1829/2003 and art. 13 of

1 I will concentrate on authorisations released under Directive 2001/18/EC on the deliberate release into the environment of genetically modified organisms and repealing Council Directive 90/220/EEC, OJ [2001] L 106, p. 1, and Regulation (EC) n. 1829/2003 of the European Parliament and the Council of 22 September 2003 on genetically modified food and feed, OJ [2003] L 268/1. Authorisations released under the Novel food regulation will not be accounted for.

2 Moreover, the guidance documents adopted by EFSA will not be accounted for, unless this is necessary for the purpose of this survey.

Directive 2001/18/EC depending on their scope (hereafter 'the GM food and feed regulation' and the 'framework Directive).[3] In giving account of the permits, focus will be placed on those released under the GM food and feed Regulation and part C of the framework Directive, dealing with the placing on the market of GMOs as or in products. Authorisations under Part B of that Directive are excluded from the scope of the survey since the placing on the market of GMOs for the purpose of research has been far less controversial than placing GMOs on the market as crops.

The survey of the EFSA's activity is divided in three periods: 2003–2006, 2007–2009 and 2010–12. In the final year of the first two periods (2006 and 2009) political requests to change specific aspects of the EFSA's strategy on GMOs were put forward by the Commission or the Council. Special attention will be placed to show how EFSA actually addressed the concerns expressed by the political institutions. The ultimate purpose is to verify whether by taking into consideration the criticisms that stakeholders addressed to EFSA, the latter has fulfilled its task of providing 'the best possible scientific opinions in all cases provided for by Community legislation.'[4]

The GMO Scientific Panel and the EFSA: Their Interlocutors and Instruments

The GMO Panel is one of EFSA's permanent scientific bodies.[5] It is formed by independent scientists who are recruited on the basis of their excellence in the field through an open selection procedure. Additional experts may work on ad hoc basis with the GMO Panel.[6]

The Panel's task is to provide scientific opinions in relation to issues pertaining to the releases of GMOs in the environment and to GM food/feed, in accordance with the sector-related legislation[7] and the GFL. Under the latter, its opinions may be requested by the Commission, the Parliament and Member States. In the GMOs sector, the practice is that requests are always submitted by the Commission.[8] Exceptionally, in December 2008 the Council directly addressed the EFSA.[9] By

3 If the scope of the application is to place GMOs on the market to use them as food/feed, then Reg. 1829/2003 applies. By contrast, if the scope is the cultivation, or their import and processing, then, Directive 2001/18 is the applicable law.

4 Art. 23a) of the GFL.

5 Art. 28(4) d) of GFL.

6 Currently, 40 scientists with specialisation in areas, such as the environment, allergenicity and statistics collaborate with the GMO Panel. http://www.efsa.europa.eu/en/faqs/faqgmo.htm.

7 See *supra* note 1.

8 115 Commission's requests may be counted on the EFSA's database between 2003 and 2012 [last accessed on 15 October 2012].

9 See *infra*, section 5.

contrast, the Parliament has never formally asked for an opinion to the GMO Panel but members of the Parliament have addressed at times critical written questions on the work of EFSA to the Commission.

The Authority has never declined to issue an opinion. Under Article 29(5) of the GFL, the Food Authority is entitled to refuse to deliver an opinion if there are no new scientific elements justifying the re-examination of an opinion. EFSA[10] had many chances to exercise this power in the area of GMOs. Indeed, in more than one occasion, the Commission asked EFSA to re-assess a request for authorisation in relation to a given GMO or the data supporting a national measure, restricting the use of an authorised GMO. EFSA has never declined to address the Commission's request, although in several instances it released a statement rather than a full blown scientific opinion.[11]

It should be stressed that the request for reconsideration is totally justified in the area of risk regulation since scientific evidence is evolving at a rapid pace and should new data come up they are expected to invalidate a previous risk assessment. But in many cases one could have doubted that the information submitted to EFSA by Member States through the Commission was truly different from the one previously assessed by the risk assessors.

The Authority's complacent attitude is similar to that of the Court of Justice in the framework of the preliminary ruling procedure, under art. 267 TFEU. Where the questions submitted by the referring court concern the interpretation of EU law, the EU judicature is, in principle, bound to give a ruling. Nevertheless, the Court has no jurisdiction to give a preliminary ruling on a question submitted by a national court where it is quite obvious that the interpretation of EU law sought by that court bears no relation to the actual facts of the main action or its purpose or where the problem is hypothetical and the Court does not have before it the factual or legal material necessary to give a useful answer to the questions submitted to it.[12] Yet, the Court is very reluctant to declare that it does not have jurisdiction to answer the questions referred by a national court. Indeed, a liberal use of its discretion on this issue will undermine the trust that national judges have in the ECJ and which is so vital for the working of the procedure.

In a similar vein, EFSA is parsimonious in its use of the power of rejection. This may be praised given the high level of contestation of the GMO decisions. A refusal would be detrimental for the building of public trust in the Authority. It is easily predictable that a denial to issue an opinion would give rise to the suspicion that EFSA is trying to protect biotech firms. EFSA's credibility would inevitably be affected and the independent work carried out by the GMO Panel would be rapidly obliterated.

---

10 About 20 written questions were addressed by members of the Parliament to the Commission on EFSA's activity between 2006 and 2009 (eur-lex data).

11 See *infra* section 4.

12 Case C-415/93 *Union Royale Belge des Sociétés de Football Association ASBL and Others v. Bosmann and others* [1995] ECR, p. I-4921, par. 59–61.

Opinions may not only be delivered upon request but also as a result of the Panel or the EFSA's initiative.[13] Although the Commission sees EFSA's self-tasking with disfavour,[14] this practice is not uncommon. Most often, an autonomous initiative is taken by the EFSA when an issue requires further analysis and research.[15] In the area of GMOs at least two instances of self-tasking activity may be identified. In 2004 the GMO Panel decided to task itself to deliver a scientific opinion on antibiotic resistance genes with the potential to be used as marker genes for genetically modified plants and which may or may not have adverse effects on human health and the environment, taking into account the limited availability of alternatives. As a result an ad hoc working group was created.[16]

In 2008, EFSA asked the GMO Panel to establish a self-tasking Working Group that, amongst others things, assessed potential impacts of genetically modified plants on Non-Target Organisms (2008)[17] and reviewed the current guidance document of the EFSA GMO Panel for Environmental Risk Assessment (ERA).

Although the Meroni doctrine acts as a constraining factor on the Commission's attitude toward EFSA's autonomous initiatives, it is submitted that the EU executive should not discourage the Authority from engaging in self-tasking activities. Indeed, the latter is often better placed than the risk manager to know possible gaps or deficiencies that need to be addressed in order to improve the risk assessment procedure. Even more, the self-tasking activities of the Authority should also be given more visibility so that the public and national authorities are aware of EFSA's proactive role.[18] Visibility is an essential ingredient in the trust building process in the work of the Authority.

The release of an opinion is not the only form through which EFSA carries out its tasks. The Authority has adopted acts not provided for by GFL, such as 'statements'[19] to reply to Commission requests and 'guidance documents.'[20]

EFSA's Role in the Sectoral Legislation

GM food and feed may be authorised for the placing on the market on ad hoc basis through a procedure centralised at EU level in which EFSA is responsible for the

13 Art. 29 of the GFL.

14 A. Alemanno, 'The EFSA at five', *European Food and Feed Law Review*, 2008, 14.

15 Ernst & Young, External evaluation of EFSA, Final Report, 2012, p. 40.

16 *EFSA Journal* (2004) 48, 1–18.

17 *EFSA Journal* 2010; 8(11), 1877.

18 See along these lines, Ernst & Young, *External Evaluation of EFSA*, above n.15, p. 9 and 47.

19 This happened, for example, in the case of the emergency measures adopted by the Commission in 2005 and 2006. See the contributions of Lawless (Chapter 6) and Pintado (Chapter 3).

20 See *infra* section n. 4 for an example.

risk assessment. Therefore, the structure of the procedure set out by the GM food and feed Regulation is different from that of the framework Directive, providing that the risk assessment is carried out by national competent authorities.

Under the GM food/feed regulation the application for authorisation or for a renewal is sent to a national authority which in its turn forwards it to EFSA. The latter is due to release an opinion in which it assesses the information provided by the applicant. The purpose of this examination is to consider whether the GM food/feed does not pose more risks than the conventional counterpart and is thus safe for consumption.

In principle, the EFSA is given six months to come up with its opinion. This time limit may be extended and in any case it runs only when the firms have submitted a completed application. In 95 per cent of the cases the EFSA is not satisfied with the original dossier.[21] Then, in case a positive position is given, the Commission has three months to decide under the comitology rules.[22] It should be pointed out that there has always been a remarkable asynchrony between the release of an EFSA's opinion and the adoption of the Commission decision on applications for authorisation or renewals. Even in the post GMO-moratorium era, in many cases the Authority delivered a favourable opinion that was followed by an authorisation only several years later.

The reasons for this backlog are different: the number of applications is numerous since stacked events[23] in the EU are not automatically authorised if single events have already been authorised, as it happens in the USA. Stacked events must be authorised on a case by case basis in order to minimise uncertainty about possible risks.[24] The second reason for delay is that despite EFSA's positive positions, objections to the authorisation may be raised at the level of the Standing committee on the food chain and animal health or by the Council as a result of which EFSA is asked to carry out additional assessments. This lengthens the process of the authorisation releases. Of course extreme caution vis-à-vis GM food/feed contributes to ensure a high level of health protection that the Treaty imposes on the Institutions and is therefore welcome. However, the average duration of authorisations in weeks exceeds by more than three times the timing set out in the legislation.[25] One of the applications that manifestly exceeded the

21 http://www.efsa.europa.eu/en/topics/topic/gmo.htm [last accessed on 30 September 2012].

22 For a survey on the application of these rules see, T. Christiansen, J. Polak, 'Comitology between political decision-making and technocratic governance: Regulating GMOs in the European Union', *Eipascope*, 2009/1.

23 A stacked event is produced by combining, through classical breeding, two or more events individually produced by biotechnology. 'Guidance Document of the Scientific Panel on Genetically Modified Organisms for the risk assessment of genetically modified plants containing stacked transformation events', *EFSA Journal*, 2007, 512, 1–5.

24 Agra Ceas Consulting, *Evaluation of the EU legislative framework in the field of GM food and feed*, Final Report, 12 July 2010, p. 61.

25 Ibid., p. 67.

reasonability is that of the GM potato EH92–527–1 (so-called 'Amflora potato') for which there is a four-year gap between the release of the opinion (2006)[26] and the authorising decision (2010).[27] It should be emphasised that this is the second crop to be authorised for cultivation in the EU and these kinds of authorisations raise lots of controversies.

The vast majority of notifications are submitted by applicants to place GM food/feed on the market; therefore, the legal basis of their application is the GM food and feed Regulation. In few cases applicants submitted requests for authorisation for the purpose mentioned above and to cultivate the GM crop. In these cases, EFSA is required to ask national competent authorities to carry out an environmental risk assessment. It results from a report of the Commission that EFSA experiences difficulties in finding a NCA willing to carry out this assessment.[28] Finally, in a minority of cases, applications were introduced, under the framework Directive, to place products other than food and feed related to GMOs on the market.[29]

As to the content of the authorisations, it is worthwhile stressing that the Authority does not state that there are no reasonable doubts that GM food and feed are safe for human consumption. EFSA gives its green light to applications when the GM product does not bear more health risks than the conventional one. In a similar vein, when the purpose of the application is to cultivate GM crops, the GMO Panel does not declare that these crops will not affect the environment but that it concludes that that subject to appropriate management measures, the cultivation of the concerned GM plants is unlikely to raise additional safety concerns for the environment compared to conventional maize.

EFSA's Activity Between 2003 and 2006

In 2003–2004 most of the Commission's requests to EFSA concerned the preparation of guidelines necessary to apply the two new Regulations on food and feed and traceability/labelling[30] requirements. Since these are the first years of EFSA's activity it is quite natural that the Authority devoted many efforts to adopt guidelines, upon the request of the Commission. For example, on 8 November 2004,

26 *EFSA Journal*, 2006, 324, 1–20.

27 Commission decision n. 2010/136, OJ [2010] L53/15.

28 COM (2006) 626, Report from the Commission to the Council and the European Parliament on the implementation of Regulation (EC) n. 1829/2003, p. 10.

29 For examples, see E. Waigmann, C. Paoletti, H. Davies, J. Perry, S. Kärenlampi, H. Kuiper, 'Special issues-Risk assessment of Genetically Modified Organisms (GMOs)', *EFSA Journal*, 2012;10(10): s1008, p. 4.

30 Regulation (CE) n. 1830/2003 of the European Parliament and of the Council of 22 September 2003 concerning the traceability and labelling of genetically modified organisms and the traceability of food and feed products produced from genetically modified organisms and amending Directive 2001/18/EC, OJ [2003] L 268/24.

the Scientific Panel on genetically modified organisms (GMO Panel) finalised the first guidance document for the risk assessment of GM plants and derived food and feed to assist the applicant in the preparation and presentation of applications.[31]

In 2003, the Commission put only two requests for opinions to assess notification for authorisations forward. No authorisations were released in this year since the new Regulation mentioned above on the placing on the market of GM food/feed was under discussion. This unofficial suspension of the authorisations was to be kept until the new legal framework was not in place.

In 2003, upon request, EFSA exercised for the first time its powers under Article 1(5)c of the GFL whereby the Authority can be consulted on products other than food and feed related to GMOs as defined by the framework Directive. EFSA released the first of a series of scientific opinions concerning measures banning the use of GMOs or their cultivation. The Commission requested EFSA's opinion after Austria notified a request for derogation from the framework Directive, under art. 114(5) TFEU.[32] The notified measures concerned a draft legislation banning the use of (authorised) genetically modified organisms in the region of Upper Austria.[33] The regional legislation did not concern GM food/feed but focused on the cultivation of GM seeds and propagating material, the use of transgenic animals for breeding purposes and the release of transgenic animals. EFSA inaugurated an answer to the request that would be often used in the assessment of Member States' safeguard measures in the years to come. EFSA responded as follows: the information provided by Austria did not supply any new scientific evidence, in terms of risk to human health and the environment, that would justify a general prohibition of cultivation of genetically modified seeds and propagating material, the use of transgenic animals for breeding purposes and the release of transgenic animals, authorised for these purposes under Directive 90/220/EEC or Directive 2001/18/EC.[34] EFSA stated that the notifier had not provided any new scientific evidence that could show that in the Upper Austria there was an environmental problem specific to that Region. On the other hand, the Authority indirectly conceded that the cultivation of GMOs could create problems of coexistence between different forms of agriculture and that this was an important agricultural

31 The EFSA guidance document has been updated, on December 2005, with a section on general surveillance of unanticipated effects of GM plants as part of the post market environmental monitoring.

32 The Commission has always asked EFSA's opinion in relation to all requests of derogation under art. 114(5) except for those considered inadmissible (such as 2006/255/EC: Commission Decision of 14 March 2006 concerning national provisions imposing on supermarkets an obligation to place genetically modified foods on separate shelves from non-genetically modified foods, notified by Cyprus pursuant to Article 95(5) of the EC Treaty, OJ [2006] L 092/12).

33 See Chapter 15.

34 Opinion of the scientific Panel on GMOs on a question from the Commission related to the Austrian notification of national legislation governing GMOs under Article 95(5) of the Treaty, *EFSA Journal*, 2003, 1.

issue. Yet, the Commission had not asked EFSA to comment on this specific issue. The Commission could have not made such a request to EFSA being it outside the Authority's mandate.

This first scientific opinion is interesting since it illustrates the limits of the EFSA's remit. On the one hand, the Food Authority cannot address the problems of coexistence that GMOs may give rise to. On the other, the Commission has never exercised its discretion of risk manager in single instances so as to accommodate socioeconomic concerns. Throughout the years this has generated a sense of frustration in Member States seeking to exclude the use/or the cultivation of GMOs in their territory.

A radical attempt to break this vicious circle was made in 2008 when a group of Member States asked the Commission to change the EU legislation so as provide more freedom to national authorities wishing to restrict the cultivation of GMOs due to the socioeconomic implications for conventional and organic agriculture.[35]

Notwithstanding the Upper Austria's failure to justify the setting up of a GMO-free area in the territory of the Land, the number of GMO-free regions increased after 2003. As of 2010, in most of the EU countries,[36] there was at least one region that declared itself GMO-free. Poland adopted in 2003 the Seed law that prohibited the seeds of genetically modified varieties and continued the anti-GMO policy throughout the years.[37]

The EFSA opinion on the Upper Austria is interesting for a second reason. For the first time it raised the thorny issue of conflicting scientific evidence between the European and national authorities. The tension between the two different levels of governance is particularly acute in the area of GMOs, whereas in other areas such as that of food additives and contaminants this does not happen.[38] EFSA decisions are accused of being self-contained and the Authority is considered unwilling to engage with competing science from the Member States.[39]

The duty of the EFSA to cooperate with the Member States with a view of addressing substantive divergence over scientific issues[40] was not sufficient to diffuse this tension. Alemanno considers that EFSA is not the body that should

35 See *infra*.

36 The exceptions are the following; Bulgaria, Cyprus, Denmark, Czech Republic, Estonia, Germany, Latvia, Lithuania, the Netherlands, Malta and Romania. These data are extrapolated from the list of GMO-free regions published in the http://www.gmo-free-regions.org/fileadmin/files/gmo-free-regions/full_list/List_GMOfree_regions_Europe_update_September_2010.pdf [last accessed 25th September 2012].

37 Case 165/08 *Commission v. Poland,* [2009] ECR, I-06843, par. 16.

38 S. Gabbi, *L'Autorità europea per la sicurezza alimentare*, 2009, Milano, p. 173.

39 M. Lee, 'Multi-level governance of genetically modified organisms in the European Union: Ambiguity and hierarchy', in L. Bodiguel and M. Cardwell, *The Regulation of Genetically Modified Organisms*, 2010, Edward Elgar, p. 111.

40 Art. 30(4) of the GFL.

solve these conflicts.[41] This author is convinced that the Authority has the responsibility to take the lead and try to address these conflicts through various means/techniques, such as the harmonisation of risk assessment procedures, exchange of information, meetings with national competent authorities.

A second situation in which the divergence of the scientific opinions provokes tension between the EFSA and the Member States concerns the safeguard measures invoked by Member States with respect to authorised GMOs.

Since 2004, EFSA has examined Member States' documentation in which it was claimed that the environmental risk assessment carried out by EFSA in relation to specific GMOs was vitiated or incomplete or did not take into consideration new scientific evidence.

EFSA has always confirmed the safety of authorised GM crops when Member States raised doubts on their neutrality for human health and the environment on the basis of new scientific evidence. The first country to prohibit the placing on the market of authorised GMOs was Austria. Between 1998 and 2010, this country banned the cultivation and/or the import of 9 GMOs. France, Luxembourg and Greece were also 'early birds' in taking restrictive measures vis-à-vis GMOs. Germany restricted the cultivation of Bt176 in 2000; later on, it suspended the cultivation of GM MON 810. Hungary invoked the safeguard measure against GM maize MON 810 one year after its accession to the EU. The EFSA was asked to assess the new information provided by these countries.[42] No new evidence of risks was identified by EFSA in these cases.

Yet, the Commission's request to abolish eight restrictive measures enacted by Austria, Germany, France, Luxembourg and Greece against varieties of GM maize and colza was not upheld by the Council on 24 June 2005. On the GM maize (Zea mays L. line MON 810) the Council took a special position. It held that there was a state of uncertainty on the safety of this GMO and urged the Commission 'to gather further evidence on the GMOs in question and further assess, whether the measure taken by [Austria] aimed at suspending as a temporary precautionary measure [its] placing on the market [was] justified and, whether the authorisation of such [an] organism still [met] the safety requirements of Directive 2001/18/EC'.[43] At the time, the Commission asked for a new opinion in relation to the new information submitted by Austria. Yet, EFSA's answer remained unchanged.[44] As a result, the Commission proposed the abolishment of the safeguard measure. The Council decision was to be taken in December 2006.

41 A. Alemanno, The European Food Safety Authority at five, *European Food and Feed Law Review*, 1, 2008, p. 24.

42 EFSA Journal (2004) 78, 1–13.

43 Proposal for a Council Decision concerning the provisional prohibition of the use and sale in Austria of genetically modified maize (Zea mays L. line MON 810) pursuant to Directive 2001/18/EC of the European Parliament and of the Council, (2006) 509, recital n. 12.

44 *EFSA Journal*, 2006, 338, 1–15.

The GM food and feed Regulation and the 'labelling and traceability' Regulation[45] entered into force in April 2004. As from this year, the authorisation flows started. Yet, it could hardly be described as a flow. Indeed, between 2004 and 2006 the Commission released nine authorisations (one under the framework Directive and eight under the food and feed Regulation) and many of them were the results of a special procedure for existing products. For each decision the Commission asked and obtained EFSA's positive opinion.

Between 2004 and 2006, the authorisation process is characterised by lights and shadows. The light came from the increase in the number of authorisations to place GMOs on the market for the purposes permitted by the EU legislation with respect to those released between 1999 and 2003 when the Council was blocked. Yet, the authorisation process was very slow. This was not so much due to the long time required by EFSA to deliver an opinion but to the fact that the Council and Standing committee's activity were slowed down.

In a single instance the release of an authorisation was contested both by some NGOs and by some members of the European Parliament. This happened in relation to GM maize 863 for which in 2004 the German competent authority had given the green light to its placing on the market for import and feed use, under the framework Directive and the GM food feed Regulation. Since a number of Member States contested the quality of the risk assessment conducted by this national authority, the Commission asked EFSA to examine the soundness of Member States' objections. In an opinion of 2004 EFSA examined the objections and concluded that there were no reasons to believe that the GMO concerned would affect human health or the environment.[46] On the basis of this statement, the Commission went on with the authorisation procedure and in 2005 the approval was released.[47]

In the first years of operation, EFSA received severe criticism from NGOs. For example, the experts of the GMO Panel were accused by Greenpeace of neglecting relevant scientific information available in the EFSA's risk assessment of the GM maize NK603.[48] Friends of the Earth questioned the scientific independence of the Authority, it criticised EFSA's work on applications for authorisation related to Monsanto's GT73 oilseed rape, Syngenta's Bt176 maize and Monsanto's MON 863 maize. This NGO accused the Authority of not outlining the degree of uncertainty in its opinions and neglecting long-term effects of GMOs. The Commission was blamed for using EFSA to push new GM products onto the market.[49]

---

45 Regulation (EC) n. 1830/2003, above n. 30.

46 *EFSA Journal* (2004) 49, 1–25.

47 2005/608/EC: Commission Decision of 8 August 2005, OJ [2005] L 207/17.

48 A. Alemanno, L'Autorité européenne de sécurité des aliments souffle ses cinq premières bougies – Un bilan d'activité, 3 *Revue du Droit de l'Union Européenne*, 2007, p. 604.

49 Friends of the Earth Europe, 'Throwing caution to the wind: A review of the European Food Safety Authority and its work on genetically modified foods and crops,' November 2004.

Notwithstanding this criticism, as illustrated by a study which evaluated the food and feed legislation, there was an overall appreciation by stakeholders on the working of the risk assessment phase of the legislation whereas criticism were addressed to the risk management stage.[50] A further interesting conclusion of the study is that the majority of stakeholders were in favour of leaving the responsibility for risk assessment to EFSA rather than to national competent authorities.[51] A further example showing that the activity of the Food Authority is appreciated by Member States is provided in another report and concerns one of the sources of major concerns for the Member States: the anti-biotic resistance marker genes.[52] On this issue, EFSA released an opinion by its own motion and the majority of Member States considered it useful for the phasing-out of such genes,[53] as required by Article 4(2) of Directive 2001/18.

In 2006, the Commission for the first time showed uneasiness with respect to the EFSA's activity. In April, this Institution criticised EFSA, taking up the proposals of the Health and Consumer Protection Commissioner Kyprianou and Environment Commissioner Dimas. Indeed, the announcement was made that there was a need to improve the scientific consistency and transparency of the decision-making process in this area. The Commission identified a number of problematic aspects of the EFSA's activity and invited the Authority 'to liaise more fully with national scientific bodies, with a view to resolving possible diverging scientific opinions with Member States; to provide more detailed justification, in its opinions on individual applications, for not accepting scientific objections raised by the national competent authorities; to clarify which specific protocols should be used by applicants to carry out scientific studies (for example regarding toxicology) demonstrating safety.'[54] Finally, applicants and EFSA are asked to address more explicitly potential long-term effects and bio-diversity issues in their risk assessments for the placing on the market of GMOs.

In turn, the Commission also made commitments. It stressed the need to better address Member States' concerns vis-à-vis specific risks identified in the risk assessment or substantiated by national authorities by introducing on a case by case basis additional proportionate risk management measures (emphasis added) in draft decisions to place GMO products on the market, as appropriate. In addition, where in the opinion of the Commission a Member State's observation raises important new scientific questions not properly or completely addressed by

50 For more details see Agra Ceas Consulting, above n. 24, pp. 34–8.

51 Ibid., p. xix.

52 Second report from the Commission to the Council and the Parliament on the experience of Member States with GMOs placed on the market under Directive 2001/18/EC on the deliberate release into the environment of genetically modified organisms, COM(2007) 81 final.

53 *EFSA Journal*, 2004, 48, 1–18.

54 COM (2006) 626, above n.28, pp. 10–12.

the EFSA opinion, the Commission may suspend the procedure and refer back the question for further consideration.

The most contentious matter of discussion between the Commission and the Council was generated by the contention about the adoption of safeguard measures by the Member States. Between 2006 and 2007 a new round of measures were licensed by the Council, in opposition to the Commission. In December 2006 the Council rejected the Commission's proposal to abolish the Austrian safeguard measure against GM maize 810. In February 2007, the Council also upheld the Hungarian banning measure against GM maize MON 810. This time the reasons for confirming Member States' bans were the following: the first was that the concerned maize MON 810 had not undergone a procedure of re-assessment. The second concerned the need to take 'the different agricultural structures and regional ecological characteristics in the EU into account in a more systematic manner in the environmental risk assessment of GMOs.' The latter reason was the first warning launched by the Council to the Commission that the risk assessment of GMOs has to be integrated with other non- scientific considerations.

Finally, in the referring period, EFSA was involved twice by the Commission in the procedure that led to the adoption of emergency measures, as enshrined in Article 53 GFL, and this despite the fact that the intervention of the Authority is not specifically foreseen in this provision.[55] The Authority must have found itself in an uncomfortable position in examining whether trade restrictive measures were necessary (and subsequently could be removed) with respect to two illegal GMOs that were imported from the USA. Indeed, in both cases, the Authority had to take a position in a situation of scientific uncertainty or of lack of information.

In March 2005, EFSA was requested an opinion in relation to emergency measures that the Commission intended to propose with respect to the non-authorised genetically modified organism Bt10 in maize products.[56] This product was imported from the USA where it was also illegal. The maize Bt10 was supposed to be mixed up with GM maize Bt11 which was by contrast legal in the USA and in the EU. The initial position of the EFSA, formalised in a statement of April 2005, was that it could not confirm the safety of the concerned product since it did not have at its disposal the scientific data necessary to carry out such an assessment.[57] Neither the US authorities nor the developer of the GM maize Bt had provided this information. Since products that are not authorised are presumed to

55 The Commission relied on other provisions of the general food law: Articles 29(1) and 22(5)(c).

56 2005/317/EC: Commission Decision of 18 April 2005 on emergency measures regarding the non-authorised genetically modified organism Bt10 in maize products, OJ [2005] L 101/14.

57 Statement of the European Food Safety Authority issued on 12 April 2005, not anymore available on the EFSA database.

pose risks for human health or the environment, the Commission took emergency measures to prevent the placing on the market of the contaminated products. In a new statement, the EFSA concluded that it was not likely that Bt 10 could pose safety concerns for animals and consumers. EFSA reassured on the risks of Bt10 on the basis of information provided by Syngenta.[58] Yet, it is noteworthy that the Authority warned the risk managers that its conclusions were based on the assumption that the information provided by the developer was correct and EFSA could not independently verify it.

In 2006 a new case of unauthorised genetically modified organism LL RICE 601,[59] coming from the USA, made it necessary to request another opinion to EFSA. This time the Commission did not check the Authority's position before adopting emergency measures.[60] In August 2006, the Commission had provisionally banned the placing on the market of the contaminated products. In the meantime, the Commission had asked the EFSA to state its position on the scientific data available on the safety of this product. Once again, in a statement issued on 14 September 2006, the GMO Panel considered that it had inadequate data for 'a full risk assessment in accordance with EFSA's GM guidance'. Yet, it concluded that the consumption of imported long grain rice containing trace levels of 'LL RICE 601' was not likely to pose an imminent safety concern to humans or animals.[61] This statement, which was reiterated in subsequent emergency measures,[62] appears contradictory and probably did not contribute to gain the public trust that was so necessary for the EFSA in the first years of activity. On the basis of this assessment the emergency measures were amended and the import of rice from the USA was made subject to a number of conditions.

58 See EFSA's press release of 9 June 2005 published on http://www.efsa.europa.eu/en/press/news/gmo050609.htm.

59 2006/754/EC: Commission Decision of 6 November 2006 amending Decision 2006/601/EC on emergency measures regarding the non-authorised genetically modified organism LL RICE 601 in rice products, OJ [2006] L 306/17.

60 2006/601/EC: Commission Decision of 5 September 2006 on emergency measures regarding the non-authorised genetically modified organism LL RICE 601 in rice products, OJ [2006] L 244/27; 2006/578/EC: Commission Decision of 23 August 2006 on emergency measures regarding the non-authorised genetically modified organism LL RICE 601 in rice products, OJ [2006] L 230/8.

61 Recital n. 5 of Decision 2006/754, [2006] L 306 17.

62 Three emergency measures were enacted with respect to illegal GMOs coming from the USA in 2007 and 2008. The EFSA was systematically consulted by the Commission and opined that the concerned unathorised GMO did not pose risks, without sufficient data to carry out a complete risk assessment. See for all Response to the request from the Commission on the unauthorised genetically modified event DAS 59123–8 in US maize-scientific Panel on GMOs, in *EFSA Journal*, 2008, p. 713, 1–10.

EFSA's Activity Between 2007 and 2009

Between 2007 and 2009, 11 GMOs were approved (six authorisations were released under the framework Directive and eight under the food and feed Regulation). This was a relative improvement in the functioning of the authorisation systems. However, this did not imply that the wind was changing in favour of biotechnology. On the contrary, these are the years in which the intolerance towards transgenic agriculture consolidated in the EU. The occasion was provided by the notification to renew the permit to cultivate GM maize MON 810.[63]

Before examining these developments, it is appropriate to delve into the way the Commission's 'new deal' on GMOs, as announced in 2006 was implemented by the same Commission and how EFSA responded.

As to the former, it took a proactive approach to address Member States' concerns. For example, in 2008 the Commission asked EFSA to review the scientific studies on the impact of maize Bt11 1507 on the environment upon which the Authority had based its positive opinion of 2005. Indeed, Member States had raised objections to the original risk assessment. The Commission asked EFSA to evaluate scientific publications that came out after the 2005 opinion. The EFSA's new opinion did not alter the original conclusions.[64]

In March 2008, the Commission gave a 24-month mandate to EFSA to further develop and update its guidance document as regards the environmental risk assessment (ERA) of GM plants. 'The purpose of this evaluation is to generate, collect and assess information on a GM plant in order to determine its impact on human/animal health and the environment relative to non-GMOs.'[65]

Let us come to EFSA's response. As we learn from the Council's recollection in the conclusions of December of 2008,[66] in 2006 EFSA made efforts to improve transparency. EFSA's news on its website confirms that in order to ensure transparency EFSA provides a summary of how comments from Member States are followed up in each of its GMO opinion.

However, the changes in strategy undertaken by the Authority were not formalised in a single document. Indeed, nowhere in the website it is possible to find a statement giving details of the strategy that EFSA envisaged to address the Commission's concerns. This is regrettable since making EFSA's changes visible is crucial to gain public trust.

The Authority's modest communication efforts came at a difficult time. Indeed, in 2008 the authorisation to cultivate GM maize 810 expired but under the rules of the framework Directive a renewal could be issued, subject to a new risk assessment. Yet, the procedure leading to the renewal was not at all smooth.

63 Between 2007 and 2008 EFSA received 25 renewal applications, including amongst others, an application to cultivate the GM maize MON 810.

64 *EFSA Journal*, 2008, 851, 1–27.

65 *EFSA Journal*, 2010;8(11):1879.

66 Council Meeting of 4 December 2008, point 8.

Member States such as Austria, France, Hungary and later Germany made every effort to avoid the renewal.

In particular, the French opposition was strenuous. In February 2008 this country invoked emergency measures, under art. 34, prohibiting the cultivation of GM maize MON 810 until its permit was not renewed. This legal basis was in reality inappropriate since it concerned food and feed rather the cultivation of a GMO. In fact, later on, France switched to art. 23 of Directive 2001/18 as a basis for its prohibition and reiterate it, although the national scientific committee, set up by the government, found that the French claims to rely on the safeguard measures had not scientific basis.[67] Germany followed the French move in 2009.[68] The German move was also criticised by the national scientists.[69]

EFSA's opinion was requested by the Commission and 8 months later the Authority answered that there was no new scientific elements highlighting that the concerned GMO posed greater risks than conventional counterpart.[70] The Commission proposed the abolishment of the French (and Greek) measures to the standing committee but the procedure was blocked by a group of Member States that asked to postpone the discussion on the proposal until the results of the renewal of the authorisation were known.

In the end, the permission to cultivate the GM maize MON 810 was officially renewed in 2010, after the Commission acquired a new EFSA's positive assessment.[71] The latter was carried out taking into consideration factors that were not accounted for in the original risk assessment. Moreover, as we learn from EFSA's website, meetings with the Member States were organised in order to take the concerns expressed by a group of 15 Member States into consideration.[72] In particular, in a letter sent to EFSA these Member States identified a number of issues which were not identified by the Spanish authority that had carried out the ERA of GM maize MON 810. These related for example to the impact of this crop on insect resistance and on target-species.[73] As a result, EFSA in a spirit of

---

67 S. Morris, C. Spillane, 'EU crop regulation: A road to resolution or a regulatory roundabout?', *EJRR*, 4/2010, p. 364.

68 The bans in France and Germany were appealed against by Monsanto in both countries. In Germany the request for an injunction was rejected; by contrast, in France the highest courts upheld Monsanto's appeal, yet with no effects on the governmental decision to continue the ban (July 2012).

69 S. Morris, C. Spillane, above n. 67, p. 364.

70 *EFSA Journal*, 2008, 850, 1–45.

71 *EFSA Journal*, 2009, 1149, 1–84.

72 For the text of the letter see http://www.efsa.europa.eu/en/events/documents/gmo090526-ax1.pdf [last accessed on 30 September 2012].

73 It should be noted that in 2011 the Commission asked EFSA to clarify if sufficient data on the impact of the GM maize MON 810 were available to conclude on the safety of of MON810 pollen as or in food. EFSA released a positive opinion. See *EFSA Journal*, 2011;9(11): 2434. It is possible that the Commission's request was asked as a precautionary step taken for the doubts on the safety of GM pollen instilled by the ECJ in the Bablok case

cooperation invited GMOs risk assessment experts designated by the members of EFSA's Advisory Forum to a scientific meeting with the environmental experts of the EFSA GMO Panel to address the issues raised collectively in the letter.

The scientific underpinning of EFSA's positive opinion was heavily criticised by Greenpeace which accused EFSA of being selective in the use of scientific literature (the Authority admittedly would omit studies that indicate risks, make conflicting statements in the opinion, carry out an invalid toxicological assessment and so on), and eventually underestimating the level of uncertainty surrounding the effects of GM plant such as maize MON 810 on the environment.[74] EFSA reviewed also the report presented by Greenpeace and rebutted the allegations.[75]

At the same time, the Commission asked EFSA to consider new evidence provided by Austria, Greece and Hungary in support of their safeguard measures against GM maize MON 810. In all three cases EFSA concluded that no new scientific evidence was presented that would invalidate the previous risk assessment of the concerned GMO.[76]

The Environment Council of December 2008 was a turning point for EFSA's activity on GMOs and for that of the Commission. The Council made recommendations/invitations to the Commission and to the EFSA on how to improve the legal framework for the authorisations of GMOs. The discontent of the Member States concerned the cultivation of GMOs rather than GM food and feed.

This time in February 2009 EFSA boosted its efforts to give accountability of its action. It provided a clear and detailed account of what it would do to meet the Council concerns. In a document entitled 'EFSA actions on Council … conclusions on GMOs', published on its website[77] we found the following indications. The Authority interpreted the Council conclusions as requiring action from the EFSA on two issues: (a) strengthening of environmental assessment and monitoring arrangements and (b) making better use of expertise.

(Case C-442/09, *Bablok and Others v. Freistaat Bayern*, nyr.). In this judgment the ECJ considered that the presence of GMO material in the end product (honey) was sufficient to require that honey was subject to the authorisation procedure of reg. 1829/2003 and regardless of the proportion of genetically modified material contained in the product in question.

74 See the study commissioned by Greenpeace and Friends of Earth, *A critique of the European Food Safety Authority's opinion on genetically modified maize MON810*, 2009 available on http://www.greenpeace.at/uploads/media/Critique-on-EFSA-MON810.pdf, [last visited 31 August 2012].

75 See 'Re-evaluation of genetically modified maize MON810: EFSA to invite stakeholders to meeting in September for scientific discussion on its opinion, published in the news of the EFSA's website, 31 July 2009.

76 See *EFSA Journal*, 2008, 756, 1–18 (Hungary); *EFSA Journal*, (2008) 891, 1–64 (Austria); *EFSA Journal*, 2008, 757, pp. 1–12 (Greece).

77 See 'EFSA action on Council of the European Union conclusions on genetically modified organisms', 11 February 2009.

As to the first issue, the Authority referred to the guidelines on the ERA of GM plants. This represented the best example of how the importance of the environment was strengthened in the EFSA risk assessment. The commitment was made to subject the draft guidelines to a public consultation before delivering it to the European Commission. The adoption process of these guidelines was remarkably open to the public. For example, in addition to examining the comments received on the draft guidelines, the EFSA invited NGOs to a meeting in order to discuss the draft guidelines.[78]

The Council's vague concern on the use of expertise was also addressed by EFSA's response. The Authority stated that it had widened the range of actors to be consulted as normal work practice.[79] In addition, the Authority suggested that when an ERA has to be carried in relation to application for cultivation of GMOs, the Member State responsible for the ERA could perform this assessment with another Member State. Indeed, this would reinforce mutual trust between Member States and would enable national authorities to cooperate with EFSA.

On the expertise issue, the Council also advocated the formation of a network of European scientific organisations representing all disciplines, thus ensuring effective coordination and cooperation between scientists. The EFSA's answer on this point recalls that the GMO EFSA net, enabling the participants to share all documentation related to applications with national authorities and organisations, was working. Further initiatives in the areas of GMOs were also pointed out.

Finally, in an effort to strengthen the harmonisation of risk assessment of GMOs, EFSA underlined that it had organised joint meeting sessions with the Meeting of European Advisory Committees on Biosafety (MEACB; yearly since 2007), as well as special EFSA Advisory Forum Meetings on GMOs (2006, 2007 and planned 2010). A further initiative taken by the Authority to address diverging scientific opinions was the organisation of bilateral meetings with Member States scientists in the context of the examination of safeguard measures.[80]

The mentioned actions show that the complaints on the lack of transparency in EFSA's activity and on its unwillingness to take Member States' scientific opinions into consideration are overstated. Of course, EFSA's efforts to ensure openness do not guarantee that the public opinion will be incorporated in EFSA risk assessment. EFSA's task is to provide the best scientific and independent advice. Therefore, it is obvious that 'elite views are better represented than popular views and peers can exercise more pressure than the public'.[81]

---

78 http://www.efsa.europa.eu/en/press/news/gmo20100706.htm [last accessed on 28 September 2012].

79 These were be limited are not limited to National Competent Authorities under directive 2001/18 but also to other GMO Member State Competent Authorities and Member State organisations.

80 The reports of these meetings were published on its website.

81 M. Lee, above n. 39, p. 111.

A further interesting development of the years 2007–2009 is that in March 2009 the Council opposed once again the Commission proposal to repeal Austria and Hungary's bans on the cultivation of GM varieties of maize. A new Council decision was needed since EFSA had been consulted again by the Commission in 2006 and 2008 and had confirmed that the safeguard measures enacted by the countries were not justified.

The discontent shown at the Environment Council of December 2008 reached its peak at the Council meeting held in June 2009. A front of 13 Member States, led by Austria,[82] put forward a radical request: they argued that individual countries should be enabled to prohibit or restrict the cultivation of authorised GMOs throughout the whole territory or in certain areas, on the basis of the principle of subsidiarity. In addition, they advocated that 'socioeconomic criteria' could justify a partial or total ban of the cultivation of GMOs.[83]

'The group of 13' requested the Commission to submit a proposal designed to entrust to Member States the authority to take decisions on the cultivation of GM crops. This request, whose legal basis is Article 114 TFEU,[84] may be considered as an intergovernmental initiative designed to ask the EU institutions to cease exercising their powers in an area of shared competence, on the basis of the principle of subsidiarity and in line with declaration n. 18 of the Lisbon Treaty. In the light of the Member State' request, it would not be legitimate for the Commission to reject it.

Certainly, the collapse of trust in the working of the EU authorisation procedure leading to the cultivation of GMOs is a failure that involves all the EU actors involved in the GMOs legislation, including EFSA. However, the impact on this decision, in the event it is finally taken at Council level, may also be positive on the approvals of GM food/feed, once that the 'hot potato' of the cultivation of GM crops reverts to the Member States competence.

The last noteworthy event of the referring period concerns a notification by Portugal, on the basis of Article 114 (5) TEC for the prohibition of cultivation of Genetically Modified Plants in the Autonomous Region of Madeira. The Commission issued an interlocutory decision in which it stated:

> ... the adoption of the EFSA Opinion is necessary before the adoption of a decision on the Portuguese notification. In view of the extended scope of the potential adverse environmental effects indicated by the Portuguese notification and the complexity of the scientific aspects related to the cultivation of GMOs in the Autonomous Region of Madeira, it is necessary that EFSA is granted

82 Bulgaria, Cyprus, Ireland, Greece, Latvia, Lithuania, Hungary, Luxembourg, Malta, Slovenia and Poland.

83 Council document n. 11226/2/09 REV 2.

84 Art. 2(2) third sentence of the TFEU is also mentioned in the recital of the draft regulation.

> a reasonable period of time before adopting its Opinion. For this reason, the Commission asked EFSA to deliver its Opinion by 31 January 2010.[85]

In line with other cases, the EFSA released its opinion concluding that there was no new scientific evidence that could justify the restrictive legislation of Portugal.[86] However, the Commission has never issued a decision in which it explicitly rejected the request for notification. This implies that the Portuguese request was accepted and the Isle Madeira benefits of a legal GMO-free status with respect to the cultivation of GMOs. Probably, the decision of the Commission to de facto accept the Portuguese request is the result of its conviction that a partial de-harmonisation of the EU rules on the cultivation of GMOs was to be approved by the Council, in light of the Member State's request to provide more freedom on national authorities in this area.

EFSA's Activity Between 2010 and 2012

The years from 2010 to 2012 were characterised by contradictory political trends in the area of GMOs. On the one hand, the number of authorisations increased with respect to previous years. Between 2010 and 2012,[87] 23 authorisations, mostly concerning GM food and feed were approved. Perhaps, the most important release for its symbolic value is that of the so-called Amflora potato (2010), which is the second authorised crop for cultivation. In addition, the GMO Panel, together with the EFSA Animal Health and Welfare Panel, developed guidance for the first time on the food and feed risk assessment of genetically modified animals, including health and welfare aspects.[88]

However, in contrast with these developments (and perhaps as an overall reaction to the long and tormented approval process of the Amflora potato), Member States persuaded the Commission to shift regulatory authority from the EU level back to the national one when taking decisions on the cultivation of GMOs.[89]

The Commission tabled a proposal to amend Directive 2001/18 in July 2010 so as to confer greater discretion on the EU Member States wishing to ban the cultivation of GMOs in their territories. The Parliament supported the initiative

85 2009/828/EC: Commission Decision of 3 November 2009 relating to the draft Regional Legislative Decree declaring the Autonomous Region of Madeira to be an Area Free of Genetically Modified Organisms, notified by the Republic of Portugal pursuant to Article 95(5) of the EC Treaty, OJ [2009] L 294/16.

86 *EFSA Journal*, 2010; 8(2): 1500.

87 The cut-off date is 30 September 2012.

88 *EFSA Journal*, 2012, 10(1): 2501 [43 pp.] For a short comment see E. Waigmann, C. Paoletti, H. Davies, J. Perry, S. Kärenlampi, H. Kuiper, above n. 29, p. 6.

89 See contributions written by S. Poli, M. Weimer, J. Varela, S. Morris and C. Spillane, 'Symposium on the EU's GMOs reform', *EJRR* 4/2010, pp. 339–69.

but introduced a number of changes on the proposal designed to detail the grounds that could justify restrictions on cultivation and to better reflect the Member States' concerns vis-à-vis transgenic crops.[90] At the moment of writing the proposal is in a stalemate situation. Indeed, under the Danish presidency, the draft regulation was revisited in order to be approved at first reading by the Council. Yet, at the Environment Council of March 2012 France, Germany, Belgium, Spain and the UK prevented the achievement of the required qualified majority threshold.[91] No progress in the discussion was made at the following Environment Council of June 2012.[92] Despite this, the political decision to regain autonomy in the cultivation of GM crops looks irreversible and will be implemented, although not necessarily in the near future.

Looking more closely at the work of the EFSA in the reference period, the following trends may be highlighted.

The Authority seems to pay greater attention than in the past to the interactions between the GMO crops and the environment, in line with its commitment to strengthen the environmental monitoring, as requested by the Council of December 2008.

For instance, after two years of preparations, in 2010 EFSA delivered a report on the potential impact of GM plants on non-target organisms, which is one of the most important concerns for Member States. This version superseded the 2006 guidance document on GMOs.[93]

Secondly, it seems possible to detect a change in the opinions of the Authority. This idea is suggested by an author who argues that in recent opinions EFSA did not position itself as a technocratic body but it made efforts to answer concerns raised by Member States and NGOs.[94]

These acts continue to give the green light to authorisations and renewals as well as to reject new scientific evidence of Member States invoking safeguard measures in line with the past. However, the news is that they are more explicit on the possible problems for the environment that GMOs may cause and they

90 See, for example, the emphasis on the need to evaluate the long term environmental effects of GM crops, the emphasis on the precautionary principle, and the liability requirements in case of unintended effects or damage that might occur due to the deliberate release or the placing on the market of GMOs. European Parliament legislative resolution of 5 July 2011 on the proposal for a regulation of the European Parliament and of the Council amending Directive 2001/18/EC as regards the possibility for the Member States to restrict or prohibit the cultivation of GMOs in their territory (COM(2010)0375 – C7–0178/2010–2010/0208(COD)), of 5 July 2011.

91 The proposal for a regulation as regards the possibility for the Member States to restrict or prohibit the cultivation of GMOs in their territory (Council document n. 7153/12, 2 March 2012).

92 Council document n. 10883/1/12, 6 June 2012.

93 *EFSA Journal*, 2010;8(11): 1877 [72 pp.].

94 M. Groenleer, The autonomy of the European Union agencies, Eburon academic publishing, Delft, 2009, p. 205.

recommend risk mitigation measures. Thirdly, they place emphasis on the limits of EFSA's conclusions that a GMO is no more risky than the conventional counterpart. Fourthly, efforts are made to highlight the reasons of scientific uncertainty.

For instance, in the opinion on the renewal of authorisation to cultivate soybean 40–3-2,[95] the GMO Panel concludes that soybean 40–3-2 is unlikely to raise additional environmental safety concerns compared with conventional soybean, but that management of its cultivation could result in environmental harm under certain conditions. The EFSA GMO Panel therefore recommends managing the use of glyphosate on soybean 40–3-2 in ways that result in similar or reduced environmental impacts compared with conventional soybean cultivation. A second important concession was made on the presence of scientific uncertainty on the environmental effects of the concerned GM plant.

A similar wording is used in another 2012 opinion in which EFSA carried out an evaluation of a risk assessment for placing on the market of genetically modified maize MON 88017 for cultivation.[96] In this act, we read:

> The EFSA GMO Panel considers that maize MON 88017 is unlikely to have any adverse effect on the environment, except for the possible resistance evolution to the Cry3Bb1 protein in coleopteran target pests; resistance evolution may lead to altered pest control practices that may cause adverse environmental effects. The cultivation management of maize MON 88017 could result in environmental harm.

Several risk mitigation measures are suggested to address these problems.

By contrast with the changes appearing in the opinions on request for authorisations/renewals, the six opinions adopted in 2012 concerning safeguard measures do not appear different from those of the past. EFSA assessed the Austrian French and Luxembourg's restrictions on the Amflora potato,[97] the Greek ban of GM maize MON 810,[98] the prolongation of prohibition of genetically modified oilseed rape event GT73 for import, processing and feed[99] and the ban of genetically modified oilseed rape events Ms8, Rf3 and Ms8 x Rf3 for import, processing and feed uses.[100]

The third 'green development' of the EFSA's activity concerns the reinforcement of the environmental monitoring tasks of EFSA. As is known, the framework Directive introduces the requirement for Post Market Environmental Monitoring (PMEM) of GMOs in order to deal with possible residual uncertainties about environmental risk and harm associated to authorised GM crops. After

---

95 *EFSA Journal*, 2012; 10(6): 2753.

96 *EFSA Journal*, 2011; 9(11): 2428.

97 *EFSA Journal*, 2012; 10(5): 2705 (France); *EFSA Journal*, 2012;10(3): 2627 (Austria), *EFSA Journal*, 2012; 10(9): 2874 (Luxembourg).

98 *EFSA Journal*, 2012; 10(9): 2877 (Greece).

99 *EFSA Journal*, 2012; 10(9): 2876.

100 *EFSA Journal*, 2012; 10(9): 2878.

Commissioner Dalli's first visit to EFSA, the Authority announced its availability to review the 2006 PMEM guidance. Moreover, and most importantly, EFSA offered to support the risk managers to conduct a regular assessment of the data resulting from the PMEM for each authorised GMO. The Commission took up EFSA's suggestion and asked the Authority to deliver an opinion on each yearly monitoring report related to GM cultivation and to the appropriateness of the methodology.

As from 2010, the EFSA has accepted to deliver scientific opinions on the PMEM related to the GM MON 810 and the Amflora potato. The developers of the two GM crops submitted their PMEM reports to EFSA on the basis of the 2010 guidelines. The GMO Panel has thus far issued three opinions.[101] As to their content, in all of them EFSA has identified shortcomings in the methodology used by the developer to monitor the effects of the GM crop on the environment and has provided recommendations to the developers. However, the EFSA's overall conclusion was that no adverse effects on the environment, human and animal health due to the cultivation of two concerned crops may be identified.

It should not go unnoticed that the changes highlighted above concern a minority of GMOs, those authorised for cultivation. By contrast, since EFSA's approvals on GM food and feed did not receive the same attention from Member States and NGOs, there are no special changes to pinpoint in the corresponding EFSA's opinions.

A final trend that may be observed in the EFSA's recent activity in the area of biotechnology concerns the greater attention to open itself up to the Institutions other than the Commission and the Council. Greater attention is paid by EFSA to liaise with the European Parliament. In January 2011, the ALDE (Alliance of Liberals and Democrats for Europe) group of the European Parliament on January 2011 organised a meeting in which invited EFSA to debate on the risk assessment of genetically modified plants (GMOs). During 2011, the Commission promoted the organisation of conferences at the Parliament on GMOs related issues.[102] More recently, the relationship between the Parliament and the EFSA suffered due to a series of event that questioned EFSA's independence.[103] As a symbolic act of protest, the budget committee of the Parliament postponed the approval of the budget waiting for these problems of conflicts of interest to be addressed. However, EFSA was granted the

---

101 Two of them concern the 2009 and 2010 growing season of GM MON 810 (2011 and 2012) whereas the third was adopted with respect the 2010 Amflora potato growing season (2012).

102 See Commissioner Dalli's speech n. SPEECH/11/674, of 18 October 2011, published on http://europa.eu/rapid/pressReleasesAction.do?reference=SPEECH/11/674 [last accessed on 30 September 2012].

103 The former scientific coordinator of the GMO Panel, Suzy Renckens, took up a job for Syngenta after serving five years for the EFSA. The Commission nomination as Mella Frewen as member of the management board was also contested given her past of lobbyist in the EU food sector.

discharge for the 2010 budget as both the environment and budget committees acknowledged the efforts put by the Authority into ensuring independence.

Conclusion

EFSA has fully used all instruments and techniques at its disposal to provide the best possible scientific opinions in the area of GMOs. As illustrated by our analysis, it has assessed and reconsidered scientific evidence; it made use of self-tasking instruments to clarify certain aspects of the risk assessment procedure and it progressively boosted the transparency of its internal decision-making process. Overall, the risk assessment is quite smooth with respect to authorisations of GM food and feed; by contrast, it is tormented as far as the cultivation of GM crops. The relationship between the Food Authority and a few Member States remain problematic in this area. EFSA has gradually established a dialogue with competent national authorities trying to address their concerns. Yet the divergence of scientific opinions remain a reality. This trend is not without exceptions: the political decision to prohibit the GM maize MON 810 in France and Germany was considered not scientifically sound not only by the scientists who sit in the GMO Panel but also by some national scientists sitting at national food safety authorities.

In light of the initiatives taken by EFSA to address the problem of scientific divergence of opinions, it is submitted that it is not entirely appropriate/acceptable to put the blame on the Authority for not having properly addressed Member States' concerns. Indeed, these concerns are only in part related to the impact of GMOs on the environment; often, these fears are a fig's leaf for other non-scientific concerns (such as the coexistence between different forms of agriculture or public opinion aversion to GMOs).

EFSA has never taken an explicit stance upon Member States' non-scientific concerns as this kind of considerations fall outside its mandate. The EFSA keeps away from the discussion on how to integrate socioeconomic concerns into the EU decision-making in the cultivation of GMOs. It is not up to Authority to take these factors into consideration in the current EU food law architecture. Often, Member States and commentators blame EFSA because it provides scientific advice without considering socioeconomic factors.

Therefore, it is somewhat surprising the opinion of an author claiming that 'the creation of the European Food Safety Authority (EFSA) has dramatically altered the European Union's (EU) adherence to science-based regulations, encouraging movement towards socioeconomic-based regulation of agricultural products and, hence, the politicization of risk'.[104]

Of course there is scope of improvements in EFSA's GMO-related activities. For example, additional steps could be taken to ensure a greater degree of transparency in the EFSA's database of questions[105] submitted by the Commission in the area of GMOs. In addition, the meetings of the GMO Panel could be held in public. To the extent that this is possible, greater efforts to harmonise risk assessment procedure, would also be a welcome move to address the problem of scientific divergence of opinions.

A final word of comment on the relationship between the EFSA and the Commission in the area of GMOs. An author uses the following metaphor to describe the relationship between the two bodies: the Commission is a blind driver with a passenger, the EFSA, giving directions to it.[106] Does this evaluation give us a correct picture of this relationship? Taken at face value all Commission decisions have always followed EFSA's opinions. This is true for requests of authorisation to place GMOs on the market, notifications under 114(5) TFEU, safeguard and emergency measures. Yet, the metaphor of the blind driver and the passenger gives a misleading picture of the Commission-EFSA's relationship. A blind driver does not question the route but he confines himself to follow instructions. The Commission has on many occasions asked EFSA to review the scientific information at the basis of its opinions, especially after 2006, or to update its findings on the impact of GMOs on the environment, without considering the possibility of proposing new legislation. This has given an important impulse to the EFSA's changes of strategy vis-à-vis Member States and stakeholders.

104 S. Smyth, International Considerations of Food Biotechnology Regulatory Frameworks, paper presented at the Conference of the ECPR Standing Group on Regulation & Governance, held at the University of Exeter in June 2012. The text of the paper can be downloaded from the website of the conference: http://www.exeter.ac.uk/reggov2012 [last accessed on 28 September 2002]. The quote is taken from p. 7.

105 The database reports the number and the date of the questions asked by the Commission to EFSA but it is difficult to identify the content of the questions and there is no reference to EFSA's answers.

106 E. Vos and F. Wendler, *Food Safety Regulation in Europe: A Comparative Institutional Analysis*, Antwerpen, Intersentia, 2006, p. 122.

Chapter 8

From BSE to Obesity: EFSA's Growing Role in the EU's Nutrition Policy

Marine Friant-Perrot and Amandine Garde

Introduction

It is only from 2007 onwards that the work of EFSA in the field of nutrition has grown considerably. This largely reflects the EU's increasing concern for the nutritional quality of food. Nevertheless, EFSA has had to face the challenge that it is particularly difficult in this field of policy intervention to distinguish the provision of independent scientific advice with decision pertaining to the normative process.

The EU's Developing Nutrition Policy as a Catalyst for Change in EFSA's Role

When EFSA was set up in 2002, the focus of its work was largely on food safety issues, as the name 'European Food Safety Authority' itself indicated. As MacMaoláin wrote in 2008:

> The first element of quality is actually nutritional value, yet … nutritional value has remained for the most part outside the factors that are taken into account in determining what qualifies as safe or high quality food[1] … As a consequence of this misinterpretation of the extent to which the [Union] is responsible for the protection of human health through the consumption of safe or quality food, the issue of nutrition has become side-lined, when in fact it should be the key component of any food quality programme.[2]

Nevertheless, the last five years have been characterised by a notable change in emphasis. The growing burden of non-communicable diseases (NCDs) in the

1 In some cases, food safety and nutrition concerns may overlap. For instance, doubts have been raised regarding the safety of aspartame, thus raising questions about the extent to which nutrition-conscious consumers should use this sweetener as a sugar replacement. Nevertheless, this overlap tends to be the exception rather than the rule.

2 MacMaoláin, C., *EU Food Law – Protecting Consumers and Health in a Common Market* (Oxford: Hart Publishing 2007) at p. 223 and 224.

EU has contributed to a significant re-evaluation of the initial position. The rapid increase of overweight and obesity rates and the recognition that poor diets have become one of the main risk factors for NCDs across the EU have led to the development of an EU nutrition strategy, culminating in the publication of a White Paper laying down a strategy on Nutrition, Overweight and Obesity-related health issues (the Nutrition White Paper),[3] which places at its heart the provision of food information to consumers.

The EU's Developing Nutrition Strategy

The EU is particularly affected by unhealthy diets, with overweight affecting 30–70 per cent and obesity affecting 10–30 per cent of adults in EU countries.[4]

Aware that public intervention limiting obesity is important not only in public health terms, but also to 'reduce the long-term costs to health services and stabilise economies by enabling citizens to lead productive lives well into old age',[5] the European Commission initiated a consultation in December 2005,[6] which led to the publication of the Nutrition White Paper in May 2007.[7]

The Nutrition White Paper emphasises the role of prevention and notes that public authorities should support individuals in their attempt to make healthier choices. It then identifies a range of relevant EU policies playing a role in addressing nutrition and physical activity, including public health, food, agriculture, transport, regional policy, sport, media and education.

The Nutrition White Paper stresses the important role which nutrition has to play in promoting healthier lifestyles. This requires, however, that consumers realise what constitutes a balanced diet and how each food they eat can contribute to such a diet. Hence the recognition that the provision of food information should be at the heart of the EU's nutrition strategy.

---

3 Commission 'White Paper on a Strategy for Europe on Nutrition, Overweight and Obesity Related Health Issues' COM (2007) 279 final.

4 European Commission, Implementation Progress Report of the Strategy for Europe on Nutrition, Overweight and Obesity Related Health Issues, Brussels, December 2010: http://ec.europa.eu/health/nutrition_physical_activity/policy/implementation_report_en.htm.

5 Improving public health and tackling obesity more specifically are an essential part of the work required to meet the Lisbon Agenda objective of boosting EU competitiveness: European Commission Memorandum, 'Questions and Answers on the EU Approach to Tackling Obesity', Memo/05/470, 8 December 2005. See also the Impact Assessment Accompanying the Nutrition White Paper of 30 May 2007, SEC(2007) 706/2, at 16.

6 European Commission Green Paper 'Promoting Healthy Diets and Physical Activity: A European Dimension for the Prevention of Overweight, Obesity and Chronic Diseases', Brussels, December 2005, COM(2005) 637 final.

7 On the Nutrition White Paper, see Garde, A., *EU Law and Obesity Prevention* (Alphen aan den Rijn: Kluwer Law International 2010).

The Key Role of Consumer Information in EU Nutrition Policy Requiring that consumers be provided with specific information about a product or a service is a regulatory technique that has enjoyed considerable popularity in the development of EU measures affecting the protection of consumers' interests. The 'information paradigm', which is at the heart of the EU Consumer Strategies for 2007–13[8] and 2012–14,[9] places the onus on consumers to decide what is good for them and their families, expecting them to read the information and process it whilst taking their personal circumstances into account. The provision of information is seen as a compromise: protection is provided as a result of the introduction of duties on traders to inform consumers of the qualities of their goods and services, whilst avoiding intrusive controls likely to diminish consumer choice.[10] Applying this rationale to food choices, the assumption is that if consumers are aware of what each foodstuff contains, they should be trusted to apply their nutrition knowledge and make appropriate choices. This reflects the view that in a society where individuals are autonomous and dislike limitations, it is expected that they take primary responsibility for their dietary choices. It also explains the focus which the Nutrition White Paper has placed on the importance of providing information to consumers. Finally, it reflects the findings that EU citizens feel confident about being able to take personal steps to avoid diet and health-related issues.[11]

However, the information paradigm promoted at EU level requires that the information made available to consumers be of sufficient quality to guide their choices and effectively allows them to 'protect' themselves. Consumer empowerment may therefore justify public intervention requiring the disclosure of a certain standard of information. Thus, Regulation (EU) No 1169/2011 on consumer food information[12] and Regulation (EC) No 1924/2006 on nutrition and health claims made on foods[13] are intended to ensure that the information on food

8 Commission 'EU Consumer Policy Strategy 2007–2013 on Empowering consumers, enhancing their welfare, effectively protecting them' COM (2007) 99 final.

9 Commission 'A European Consumer Agenda – Boosting confidence and growth' COM (2012) 225 final.

10 Weatherill, S., *EU Consumer Law and Policy* (Cheltenham: Edward Elgar 2005) at p. 84. On consumer information, see also Howells, G., 'The potential and limit of consumer empowerment by information' (2005) *Journal of Law and Society*, 32(3) 349–70.

11 http://www.efsa.europa.eu/fr/riskcommunication/riskperception.htm, summary at p. 7.

12 Regulation (EU) No 1169/2011 of the European Parliament and of the Council of 25 October 2011 on the provision of food information to consumers [2011] L 304/18.

13 Corrigendum to Regulation (EC) No 1924/2006 of the European Parliament and of the Council of 20 December 2006 on nutrition and health claims made on foods [2007] OJ L 12/3.

provided to consumers is clear, sufficient and trustworthy[14] and constitute major components of the EU's nutrition strategy.[15]

The regulation of how consumer information is provided and what it should contain ultimately allows the responsibility for healthy choices to be shared between, on the one hand, consumers, who are expected to process the information made available to them when purchasing goods and services, and, on the other, regulatory authorities, which must ensure that enough information is made available to consumers and that such information is neither false nor misleading.

The food information paradigm nonetheless presupposes that the fundamental question of what constitutes nutritious food is answered.

Food must be categorised on the basis of scientific evidence. There is a general agreement that energy-dense, micronutrient-poor foods which are high in fat, sugar or salt are not nutritious and may have detrimental effects on human health, but proposals for actions to limit their promotion and availability remain not merely controversial but hotly disputed by those having commercial interests in these products. It is all the more important to fight 'miraculous' foods in the current context of the medicalisation of diets.[16] Hence the importance of having EFSA as the EU's independent, scientific authority to help policy makers at EU and national level develop evidence-based nutrition profiles, support their regulatory decisions, develop effective nutrition policies, set diet-related public health targets or develop educational programmes on healthy diets.

EFSA's Main Areas of Nutrition Intervention

Regulation (EC) No 178/2002 on food safety provides that the mission of EFSA, which 'shall contribute to a high level of human life and health', includes the provision of 'scientific advice and scientific and technical support on human nutrition in relation to [EU] legislation and, at the request of the Commission, assistance concerning communication on nutritional issues within the framework

14 The principle that information must be loyal is at the heart of EU food law: see Article 16 of Regulation (EC) No. 178/2002 of the European Parliament and of the Council of 28 January 2002 Laying Down the General Principles and Requirements of Food Law, Establishing the European Food Safety Authority and Laying Down Procedures in Matters of Food Safety [2002] OJ L31/1. See also Article 7 of Regulation (EU) No 1169/2011 (OJ 2011 L 304/18) and Regulation (EC) No 1924/2006 on nutrition and health claims, discussed below (OJ 2007 L 12/3).

15 At pp. 5 and 6.

16 In 2010, the global worth of health food amounted to between EUR 55 and 96 billion, depending on the exact definitions given to this term, and was expected to grow by 20% a year within the next 10 years. It was then estimated that by 2011, 6 to 10% of the overall food market would be made of health food: http://www.industrie.gouv.fr/techno_cles_2010/html/viv_53.html.

of the [EU] health programme'.[17] In particular, EFSA's Scientific Panel on Dietetic Products, Nutrition and Allergies ('the NDA Panel') deals with questions relating to dietetic products, nutrition and food allergies as well as associated topics such as novel foods. The Nutrition Unit provides administrative and scientific support to the NDA Panel.

In recent years, the NDA Panel has dealt with three issues of major significance for the development of EU nutrition policy: determining the scientific substantiation of food claims; the establishment of nutrient profiles; and the setting of dietary reference values.

Determining the Scientific Substantiation of Food Claims Regulation (EC) No 1924/2006 defines a claim as 'any message or representation, which is not mandatory under [Union] or national legislation, including pictorial, graphic or symbolic representation, in any form, which states, suggests or implies that a food has particular characteristics'.[18] The Regulation then divides food claims into two main sub-categories: nutrition claims[19] and health claims.[20] As claims are voluntarily provided by food operators, they must be distinguished from the information disclosed as part of a legal requirement, such as the nutritional declaration provided for in Regulation (EU) No 1169/2011.[21]

Relying on food claims may be seen as a positive evolution insofar as these claims have the potential to inform purchasing decisions. This, in turn, may encourage food manufacturers to reformulate their products and place more nutritious foods on the market. Nevertheless, food claims also are a powerful marketing tool for food industry operators. It is consequently imperative to ensure that the claims in question are reliable and do inform consumer choices rather than mislead them.

After more than three years of intense debate, the Council and the European Parliament adopted Regulation (EC) No 1924/2006, which lays down the overriding principle that nutrition and health claims may only be used if they are not misleading[22]

17 Article 22 of Regulation (EC) No. 178/2002 of the European Parliament and of the Council of 28 January 2002 Laying Down the General Principles and Requirements of Food Law, Establishing the European Food Safety Authority and Laying Down Procedures in Matters of Food Safety [2002] OJ L31/1.

18 Article 2(2) of Corrigendum to Regulation (EC) No 1924/2006 of the European Parliament and of the Council of 20 December 2006 on nutrition and health claims made on foods [2007] OJ L 12/3.

19 Article 2(4) of Regulation (EC) No 1924/2006.

20 Article 2(5) of Regulation (EC) No 1924/2006. In Case C-544/10 *Deutsches Weintor* [2012] ECR I-xxx, 6 September 2012, the Court of Justice of the European Union adopted a broad interpretation of what constituted a health claims.

21 Article 9(l) and Articles 29 to 35 of Regulation (EU) 1169/2011 of the European Parliament and of the Council of 25 October 2011 on the provision of food information to consumers [2011] OJ L 304/18.

22 Articles 3, 4 and 5 of Corrigendum to Regulation (EC) No 1924/2006 of the European Parliament and of the Council of 20 December 2006 on nutrition and health

and if they are scientifically substantiated.[23] The NDA Panel assesses whether claims relating to *the nutrition and health benefits of foods* are substantiated by scientific evidence. It is on the basis of this scientific evaluation that the EU Commission then decides whether or not such claims should be authorised at EU level.

Nutrition claims are only permitted if they are listed in the Annex and if they respect precise and quantifiable values.[24] For example, a claim that a food is a 'source of fibre' may only be made 'where the product contains at least 3 grams of fibre per 100 grams or at least 1.5 grams of fibre per 100 kcal'.[25] Amendments to the Annex may be made subject, where appropriate, to the consultation of EFSA.[26] To date, five nutrition claims have been added to the original list of 24.[27]

As far as health claims are concerned, a positive list of health claims other than those referring to the reduction of a disease risk has been drawn up by the Commission, on the basis of claims submitted by Member States. These health claims have then been allowed on labels, provided that the producer can verify the link between the claim and a given product. For health claims referring to the reduction of a disease risk, authorisation will need to be requested on a case-by-case basis, following the submission of scientific evidence to EFSA for assessment. EFSA is responsible for verifying the scientific substantiation of the claims submitted.[28]

The Commission has established an EU register of nutrition and health claims made on food which will be updated regularly to include the list of permitted nutrition and health claims together with the conditions applying to them, as well as

---

claims made on foods [2007] OJ L 12/3.

23 Article 6 of Regulation (EC) No 1924/2006.

24 Article 8(1) of Regulation (EC) No 1924/2006.

25 Annex to Regulation (EC) No 1924/2006.

26 Article 8(2) of Corrigendum to Regulation (EC) No 1924/2006 of the European Parliament and of the Council of 20 December 2006 on nutrition and health claims made on foods [2007] OJ L 12/3.

27 Commission Regulation (EU) 116/201 of 9 February 2010 amending Regulation (EC) No 1924/2006 of the European Parliament and of the Council with regard to the list of nutrition claims. [2010] OJ L 37/16. By contrast, the claim 'now contains X% less of [nutrient]' was rejected following the objection of the European Parliament on 2 February 2012 (P7_TA (2012)0022) on the basis that such a claim 'runs counter to the purpose and content of the basic instrument by being ambiguous, misleading and confusing to the average consumer' and that it 'could act as a disincentive to producers to reformulate their products more substantially in order to meet the requirements for the 'reduced [nutrient]' or 'light' claims, as it is easier to reduce a nutrient by 15% than by 30%' (15% being the threshold proposed by the Commission).

28 Four types of health claims are identified in Regulation (EC) No 1924/2006: general function claims; new function claims; disease reduction claims; and child development or health claims. For more information, see Articles 13 and 14 of the Regulation, as well as EFSA's webpage on nutrition and health claims: http://www.efsa.europa.eu/en/topics/topic/nutrition.htm.

a list of rejected health claims and the reasons for their rejection. A first list of 222 health claims was published in May 2012.[29] Overall, the amount of health claims EFSA has had to assess has exceeded all expectations: out of the 4,637 claims (of a total of 44,000 health claims Member States had proposed) the Commission submitted to EFSA between July 2008 and March 2010, the Commission asked EFSA to evaluate 2,758 claims by June 2011, 331 claims were withdrawn and 1,548 claims on 'botanicals' have been placed on hold by the Commission pending further consideration on how to proceed with these. As Professor Albert Flynn, then Chair of the NDA Panel, said on 28 July 2011 when EFSA published the final series of 35 evaluations of a total of 2,758 food-related general function health claims: 'This very challenging task was completed thanks to the dedication and commitment of the experts on the NDA Panel in collaboration with EFSA staff, who have had to cope with an unprecedented workload, coupled with very tight deadlines and often poor information'[30] – a mammoth task the EU did not seem to have anticipated.[31]

Setting Nutrient Profiles Article 4 of (EC) No Regulation 1924/2006 provides that food must have appropriate nutrient profiles to bear nutrition or health claims. The term 'nutrient profile' refers to the nutrient composition of a food or diet. 'Nutrient profiling' therefore is the classification of foods for specific purposes based on their nutrient composition.[32]

The need for nutrient profiles rests on the principle that food containing high levels of nutrients whose excessive intakes as part of the overall diet is not recommended should not be able to be marketed as providing nutrition or health benefits if, ultimately, such consumption is not healthy. Thus, Article 4 of the Regulation provides that the European Commission will establish nutrient profiles by 19 January 2009.[33] EFSA was consulted and in preparing its scientific

29 Commission Regulation (EU) 432/2012 of 16 May 2012 establishing a list of permitted health claims made on foods, other than those referring to the reduction of disease risk and to children's development and health [2012] OJ L 136/1. The EU Register is available at: http://ec.europa.eu/nuhclaims/.

30 EFSA delivered 341 opinions on the health claims thus submitted: http://www.efsa.europa.eu/en/press/news/110728.htm.

31 Ernst & Young, External Evaluation of EFSA – Final Report, 5 September 2012: http://www.efsa.europa.eu/en/keydocs/docs/efsafinalreport.pdf, at p. 160.

32 This definition is taken from the Scientific Opinion of the NDA Panel of 31 January 2008 on the Setting of Nutrient Profiles for Foods Bearing Nutrition and Health Claims Pursuant to Article 4 of the Regulation 1924/2006, (2008) *EFSA Journal*, 644. See also the dedicated webpage of the WHO on nutrition profiling: http://www.who.int/nutrition/topics/profiling/en/ For different models of nutrition profiling, see in particular the Nutrition Profiling Report of a Technical WHO/IASO Meeting published by WHO in 2011: http://www.who.int/entity/nutrition/publications/profiling/WHO_IASO_report2010.pdf.

33 The delegation by the Commission of its implementing powers, as derives from Articles 290 and 291 TFEU, is referred to as 'comitology'. On this procedure, see Alemanno,

advice to the Commission, the NDA Panel reviewed a wide range of reports and papers on nutrient profiles and considered views from stakeholders. It delivered its opinion in January 2008, focusing as Article 4(1) requires, on:

- whether profiles should be set for food in general and/or categories of food
- the choice and balance of nutrients to be taken into account
- the choice of reference quantity/basis for profiles
- the approach to the calculation of the profiles
- the feasibility and testing of a proposed system.

As EFSA summarised:

> The nutrient profile of the overall diet is an important determinant of health and the nutrient profile of a "balanced" diet is defined by science based recommendations for intakes of energy and nutrients. Because diets are composed of multiple foods, overall dietary balance may be achieved through complementation of foods with different nutrient profiles so that it is not necessary for individual foods to match the nutrient profile of a "balanced" diet. Nevertheless, individual foods might influence the nutrient profile of the overall diet, depending on the nutrient profile of the particular food and its intake. Thus, when classifying food products as eligible to bear claims, the potential of the food to adversely affect the overall dietary balance is the main scientific consideration.[34]

However, in setting the nutrient profiles, the Commission is also required to 'carry out consultations with interested parties, in particular food business operators and consumer groups'.[35] The setting of nutrient profiles is a complex task requiring that account be taken of scientific evidence on which EFSA based its opinion, but also of industrial/commercial considerations, including innovation, cultural and dietary/culinary considerations. Thus, the Commission has conducted specific and extensive consultations of stakeholders on the setting of nutrient profiles, including two meetings of a working group on nutrient profiles.[36] Member State experts were also consulted within the Commission expert working group on nutrition

A. and Meuwese, A., 'Impact assessment of EU non-legislative rulemaking: The missing link in "new comitology"', (2013) *European Law Journal*, 19, 76–92.

34 Opinion of the NDA Panel on the setting of nutrient profiles for foods bearing nutrition and health claims pursuant to Article 4 of the Regulation (EC) No 1924/2006, adopted on 31 January 2008 in answer to EFSA-Q-2007–058: http://ec.europa.eu/food/food/labellingnutrition/claims/nut_profiles_en.htm.

35 Article 4(1) of Corrigendum to Regulation (EC) No 1924/2006 of the European Parliament and of the Council of 20 December 2006 on nutrition and health claims made on foods [2007] OJ L 12/3.

36 http://ec.europa.eu/food/committees/advisory/sum_wg_11072008.pdf.

and health claims, in which EFSA participated. Nevertheless, no nutrient profiles have yet been adopted. The difficulties facing the Commission largely stem from the fact that the boundary between the scientific and the policy decision spheres is particularly difficult to draw in this area, as discussed below. The difficulties are further compounded by the fact that nutrient profile schemes need to be adaptable.[37]

Establishing Dietary Reference Values and Food-Based Dietary Guidelines Each food must be considered as part of an overall diet. This requires a series of estimates of the amount of energy and nutrients which different population groups need to be healthy.[38] Food-based dietary guidelines translate nutritional recommendations into messages about foods and diet, and can guide consumers on what to eat and help them make healthy dietary choices.[39]

The Commission asked EFSA to review and update the reference values for nutrient and energy intakes established in 1993 by the Scientific Committee on Food.[40] In performing this task, EFSA has taken account of new scientific evidence and recent recommendations issued at national and at international level. The Commission has also requested EFSA to help Member State authorities translate nutrient-based recommendations into practical food-based dietary guidelines. In order to ensure a consistent approach throughout, the NDA Panel has laid down general principles for establishing dietary reference values,[41] has set dietary reference values for carbohydrates, dietary fibre, fats and water, has published an opinion on food-based dietary guidelines providing advice to policy makers on how to translate nutritional recommendations into messages about foods[42] and has given scientific advice on the establishment of tolerable upper levels of intakes (UL) for vitamins and minerals which represent the highest level of daily intake likely to pose no risk of adverse health effects.[43]

---

37 Opinion of the NDA Panel on the setting of nutrient profiles for foods bearing nutrition and health claims pursuant to Article 4 of the Regulation (EC) No 1924/2006, adopted on 31 January 2008 in answer to EFSA-Q-2007–058: http://ec.europa.eu/food/food/labellingnutrition/claims/nut_profiles_en.htm.

38 It is important to note that dietary reference values are not individual recommendations.

39 http://www.efsa.europa.eu/en/topics/topic/drv.htm.

40 http://ec.europa.eu/food/fs/sc/scf/out80_en.html.

41 NDA Panel, Scientific Opinion on establishing food-based dietary guidelines, adopted on 4 December 2009 and published on 25 March 2010.

42 http://www.efsa.europa.eu/en/press/news/nda100326.htm.

43 Tolerable Upper Intake Levels for Vitamins and Minerals by the Scientific Panel on Dietetic products, nutrition and allergies (NDA) and Scientific Committee on Food (SCF), February 2006: http://www.efsa.europa.eu/en/ndatopics/docs/ndatolerableuil.pdf. Such advice is particularly important in light of the tendency of many food operators to enrich food in vitamins and minerals, and will assist the Commission and Member States in setting maximum levels of nutrients authorised in fortified foods and food supplements.

Nutrition as a Sensitive Issue at the Crossroad between Science and Cultural Values

In all these areas, EFSA works independently, openly and transparently to deliver the scientific advice required to support the policies and decisions of risk managers in the field of nutrition. This section discusses difficulties EFSA has encountered in performing its nutrition-related tasks.

Transparency as a Pre-Requisite to EFSA's Credibility

The principle of transparency is expressly laid down in Regulation (EC) No 178/2002, which provides in Article 9 for 'open and transparent public consultation, directly or through representative bodies, during the preparation, evaluation and revision of food law', whilst Articles 3(13) and 10 lay down the requirement that the public should be informed of hazards and risks.[44] This general principle translates into specific obligations for EFSA. In particular, Article 23(j) requires that it shall 'ensure that the public and interested parties receive rapid, reliable, objective and comprehensible information in the fields within its mission'.[45] Not only does the transparency requirement benefit consumers in that it ensures that they are confident in existing food risk assessment mechanism, but it also strengthens EFSA's relationship with food operators – who clearly are 'interested parties' within the meaning of Regulation (EC) No 178/2002 – particularly when they apply for an authorisation to use food claims.

Transparency towards Food Operators EFSA has developed a good working relationship with food operators, in accordance with Article 42 of Regulation (EC) No 178/2002,[46] via the intermediary of the consultative platform of interested parties created in 2005 which brings together EU-wide stakeholder organisations working in areas related to the food chain.[47] This mechanism of public consultation, which takes the form either of online consultations or of technical meetings, allows food operators inter alia to ask for clarifications relating to the scientific assessment of food claims.

44 H. Muñoz, *Principe de Transparence et Information des Consommateurs dans la Législation Alimentaire Européenne* (San José, Costa Rica: INIDA 2011) (as part of the work of the Lascaux Programme: http://www.droit-aliments-terre.eu/).

45 For a variation on the transparency theme, see also Article 38 entitled 'Transparency' which enumerates the documents which EFSA shall make available to the public without delay as part of its duty to carry out its activities 'with a high level of transparency'.

46 'The Authority shall develop effective contacts with consumer representatives, producer representatives, processors and any other interested parties.'

47 The Platform meets three times per year in plenary meetings and provides a forum for dialogue, exchange of ideas, information and views. For more information, see: http://www.efsa.europa.eu/en/stakeholders/cp.htm.

In the last few years, the dialogue EFSA has established with food operators has intensified, which in turn reinforces the acceptability of its decisions. Thus, the restrictive position which EFSA has adopted on health claims is arguably compensated by a better dialogue with food operators on what is required from them in this field both from a formal and from a substantive point of view. EFSA has published a range of guidance documents and organised scientific meetings. The outcome of this increased interaction has led to the publication of general guidelines on the nature and the standard of proof required by EFSA to exercise its review and determine the accuracy of food claims,[48] as well as guidance on the substantiation of specific types of health claims.[49] In light of the significant costs food operators incur to prepare and present an application to EFSA for the authorisation of a health claim, it is of the utmost importance that they understand: (i) which of the effects invoked EFSA will consider beneficial to health and (ii) what studies or criteria may be relied upon to justify the claim in question.[50]

Transparency towards Consumers EFSA's transparency is a key element to measure the success of the institution. The loss of consumer confidence following the BSE scandal may only be regained if EFSA works openly and independently from external pressure, and is perceived as doing so by consumers. The transparency of EFSA's working practices manifests itself in different ways, both in relation to the appointment of experts[51] and the scientific advice they give.

---

48 Scientific and Technical Guidance for the Preparation and the Presentation of the Application for an Authorisation of Health Claim of the NDA Panel, 6 July 2007: the purpose of this guidance is to assist applicants in preparing and presenting their applications for authorisation of health claims falling under Article 14 of the Regulation 1924/2006. General guidance for stakeholders on the evaluation of Article 13.1, 13.5 and 14 health claims, (2011) *EFSA Journal*, 9(4), 2135.

49 Guidance on gut and immune function (2011) *EFSA Journal*, 9(4), 1984; on antioxidants, oxidative damage and cardiovascular health (2011) *EFSA Journal*, 9(12), 2474; on appetite ratings, weight management, and blood glucose concentrations (2012) *EFSA Journal*, 10(3), 2604; on bone, joints, skin, and oral health, (2012) *EFSA Journal*, 10(5), 2702; on physical performance (2012) *EFSA Journal*, 10(7), 2817; and on functions of the nervous system, including psychological functions, (2012) *EFSA Journal*, 10(7), 2816.

50 Nevertheless, the food industry has expressed concern that the criteria EFSA has upheld are similar to those used for pharmaceuticals, leading some major food operators to stop all health communication: 'Food Industry representatives … find the process of opinions, specifically on health claims and procedures, inefficient, costly and highly bureaucratic and thus entailing a significant burden as well as lacking of clarity and transparency': Ernst & Young, External Evaluation of EFSA – Final Report, September 2012: http://www.efsa.europa.eu/en/keydocs/docs/efsafinalreport.pdf, at p. 43.

51 De Munagorri Rafael, E. and Leclerc, O., Les Apports de la Théorie Juridique à la Délimitation de l'Expertise: Réflexions sur le Lien de Droit: http://halshs.archives-

Firstly, compliance with the principle of transparency allows for the detection of potential conflicts of interests which could affect the independence and impartiality of the experts. EFSA must act 'independently of outside pressures'.[52]

One should note that consumer organisations or other members of civil society which have identified various connections between prominent EFSA members and the food industry have not targeted the NDA Panel as raising particular concerns.[53] Rather, the high percentage of applications for health claims which have been rejected suggests that EFSA has acted independently. Furthermore, in February 2012 when the impartiality of Diana Banati as member and chair of EFSA's Management Board was challenged,[54] EFSA reinforced its rules on the prevention of conflicts of interest, not least the obligation resting on all providers of scientific advice to EFSA to disclose any such conflicts.[55] An independent report published in September 2012 noted the high quality of EFSA's scientific outputs as well as the Agency's culture of transparency and robust systems to ensure impartial scientific advice.[56]

Secondly, compliance with the principle of transparency enables consumers to get acquainted not only with the opinions EFSA delivers but also with the scientific approach it follows. The arguments used to substantiate its opinions are all the more important as the methodology and the reasoning adopted by its experts are likely to influence their content. Science is not neutral, and this is particularly true in the field of nutrition. Even at the risk assessment stage, the consensus which scientific experts express in their opinions reflect choices which derive from the normative process.[57] In a context of scientific uncertainty, the

---

ouvertes.fr/halshs-00538472/en/ 2010.

52 COM(1999) 719 final, at par. 41.

53 See the website of the NGO Corporate Europe Observatory which identified conflicts of interest about the safety of food additives, including aspartame, in September 2011: http://corporateeurope.org/pressreleases/2011/ngos-demand-dismissal-two-efsa-experts-who-failed-declare-food-industry-links. See also the response of Catherine Geslain-Lanéelle, 'I claim with conviction that EFSA is not infiltrated by the industry' ['Je le dis avec force, l'EFSA n'est pas infiltrée par l'industrie'], *Le Monde*, 2 December 2011, p. 10.

54 On the relationship with ILSI, see the Report *Conflicts on the Menu* published in February 2012 by the Corporate Europe Observatory (ou *l'Observatoire Européen des Multinationales*) and Earth Open Source: http://corporateeurope.org/publications/conflicts-menu. See also the letter Catherine Geslain-Lanéelle sent to ILSI on behalf of EFSA on 10 May 2012: http://www.efsa.europa.eu/en/edinterviews/docs/corporateilsi120510.pdf.

55 Decision of the Executive Director implementing EFSA's Policy on Independence and Scientific Decision-Making Processes regarding Declarations of Interests, 21 February 2012. See http://www.efsa.europa.eu/en/topics/topic/independence.htm, as well as Gabbi, S. 'Independent scientific advice: Comparing policies on conflicts of interest in the EU and the US', (2001) 1 *European Journal of Risk Regulation*, 2, at p. 213.

56 Ernst and Young, External Evaluation of EFSA – Final Report, 5 September 2012: http://www.efsa.europa.eu/en/keydocs/docs/efsafinalreport.pdf, at p. 182.

57 Jasanoff, S., *The Fifth Branch – Science Advisers as Policymakers* (Cambridge: Harvard University Press 1994); Truihe-Marengo, E. (ed.), *Preuve Scientifique, Preuve*

level of scientific evidence required corresponds to existing knowledge. However, knowledge is often incomplete, even partial when the food industry has financed the research on which it rests. Determining causation becomes extremely complex and the path leading from knowledge to decision requires that a range of choices be made. The publication of opinions and their substantiation therefore allows for the identification of these 'negotiated' elements of the process. This is all the more so as minority opinions are also communicated to the public.[58]

The establishment of dietary reference values clearly illustrates this notion of relativity of scientific truth. The outcome of the public consultation on the draft opinion of the NDA Panel on principles for deriving and applying dietary reference values[59] shows how significant selecting one criterion over another may be.[60] Depending on whether one chooses an evaluation based on Population Reference Intake (PRI) or an evaluation based on Average Requirement (AR), the assessment of the dietary intake will vary. The PRI indicates the level of nutrient intake that is adequate for virtually all people in a population group; as such, it tends to overestimate the needs of the overall population to ensure that its needs for certain nutrients are satisfied. By contrast, the AR combines a statistical approach applicable to certain segments of the population with an analysis of actual under- or over-consumption of certain nutrients, whilst offering a personalised support to populations suffering from a risk of under- or over-nutrition.[61] This explains why consumers should be able to identify the scientific criteria on which EFSA relies: they influence the recommended intakes in macro- and micro-nutrients and are likely to modify significantly the political decisions which are taken in relation to food-based dietary guidelines, nutrient profiles and food claims.

In determining the method and the evidence required, EFSA's scientific experts are also strongly influenced by cultural considerations pertaining to the food models they are familiar with. Some authors have highlighted the influence that a food model, be it Latin or Anglo-American,[62] has on the scientific choices

---

Juridique (Brussels: Larcier 2012) at p. 17.

58 Article 38(b) of Regulation 178/2002.

59 (2010) 8(5) *EFSA Journal*, 1504.

60 See also the Scientific Opinion on Principles for Deriving and Applying Dietary Reference Values, 2010 8(3) *EFSA Journal*, 1458: 'in defining nutrient requirements the selection of criteria to establish nutrient adequacy is an important step' (at p. 2).

61 Martin, A. 'Les apports nutritionnels conseillés (ANC) – un modèle alimentaire scientifique?', in Poulain, J.P. (ed.), *Dictionnaire des cultures alimentaires* (Paris: Presses Universitaires de France 2012).

62 Fischler, C. and Masson, E. (eds), *Manger: Français, Européens et Américains face à l'alimentation* (Paris: Editions Odile Jacob 2008). See also Rozin, P., Fischler, C., Imada, S. et al., 'Attitudes to food and the role of food in life in the USA, Japan, Flemish Belgium and France: Possible implications for the diet health debate' (1999) *Appetite*, 33, 163.

confronting them.[63] Any attempt to separate the analysis of the nutrient content from the analysis of the foods and food model is unavoidably artificial. In this field, a complex mutual relationship exists between the choice of scientific data by an expert and the reference food model he uses, depending on whether he is influenced by a Latin or an Anglo-American approach to food. Apart from the transparency requirement, this confusion may also render the definition of EFSA's role in the field of nutrition much more difficult and contentious.

A Role which Remains to Be Clearly Defined

EFSA's expertise helps support the decisions whose main objective is to contribute to the discovery of relevant technical and scientific data in the definition of EU and national nutrition policies. One of EFSA's main tasks is to define the dietary reference values to identify and address any deficiencies in key nutrients. As a result of better nutrition knowledge, the objectives of protecting and promoting public health work in tandem: the definition of the levels of nutrients required to optimise the normal functions of the organism enables a reduction of the risk of occurrence of certain illnesses resulting from nutrition deficiencies. The definition of nutrient profiles and scientifically supported food claims complete the picture: they constrain the nutrition communication strategies that food operators have put in place. In performing all these tasks, the NDA Panel must focus on the *nutrient* to define the optimum quantity and its role in the proper functioning of the organism. Defining a good *diet* is the responsibility of policy makers who bear the primary responsibility to influence food choices to protect the health and the security of consumers.[64]

The Influence of the Food Model on the Scientific Methodology Nutrition expertise is characterised by an interaction between nutrition and social norms, and this interaction is reflected in the scientific choices which are made. In a nutshell, one can observe an opposition between 'an Anglo-American and Nordic model which views a given food as a set of nutrients whose quantities will vary and

63 For example, see the lecture delivered by Ambroise Martin on 6 April 2011: http://html5.ens-lyon.fr/Acces/FormaVie/20110406/ambroise_martin/video.html. See also Martin, A. 'Les apports nutritionnels conseillés (ANC) – un modèle alimentaire scientifique?, in Poulain, J.P. (ed.), *Dictionnaire des cultures alimentaires* (Paris: Presses Universitaires de France 2012).

64 This being said, the mutual influences between the risk assessment and the risk management stages of the process further highlight the difficulties involved in drawing a clear line between what should fall within the sphere of the scientific expertise and what should fall within the sphere of the policy making process. There is a vast literature on the separation between risk assessment and risk management; see in particular: Gabbi, S., 'The interaction between risk assessors and risk managers' (2007) EFFL, 3, 126; Alemanno, A., 'The European Food Safety Authority at Five' (2008) EFFL: 1, 8; and Noiville, C., *Du bon gouvernement des risques* (Paris: Presses Universitaires de France 2003), at p. 62.

whose nutrition properties consumers must assess',[65] and 'a Latin model for which a food is part of an overall diet resting on food variety, as well as the pleasure and the conviviality deriving from their consumption'.[66] A close look at its scientific opinions suggests that EFSA arbitrates whether to rely on one or the other model.

For example, in relation to micro-nutrient enrichment, we note a tension between the two approaches, as they rely on different criteria. What is at stake is to determine the dietary reference values which should be relied upon at European level to authorise, or not, the enrichment of food in vitamins and minerals under Regulation (EC) No 1925/2006. The Anglo-American approach (prevalent in the UK, in the USA and in Canada) relies on the PRI criterion and focuses on whether the entirety of the needs of the population are satisfied, even though this means that some individuals will ingest certain micro-nutrients in excess.[67] For food industry operators, this criterion is preferable: it offers more opportunities for the development of a diet based on processed food enriched in vitamins and minerals. By contrast, in France, the AFSSA (the national food safety agency, now the ANSES) underlined that there was no advantages to be gained from exceeding the recommended dietary intakes based on the AR criteria.[68] This analysis rests on the assumption that a balanced diet covers all the average needs of most individuals and that enriching food should only be recommended for certain specific population categories.[69] Vitamin enrichment for the overall population, even below levels raising safety concerns, would not be advantageous on the basis of a cost-benefit analysis. EFSA's opinions reflect these tensions, highlighting how difficult it is to reach a consensus among experts coming from different

---

65 ['un modèle alimentaire anglo-saxon et nordique qui conçoit l'aliment comme un ensemble de nutriments différemment dosés dont il appartient au consommateur d'évaluer l'intérêt diététique'].

66 ['le modèle latin pour lequel l'aliment s'inscrit dans un **équilibre** global fondé sur la variété des produits consommés, le plaisir de leur goût et la convivialité']. See the Report of the French *Sénat* on Nutrition Profiles (n°336), 8 April 2009, at p. 11: http://www.senat.fr/rap/l08–336/l08–336.html.

67 See the lecture delivered by Ambroise Martin: http://html5.ens-lyon.fr/Acces/FormaVie/20110406/ambroise_martin/video.html.

68 See Opinion of 3 July 2009 (avis relatif à l'évaluation des teneurs en vitamines et minéraux des denrées alimentaires enrichies et des compléments alimentaires: synthèse) (Request 2007-SA-0315): 'No data provides any basis for concluding that there is any nutrition advantage to exceed the *apports nutritionnels conseillés* (or French dietary reference values). Thus, the Afssa considers that relying exclusively on safety limits to the detriment of the *apports nutritionnels conseillés* is *neither scientifically coherent nor compatible with the Regulation*' (at p. 2) (our translation and our emphasis).

69 This approach is statistical; if the deficiency is statistically relevant, it is necessary to support the finding by individual clinical studies to identify the population groups affected and focus corrective measures on them (for example, the deficiencies affecting pregnant women).

food cultures. Thus, the NDA Panel stressed that an assessment based on the PRI criterion risked overestimating dietary needs:

> In dietary assessment of groups the Average Requirement can be used to estimate the prevalence of inadequate intakes of micronutrients (the Average Requirement cut-point method), if the distribution of nutrient intakes is normal, and intakes are independent from requirements. The Population Reference Intake should not be used for this purpose as this would result in overestimation of the proportion of the group at risk of inadequacy.[70]

The Panel nonetheless tampered its concerns:

> For nutrients such as vitamins, minerals, and protein, the PRI can be a practical starting point. However, target median intakes higher than the Population Reference Intake might be considered, especially in case of a skewed intake distribution.[71]

These statements clearly illustrate that scientific choices are not neutral and that the emphasis is moving from the policy makers to the scientific experts even though the aim is to agree on the methods and the criteria to be used for dietary reference values.

For a Multidisciplinary Approach in Support of a European Nutrition Policy If science is not neutral, it also needs to be complemented by other types of analyses to fully account for the complexity of the policy-making process.[72] The 'incompleteness' of science is particularly obvious when one considers the highly politicized issue of nutrition profiling.[73]

The establishment of nutrient profiles requires the combination of a quantitative with a qualitative nutrition analysis, and the inclusion of this analysis within an overall vision of what a balanced diet entails. The notion of nutrient profile rests on the idea that it is possible to assess whether or not a given food favours a

70 'Scientific Opinion on the Principles for Deriving and Applying Dietary Reference Values' (2010) *EFSA Journal*, 8(3), 1458, at p. 3.

71 Ibid.

72 Jasanoff, S. (ed.), *States of Knowledge: The Co-Production of Science and the Social Order* (International Library of Sociology 2004); Jasanoff, S., *Science and Public Reason* (Routledge 2012); Wynne, B., *Rationality and Ritual* (Routledge 2010).

73 This example is not isolated in EU food law: see also the ongoing debates on GMOs, Friant-Perrot, M., 'The European Union regulatory regime for genetically modified organisms and its integration into Community food law and policy', in Bodiguel, L. and Cardwell, M., *The Regulation of Genetically Modified Organisms – Comparative Approaches* (Oxford: Oxford University Press 2012), at p. 79; Hermitte, M.A., 'L'administration de la preuve scientifique dans les dispositifs juridiques', in Truilhé-Marengo, E., 2012, *Preuve Scientifique, Preuve Juridique* (Brussels: Larcier 2012) at p. 97.

balanced diet depending on its specific characteristics. Recital 11 of Regulation 1924/2006 thus provides that '[t]he application of nutrient profiles as a criterion would aim to avoid a situation where nutrition or health claims mask the overall nutritional status of a food product, which could mislead consumers when trying to make healthy choices in the context of a balanced diet'. When classifying food on the basis of their ability to bear nutrition or health claims, the most important scientific criterion relied upon is whether this food could have a negative impact on the overall diet. However, to avoid a reductionist and utilitarian approach, which would reduce diets to a mere sum of nutrients, Recital 12 of the Regulation adds that '[w]hen setting the nutrient profiles, the different categories of foods and the place and role of these foods in the overall diet should be taken into account and due regard should be given to the various dietary habits and consumption patterns existing in the Member States'. This precision complements scientific with social data (cultural, religious, symbolic ...) as diets cannot be reduced to their sole nutrition function.[74] The reliance on expert reports considered to be of secondary circle (that is, from social and human sciences as opposed to hard sciences) could therefore be necessary to establish nutrient profiles. Regulation 1924/2006 provides for the extension of the scope of the assessment of experts in Recital 30: '[i]n some cases, scientific risk assessment alone cannot provide all the information on which a risk management decision should be based. Other legitimate factors relevant to the matter under consideration should therefore be taken into account'. A multidisciplinary approach, including the inputs of anthropologists, sociologists, economists ... offers the advantage of acknowledging the complexity of national food cultures.

The establishment of food-based dietary guidelines similarly illustrates the need to pay attention to a broad range of considerations alongside health considerations for the risk analysis.[75] As EFSA has indicated, 'foods and diets have cultural, ethnic, social and family aspects that individual nutrients themselves do not have ... there are wide disparities in dietary/cultural habits and the availability of food products between European Member States'.[76] For example, 'the Portuguese food consumption pattern is characterised by a high availability of plant foods and fish and a relatively low availability of animal fat and animal food products', whereas 'the French pattern is characterised by a

74 In its Opinion of 2008, EFSA explained: 'the setting of nutrient profiles is an exercise that should take into account dietary recommendations, public health considerations, generally accepted scientific evidence relative to the relationship between diet, nutrition and health as well as other considerations of an industrial/commercial, cultural and dietary/ culinary nature. Profiles should also, however, permit product innovation and should take into account the variability of dietary habits and traditions and the fact that dietary changes take time.'

75 'Scientific Opinion on Establishing Food-Based Dietary Guidelines' (2010) *EFSA Journal*, 8(3), 1460.

76 Ibid., at p. 26.

high availability of animal products'.[77] Thus, if 'food-based dietary guidelines constitute science-based policy recommendations in the form of guidelines for healthy eating', 'they are primarily intended for consumer information and education, and as such, they should be appropriate for the region or country, culturally acceptable and practical to implement'. Thus, EFSA has underlined the importance of taking into account 'psycho-social factors, cultural practices and economical and environmental considerations' when establishing food-based dietary guidelines.[78]

These remarks raise the broader question of the contribution which social sciences can make to risk analysis. If legitimate considerations other than scientific considerations (social acceptability, economic cost ...) must be taken into account at the risk management phase of the process, this does not necessarily mean that these other factors fall outside the area of expertise. They must, however, rest on a scientific approach to identify and define all the elements which can be recognised as verifiable and/or measurable (economic situation, religious prohibition, legal principle ...).[79] Thus, some Member States consider that in relation to food[80] or for other specific issues (biotechnologies and food ...)[81] a socioeconomic analysis is such as to complement scientific expertise and therefore informs the subsequent risk management decisions which may be made. At EU level, the European Group on Ethics in Science and New Technologies also extends the assessment process to considerations falling outside the scope of hard sciences.[82]

As far as nutrition is concerned, it is difficult to envisage a nutrition policy without the assistance of second-circle experts in the assessment of its economic impact (costs for food operators (reformulation ...), as well as the affordability and the social accessibility of foods for consumers).[83] To both clarify the role of

77 Ibid., at p. 9.

78 Ibid., at p. 20.

79 Conseil National de l'Alimentation, Opinion 22, *Place de la science et des autres considérations dans les décisions nationales et internationales en matière de politique de l'alimentation*, 1999.

80 See for example the Social Science Research Committee of the UK Food Standards Agency. Thus, fruit and vegetable consumption (which offers important nutritional benefits) varies considerably among countries, in large part reflecting the prevailing economic, cultural and agricultural environments.

81 See for example the French *Haut Conseil des Biotechnologies* which comprises two independent committees: one scientific committee and one economic, social and ethics council.

82 http://ec.europa.eu/bepa/european-group-ethics/index_en.htm. Their contribution has proven essential in the debate on the introduction in food of products derived from animal cloning: European Group on Ethics in Science and New Technologies, *Ethical Aspects of animal cloning for food supply*, Opinion 23, 16 January 2008.

83 For example, fruit and vegetable consumption (which is nutritionally recommended) varies considerably from one Member State to the other, reflecting in large part the prevailing economic, cultural and agricultural environments.

the NDA Panel and limit its expertise to scientific assessments, we could perhaps envisage the establishment of a specific committee with expertise in social sciences which would be distinguishable from EFSA and whose independence from the Commission would be guaranteed. Nutrition policies, and this is particularly true for the development of effective obesity prevention strategies, do require a multidisciplinary approach. Let us remember that food choices are 'total social facts'.[84]

---

84 Mauss, M., 'Essai sur le Don. Forme et Raison de l'Échange dans les Sociétés Archaïques', (1925) *L'Année Sociologique, nouvelle série* 1, 30–186.

Section 3: Scientific Communication

Chapter 9
EFSA's Communication Strategy: A Critical Appraisal

Raymond O'Rourke

Introduction

The European Food Safety Authority (EFSA) was established in the aftermath of the BSE and Belgian Dioxin food crises. A major debate took place at European and Member State level due to the lack of consumer trust in the 'food safety' governance of the food chain. These food scares undermined the faith in 'old' forms of governance that many consumers perceived as being unable to ensure food safety. Romano Prodi, the new Commission President in his first policy speech to the European Parliament in July 1999, stated that enhancing food safety would be one of the main priorities of his tenure at the Commission and suggested the establishment of a 'European FDA'. The European Parliament had advocated the creation of a similar authority some years previously in a parliamentary report by an Irish MEP, Tom Raftery. A previous Italian Commissioner, Emma Bonino had also advocated the establishment of a European FDA.

The outcome of this food safety debate was a Green Paper on Food Law (1997), a Communication on Consumer Health and Food Safety (1997), a White Paper on Food Safety (2000) followed by EP and Council Regulation 178/2002 introducing General Principles of European Food Law, re-orientating the Rapid Alert System for Food and Feed Products and the establishment of the EFSA. It is important for readers to understand that EFSA was established in the light of a major policy debate on governance structures related to food safety. This point will impinge substantially on my conclusions relating to how I argue EFSA has dealt with the issue of risk communication under its mandate.

While much commentary on the structure of EFSA begins with the White Paper, a major issue was decided in the Communication on Consumer Health and Food Safety (1997) that has a fundamental bearing on the role of EFSA in the EU governance structure for food safety. The Communication established the principle of the separation between risk assessment and risk management roles. Responsibility for legislation should be separated from that for both scientific assessment and food inspections. Regulation 178/2002 put this separation of functions into law and established that the risk analysis approach to food safety is a fundamental tenet of European Food Law.

The risk analysis framework is comprised of three interrelated but 'theoretically' functionally separated components: *risk assessment, risk management* and *risk communication.* The process of *risk assessment* has been defined by Codex Alimentarius as being a scientifically based process consisting of hazard identification, hazard characterisation, exposure assessment and risk characterisation. The Regulation requires that *risk assessment* be undertaken in an independent, objective and transparent manner based on the best available science. Against that, *risk management* is defined as the process of weighing policy alternatives in the light of the results of risk assessment and if required, selecting the appropriate actions necessary to prevent reduce or eliminate the risk to human health/food safety. Such actions will include food inspection control options and the possible adoption of specific regulatory measures. *Risk communication* is defined as the interactive exchange of information and opinions concerning 'risk' and 'risk management policy & decisions' amongst risk assessors, risk managers, consumers and other interested stakeholders.

In the past the framework in which the practice of risk analysis has been contained assumed that risk communication is shaped by, and results from, risk management, which, in turn, is informed by the outcome of risk assessments. More recent FAO/WHO studies have assumed some integration between the three elements. Lord Philips's BSE Inquiry highlighted that in the operation of the risk analysis framework in the UK, the fundamental importance of risk communication was ignored or at least played a minor role to that of risk assessment and risk management. The UK authorities wrongly declared [risk communication] that there was no risk to public health from eating beef. The Report states that UK Ministers were too preoccupied with preventing a panic reaction to BSE despite warnings from scientists for a number of years. When they finally did communicate with the public their concerns, consumers lost all faith in the risk analysis model as enacted by the UK authorities since the 'degree of risk' had not been communicated to consumers, rather the communication message had been that there was 'no risk'. By avoiding communicating 'risk' to consumers, the UK authorities inadvertently created the very panic reaction they had been hoping to avoid.

The integration of the three elements of the risk analysis model is therefore fundamental to proper functioning of the model, reflecting the importance of developing a dialogue on food safety between key stakeholders (including consumers), the various different actors in the food chain, risk assessors and risk managers. It has been argued that public trust in food safety is instilled by the functional separation of the risk analysis components in particular risk assessment and risk management. In practice the distinction between these components may be less clear cut because it is seldom possible to obtain risk assessments that are free of value-laden or political judgements and in addition often the same individuals in regulatory institutions may have responsibility for both risk assessment and risk management functions. The policy decision to advocate the functional and in some cases the structural separation of risk assessment and risk management as a means of enhancing public trust in the food safety governance structure is fundamental to the establishment EFSA. This was reflected in the risk analysis model established by EP and Council Regulation 178/2002 and within which EFSA would operate in the future. That structure I believe has had a profound effect on EFSA's risk communication function for better and worse.

The White Paper on Food Safety called for the creation of a new scientific body charged with providing independent and objective advice on food safety issues associated with the food chain. The objective of the body would be to '*contribute to a high level of consumer health protection in the area of food safety, through which consumer confidence can be restored and maintained*'.

EP and Council Regulation 178/2002 which established EFSA provides the Authority (Article 23) with the right to communicate on its own initiative and independent from the political process its own conclusions on matters within its mission. The Regulation specifies that EFSA will undertake its risk communication role in close collaboration with the European Commission and the Member States in order to promote necessary coherence and will do so without prejudice to the Commission's own competence to communicate its risk management decisions.

The Authority (Article 40) can communicate on its own initiative in the fields within its mission without prejudice to the Commission's competence to communicate risk management decisions.

EFSA is to act in close collaboration with the Commission and Member States to promote the necessary coherence in the risk communication process.

In addition, at the request of the Commission, EFSA shall provide assistance concerning communication on nutritional issues within the framework of the EU health programme (Article 22. (5)).

EFSA provides scientific support to the European Commission over food scares and in emergency situations, including drawing up a general plan for crisis management and participating in the work of a Crisis Unit established under Article 56 to deal with a major EU-wide food scare.

While EFSA has a legal obligation to work in coordination with the competent national authorities in Member States, the latter are not obliged by law to coordinate their communications activities with those of EFSA.

EFSA's Communications Strategy

In the early days, EFSA's risk communications role reflected very much the sentiment in Article 40 of EP and Council Regulation 178/2002. Article 40 seems to take the view that risk communication is simply a matter of letting the public have easy access to scientific assessments/reports of the Authority in contrast to the definition of risk communication in Article 3. (13) which understands risk communication to be a more complex and interactive process.

This approach to risk communication changed fundamentally when EFSA published a detailed and specific communications strategy in 2005. The Communications Strategy for 2005–2009 was formally adopted by EFSA's Management Board and set long-term communication objectives outlining how these will be achieved and the measures to be implemented to evaluate success. This strategy has been continued by means of EFSA's Communications Strategy 2010–13.

EFSA's Strategic Plan 2009–13 confirms as a key priority '*to reinforce confidence and trust in EFSA and the EU food safety system through effective risk communications and dialogue with partners and stakeholders*'. Working towards this goal the Communications Strategy 2009–13 builds on past experience, by means of specific consumer and qualitative research carried out amongst EFSA's target audiences. The strategy takes into account changes in organisational vision, strategy and working practices at EFSA. It also responds to future challenges based on various food safety concerns and priorities of EFSA's partners, stakeholders and the general public.

The Communications Strategy sets out the following key priorities:

- Simplicity and Transparency – aiming to increase the relevance and understanding of EFSA communications for key target audiences, e.g. consumers, national food agencies, the food industry.
- Independence – ensure the independence of EFSA's risk assessment advice.
- Visibility and outreach – enhance outreach, in the EU and beyond, by increasing awareness and recognition of EFSA and its role and work as a risk assessor.
- Coherence – further increase the coherence of risk communications across the EU and beyond.
- Dialogue – enhance dialogue with stakeholders and increase their interaction with EFSA.

In support of these priorities, EFSA is implementing its communications activities in key thematic areas thereby increasing their impact and effectiveness.

EFSA's communications strategy focuses on '*influencing the influencers*' and on providing those stakeholders in the food area with the information they require and with messages that can be further adapted and tailored to meet specific stakeholder needs.

The primary targets or recipients of EFSA's scientific advice are those who commission work from the Authority and/or have particular involvement or interest in food and feed safety issues. These include: the European institutions who can task the Authority to carry out scientific work (i.e. European Commission, European Parliament and the Member States); national food safety agencies; stakeholders with a specific interest in the food chain (including industry, consumer organisations, environmental and other NGOs); stakeholders from the scientific community and other audiences with a particular interest in food and feed safety issues (e.g. health professional groups).

The major components and tools of EFSA's Communications Strategy include the following.

Understanding Public Perception of Risk

EFSA continually initiates research to investigate the views of consumers on risk via DG SANCO's Eurobarometer surveys. For example results from the 2010 Eurobarometer on food-related concerns show that scientists and national food safety agencies and EFSA are regarded as trusted sources of information on food safety risks. However, independence is increasingly highlighted as an issue for particular stakeholders especially consumers and opinions are divided regarding the independence of scientific advice provided by EFSA.

In addition to such surveys EFSA in 2005 established an expert Advisory Group on Risk Communications (AGRC), reporting to the Executive Director. Members of this group have a wide range of expertise in risk communications. The Group assists EFSA in the implementation of its mission in respect of risk communications.

EFSA's Public Announcements

All opinions adopted by EFSA's Scientific Committee and Panels are published on the Authority's website. An Explanatory Note outlining the key findings for a non-technical reader is published along with the detailed Scientific Opinion. In 2011, EFSA provided 658 scientific outputs (Opinions, Guidance Documents, etc.), 58 per cent of which were related to regulated products highlighting the considerable work EFSA has been completing in relation to the Nutrition and Health Claims legislation.

Press statements/releases are drafted for Scientific Opinions considered to be more 'sensitive' and/or of broader public interest and published on the EFSA website. Press briefings are organised for Scientific Opinions where there is a high level of stakeholder and public interest and/or for which there may be more immediate risk management implications.

EFSA in the period 2005–11 has held press briefings on the issues of: semicarbazide and baby foods; GMO risk assessments; trans fatty acids; aspartame; pork dioxin outbreak in Ireland and E. coli outbreak in Germany.

Media Relations

In addition to press releases, EFSA makes available to journalists additional background information and Q&As to further explain complex scientific concepts and technical issues relating to Scientific Opinions. The EFSA press office also deals with ongoing media queries to the Authority on a daily basis. It has also established agreed guiding principles between the Authority and the Scientific Committee and Panels and their working groups on handling media relations related to the communication of EFSA's scientific advice. These reflect EFSA's general commitment to openness, independence, the clear communication of scientific findings and the provision of backup support to the members of the Scientific Committee and Panels.

In 2011, EFSA produced 78 press releases, as against 75 in 2010 – supporting approximately 35 per cent of EFSA scientific outputs (Opinions, Guidance Documents, scientific research, etc.) These press releases resulted in around 9,397 media articles throughout the EU, a 13 per cent increase on the figure in 2010.

Web

The EFSA website in 2011 received more than 3.5 million visitors. Subscribers can avail of an EFSA Highlights email service which had 27,993 subscribers in 2011, a thrice-weekly bulletin of latest news and related EFSA information. In that case, for a large percentage of EFSA's dedicated audience the principle experience of EFSA is not through conferences, meetings with staff etc. but rather through the EFSA website. In that case, EFSA continually monitors usage of the website and how the experience can be adapted and improved for specialist and non-specialist audiences in order that the information provided is credible, informative, timely and accessible.

Publications

Beside the numerous Scientific Opinions, press releases, etc., published every year EFSA publishes a number of corporate publications. In 2011, EFSA produced 125 publications which included: an Annual Report and Summary; a bimonthly newsletter (EFSA News); a corporate brochure presenting the Authority, its remit, organisation and work; and fact sheets on key themes related to EFSA and its development.

A growing number of ad-hoc scientific documents are being published by EFSA in addition to Scientific Opinions – these have included numerous guidance documents on risk assessments in particular relating to the Nutrition and Health Claims legislation, as well as a series of publications relating to EFSA Scientific Colloquia and an Annual Community Zoonoses Report.

Collaboration with National Food Safety Authorities

The work of the Advisory Forum Working Group on Risk Communications provides for an exchange of information and aims at promoting better coordination of communications activities between national food safety authorities and EFSA. The group strives to develop best practices in risk communications and share past learning experiences of national food agencies relating to risk communications particularly in a crisis situation.

In 2009, EFSA also implemented an international strategy recognising international cooperation in risk communications as key to building coherence in an increasingly global communications environment. EFSA has established cooperation agreements with the US Food and Drug Administration, the Food Safety Commission of Japan and is liaising closely with agencies outside the EU, e.g. Australia/New Zealand, Canada as well as with international organisations, e.g. WHO. FAO, OIE, OECD.

Review of EFSA's Communications Strategy

There is little doubt that EFSA has sufficiently established its risk communication and the Authority is seen as an independent and trusted voice on food safety matters. Its Scientific Opinions, publications, Website, Expert and Advisory Groups have all assisted in making EFSA a good communicator with a significant output of information for reference by EU institutions, Member States and stakeholders. On the other hand the Communications budget is limited as against other tasks completed by the Authority amounting to €7.9 m or 10.64 per cent of EFSA's Budget in 2010.

Yet since EFSA was established in the wake of two major food crisis – BSE and the Belgian dioxin outbreak – it is therefore imperative to assess how its risk communications strategy has worked in relation to major food crisis during the period 2005–12. Only by assessing its risk communications activities in crisis situations can we ascertain if the Authority has fulfilled the role assigned for it by the framers of the White Paper on Food Safety (2000) and EP and Council Regulation 178/2002. I propose to look at four case studies in order to constitute this assessment.

Case Studies

Semicarbazide and Baby Foods (2003)

Semicarbazide is a chemical substance which has been found at times in foods packed in glass jars with metal lids sealed with plastic (PVC) gaskets, like those utilised for baby foods.

In July 2003, EFSA was informed by the food industry that the presence of semicarbazide had been found in routine analytical monitoring carried out by a number of food manufacturers.

The presence of semicarbazide was not linked to any particular foodstuffs but rather to the form of packaging. Many foodstuffs utilise such packaging (e.g. fruit juices, jams and conserves honey, pickles, mayonnaise, sauces, ketchups and bay foods) but in particular initial concerns were highlighted regarding the possible carcinogenic effects of semicarbazide and baby foods. The origin of the semicarbarzide was traced to the breakdown of azodicarbonamide, the foaming agent in the plastic gaskets that are used to seal metal lids to glass jar packaging. The food industry informed EFSA of its intention to develop gaskets using an alternative foaming agent.

In response to the information from the food industry, EFSA convened an ad-hoc expert group meeting of the Scientific Panel on Food Additives, Flavourings, Food Processing Aids and Material in Contact with Food (AFC) on 23 July 2003 in order to review all the available data and scientific information on semicarbazide. An initial preliminary advice document was prepared on the subject prior to a full-scale risk assessment.

The full-scale risk assessment needed to take into account the particular concerns about baby foods so the AFC Panel met on a number of occasions in late September/early October. Following consultation with other EFSA scientists and taking into account nutritional and microbiological considerations, the Authority provided an update in October 2003 on semicarbazide in foods especially baby foods and its implications for human health.

EFSA held a press briefing on the topic, with the participation of the Chair of the AFC Panel, Dr Sue Barlow, in order to communicate its findings and facilitate a better understanding of any possible implications for human health. The risk assessment recommended that it would be prudent to reduce exposure to semicarbazide and this could be best done changing the packaging for such foodstuffs. EFSA's scientific experts informed the public that there was very limited exposure to semicarbazide when utilising such packaged foodstuffs and that therefore the risk to human health was 'very low'.

On the question of a cancer risk, the assessment stated that there was no definitive research proving that semicarbazide was a genotoxic carcinogen but EFSA agreed to continue to monitor the situation and advise consumers if there was need to change this advice.

In terms of possible risk management decisions, EFSA recommended to the European Commission that they should put in place a programme to ensure that semicarbazide would ultimately no longer be found in the sealing gaskets of glass jars utilised for the packaging of various foodstuffs, in particular baby foods.

EFSA's risk assessment and recommendations regarding semicarbazide and glass jar packaging published on 15 October 2013, was published at the same time by various different national food agencies in different Member States, e.g. Afssa (France); BfR (Germay); FSAI (Ireland); FSA (UK); NSAF (Finland); VWA (Netherlands). Other Member States or National Food Agencies chose not to publish any information on the topic and EFSA's risk assessment, considering that semicarbazide represented a very small potential human health risk and for fear of thereby drawing unwarranted public attention to the issue.

EFSA's risk assessment on semicarbazide was given great prominence in European media in October 2013. Media analysis showed that generally the media approach to the issue was balanced and factual. Although some comment in the UK media was alarmist reflecting a specific style of journalism and the outcome of the BSE crisis.

The issue ceased to be topical after the EFSA risk assessment in October 2003. EFSA's Scientific Panels carried out further reviews of the issue and assessed the possible human health risks associated with levels of semicarbazide found in various foodstuffs. The AFC Panel provided a new risk assessment on the issue in July 2005, highlighting that that semicarbazide was not a carcinogenic risk given the levels of the substance found in foodstuffs packaged in glass jars in 2003 and 2004. In addition, the adoption of EC Directive 2004/1/EC banning the use of azodicarbonamide in plastics used as food contact materials would eliminate this source of semicarbazide in foodstuffs. This legislation was proposed in the original EFSA risk assessment in October 2003.

Aspartame Scare (2005)

Aspartame even today remains a highly controversial sweetener used by the food industry and which is thought by many consumer/public health groups to have possible carcinogenic effects.

In 2005, the Ramazzini Foundation [European Foundation of Oncology and Environmental Sciences] published initial findings of a study that concluded that aspartame caused cancer in laboratory animals, which was taken up by European media with headlines such as '*Cancer linked to sweetener*'. In the media frenzy there were calls for Member States and the European Union to ban the use of aspartame as a sweetener in all foodstuffs.

Initially in April and June 2005, the Ramazzini Foundation made short presentations of their findings to the Italian Ministry of Health, EFSA and other global stakeholders. On 11 July 2005, the Foundation held a press conference announcing the results of their study on aspartame consumption and the link with cancer – the study consisted of 8 years of research involving 1,800 rats, 34,000 slides and costing approximately €1m.

Following the press conference, EFSA put out a press statement advising the public that it would immediately undertake its own evaluation of the important Ramazzini Foundation study when it obtained the research data.

The International Sweeteners Association (ISA) and other industry groups in response to the Ramazzini Foundation press release stated that there was no link between aspartame consumption and cancer. The Ramazzini Foundation informed interested parties that their findings would be published in a forthcoming issue of the *European Journal of Oncology*.

The aspartame issue was highlighted extensively by the European media due to the contested regulatory history of aspartame, the scientific reputation of the Ramazzini Foundation and the decision by EFSA to publish a press release at the same time signalling the possible international importance of the research findings.

In the period July–November 2005, EFSA sought access to the research data of this study in order to begin its own risk assessment on aspartame. In an unprecedented move, EFSA issued a press release on 29 November 2005 urging the Ramazzini Foundation to provide the Authority with this data.

The Foundation in response confirmed EFSA would receive the full 900-page research study, but when EFSA obtained a copy of the study it did not contain any of the 34,000 slides fundamental to the research. The Ramazzini Foundation stated the slides were not available to EFSA as it did not think it appropriate for such data to be open to third-party review. Despite various interactions between EFSA and the Ramazzini Foundation in the period January–May 2006, EFSA was still not provided with the full data on the aspartame research.

On 5 May 2006, EFSA held a press conference in Rome summarising its Scientific Opinion on the aspartame research undertaken by the Ramazzini Foundation. The press release stated that EFSA concluded that '*based on all the available data to date there is no reason to further review the previous scientific opinion on the safety of aspartame*'. In response the Ramazzini Foundation attacked EFSA's opinion and continued to state that aspartame was potentially carcinogenic.

The issue was further highlighted in 2007 when the results of a second aspartame study by the Ramazzini Foundation was published in *Environmental Health Perspectives* but as before the Foundation refused to share the research data with EFSA or other authorities in the USA or Canada.

EFSA Scientific Panels have continued to issue advice on new scientific studies or research relating to aspartame in 2006, 2009 and 2011. The Authority continues to take the view that the new scientific data has not been sufficient to change its safety evaluation of aspartame for use as a sweetener in foodstuffs.

Irish Pork Contamination (2008)

On 19 November 2008 routine sampling of pork fat from slaughtered pigs indicated the presence of dioxin or PCBs. These initial results were communicated to the Food Safety Authority of Ireland (FSAI). Sampling was then done on the animal feed used on the pig farm detected as having high levels of dioxins.

Dried bread fed to pigs was found to be the source of the dioxin – the feed contamination was caused by the use of recycled mineral oil as fuel in the direct flame drying of food waste during the processing of animal feed.

By 4 December the authorities had identified all the pig and cattle farms which had received the contaminated animal feed – 10 pig farms and 38 cattle farms. On the same day a joint Department of Agriculture and Food and FSAI press release announced restrictions on all these farms due to the detection of dioxin contaminated animal feed. The following day the Dutch food safety authority informed the Irish authorities they were investigating dioxin contamination of pork which was Irish in origin. With this information, the Irish authorities immediately informed the EU's Rapid Alert System for Food and Feed (RASFF) of the potential EU-wide implications of this dioxin contamination in Ireland.

On 6 December when Irish and Dutch samples tested positive for dioxin in the region of 80–200 picograms, well in excess of the 1 picogram permitted by Commission Regulation 1881/2006, the Irish authorities ordered that all Irish pork products from pigs slaughtered after 1 September 2008 should be recalled. The aim of the Irish authorities in implementing a full product recall was to assure consumers about food safety with the added message that a 'short term' exposure to dioxins was not adverse to human health. The product recall for pork was necessitated by the fact that there was not full traceability of pork products – it was not possible to link pork products to specific farms as was the case in relation to cattle.

On 8 December, the EU made a request to EFSA under EP and Council Regulation 178/2002 for an independent risk assessment on the Irish dioxin contamination. EFSA concluded that even in an extreme situation where someone was exposed to dioxin contaminated pork over an extended period, e.g. 90 days, there was no certainty of adverse health effects. The risk assessment in general supported the decision for a full product recall of Irish pork products as a means of stopping any ongoing exposure. EFSA's risk assessment reassured regulators, industry and consumers EU-wide that the correct decisions had been made in the interests of food safety and consumer health.

German E. coli Outbreak (2011)

Between May and June 2011, a serious outbreak of food borne illness causing a number of deaths, took place in Northern Germany due to a specific strain of E. coli. Initially German officials without definitive results of test samples stated that the source of the E. coli strain was linked to organic cucumbers imported from Spain. Subsequently, they stated that instead the Spanish greenhouses located in Andalusia were the source of the E. coli. Both statements were incorrect and tremendous financial damage was done to Spanish vegetable exports.

On June 4, German and EFSA officials examined samples locating the source of the E. coli to a restaurant in Lubeck, Germany. The following day an Agriculture Ministry official advised consumers to stop eating bean sprouts since they had become the latest suspected source of the E. coli outbreak.

This was an example where the Commission and German authorities not only asked for EFSA to provide urgent scientific advice but for the first time, asked EFSA staff to provide technical assistance to support the German authorities. EFSA staff worked alongside officials in the German agencies to help trace the source of the E. coli outbreak.

Later on 29 June a joint EFSA/European Centre for Disease Control and Prevention risk assessment implicated fenugreek seeds imported from Egypt in 2009 and 2010 from which sprouts were grown, as a cause of this E. coli outbreak. The risk assessment cautioned that '*there is still much uncertainty about whether this is truly the common cause of the infections*' as tests on the seeds had not found the exact E. coli strain responsible for the deaths of people in Germany, Austria, Sweden, UK and Denmark.

Following further preventative measures, tests and investigations, the German authorities as of 26 July declared that the E. coli outbreak was finished.

The EFSA/European Centre for Disease Control and Prevention risk assessment notes that the preparation of fresh bean sprouted seeds does not totally eliminate the possibility of bacterial contamination. Equally the fact that sampling and bacteriological methods failed to detect the E. coli strain point to the importance of good production and handling practices for such products, especially with the difficulty of tracing pathogens in seeds.

EFSA released a number of urgent scientific assessments during the E. coli outbreak and post-crisis published a Scientific Opinion on the health risk associated with bean sprouts.

Analysis of Case Studies

In analysing the communications response of EFSA to these four crises it is possible to look at them in pairs – semicarbazide and aspartame and Irish pork contamination and German E. coli outbreak. The crises regarding semicarbazide and aspartame emerged due to industry concerns following scientific tests or in the case of aspartame following a major scientific study. The other two examples came about via tests or scientific evidence obtained by national authorities and which pitted EFSA against Member States.

Semicarbazide and Aspartame

In the cases of semicarbazide and aspartame EFSA reacted quickly and demonstrated that its communications strategy was working effectively. It took the view that in both cases, the best approach was for EFSA itself to undertake a thorough risk assessment of the issue in order to assess the risk and thereby inform stakeholders (Commission, Member States, industry and consumers) of any potential risks.

In the case of semicarbazide many of their recommendations were ultimately taken on board by the European Commission. By reacting so quickly EFSA was able to lower the panic that could have emerged in the media regarding baby foods.

In the case of aspartame EFSA was hampered by the fact that the Ramazzini Foundation refused to provide the Authority with the full research data from its study. By proactively highlighting this EFSA maintained their independence and reputation despite the fact any subsequent risk assessment on aspartame was limited due to this non-cooperation by the Foundation. In essence, whether to ban the use of aspartame was a risk management decision for the European Commission, EFSA by its actions ensured that its scientific assessment was fundamental to any such decision. The issue got media traction due to the reputation of the Ramazzini Foundation and the complex regulatory history of aspartame, but even so EFSA's views were continually articulated in media discussions.

In both cases, EFSA's communications strategy worked effectively as a means of 'influencing the influencers'; demonstrating its independence from the Commission and other stakeholders as it certainly did not get itself aligned with industry lobbies like the ISA; and its messages were clear and coherent allaying possible consumer fears over the linkage made between aspartame or semicarbazide and cancer.

Since both issues were highly scientific EFSA was able to demonstrate its competence and to utilise its powers under Article 23 of EP and Council Regulation to comment independent of the political process or any potential risk management decisions by the European Commission. In many ways, I would suggest that EFSA's independent actions were an immense benefit, indeed I would suggest a 'shield' behind which the Commission and even Member States could hide when confronted with suggestions to recall all foodstuffs sold in glass jar or ban the use of the sweetener aspartame in foodstuffs. The Commission or Member States were able to respond that 'we await the risk assessment of EFSA'

Irish Pork Contamination and German E. coli Outbreak

These two incidents demonstrate a very different communications scenario for EFSA. Both cases involve Member States and the Commission in scenarios like BSE/Belgian Dioxin crisis which were instrumental in the creation of EFSA.

Under EP and Council Regulation 178/2002, EFSA's risk communication role is much more circumspect. The Authority does not have the luxury of utilising Article 23 to give its independent risk assessment of the situation.

Its risk assessments are dependent on obtaining scientific data from the Member State. Yet unlike in the case of aspartame where it can play EFSA scientists against the Foundation scientists, in these cases to take on a Member State would be in opposition to the philosophy established in the Regulation that where there is conflicting scientific assessment between a Member State and EFSA, that the conflict should be ironed-out in a cooperative fashion. In a case of a major food crisis like pork contamination or E. coli there is little time to begin such cooperative procedures. EFSA is dependent on the openness of the Member State and more importantly on the Commission to fight its case with the Member State. In that sense, EFSA is more an on-looker than a participant in the process.

The Irish pork contamination demonstrates the best scenario for EFSA. The Irish authorities cooperated fully with the Commission, utilising the RASFF system and once the Dutch Food Agency had found Irish-origin pork samples that tested positive for dioxin they decided on a full recall of all Irish pork products as the best means of allaying consumer fears. EFSA's role then was to provide a risk assessment to analyse the potential health effects on consumers who may have inadvertently eaten Irish pork products over the previous months. The risk assessment was comprehensive that while the positive samples had very high levels of dioxin, a consumer would have had to have eaten almost on a daily basis for weeks to have had an adverse health effect.

The German E. coli outbreak demonstrates the worst case scenario for EFSA. The German authorities made crazy and unsubstantiated statements as to the source of the E. coli. The Commission sat on the sidelines and never really took the issue seriously in terms of food safety, being diverted into the issue of compensation for Spanish farmers. The outbreak seemed to demonstrate that the lessons of BSE/Belgian dioxin had been forgotten. The Andalusian Agriculture Minister went on television and ate a cucumber to prove to consumers that it was safe. The German authorities in the guise of different Lander and Federal agencies continued to give out mixed messages as to the source of the E. coli. The Commission never sought to take control of the issue and establish a Crisis Unit as was available to it under Regulation 178/2002. While EFSA may highlight in its Annual Activity Report 2011, it was the first occasion when EFSA officials provided technical assistance to Member State authorities, that is a pyrrhic victory for the Authority.

Like the common flu, the E. coli outbreak defused itself out of the general populace so that the German authorities could declare it was finished. They were lucky it was not a more virulent food safety scare as their actions aped those of the UK and Belgian authorities in the past. It seemed they had forgotten the lessons of the BSE and Belgian Dioxin crisis. Unfortunately, EFSA was sidelined since the European Commission failed to prioritise the issue preferring to await actions of the German authorities rather than proactively decide it was a wider issue needing an EU-wide response. Alas, the neutering of EFSA's potential role in this crisis reflected the demarcation made between risk assessment and risk management in the Communication on Consumer Health and Food Safety (1997) and the structure of the Authority established in Regulation 178/2002 where EFSA is dependent on the European Commission in relation to the actions of Member States and conflicting scientific advice.

Conclusions

As it was highlighted in the introduction, there had been considerable debate about establishing a European FDA-type structure in the late 1990s following the BSE and Belgian Dioxin crisis. While Regulation 178/2002 introduced a risk analysis model as the basis for European Food Law, there was considerable pressure from Member States to retain their risk management food control functions. Commissioner David Byrne could argue that the US FDA model would have led to an 'unwarranted dilution of democratic accountability' but the reality was that the Member States were not prepared to share their risk management powers.

Regulation 178/2022 stated clearly that EFSA in the exercise of its tasks including risk communication, should act '*in close cooperation with the competent bodies in the Member States carrying out similar tasks to those of the Authority*' [Article 22(7)]. In that case, EFSA, the European Commission and the Member States must cooperate in order to ensure effective coherence between risk assessment, risk management and risk communication functions.

Additionally, in the case of risk communication it is mandated to work in close collaboration with the Commission and the Member States '*to promote the necessary coherence in the risk communications process*' [Article 40].

EFSA has done well in 10 years communicating risk when it has not been a case of shared competence. Semicarbazide and aspartame demonstrate that the Communications Strategy the Authority adopted in 2005 was robust enough to take on a potentially difficult issue like semicarbazide with linkages to baby foods and cancer. Equally, in the case of aspartame EFSA defended its position well against a formidable scientific body like the Ramazzini Foundation.

Yet it is in the case of food crises such as the Irish Pork contamination and the German E. coli outbreak where the limitations placed upon its risk communication mandate in Regulation 178/2002 can be seen to be a hindrance. In the Irish case, a cooperative Member State meant there was coherence in the risk communication message provided for consumers on this issue. In the case of the German E. coli outbreak, we saw all the mistakes of BSE/Belgian dioxin re-enacted once again, leaving EFSA in a limbo area between the Commission and the German authorities. EFSA's position was not helped by a European Commission reluctant to take on powers granted to it under Regulation 178/2002 to establish plans for crisis management of an EU-wide food scare.

Transparency and credibility are inextricably linked with both risk assessment and risk management decisions. EFSA has from its beginnings always aimed at the highest transparency standards. Credibility is a more difficult concept to define but in the context of the food governance area it consists of three components: credibility of data; credibility of the risk assessment process and credibility of the resulting decision-making process.

Using this framework when analysing the German E. coli outbreak it is clear that there were credibility problems with the data since the German authorities made decisions before having complete scientific data. This undermined EFSA's risk assessment and meant the ensuing decisions of the European Commission or German or Spanish authorities were not seen as credible. Credibility lost cannot be regained. In the absence of a clearly communicated risk management decision process then criticism can often fall back on the more transparent risk assessment process. Unfortunately that is the situation that occurred for EFSA in the case of the German E. coli outbreak. Since the European Commission refused to take control of the situation, mixed messages were communicated in Germany, Spain and other Member States. With EFSA 10 years old it may be time again to review the risk communications role provided to the Authority in Regulation 178/2002 and establish a structured template for the role and responsibilities of all parties [Commission, Member States and EFSA] in the case of EU-wide food emergencies/scares.

Chapter 10
EFSA Stakeholder and Public Involvement Policy and Practice: A Risk Governance Perspective

Marion Dreyer and Ortwin Renn

Introduction

Since the second half of the 1990s, stakeholder involvement in the regulation of health and environmental risks has gained momentum in Europe. This is in large part due to increased public awareness of such risks, growing demands of civil society to have a voice in the risk handling process, and the explicit acknowledgement of scholars and policy makers alike that both facts and values play a role in all types of risk decisions. Revised EU regulatory frameworks such as those for chemicals control,[1] safe use of biotechnology in agriculture,[2] and food safety[3] offer new possibilities for interested individuals and socially organised groups to scrutinise relevant parts of the risk decision process and provide an input into the process. This can be highlighted by the following quote pointing to:

> the gradual opening up of public expert institutions to societal engagement practices in order to meet societal demands for reliable, unbiased and transparent information and an active role of citizens in the construction of knowledge, in particular in the field of risks and environmental issues.[4]

---

1 Renn, O. and Elliott, E.D., 'Chemicals' In: Wiener, J.B., Rogers, M.D., Hammitt, J.K. and Sand, P.H. (eds), *The Reality of Precaution: Comparing Risk Regulation in the United States and Europe* (London: Earthscan 2011), pp. 223–56; Heyvaert, V., 'The EU chemicals policy: Towards inclusive governance?' In: Vos, E. (ed.), *European Risk Governance: Its Science, its Inclusiveness and its Effectiveness* (Connex Report Series No. 6. Mannheim: University of Mannheim 2008), pp. 185–221.

2 Steffek, J. and Ferretti, M.P., 'Accountability or 'good decisions"? The competing goals of civil society participation in international governance' (2009) 23(1) *Global Society*, 37–57.

3 Dreyer, M. and Renn, O. (eds), *Food Safety Governance: Integrating Science, Precaution and Public Involvement* (Berlin, Heidelberg: Springer 2009a).

4 Hériard-Dubreuil, G. and Baudé, S., 'Innovative approaches to stakeholder involvement in risk governance: Lessons from TRUSTNET IN ACTION European research project' In: Vos, E. (ed.), *European Risk Governance: Its Science, its Inclusiveness*

The focus of this chapter is on the role of stakeholder and public involvement in the EU level food safety governance. The Directorate General Health and Consumers (DG SANCO), the food risk management authority at EU level, has promoted this trend towards more open governance since the late 1990s. This is also true for EFSA, the scientific expert body responsible for risk assessment since its establishment in 2002. EFSA has the dual role of both risk assessor and risk communicator. Its mandate is to provide the European Commission, the Member States and the European Parliament with independent, high quality scientific advice *and* to communicate about its findings. It has adopted a set of mechanisms of stakeholder and public involvement. The opening up of the scientific advice producing process to non-scientists – albeit in a clearly limited manner – is a true procedural innovation in the regulation of food safety at EU level. Prior to the 'BSE-turning point', this process was the exclusive domain of scientific experts and lobbyists, forming a 'black box' to all those not directly involved in the process.[5]

This trend towards more inclusive governance is for instance not (or not as clearly) observable in the United States. This observation relates to the field of environmental risk regulation where 'most risk assessors appear still to follow the old expert-dominated risk paradigm, in which the public has little or no voice'.[6] The paper by Shrader-Frechette contrasts this practice with the mandate of the famous 1996 report 'Understanding Risk' of the U.S. National Academy of Sciences[7] that advised agencies to involve the public throughout the entire risk handling process.

Being inclusive does not contrast with EFSA's and the EU Commission's position that risk assessment is essentially a scientific and objective activity. This position is upheld in the European Parliament and Council Regulation 178/2002, widely known and referred to as the 'General Food Law Regulation' (EC 2002),[8] and a prominent view advocated by the responsible authorities. The question of whether EFSA's interaction with stakeholders is compatible with the formal mandate and declared aim of safeguarding the independence of risk assessment has remained a contentious issue since the Authority's inception. Currently, however,

and its Effectiveness (Connex Report Series No. 6. Mannheim: University of Mannheim 2008), pp. 123–52.

5 Millstone, E. and van Zwanenberg, P., 'The evolution of food safety policy-making institutions in the UK, EU and Codex Alimentarius' (2002) *Social Policy and Administration*, 593–609.

6 Shrader-Frechette, K., 'Analyzing public participation in risk analysis: How the wolves of environmental justice hide in the sheep's clothing of science' (2010) 3(4) *Environmental Justice*, 119–23.

7 Stern, P.C. and Fineberg, H.V. (eds), *Understanding Risk: Informing Decisions in a Democratic Society* (National Research Council, Committee on Risk Characterization. Washington, DC: National Academy Press 1996).

8 Here it says: 'In order for there to be confidence in the scientific basis for food law, risk assessment should be undertaken in an independent, objective and transparent manner, on the basis of the available scientific information and data' (EC 2002, Recital 18).

the most prominent issue is not the potential conflict between EFSA's scientific risk assessment mandate and involvement of external stakeholders. Rather a debate has unfolded, instigated by some press coverage and political observers, on whether the independence of EFSA's work is threatened by too close links between the scientific experts and the members of the Management Board (amongst others responsible for appointment of the members of the Scientific Committee and the Scientific Panels) on the one side and industry on the other. This debate has caused EFSA to undertake a new initiative in 2012 and open up its scientific meetings to observers from interested parties. This initiative has been introduced as a means of providing greater insights to the risk assessment process. Indirectly, it has been directed towards re-building trust and towards demonstrating transparency and openness. It is still an open question whether the new EFSA's 'glass house'[9] policy will reach its targeted goals.

In this paper we discuss issues of legitimisation that EFSA faces in regard to its policy on stakeholder and public involvement. We argue that a successful involvement policy requires that EFSA's risk assessment activities are embedded in a multistage risk governance process in which stakeholder involvement in assessment-related activities should serve mainly the purpose of collecting relevant knowledge from stakeholders without being influenced by their evaluations or policies. To develop this argument we draw on a concept of risk governance that distinguishes four main governance stages[10] and is inspired by the idea of an analytic-deliberative process, first developed by the US-Academy of Sciences.[11]

In order to explain the rationales underlying EFSA's stakeholder policy we, firstly, describe the socio-political context within which EFSA had been established and which favoured a positive stance towards interacting with stakeholders (second section). Next, we outline the Authority's stakeholder policy and describe it as supplementary to DG SANCO's stakeholder initiatives (third section). Then, we reflect on the contentious issues in regard to EFSA's stakeholder policy by reference to the multistage IRGC risk governance concept (fourth section).

Stakeholder and Public Involvement in EU Food Risk Governance

By the late 1990s, academics and policy makers alike diagnosed serious problems of legitimacy and transparency in the decision-making processes about food safety

9 EFSA's approach on Public Consultations on scientific outputs, EFSA website at: http://www.efsa.europa.eu/en/keydocs/docs/consultationpolicy.pdf.

10 IRGC (2005). *White Paper on Risk Governance: Towards an Integrative Approach.* Geneva: International Risk Governance Council; Renn, O. and Walker, K. (eds), *Global Risk Governance* (Berlin, Dordrecht: Springer 2008).

11 Stern, P.C. and Fineberg, H.V. (eds), *Understanding Risk: Informing Decisions in a Democratic Society* (National Research Council, Committee on Risk Characterization. Washington, DC: National Academy Press 1996).

in Europe. Two main (interrelated) shortcomings were identified in connection with the management of the series of food scares that had occurred in the 1990s, with the prion disease BSE (Bovine Spongiform Encephalopathy, known as 'mad cow disease') and the human variant CJD (Creutzfeldt-Jakob Disease) as the politically most delicate and contentious issue. First, the scientifically driven process of understanding and characterising food risks and the way in which the outcome of this process was used in decision-making on risk management were criticised as opaque and secretive.[12] Second, there was the widely shared supposition that risk management decision-making was biased towards economic interests – in particular in the BSE case.

These shortcomings were believed to exist in risk decision-making at member state level (in the BSE case it was the UK which was caught in a cross-fire of criticism); but also the European Union was strongly accused of being at fault:

> The Commission was faced with accusations stemming from the [European] Parliament, of being biased towards industrial interests and of giving priority to the objective of achieving the Single Market over public health.[13]

It was a widely expressed concern at the time of the food scares that, as a result of economic globalisation and trade liberalisation, the EU would advance powerful industry interests at the expense of public health and consumer interests. Food safety regulators giving precedence to the goals of economic growth and competitiveness were criticised as being too lax in controlling compliance to food laws and too lenient for fast approvals even when lacking the necessary evidence. Uncertainties were seen as being ignored and public health protection compromised.[14] Further, the public's diverse attitudes and values were not sufficiently recognised and respected in the handling of food safety issues.[15]

These worries were interpreted in European policy circles as manifestations of serious problems of trust and legitimacy. In its White Paper on European

12 Vos, E., 'The EU regulatory system on food safety: Between trust and safety' In: Everson, M. and Vos, E. (eds), *Uncertain Risks Regulated* (Milton Park: Routledge-Cavendish 2009), pp. 249–67.

13 Demortain, D., 'European Agencies. The European Medicines Agency (EMEAI and the European Food Safety Authority (EFSA)' In: Benamouzig, D. and Borraz, O. (eds), *Food and Pharmaceutical Agencies in Europe: Between Bureaucracy and Democracy. Cross-national Perspectives*. A Commented Bibliography (Grenoble: CNRS – Maison des Sciences de l'Homme-Alpes 2007) pp. 15–100.

14 van Zwanenberg, P. and Millstone, E., *BSE: Risk, Science and Governance* (Oxford: Oxford University Press 2005).

15 Hansen, J., Holm, L., Frewer, L.J. and Sandøe, P., 'Beyond the knowledge deficit: Recent research into lay and expert attitudes to food risks' (2003) 41 *Appetite*, 111–21; Vos, E., 'EU food safety regulation in the aftermath of the BSE crisis' (2000) 23(3) *Journal of Consumer Policy*, 227–55.

Governance the Commission[16] even identified the widely perceived failure of the EU to manage food incidents effectively as one of the reasons for rising public misgiving and reticence about EU policies and institutions.[17] One major objective of the thorough reform process to which EU food risk decision-making principles and institutional arrangements were subjected in the wake of the BSE crisis was to restore what had come to be perceived as a most valuable, however, increasingly scarce resource: *public trust* in food safety and those responsible for protecting the public from food safety-related risks.

The core of the reforms at the EU level was the allocation of responsibilities for risk assessment and risk management to separate institutions. This division of responsibilities is codified in the General Food Law Regulation, the EU's overarching legal instrument that the European Parliament and the Council adopted in January 2002 (EC 2002). The stated aim of the 'two-body solution'[18] is to assure the *independence* of science-based food risk assessment. This independence is related to the objective of trust restoration. The European Commission's White Paper on Food Safety had identified scientific advice 'being produced to the highest standards of independence, excellence and transparency'[19] as a basic requirement for consumers' confidence in EU food safety policy.

The EU (and among the member states also very much the UK) also resorted to reforms designed to uphold the *procedural legitimacy*[20] of food safety governance by incorporating or strengthening democratic norms in the process of dealing with food safety issues.[21] Advancement of the *democratic quality* of the governance process forms another major response to the situation of 'contested governance' and

16 Commission of the European Communities, 'European Governance. A White Paper' COM (2001) 428 final, 25 July 2001, Brussels.

17 Vos, E., 'The EU regulatory system on food safety: Between trust and safety' In: Everson, M. and Vos, E. (eds), *Uncertain Risks Regulated* (Milton Park: Routledge-Cavendish 2009) pp. 249–67.

18 Millstone, E., 'Science, risk and governance: Radical rhetorics and realities of reform in food safety governance' (2009) 38 *Research Policy*, 624–36.

19 Commission of the European Communities, 'White Paper on Food Safety', COM (1999) 719 final, 12 January 2000, Brussels.

20 The exposition adopts here the argumentation by Grace Skogstad (2003, p. 324), who suggests in her analysis of GMO regulation in the EU that, 'all strategies to render policies acceptable by virtue of democratising the procedures by which they are arrived at can be viewed as input-oriented legitimation'. While the 'test of appropriateness' under output (or results-based) legitimation standards was the perceived merit of policy outcomes, the merit of this test under input (or procedure-oriented) legitimation standards was the conformity of decision-making procedures with democratic norms of public participation and control (ibid., pp. 324–5).

21 The same holds true for the UK and Germany, and to a lesser extent for France, which have also declared the (re-)establishment of consumer confidence as one objective of their revised food safety policy (cf. Dreyer et al. 2006, p. 57).

the perceived loss of public trust.[22] It is formulated on the website of the European Commission's Directorate General for Health and Consumer Protection (DG SANCO) as follows: 'Transparency of legislation and effective public consultation are essential elements of building this greater [consumer] confidence'.[23]

There are three major modes by which this purpose was served in future food safety policy and regulation:[24]

- by making the risk handling process, including risk assessment,[25] more transparent through wider public documentation;
- by offering more readily comprehensible and process-oriented information on risks to the public at large, specifically addressing major consumer concerns;
- and by providing more and improved opportunities for the consultation of economic and civil society actors in relation to food policy, legislation, and risk assessment and risk management activities.

Hence, the new provisions on food safety were tied up with two main objectives both related to re-building public trust: Strengthening of the expertise and independence of scientific advice and the introduction of more transparency, consumer-oriented risk communication, and stakeholder involvement in the risk handling process.[26]

---

22 Ansell and Vogel refer to the situation of 'both sudden and pervasive loss of trust and legitimacy and an uphill battle to restore it' (2006, p. 20) as 'contested governance' and argue that European food safety regulation over the turn to the new millennium exemplified such a case. Ansell, C. and Vogel, D. (eds), (2006). *What's the Beef?: The Contested Governance of European Food Safety* (Cambridge: MIT Press).

23 DG SANCO website: http://ec.europa.eu/food/food/foodlaw/principles/index_en.htm (accessed on 15 March 2012).

24 Dreyer M., Renn, O., Borkhart, K. and Ortleb, J. (2006), 'Institutional re-arrangements in European food safety governance: A comparative perspective' In: Vos, E. and Wendler, F. (eds), *Food Safety Regulation in Europe: A Comparative Institutional Analysis* (Series Ius Commune. Antwerp and Oxford: Intersentia Publishing), pp. 9–64.

25 EFSA's current practice is to publish scientific opinions as well as the agendas and minutes of meetings and other key documents on its website; the Authority also broadcasts through its website important meetings (including all Management Board meetings) and events (see EFSA's website at: http://www.efsa.europa.eu/en/values/transparency.htm; accessed on 15 March 2012). The Register of Questions database provides information about each request to EFSA including supporting documents and the current status (see EFSA's website at: http://www.efsa.europa.eu/en/request/requests.htm; accessed on 15 March 2012).

26 Vos, E., 'The EU regulatory system on food safety: Between trust and safety' In: Everson, M. and Vos, E. (eds), *Uncertain Risks Regulated* (Milton Park: Routledge-Cavendish 2009) pp. 249–67; Vos, E. and Wendler, F., 'Food safety regulation at the EU level' In: Vos, E. and Wendler, F. (eds), *Food Safety Regulation in Europe: A Comparative*

Reforms of Stakeholder and Public Involvement Policy and Practice

Since the 2002 reform, efforts to involve stakeholders in EU food risk governance have constantly gained weight. These efforts are accompanied by verbal declarations highlighting the value of and the need for connecting with citizens and stakeholders, open dialogue, and understanding and addressing the concerns of stakeholders and consumers. Since the mid 2000s, these declarations present a standard part of the official rhetoric of many European policy makers, regulators and expert advisers. Involvement practice and rhetoric have a legal basis. Public consultation and interaction with stakeholders constitute one of the main pillars on which the General Food Law Regulation rests.[27] The Law stipulates that, with the exception of urgent matters, there shall be 'open and transparent public consultation, directly or through representative bodies, during the preparation, evaluation and revision of food law'.[28] Furthermore, it specifies that EFSA shall develop 'effective contacts with consumer representatives, producer representatives, processors, and any other interested parties' in the course of risk assessment.[29]

The Law is also specific about the participation in risk management. This is defined as 'weighing policy alternatives in consultation with interested parties'.[30] This is in line with the concept of risk communication advocated by the Commission's White Paper on Food Safety, which defines its involvement concept as an interactive and involving dialogue with and feedback from stakeholders.[31] Public consultation directly relates to participation as one of the five normative principles of 'good governance' which the European Commission has identified in its White Paper on European Governance. It requires governance institutions to ensure wide participation from the conception of policy options to the implementation of decisions.[32]

The opportunities that EFSA provides for involvement is not related to risk management but to risk assessment. The involvement concept consists mostly

Institutional Analysis (Series Ius Commune. Antwerp and Oxford: Intersentia Publishing 2006), pp. 65–138.

27 Two further major cornerstones are the application of the principles of independence, objectivity and transparency in risk analysis, and the application of the precautionary principle in the face of scientific uncertainty.

28 Council Regulation (EC) 178/2002 of 28 January 2002 laying down the general principles and requirements of food law, establishing the European Food Safety Authority and laying down procedures in matters of food safety [2002] OJ L31/1.

29 Ibid.

30 Ibid.

31 Commission of the European Communities, 'White Paper on Food Safety', COM (1999) 719 final, 12 January 2000, Brussels.

32 Commission of the European Communities, 'European Governance. A White Paper' COM (2001) 428 final, 25 July 2001, Brussels.

of an 'elicitation of responses to pre-formed proposals'[33] (i.e. of consultation), which has been contrasted to 'symmetrical two-way deliberation' (ibid.) with the potential to empower inputs from different social actors.[34] Empowerment of civil society and economic actors to influence decision-making is restricted to being part of EFSA's management. Four of the Management Board members, out of 15, are required to have a background in organisations representing consumers and other interests in the food chain (EC 2002, Art. 25(1)). However, these (as all other) members are mandated to act independently in the public interest (EC 2002, Art. 37(1)) and do not formally represent a specific sector or particular concern – though their particular background will inevitably have an impact on their views as Board members.[35] However, the influence of stakeholders is consultative, stakeholder interests are not supposed to interfere with the scientific decision-making process.

There is *change* from the earlier involvement practices in three respects. First, consultation occurs on a more regular basis and also increasingly in a more open manner, with EFSA's Stakeholder Consultative Platform taking a prominent position in regard to risk assessment matters, and DG SANCO's Advisory Group playing a more influential role in regard to risk management matters. This contrasts with ad-hoc, informal and confidential 'behind closed doors' consultations, which are highly dependent on the discretion of individual risk managers. This ad-hoc mode of including stakeholders was typical for SANCO policy making style and still is to a large extent.

Second, the European institutions also seek advice from stakeholders on how to improve their system of consultation. The Stakeholder Consultative Platform advises EFSA in regard to the Authority's stakeholder policy and assists EFSA to better tailor its stakeholder involvement procedures to stakeholders' concerns in the area of food safety. DG SANCO consults the Stakeholder Dialogue Group[36]

33 Stirling, A. (rapporteur), *From Science and Society to Science in Society: Towards a Framework for 'Cooperative Research'*. Report of a European Commission Workshop, Governance and Scientific Advice Unit of DG RTD (Directorate C2, Directorate General Research and Technology Development, Brussels, 24–5 November 2005, report of February 2006).

34 A. Stirling uses these terms to describe the 'bottom line recommendation' of a European Commission Workshop dealing with the topic of 'From Science and Society to Science in Society: Towards a Framework for "Cooperative Research"' (24–5 November 2005): '… European activities in these areas [the governance of research and the scientific advice process] should be informed by, and should themselves incorporate, more effective forms of symmetrical two-way deliberation, empowering inputs from a wide diversity of social actors', p. 4.

35 Alemanno, A., 'The European Food Safety Authority at five' (2008) 1 *European Food and Feed Law Review*, 2–24.

36 Commission (EC) 2007/602 Decision of 5 September 2007 setting up the stakeholder dialogue group in the areas of public health and consumer protection. [2007] OJ L 234/13.

on how to improve the quality of its consultations in the areas of public health and consumer protection including safety of the food chain.

The third and most notable change, connected with the two others, is the actual opening of the former 'black box' of risk assessment to outside parties. Statements such as this: 'As for transparency and participation, scientific committees remain opaque and the participation of civil society and stakeholders is obviously not developed'[37] are no longer a proper description of EFSA's performance in these regards. As will be highlighted in the next section, EFSA's public involvement procedures have expanded significantly in the recent past.[38]

EFSA's Involvement Approach

EFSA's practice of stakeholder and public involvement as it has evolved over the past decade comprises a variety of procedures and provisions. These include multilateral discussions at scientific conferences, face-to-face technical meetings, public consultations via the Authority's website, an annual Stakeholder Colloquium and the Stakeholder Consultative Platform.[39]

With the establishment of the Platform, EFSA institutionalised stakeholder consultation through a permanent body. The Platform was established in 2005 as a 'forum of regular dialogue and exchanges'.[40] It is composed of EU-wide stakeholder organisations operating in the food chain and within EFSA's remit. As indicated above, its main task is to assist the Authority in developing its overall relations and policy with regard to 'civil society stakeholders'. According to EFSA terminology, these include 'consumer groups, non-governmental organisations (NGOs), and market operators such as farmers, food manufacturers, distributors

37 Demortain, D., 'European Agencies. The European Medicines Agency (EMEAI and the European Food Safety Authority (EFSA)' In: Benamouzig, D. and Borraz, O. (eds), *Food and Pharmaceutical Agencies in Europe: Between Bureaucracy and Democracy. Cross-national Perspectives*. A Commented Bibliography. (Grenoble: CNRS – Maison des Sciences de l'Homme-Alpes 2007) pp. 15–100.

38 Klintman, M. and Kronsell, A., 'Challenges to legitimacy in food safety governance? The case of the European Food Safety Authority (EFSA)' (2010) 32(3) *European Integration*, 309–27.

39 See EFSA's website: http://www.efsa.europa.eu/en/values/transparency.htm (accessed on 13 March 2012).

40 The inaugural meeting took place in Parma, 6–7 October 2005. The Platform holds meetings three times a year (EFSA website: http://www.efsa.europa.eu/en/stakeholders/cp.htm (accessed on 15 April 2012); EFSA (2010). Stakeholder Consultative Platform: Terms of Reference, mb 17.06.10 item 4 doc 3 – Stakeholder Consultative Platform: new terms of reference. [Online, EFSA website]. Available at: http://www.efsa.europa.eu/en/consultativeplatform/docs/cptor.pdf (accessed on 3 April 2012).

or processors and science professionals'.[41] Its mandate includes commenting on EFSA's work program and annual management plant, advising on risk assessment methodologies and providing information and cooperation at the technical level.[42] EFSA has been quite rigorous in designing a selection process for stakeholder involvement on the basis of fair representation and competence.

Increasingly, EFSA has also sought advice and input on general and issue-specific risk assessment approaches and methodologies from stakeholders. To date, the Authority has launched public consultations on issues such as the scientific and technical guidance documents for the application for authorisations of a health claim; the guidance for risk assessment of genetically modified plants and derived food and feed; the methodology for conducting Geographical BSE risk and others.[43] EFSA also invites public comments on draft scientific opinions. For instance, the Authority has carried out a public consultation to receive input on the draft Scientific Opinion on Dietary Reference Values (DRVs) for protein (in 2011)[44] and on the draft Scientific Opinion on the assessment of allergenicity of GM plants and micro-organisms and derived food and feed (in 2010).[45]

In addition to web-based public consultations, EFSA resorts also to a more targeted approach to invite comments and input in regard to scientific outputs or procedures such as technical meetings with its Stakeholder Consultative Platform or establishment of working groups of the Platform. In the second half of the 2000 decade, EFSA established a working group with Platform members mandated to provide EFSA's Scientific Committee with advice on how to draft EFSA's recommendations for Transparency in Risk Assessment.[46] EFSA also

---

41 See EFSA website at: http://www.efsa.europa.eu/en/networks/stakeholders.htm (accessed on 15 April 2012). EFSA distinguishes civil society stakeholders from 'institutional stakeholders' referring to 'those to whom the Authority has a legal obligation to work with under Community rules, e.g. the European Commission, the European Parliament and the Member States' (ibid.).

42 EFSA (2010). Stakeholder Consultative Platform: Terms of Reference, mb 17.06.10 item 4 doc 3 – Stakeholder Consultative Platform: new terms of reference. [Online, EFSA website]. Available at: http://www.efsa.europa.eu/en/consultativeplatform/docs/cptor.pdf (accessed on 3 April 2012).

43 See EFSA website at: http://www.efsa.europa.eu/en/values/transparency.htm (accessed on 15 April 2012). In 2010, EFSA launched 91 public consultations (EFSA 2011, p. 9).

44 See EFSA website at: http://www.efsa.europa.eu/de/supporting/pub/225e.htm.

45 See EFSA website at: http://www.efsa.europa.eu/en/efsajournal/pub/1699.htm.

46 EFSA (2009). Management Board, 18 June 2009, Athens, Greece, mb 18.06.09 item 9 doc 7a – Renewal of Stakeholder Platform – Review of activities 2006–2009. [Online, EFSA website]. Available at: http://www.efsa.europa.eu/en/090618/docs/mb090618-ax10b.pdf (accessed on 3 April 2012); EFSA (2010). Stakeholder Consultative Platform: Terms of Reference, mb 17.06.10 item 4 doc 3 – Stakeholder Consultative Platform: new terms of reference. [Online, EFSA website]. Available at: http://www.efsa.europa.eu/en/consultativeplatform/docs/cptor.pdf (accessed on 3 April 2012).

held a technical meeting with all Platform members on its draft Opinion on animal cloning.[47]

In 2012, as part of its openness and transparency policy, EFSA provides interested parties with the opportunity to participate in Scientific Panel meetings as observers. In the past, this option of stakeholder involvement has been the subject of highly controversial debate.[48] EFSA has ventured into this new openness with mixed feelings: the Authority is going to 'test the feasibility' of this additional step in enhancing the transparency of the risk assessment business.[49] The observer status does not allow stakeholders to contribute information or data or transport their views into the expert discussions. However, it does give them formal access to the expert exchanges and strengthens their 'monitoring power'.[50] Further, it enables them to increase their constituency's knowledge about specialised information and the argumentative basis of risk assessment outcomes.

Critical Reflection of EFSA's Involvement Policy and Practice from a Risk Governance Perspective

The Notion of Food Risk Governance

In the last decade, the term 'governance' has experienced tremendous popularity in various research fields including risk research. While there is no generally agreed definition of what constitutes 'risk governance', this concept is typically understood as involving the translation of the substance and core principles of the governance term to the context of risk and risk-related decision-making.[51]

This implies that the concept of risk governance pays special attention to collective decision-making on risk as a multi-actor and multi-level process involving new modes of regulation and collaboration. Within a broad notion, risk governance refers to the complex web of actors (governmental and non-

47 See EFSA website at: http://www.efsa.europa.eu/en/events/event/stakeholder080207.htm.

48 Vos, E., 'The EU regulatory system on food safety: Between trust and safety' In: Everson, M. and Vos, E. (eds), *Uncertain Risks Regulated* (Milton Park: Routledge-Cavendish 2009) pp. 249–67.

49 EFSA (2011). Policy on Independence and Scientific Decision-Making Processes of the European Food Safety Authority, mb 15.12.11 – Policy on independence and scientific decision-making process – ADOPTED [Online, EFSA website]. Available at: http://www.efsa.europa.eu/en/keydocs/docs/independencepolicy.pdf (accessed on 3 April 2012).

50 Tamm Hallström, K. and Boström, M., *Transnational Multi-Stakeholder Standardization: Organizing Fragile Non-State Authority* (Cheltenham: Edward Elgar 2010).

51 Renn, O., *Risk Governance: Coping with Uncertainty in a Complex World* (London: Earthscan 2008); van Asselt, M.B.A. and Renn, O., 'Risk governance' (2011) 14(4) *Journal of Risk Research*, 431–49.

governmental), rules, conventions, processes and mechanisms concerned with how relevant food risk information is collected, analysed and communicated and with how decisions on risk management are taken and implemented at different policy levels.

Food Risk Governance (or the similar term of Food Safety Governance) in this perspective is understood to include but also to extend beyond the three conventionally recognised interrelated components of risk analysis (risk assessment, risk management, and risk communication). Food risk governance also involves the collaboration of and coordination between public authorities and commercial and civil society actors and wider contextual factors such as institutional arrangements, regulatory styles, legislative procedure and political culture.[52]

It has been underlined that in the context of risk the notion of 'governance' is used 'both as a description of how decisions are made and as a model for how to improve decision-making structures and processes'.[53] In this paper we rely on a specific framework of risk governance that has been developed and promoted by the International Risk Governance Council.[54] One of the principles that this concept endorses is that the pursuit of risk governing purposes cannot be confined to public authorities but requires the inclusion of a wider array of actors. The idea of *inclusive governance* is inherent to this concept. It is based on the assumption that affected and interested parties have something valuable to contribute to all major steps of the governance process. Of course, not all stakeholders are interested in providing constructive advice and feedback, yet the system is built on the assumption that stakeholder input in general can enrich the process and enlighten the responsible authorities. Particularly in cases of risks surrounded by complexity, uncertainty and ambiguity, the argument goes, mutual communication and exchange of ideas are likely to significantly improve the final decisions, rather

52 Millstone, E., van Zwanenberg, P., Marris, C., Levidow, L. and Torgersen, H., *Science in Trade Disputes Related to Potential Risks: Comparative Case Studies* (Seville: Institute for Prospective Technological Studies 2004. Available online at: http://ftp.jrc.es/EURdoc/eur21301en.pdf (accessed on 10 January 2012)); Millstone, E., 'Science, risk and governance: Radical rhetorics and realities of reform in food safety governance' (2009) 38 *Research Policy*, 624–36; Ansell, C. and Vogel, D. (eds), (2006). *What's the Beef?: The Contested Governance of European Food Safety* Cambridge: MIT Press; Dreyer, M. and Renn, O. (eds), *Food Safety Governance: Integrating Science, Precaution and Public Involvement* (Berlin, Heidelberg: Springer 2009a); Klintman, M. and Kronsell, A., 'Challenges to legitimacy in food safety governance? The case of the European Food Safety Authority (EFSA)' (2010) 32(3) *European Integration*, 309–27.

53 van Asselt, M.B.A. and Renn, O., 'Risk governance' (2011) 14(4) *Journal of Risk Research*, 431–49.

54 IRGC (2005). White Paper on Risk Governance: Towards an Integrative Approach. Geneva: International Risk Governance Council; Renn, O. and Walker, K. (eds), *Global Risk Governance* (Berlin, Dordrecht: Springer 2008).

than impede the decision-making process or compromise the quality of scientific input and the legitimacy of legal requirements.[55]

Designing inclusive risk governance consists according to the IRGC framework of a chain of four central activities to handle risks: Framing, risk appraisal, risk evaluation, and risk management. The risk process has an iterative nature and communication is linked to all activities. We draw on this four-stage design for suggesting how a structured approach to public and stakeholder involvement in food safety governance could look like.

Tailoring Involvement to the Different Risk Governance Stages[56]

Specifying the role of stakeholder and public involvement in each of the four different stages is essential since 'public engagement is not a stage of governance that can be completed, tidied up and filed away'.[57] Therefore, one needs to distinguish between *different purposes* served at the four governance stages to which public involvement needs to be tailored. In order to define the purposes served at these four stages we propose to distinguish between four discourse categories.[58] The following paragraphs provide a brief description of the four discourse categories and the way public involvement should be related to them. Each of the four discourses produces different types of outcomes that are fed into the next governance stage.

Involvement at the stage of *framing* requires a *design discourse*. This discourse is aimed at defining the food safety threat, setting the terms of reference (including the scope, focus and design of Appraisal), and at specifying the way (breadth, concrete procedures) in which stakeholders and/or the wider public may be included in the further steps of the governance process.[59]

---

55 Webler, T., 'The craft and theory of public participation' (1999) 2(1) *Risk Research*, 55–71; Renn, O., 'The challenge of integrating deliberation and expertise: Participation and discourse in risk management' In: MacDaniels, T.L. and Small, M.J. (eds), *Risk Analysis and Society: An Interdisciplinary Characterization of the Field* (Cambridge: Cambridge University Press 2004) pp. 289–366.

56 This subsection draws on Dreyer and Renn 2009b and Dreyer and Renn 2008; see also König et al. 2010.

57 Stilgoe, J., Irwin, A. and Jones, J., *The Challenge is to Embrace Different Forms of Expertise, to View them as a Resource rather than a Burden ... The Received Wisdom: Opening up Expert Advice* (London: Demos 2006); Jasanoff, S., 'Relating risk assessment and risk management. Complete separation of the two processes is a misconception' (1993) 19 *EPA Journal*, 35–7.

58 Renn, O., 'Diskursive Verfahren der Technikfolgenabschätzung' In: Petermann, T. and. Coenen, R. (eds), *Technikfolgenabschätzung in Deutschland: Bilanz und Perspektiven* (Frankfurt/M.: Campus 1999), pp. 115–30.

59 König, A., Kuiper, H.A., Marvin, H.J.P., Boon, P.E., Busk, L., Cnudde, F., Cope, S., Davies, H.V., Dreyer, M., Frewer, L.J., Kaiser, M., Kleter, G.A., Knudsen, I., Pascal, G., Prandini, A., Renn, O., Smith, M.R., Traill, B.W., van der Voet, H., van Trijp, H., Vos, E.

The *epistemic discourse* is generic to the stage of *appraisal* which is aimed at understanding risk (including both possible physical impacts and social concerns and impacts). It comprises communication processes in which experts of knowledge (not necessarily scientists) grapple with the clarification of a factual issue. The goal of such a discourse is the representation and explanation of a phenomenon as close to reality as possible. By knowledge, we refer to *systematic* knowledge collected by established means of natural and social sciences and *experiential* knowledge collected by interactive techniques such as hearings or focus groups.[60] Both types of knowledge are important for describing what we generally know about the food safety issue and what we have learned in dealing with the risk or a similar risk in the past. Subject to the provisions of framing, civil society actors and also the wider public may contribute to the broadening and refining of the infrastructure of knowledge and information upon which evaluation and management decisions will then draw. It is important to note, that it is *not* the task of stakeholders and representatives of the wider public in the epistemic discourse to deal with normative questions pertaining to the acceptability or tolerability of either the risk itself, possible alternatives to the risk source in question (substances, processes, practices), or management measures for dealing with the risk. These normative issues need to be dealt with at the evaluation and management stages. They are based on value judgements about what is 'desirable' rather than what is 'true' (this is also a prominent justification of the allocation of risk assessment and risk management responsibilities to different institutions in EU food safety regulation).

The *reflective discourse* is generic to the *evaluation* stage. This stage is concerned with arriving at a balanced judgement on the risk on the basis of the outcome of the epistemological discourse and social values and preferences. The reflective discourse encompasses communication processes dealing with the interpretation of factual issues, the clarification of preferences and values, and a normative judgement of the risk's tolerability or acceptability.[61] The tolerability or acceptability judgement is informed by the results of the scientific assessment process (for which EFSA is responsible), but it is not determined by it. Other important considerations on wider social and economic issues (e.g. benefits, societal needs, quality of life factors, sustainability, distribution

and Wentholt, M.T.A., 'The SAFE FOODS framework for improved risk analysis of foods' (2010) 21(12) *Food Control* (Special Issue: Safe Foods – Towards a new risk analysis framework for food safety), 1566–1587.

60 Renn, O., 'The contribution of different types of knowledge towards understanding, sharing and communicating risk concepts' (2010) 2(2) *Catalan Journal of Communication and Cultural Studies*, 177–95.

61 The term 'tolerable' refers to an activity that is seen as worth pursuing (for the benefit it carries), yet it requires additional efforts for risk reduction within reasonable limits. The term 'acceptable' refers to an activity where the remaining risks are so low that additional efforts for risk reduction are not seen as necessary (IRGC 2005, p. 36).

of risks and benefits, social mobilisation, conflict potential) may be included in the balancing process. The main purpose of participation here is to ensure that all values and preferences are included in the weighing procedure, and that the final judgement reflects the societal balance between innovativeness and caution. This discourse would require the cooperation of risk assessors and risk managers since technical competence and value judgements are both needed to come up with a prudent evaluation.

The *practical discourse* is generic to the *management* stage which is concerned with acting on risk. It involves communication processes aimed at the identification, assessment, and selection of different management measures for reducing and managing 'intolerable risks' or 'tolerable but not acceptable' risks. This discourse looks at the variety of possible interventions, addresses the pros and cons for each measure or package of measures and suggests a set of measures that appear to be effective, efficient and fair. The main purpose of public involvement is here to assure that relevant knowledge and different preferences are considered in the conclusions on the selection of one or more management measures.

EFSA's Emphasis on Knowledge Collection and Consultation

From the outset, the issue of EFSA's engagement with stakeholders and the public has been controversial. There continues to be concern that interaction with outside parties might politicise the risk assessment process or provide an access point for industry interest representation.[62]

During the past two years, EFSA has stressed in documents explaining its policies on consultation and independence that stakeholders and the public are invited to contribute their specific *knowledge* on questions of risk assessment so that the quality of the assessments can be improved. These documents state explicitly that the Authority will not take perspectives and judgements on issues of risk management (such as whether addressing the risk requires the initiation of risk-reducing actions and how these actions should be designed) into consideration since EFSA has no mandate for risk management issues. Here we provide some examples of such statements:

> EFSA is committed to openness and regularly consults and meets its partners, stakeholders and the public at large on key issues, both scientific and otherwise. This includes EFSA's core planning and strategy documents as well as key scientific issues and all guidance documents. Consultations and scientific events

62 Vos, E. and Wendler, F., 'Food safety regulation at the EU level' In: Vos, E. and Wendler, F. (eds), *Food Safety Regulation in Europe: A Comparative Institutional Analysis* (Series Ius Commune. Antwerp and Oxford: Intersentia Publishing 2006), pp. 65–138.

> contribute to enhancing the quality and completeness of EFSA's scientific outputs.[63]

> However, EFSA creates a firewall that prevents hearing experts from exerting any undue influence over the discussions of the independent experts by excluding the former from the drafting of outputs and from the final exchanges and voting on those outputs. This allows the Authority to take stock of the data or expertise developed by industry, NGOs and other interested parties on newly developed practices, processes, substances, and products.[64]

> The [public] consultation will also need to clarify the consultation target audiences, the nature of relevant information and further operational details e.g. comments which do not relate to the contents of the document or contain information on individual cases or are related to policy or risk management aspects, which is out of the scope of EFSA's activity, will not be taken into account.[65]

This specification of EFSA's involvement policy can help to add legitimacy. Concerns that EFSA's risk assessment work is unduly influenced by 'external' considerations can be allayed, when there is clarity that EFSA does not provide a platform for participatory processes and deliberation around competing interests, values and visions but instead collects relevant knowledge from different sources to produce more informed opinions.

In addition to legitimacy, the open governance policy is meant to generate and sustain trust. The Authority's self-presentation strongly highlights the need for trust and independence of EFSA's scientific advice. This motive is also the prime rationale for the new 'observer policy':

> By providing the opportunity for interested parties to observe Panel meetings in action, how scientific opinions are developed and how various points of view are

---

63 EFSA (2011). Policy on Independence and Scientific Decision-Making Processes of the European Food Safety Authority, mb 15.12.11 – Policy on independence and scientific decision-making process – ADOPTED [Online, EFSA website]. Available at: http://www.efsa.europa.eu/en/keydocs/docs/independencepolicy.pdf (accessed on 3 April 2012).

64 EFSA (2011). Policy on Independence and Scientific Decision-Making Processes of the European Food Safety Authority, mb 15.12.11 – Policy on independence and scientific decision-making process – ADOPTED [Online, EFSA website]. Available at: http://www.efsa.europa.eu/en/keydocs/docs/independencepolicy.pdf (accessed on 3 April 2012).

65 EFSA's approach on Public Consultations on scientific outputs [Online, EFSA website.] Available at: http://www.efsa.europa.eu/en/keydocs/docs/consultationpolicy.pdf (accessed on 3 April 2012).

> debated by experts, EFSA aims to build further confidence in the risk assessment process and in its own scientific work and outputs. (EFSA website)[66]

This new policy needs to be seen against the background of the recent accusations that several of the experts working in EFSA scientific panels have too close links to the food industry, which could compromise the Authority's independence. The former head of EFSA's Management Board, Diána Bánáti, was publicly attacked to have failed to declare a conflict-of-interest situation to EFSA (caused by simultaneous work for the industry-funded think-tank International Life Sciences Institute (ILSI) Europe). Since this event,[67] EFSA has been under great pressure (amongst others from the European Parliament) to demonstrate that the scientific experts (and the Management Board members, who are amongst others responsible for the governance of the expert selection process) are not biased in their work and decisions. Whether the panel experts will accept the new observer policy or oppose it remains to be seen.

It is clear, that trust-building in regard to the independence and quality of scientific advice will remain an important rationale of EFSA's involvement policy. In 2011 and 2012 EFSA conducted two major workshops in which it invited stakeholders to discuss the new independence policies and to collect advice on how to sustain scientific integrity. The new policy indicates that the 'instrumental rationale' is complemented with a 'substantive rationale'[68] for consulting stakeholders and the wider public: From the substantive perspective, consultation leads to 'better ends',[69] i.e. in EFSA's case to improved scientific advice.[70] If EFSA is able to demonstrate that getting substantive advice is a serious motivation for

66 EFSA website at http://www.efsa.europa.eu/en/press/news/120307.htm (accessed on 10 April 2012).

67 In response to the pressure of the European Parliament, EFSA has recently strengthened its rules on transparency and conflicts of interest (EFSA 2011); on 9 May 2012, EFSA announced that Diána Bánáti had resigned from the EFSA post; see EFSA website at: http://www.efsa.europa.eu/en/faqs/faqresignationdianabanati.htm (accessed on 15 May 2012).

68 In considering the range of rationales and motivations bearing on participation in science and technology governance Andy Stirling (2007, 2009) has proposed to distinguish between three types of perspective: normative, instrumental and substantive. This analytical distinction builds on earlier conceptual work by Fiorino (1989) on different rationales and imperatives for participatory engagement of powerful institutions.

69 Stirling, A., 'Opening up or closing down? Analysis, participation and power in the social appraisal of technology' In: Leach, M., Scoones, I. and Wynne, B. (eds), *Science and Citizens: Globalization and the Challenge of Engagement* (2nd impression. London, New York: Zed Books 2007), pp. 218–31.

70 Finardi, C., Pellegrini, G. and Rowe, G., 'Food safety issues: From Enlightened Elitism towards Deliberative Democracy? An Overview of EFSA's "Public Consultation" Instrument' (2012) 37 *Food Policy*, 427–38.

their new openness policy, this could produce better outcomes but also enhance public trust in the Authority's performance.

In cases of risk associated with high levels of complexity and/or uncertainty it seems advisable to complement the currently used consultation procedures where interaction occurs mainly in an aggregate manner[71] with deliberative procedures, i.e. communication processes based on mutual exchange of arguments and reflections allowing for in-depth discussions.

Lack of Provisions for Deliberations in Regard to Risk Evaluation

A thorough reform to dismiss legitimate concerns that stakeholder and public involvement could undermine the quality and credibility of the risk assessment would be to organise risk evaluation as a risk governance phase in its own right as proposed by the IRGC risk governance framework. This would imply separate structures and processes including particular procedures of stakeholder and public involvement.

Current participatory mechanisms are not designed to capture, reflect on and deliberate over the wider concerns and expectations that individuals, social groups, and different cultures may link with food safety-related issues.[72] Deliberations around value judgements are relevant at the framing, evaluation and management stages.[73] In cases in which the food risk is associated with high levels of uncertainty, complexity and/or ambiguity, deliberations at the evaluation stage are of particularly high importance. What the current EU food safety governance system lacks is an institutional location and platforms where these deliberations can *legitimately* take place. EFSA is often challenged about non-scientific aspects of a problem or a pending decision to which it cannot respond due to its remit. Hence, the Authority appears to be insensitive and far-removed from reality as

71 Bengtsson, B. and Klintman, M. 'Stakeholder participation in the EU governance of GMO in the food chain' In: Bäckstrand, K., Khan, J., Kronsell, A. and Lövbrand, E. (eds), *Environmental Politics and Deliberative Democracy: Examining the Promise of New Modes of Governance* (Cheltenham, UK and Northampton, MA, USA: Edward Elgar 2010) pp. 105–22; Borrás, S., Koutalakis, C. and Wendler, F., 'European agencies and input legitimacy: EFSA, EMeA and EPO in the post-delegation phase' (2007) 29(5) *Journal of European Integration*, pp. 583–600.

72 Steffek, J. and Ferretti, M.P., 'Accountability or "good decisions"? The competing goals of civil society participation in international governance' (2009) 23(1) *Global Society*, 37–57; Dreyer, M. and Renn, O., 'Developing a coherent European food safety policy: The challenge of value-based conflicts to EU food safety governance' In: Frewer, L.J. and van Trijp, J.C.M. (eds), *Understanding Consumers of Food Products* (Cambridge: Woodhead, 2006) pp. 534–57; Dreyer, M., Renn, O., Cope, S. and Frewer, L.J., 'Including social impact assessment in food safety governance' (2010) 21(12) *Food Control*, 1620–1628.

73 Dreyer, M. and Renn, O., 'A structured approach to participation' In: Dreyer, M. and Renn, O. (eds), *Food Safety Governance: Integrating Science, Precaution and Public Involvement* (Berlin, Heidelberg: Springer 2009b) pp. 111–20.

it does not address these concerns. One way to resolve this problem is for EFSA to identify those concerns and bring them to the attention of SANCO or other risk management agencies that have responsibility for addressing these issues. Such a transfer of identified items to risk management authorities highlights the need for joint risk evaluation practices. In the current system, evaluation activities are exercised in a manner that is largely implicit and ad-hoc. As evaluation is a task at the interface between risk assessment and risk management[74] involvement procedures would need to be organised in cooperation and interaction between risk assessment and risk management authorities.

In those cases in which food risks are highly ambiguous and likely to trigger public controversy the results of what has been termed a 'concern assessment'[75] would be an important input into the deliberations during the phase of evaluation. In a concern assessment social scientists and economists identify and analyse risk perceptions and social concerns using social science methods such as surveys, focus groups, macro-economic modelling, or structured hearings with stakeholders. In the current EU food safety governance system there are no clear provisions for the use and performance of such concern assessments. The European Group on Ethics in Science and New Technologies has produced some opinions that could be considered relevant for addressing food safety-related concerns. It has been controversial, however, whether consideration of these opinions was within EFSA's remit or an exclusive risk management task. One way of institutionalising the identification and analysis of risk perceptions and social concerns within the current governance system would be to establish a 'concern assessment panel' in EFSA. This panel would extend EFSA's scientific panels by one and take the same format as the other panels except that this panel would comprise experts with a background in the social, psychological and economic sciences.[76] The present Advisory Group on Risk Communications has been serving this purpose since its establishment in 2002. However, it cannot substitute for a panel that would be responsible for identifying social concerns and impacts as an important input to the later stages of evaluation and subsequent management process.

---

74 This task draws on both scientific knowledge and political and socioeconomic considerations. The risk tolerability/acceptability judgement requires a good understanding of the web of evidence, residual uncertainties, and ignorance (i.e. the scientific characterisation of the risk) as well as judgemental competencies for making the necessary trade-offs between risk, benefit and other relevant impact categories (cf. Dreyer and Renn 2008).

75 IRGC (2005). *White Paper on Risk Governance: Towards an Integrative Approach.* Geneva: International Risk Governance Council; Renn, O., *Risk Governance: Coping with Uncertainty in a Complex World* (London: Earthscan 2008).

76 Vos, E. and Wendler, F., 'Legal and institutional aspects of the General Framework' In: Dreyer, M. and Renn, O. (eds), *Food Safety Governance: Integrating Science, Precaution and Public Involvement* (Berlin, Heidelberg: Springer 2009) pp. 83–109.

Summary

In this chapter we addressed the role of stakeholder and public involvement in the opinion forming process of EFSA. The inclusion of stakeholders has been reinforced by the need for additional knowledge from various stakeholders and actors in the assessment process, by the request for trustworthiness and by the requirement for public legitimization. EFSA is committed to a gradual opening of the risk assessment process to outside parties in the EU's revised food safety system. 'The scrupulous application of the general principles of openness and transparency'[77] has been one response to the perceived loss of public trust in food safety and science-based food risk assessments after the BSE scare.

However, this openness can also be interpreted as a potential threat to the independence of risk assessment (in terms of its scientific integrity). Being subject to inputs from different interest groups could compromise the impartiality of the scientific panels. To address these concerns, the Authority needs to ensure that stakeholder and public involvement is reconcilable with the protection of risk assessments from "inappropriate policy [and other] influences".[78] The independence principle is of central importance to the EU food safety system: Separate institutions for risk assessment and risk management were deliberately designed to guarantee that assessment is done independently from management. While the value of the institutional divide is debatable (due to the many interactions and interdependencies between risk assessment and risk management),[79] [80] [81] there is wide agreement on the merits of a functional distinction between the two tasks as they involve 'different goals, kinds of expertness, and operating principles'.[82]

If EFSA can convincingly demonstrate that those consulted are contributors to an 'epistemic discourse' and that their knowledge is used to improve risk assessments and risk assessment guidelines, it will enhance its credibility that the principles of independence and openness are adhered to. It may experience the risk that not all stakeholders are interested in such a role and use this discourse for public advocacy. Yet if the mandate of including relevant knowledge is made

---

77 EFSA. Call for Expressions of Interest for organizations to be considered for membership in the European Food Safety Authority's Stakeholders Consultative Platform [Online, EFSA website]. Available at: http://www.efsa.europa.eu/en/interest/docs/cfistakeholderplatform2012.pdf (accessed: 5 May 2012).

78 National Research Council, *Risk Assessment in the Federal Government: Managing the Process* (Washington DC: National Academy Press, 1983).

79 *Ibid.*, p. 6.

80 Jasanoff, S., 'Relating risk assessment and risk management. Complete separation of the two processes is a misconception' (1993) 19 *EPA Journal*, 35–7.

81 Codex Alimentarius, *Working Principles for Risk Analysis for Food Safety for Application by Governments* (Rome: World Health Organization/Food and Agriculture Organization of the United Nations, 2007).

82 National Research Council, *Risk Assessment in the Federal Government: Managing the Process* (Washington DC: National Academy Press, 1983), p. 151.

clear and transparent such strategic behavior may outmaneuver itself. Over time, the contributors to improved knowledge will become the dominant players in the epistemic discourse. At the same time, EFSA should not treat criticism by stakeholder groups as attacks against the institution and its performance. There is a fine line between unreasoned attack and well-founded criticism. Being open to critical remarks and demonstrating that critical remarks are taken seriously can also help the Authority to overcome the objections that several stakeholders have raised.[83] In particular, EFSA has been criticized that its involvement practice is restricted to 'sham involvement' in terms of a 'simple exercise in democratic legitimation and trust enhancement'. [84] EFSA's very emphasis on trust-building as a rationale for stakeholder and public involvement has partially nurtured such accusations. Explicit reference to building and sustaining trust is usually met with public skepticism. Certainly, such accusations and misperceptions can only be overcome if EFSA is able to demonstrate that its strengthened rules about conflicts of interest are consistently implemented. The two workshops on scientific integrity have been paving the path in this direction but there is certainly more evidence needed that the practice is following the rhetoric.

We have further argued that EFSA's involvement policy could gain credibility and legitimacy if the EU's food safety system included a concern assessment as part of the scientific investigation and included a separate phase of risk evaluation as a bridge between assessment and management. Hence, there is a need for clearer structures and processes through which the 'integration principle', i.e. the 'need to collect and synthesize all relevant knowledge and experience from various disciplines and various sources including uncertainty information and *articulations of risk perceptions and values*' and the 'reflection principle', i.e. a balanced risk judgment which takes into account also wider economic, social and cultural issues that requires a *collective reflection and deliberation process*[85] (emphasis added), are implemented in EU food safety governance.

---

83 Bengtsson, B. and Klintman, M. 'Stakeholder participation in the EU governance of GMO in the food chain' In: Bäckstrand, K., Khan, J., Kronsell, A. and Lövbrand, E. (eds), *Environmental Politics and Deliberative Democracy: Examining the Promise of New Modes of Governance* (Cheltenham, UK and Northampton, MA, USA: Edward Elgar 2010) pp. 112–113.

84 Everson, M. and Vos, E. (eds), *Uncertain Risks Regulated* (Milton Park: Routledge-Cavendish 2009), p. 29. The authors refer here to the Dutch government's public participation initiatives in regard to genetically modified organisms.

85 van Asselt, M.B.A. and Renn, O., 'Risk governance' (2011) 14(4) *Journal of Risk Research*, 431–49. The 'communication and inclusion principle' holds that the higher the levels of uncertainty, complexity and/or ambiguity, the greater the variety of actors that need to be involved in this process. According to van Asselt & Renn the three principles synthesize what needs to be seriously considered in organizing processes and structures to govern uncertain, complex and/or ambiguous risks in particular.

PART II
EFSA From Outside

Section 1: The Institutional Perspective

Chapter 11

The European Food Safety Authority: A View from the European Commission

Paola Testori Coggi and Patrick Deboyser[1]

Background

Although food safety was one of the very first concerns addressed by the legislator of what was then known as the European Economic Community,[2] no attempt was made, during the first four decades of European integration (1960s–1990s), to establish an integrated framework for food safety. The successive legislative programmes that were adopted in the veterinary sector[3] and in the foodstuffs sectors[4] had a clear objective: to achieve the free movement of food and food products within the internal market. This was indeed the only objective allowed under Article 100 EEC (now Article 115 TFEU), the only legal basis available at the time for the purpose of the approximation of legislations.

Thus, until the late 1980s, food safety was only a secondary objective for the European legislator. The adoption of the Single European Act, in 1986, marked an important change in this respect. The new Article 100a EEC introduced by the SEA (now Article 114 TFEU) not only allowed for the adoption by qualified majority of measures having as their object the establishment and functioning of the internal market, but it also provided that the Commission, the Council and the Parliament should, in proposing or adopting measures concerning health, safety, environmental protection and consumer protection, aim at a 'high level of protection, taking account in particular of any new development based on scientific facts'. At least from thereon, it was clear that the European legislator

1 The opinions expressed are the authors' own and do not necessarily reflect the views of the European Commission.

2 See Council Directive on the approximation of the rules of the Member States concerning the colouring matters authorised for use in foodstuffs intended for human consumption (OJ 115, 11.11.62, p. 2645).

3 Council Resolution of 12 March 1968 on Community measures to be taken in the veterinary [1968] OJ C 22 of 18.03.68, p. 18.

4 Council Resolution of 28 May 1969 (OJ C76 of 17.06.69, p. 1) and Council Resolution of 22 July 1974 (OJ C 92 of 06.08.74, p. 2).

was not only allowed to act with food safety in mind, but indeed that ensuring food safety was part of its actual mission. Nonetheless, throughout the 1990s, the EU food policy remained a piecemeal effort, mainly driven by the objectives of the common agricultural policy and the establishment of the single market.

The various food scares that shattered the EU agriculture and food market in the 1990s, mingled with consumer concerns about the use of growth-hormones in cattle and GM food, clearly demonstrated the inadequacy of the EU framework for food safety. Whilst food controls were still largely in the hands of Member States, it became clear that there was an expectation in the general public that the EU institutions should have long taken over and that the BSE and dioxin crisis, notably, were as much a failure of the EU as a failure of the most concerned Member States.

This was clearly on Mr Romano Prodi's mind, the designate-president of the European Commission when he addressed the European Parliament, in October 1999. 'The European public has lost confidence in both national and European food and drug regulators,' he said. 'They no longer trust their governments or the scientists. In my view, we have to take the initiative and look toward the idea of an independent European food and drug agency to help win back consumer confidence'.[5] By then, the European Commission had already shaken up its organisational chart to create a new Directorate-General for Health and Consumers[6] (hereafter: DG SANCO), to include the former Directorate-General for Consumer Policy and Consumer Health Protection (DG XXIV),[7] the Directorate for Public Health previously located in the Directorate for employment, industrial relations and social affairs (DG V), and the Food legislation service that was hitherto a part of the Directorate-General for Enterprises (DGIII).

Under the direction of Commissioner David Byrne, DG SANCO promptly produced a blue-print for a 'radical new approach to food safety'.[8] In sharp contrast with previous legislative programmes, the White Paper was making it clear that structural reforms were as much necessary as a legislative overhaul.

5 For a reconstruction of the genesis of EFSA, see A. Alemanno, 'The European Food Safety Authority at Five', *European Food and Feed Law Review*, vol. 1, 2008. The idea to create the European equivalent of the US-FDA had already been discussed in the European Parliament a decade earlier (see Raftery Report on the food industry, Doc. PE 128.325). In the literature, see Patrick Deboyser, '*Le marché unique des denrées alimentaires*', *Revue du Marché Unique européen*, vol. 1, 1991, at p. 86.

6 Initially known as the Directorate-General for Health & Consumer Protection.

7 Directorate-General (DG XXIV) had been created in 1997 to have the particular responsibility for consumer health. All the relevant scientific committees and responsibility for inspection and control were thus placed under the authority of the Commissioner for Consumer Policy and Health Protection. See the Commission Communication on Consumer health and food safety COM(97) 183 final of 30 April 1997.

8 White Paper on Food Safety – COM(99)719 of 12 January 2000, http://europa.eu.int/comm/dgs/health_consumer/library/pub/pub06_en.pdf.

To support the newly created DG SANCO, in which the FVO[9] was to play a major part, it was proposed to create an independent European Food Authority,[10] to streamline procedures for the adoption of EU food safety measures by the Commission, assisted by a single committee representing the Member States, and to institutionalise information mechanisms such as the all-important Rapid Alert System for Food.

There was instant and wide-spread support for the reform ideas outlined in the White Paper, which the Commission thus followed up with an appropriate proposal.[11] To their credit, Council and Parliament did not drag their feet and adopted Regulation (EC) No 178/202 in record time.[12] This Regulation includes the key elements, announced in the White Paper, which paved the way to the new food safety policy of the EU:

- It lays down the general principles and requirements of food law (including traceability and the first ever codification of the precautionary principle).
- It establishes EFSA – the European Food Safety Authority, as well as the Standing Committee on the Food Chain and Animal Health (SCFCAH).

It lays down new procedures in matters of food safety (including the Rapid Alert System for Food and Feed (RASFF), and a number of procedures to deal with emergency situation and crisis management.

This long preamble was necessary to understand that EFSA is a piece in a broader jigsaw where food safety is the primary concern.

9 FVO – the Food and Veterinary Office (now Directorate F of DG SANCO) had already been established in 1997.

10 'Authority' is actually a misnomer, for what was proposed was the classic model of an 'agency'. It seems that Commissioner David Byrne was particularly keen on the term 'authority', having been involved himself in the creation of the Irish Food Authority. The Joint Statement of the European Parliament, the Council of the EU and the European Commission on decentralised agencies actually recommends aligning names of existing agencies, particularly where this would not affect the established image of the agency which is the case of EFSA, as the acronym would not change. (Given its importance, I would suggest inserting a complete reference to the Joint Statement.)

11 OJ C 96 E of 27.3.2001, p. 247.

12 Regulation (EC) No 178/2002 of the European Parliament and the Council of 28 January 2002 laying down the general principles and requirements of food law, establishing the European Food Safety Authority and laying down procedures in matters of food safety (OJ L 31 of 1.2.2002, p. 1).

EFSA's Mission

EFSA is often compared with EMA – the European Medicines Agency (formerly known as EMEA – the European Medicines Evaluation Agency).[13] The comparison is appropriate, first and foremost because EFSA was originally modelled on the EMEA, but also because DG SANCO is now the partner DG for both agencies.[14]

There is, however, an essential difference in the original missions of EMA and EFSA, and this difference is reflected in their respective governance.

EMA was not created to improve or guarantee the safety of medicinal products in the EU, although one can contend that it has significantly contributed to such an objective. EMA was established to support a new centralised EU authorisation system for technologically advanced medicinal products, in particular those derived from biotechnology, and to provide for arbitration in cases of divergent decisions concerning medicines authorised by the Member States. Thus, the main purpose of EMA was, and still is, the functioning of the EU single market. It is important to note that the establishment of both the centralised and the decentralised procedures for the authorisation of medicinal products, to be operated by EMA and the Commission, were actually the result of an important transfer of competences from the Member States to the European Economic Community. This is clearly reflected in the governance of EMA: both the management board of EMA and its scientific committees are essentially composed of representatives of the Member States, appointed by them.[15]

In contrast, EFSA was not created to facilitate the free movement of agricultural and food products within the EU,[16] and its establishment did not require any transfer of competence from the Member States to the Union. Actually, in creating EFSA the Commission abandoned the oversight on risk assessment for food which it had had since the creation of the Scientific Committee on Food in 1974. The rationale behind such a choice is to ensure a functional separation of risk assessment and risk management, in order to ensure the scientific integrity of the risk assessment, to avoid confusion over the functions to be performed by

13 See Council Regulation (EEC) No 2309/93 of 22 July 1993 laying down Community procedures for the authorisation and supervision of medicinal products for human and veterinary use and establishing a European Agency for the Evaluation of Medicinal Products (OJ L 214 of 24. 8. 1993, p. 1).

14 The supervision of EMA was transferred from DG ENTR to DG SANCO in January 2010, alongside the competence for Pharmaceutical policy and legislation.

15 The management board of EMA also includes two representatives from the Commission, two representatives from the European Parliament, and, since 2004, two representatives of patients' organisations, one representative of doctors' organisations and one representative of veterinarian's organisations (see Article 65 of Regulation (EC) No 726/2004, OJ L 136 of 30.04.2004, p. 1).

16 Recital 34 of Regulation (EC) No 178/2002 mentions en passant that EFSA 'should assist in ensuring the smooth functioning of the internal market' but this notion is not reflected in the missions of EFSA, as outlined in Article 22 of same Regulation.

risk assessors and risk managers and to reduce any conflict of interest.[17] With such an emphasis on independence, it is logical that both the management board and the scientific committee and its panels would be constituted independently from Member States nominations. Admittedly, and apart from the Commission representative, the management board of EFSA is appointed by the Council, in consultation with the European Parliament, but they must choose its members within a list of independent personalities presented by the Commission.[18]

Whilst EFSA was created without any transfer of competence from the Member States to the Union, a number of subsequent legislations have operated such a transfer by establishing centralised EU procedures for the authorisation of genetically modified food and feed,[19] the establishment of maximum residue levels of pesticides in or on food and feed,[20] the authorisation of nutrition and health claims,[21] the addition of vitamins and minerals and of certain other substances to foods,[22] the authorisation of food additives, food enzymes and food flavourings,[23] to name but just the most significant such transfers.

Thus, it can be argued that, over the years, EFSA's role has expanded and that the Authority is increasingly involved in the operation of EU centralised procedures. Interestingly, EMA has recently undergone an exactly opposite transformation. Both then Commissioner John Dalli and the management of DG SANCO have repeatedly insisted in their contacts with EMA that they consider that the primary mission of EMA is to provide a high level of protection of human and animal health when it comes to pharmaceuticals in the EU. This shift is reflected in the

---

17 Working Principles for Risk Analysis for Application in the Framework of the *Codex Alimentarius*, para. 9. http://www.fao.org/docrep/010/a1472e/a1472e00.htm.

18 Note that four of the members should have their background in organisations representing consumers and other interests in the food chain. See Article 25(1) of Regulation 178/2002.

19 Regulation (EC) No 1829/2003 of the European Parliament and of the Council of 2 September 2003 on genetically modified food and feed (OJ L 268, 18.10.2003, p. 1).

20 Regulation (EC) No 396/2005 of the European Parliament and of the Council of 23 February 2005 on maximum residue levels of pesticides in or on food and feed of plant and animal origin and amending Council Directive 91/414/EEC (OJ L 70, 16.3.2005, p. 1).

21 Regulation (CE) No 1924/2006 of the European Parliament and of the Council of 20 December 2006 concerning nutrition and health claims made on foods (OJ L 12 of 18.01.2006, p. 3).

22 Regulation (CE) No 1925/2006 of the European Parliament and of the Council of 20 December 2006 on the addition of vitamins and minerals and of certain other substances to foods (OJ L 12 of 18.01.2006, p. 26).

23 Regulation (EC) No 1331/2008 of the European Parliament and of the Council of 16 December 2008 establishing a common authorisation procedure for food additives, food enzymes and food flavourings (OJ L 354 of 31.12.2008, p. 1).

recent legislation on pharmacovigilance,[24] and is even more obvious in the recent Commission proposals to improve the EU pharmacovigilance system.[25]

Management Board

One could perhaps wonder whether the above-mentioned evolution in the role of EFSA should not be reflected in its governance. As demonstrated by the precedent set up by the creation of EMA, there might be value in having representatives of the Member States on the management board of an EU agency, notably because it contributed to making of EMA the 'hub' of a network of agencies in charge of pharmaceutical supervision. The habit of appointing heads of national agencies to the board has both advantages and disadvantages. On the one hand, it can be assumed that the concerned individuals are highly experienced, being themselves in charge of managing an agency at home, and that they are independent from business interests as this is normally a condition for being appointed as head of a national agency. On the other hand, heads of national agencies have a clear conflict of interest where the board has to decide the remuneration for scientific services provided to the agency by national agencies, as the European Court of Auditors has repeatedly pointed out in the case of EMA[26] (more on this hereafter). As EFSA is unlikely to charge fees in the foreseeable future (this will be discussed below, § 5) and even less likely to hire the services of national agencies for the provision of scientific advice, it might be argued that there would be no such problem if the board of EFSA were mainly composed of representatives of national agencies. On this point, it is worth noting that the Joint Statement of the European Parliament, the Council of the EU and the European Commission on decentralised agencies[27]

24 Regulation (EU) No 1235/2010 of the European Parliament and of the Council of 15 December 2010 amending, as regards pharmacovigilance of medicinal products for human use, Regulation (EC) No 726/2004 laying down Community procedures for the authorisation and supervision of medicinal products for human and veterinary use and establishing a European Medicines Agency, and Regulation (EC) No 1394/2007 on advanced therapy medicinal products (OJ L 348, 31.12.2010, p. 1) and Directive 2010/84/EU of the European Parliament and of the Council of 15 December 2010 amending, as regards pharmacovigilance, Directive 2001/83/EC on the Community code relating to medicinal products for human use (OJ L 348, 31.12.2010, p. 74).

25 Proposal for a Regulation of the European Parliament and of the Council amending Regulation (EC) No 726/2004 as regards pharmacovigilance, COM(2012) 51 final of 10.2.2012, 2012/0023 (COD). Proposal for a Directive of the European Parliament and of the Council amending Directive 2001/83/EC as regards pharmacovigilance, COM(2012) 52 final of 10.2.2012, 2012/0025 (COD).

26 See paragraph 16 of the European Court of Auditors Report on the annual accounts of the European Medicines Agency for the financial year 2010, together with the Agency's reply (OJ C 366 of 15.12.2011, p. 27).

27 PE-CONS 00000/2011 – C7–0000/2011.

recommends a uniform composition of the management board of agencies very close to the EMA model:

- one representative from each Member State
- two representatives from the Commission
- one member designated by the European Parliament
- a fairly limited number of stakeholders' representatives.

In the case of EFSA, such a change – which would necessarily require an amendment to Regulation (EC) No 178/2002 – would considerably expand the size of the board. Consideration should therefore be given to another recommendation from the Joint Statement:

> in order to streamline the decision-making process in the agency and contribute to enhancing efficiency and effectiveness, a two-level governance structure should be introduced, when this promises more efficiency: in addition to the Management Board, giving general orientations for the agency's activities, a small-sized Executive Board, with the presence of a Commission representative, should operate and be more closely involved in the monitoring of the agency's activities, with a view to reinforcing supervision of administrative and budgetary management, in particular on audit matters.

The opportunity (of changing Regulation (EC) No 178/2002) would very probably be seized to align the voting rules in the board to the model recommended by the Joint Statement:[28]

- absolute majority voting for current business matters
- two-thirds majority for the appointment and dismissal of the director, the designation of the chairperson of the board, adoption of the annual budget and of the work programme.

Executive Director

The role of the Executive Director is crucial for EFSA's governance, being responsible for, amongst others, managing the agency on a day-to-day basis, drawing up and implementing the work programme, ensuring that the agency carries out its tasks, preparing the statement of revenue and expenditure, executing the budget and dealing with all kinds of staff matters.[29]

---

28 Compare with Article 25(5) of Regulation (EC) No 178/2002 (for EFSA) and Article 65(6) of Regulation (EC) No 726/2004 (for EMA).

29 Article 26(2) of Regulation (EC) No 178/2002.

Furthermore, the Executive Director is the legal representative of EFSA, and – as such – has to establish relationships with the Management Board, the European Parliament and the European Commission. He or she is, first and foremost, accountable to the Management Board, to which an annual report, including accounts, must be submitted.[30] EFSA's Director is also accountable to the European Parliament and the Council for the use of the EU contribution through the annual discharge procedure. As the European Commission is, by far, the main 'client' of EFSA, the Executive Director has also to develop and maintain regular contacts with the European Commission, and in particular the Commissioner for Health and consumers and DG SANCO. The flow of information between DG SANCO and EFSA has improved over time, and the current level of exchanges allows for a smooth planning of activities on both sides.

It can be said that the current Executive Director of EFSA has performed to the general satisfaction, and her initial mandate was recently renewed for another five years, as proposed by the Commission. In line with the overall policy on EU agencies, an Executive Director whose term of office has been extended should not participate in another selection procedure for the same post at the end of the overall period.[31]

Fees for EFSA?

Any amendment to Regulation (EC) No 178/2002 would necessarily raise again the question as to whether EFSA should be allowed to raise fees. This is indeed perhaps one the most important differences in their daily operation between EMA and EFSA: whilst EMA derives the bulk of its resources from fees paid by the pharmaceutical industry.[32] EFSA's budget is entirely provided by a contribution from the EU.[33] When EFSA was established, there were hardly any individual decisions based on EFSA opinions and therefore very little opportunity to levy fees from companies. Regulation (EC) No 178/2002[34] nonetheless provided that

---

30 Ibid.

31 See 'Joint Statement of the European Parliament, the Council of the EU and the European Commission on decentralised agencies' at paragraph 15 (PE-CONS 00000/2011 – C7–0000/2011).

32 The 2012 EMA budget totals €222.5 million (6.5% increase over the 2011 budget), which includes a general contribution from the EU budget of €23 million, a surplus of €9.9 million from 2010, and the €6 million orphan medicinal products fund. The planned fee revenue is increased by 7.5% over the 2011 budget to €173 million (EMA/MB/33634/2012 of 9 February 2012).

33 This contribution was established at €77.1 million in 2011 and €76.3 million in 2012 (PE-CONS 00000/2011 – C7–0000/2011–2011/2020(BUD)).

34 See Article 45. The text is obviously incomplete.

within three years following the date of its entry into force the Commission would publish a report on the feasibility and advisability of presenting a legislative proposal under the co-decision procedure to introduce fees. This prevented the Commission from proposing fees on requests for the authorisation of genetically modified food and feed at the time it made the proposal which lead to the adoption of Regulation (EC) 2309/2003.[35] This was all the more surprising that, until then, several Member States had been levying substantial fees on such applications under Regulation (EC) No 258/97.[36]

The opportunity to install fees was then missed with the adoption of Regulation (EC) 1924/2006[37] on nutrition and health claims.[38] A plausible explanation justifying this outcome can be found in the report which the Commission eventually presented to Parliament and Council in 2010.[39] The overall conclusion of this report was that:

> in view of the complexity of establishing a fee-system in the area of EU food legislation, the Commission [considered] that more reflection [was] needed on the range of options to be considered and that it [was] not possible to draw any definitive conclusions at [that] stage. This [would] be done in the course of an impact assessment.

Considering that most of the comments that this report generated were negative on the opportunity to introduce fees, principally because of fears that this may jeopardise the independence of EFSA, it can be safely predicted that the impact assessment, which is due by the end of 2012, will not call for the introduction of fees.

Whilst there would have been a good case for levying fees at least in those areas where a centralised EU authorisation is coupled with a period of data exclusivity for the authorisation holder (e.g. genetically modified food and feed, health claims and – in the future – novel food), this should have been done from the outset and not several years after the introduction of the said centralised procedures. Be it as it may, fees would always only concern a limited part of EFSA activities, and would probably not generate a significant increase in EFSA funding as it is likely that the European Parliament would reduce the grant from the EU budget accordingly.

---

35 See footnote 17 above.

36 OJ L 43, 14.2.1997, p. 1. Interestingly, companies were systematically introducing applications precisely in the Member States which were levying fees.

37 See footnote 19 above.

38 Possibly, the introduction of fees for applications for the authorisation of health claims would have prevented a number of frivolous applications!

39 Report on the advisability and feasibility of presenting a legislative proposal enabling EFSA to receive fees COM(2010) 496 final of 23.9.2010.

Conflicts of Interest

Both EMA and EFSA have been plagued, notably in the press and in the European Parliament, for their poor management of conflicts of interest[40] and this has caused serious reputational damage to both agencies.

Under the Staff Regulations, an official must notify any personal interest that might impair his/her independence.[41] Thus, the declaration of interest plays a key role in the management of conflict of interests, in particular in the case of EU agencies which, such as EMA and EFSA, have a high exposure to impartiality risk.

Both EMA and EFSA are continuously developing and enhancing their policies and procedures in an effort to adequately address conflict of interest. This includes: screening candidates before appointment, requiring detailed declaration of interest, monitoring the outsourcing of services, policing gifts and invitations, training staff, and addressing post-employment situations. As the two agencies grow with age, it will also be important to consider the mobility of staff in sensitive functions. It is worth noting, however, that in its Preliminary observations on 'Management of conflict of interest in selected EU Agencies', the Court of Auditors noted that 'out of the selected Agencies, EMA and EFSA developed the most advanced policies and procedures for declaring, assessing and managing conflict of interest'.[42]

Conclusion

EFSA was created as an essential component of a broader plan aiming at restoring consumer confidence in the EU food safety system. Ten years on, it appears that this goal was achieved. While the last decade has not always been plain sailing, it was certainly not plagued with food scares like the previous one. EFSA has contributed significantly to this achievement.

Over the last five years or so, the working relation between EFSA and the Commission has improved and has now reached a satisfactory level.[43]

---

40 A conflict of interest may arise between the public duty and private interests of a public official. This conflict arises when the public official has private-capacity interests which could improperly influence the performance of his official duties and responsibilities. (Managing Conflict of Interest in the Public Service: OECD Guidelines and country experiences, OECD, Paris, 2003, p. 24.)

41 Article 11a.

42 Preliminary observations adopted on 29 May 2012 (not yet published).

43 For an assessment of EFSA–Commission relations during the first five years of EFSA see A. Alemanno, 'The European Food Safety Authority at Five', *European Food and Feed Law Review*, vol. 1, 2008.

Being relied upon as it is to provide the EU institutions, Member States and the general public with the best possible independent scientific advice on all food safety matters, it is paramount that EFSA is equipped with the best possible governance structure. Time seems to have come to consider making some improvements in this respect. The Commission is currently reflecting on the opportunity to present a proposal to Parliament and Council amending Regulation (EC) No 178/2002 in order to take into account the recommendations of the Joint Statement of the European Parliament, the Council of the EU and the European Commission on decentralised agencies.[44] However, for the reasons illustrated above, the proposal is unlikely to call for the introduction of fees for EFSA.

Finally, EFSA is expected to continue enhancing its policies and procedures for declaring, assessing and managing conflicts of interest in order to ensure the highest independence of the scientific advice.

44 PE-CONS 00000/2011 – C7–0000/2011.

Chapter 12
Scientific Expertise and Open Government in the Digital Era: A View from the EU Agencies

Alessandro Spina[1]

Introduction

Scientific methods evolve and change over time. Were Aristotle's deductive logic still the dominant method of investigation in science, the scientific opinions of the European Food Safety Authority (EFSA) would be replete with syllogisms rather than assessments of data. However, the mere obsolescence of the scientific method might not be a sufficient cause to challenge the legality of administrative acts. This paradoxical observation invites us to reflect upon how scientific expertise is sourced and organised within EFSA, also in the light of the broad discretion in delivering the '*best possible scientific opinion in all cases provided for by the Community legislation and on any question within its mission*' (see Article 23(a.) of Regulation (EC) 178/2002).

Public institutions adopt decisions on technically complex issues by relying on experts and science advisers. In the aftermath of the BSE crisis in Europe, EFSA has been established in order to guarantee the independence of the scientific expertise integrated in the public decision-making on food safety.[2] Hence, the organisational elements of EFSA and of other EU agencies to obtain the best available scientific expertise in a specific field are fundamental to accomplish the institutional task. This chapter will examine the scientific advisory model in the light of two profound socioeconomic transformations occurring in both science and government.

In our times, characterised by the hyper-connectivity of individuals to the Internet, the extraordinary capacity of personal devices to collect and process data, and the socioeconomic relevance of social networking and online gaming,

1 The views expressed in this Chapter are those of the Author and do not necessarily represent the views, and should not be attributed, to the European Medicines Agency.

2 Alemanno, A., 'The Evolution of European Food Regulation: Why the European Food Safety Authority is not a EU-Style FDA', in C. Ansell and D. Vogel (eds), *What's the Beef? The Contested Governance of European Food Safety* (Cambridge, MA: MIT Press, 2006), pp. 237–58.

the relationship between scientific experts and non-expert is changing. Websites, blogs and social media enable a direct communication of unfiltered scientific opinions to citizens and novel mechanism for testing new scientific theories or to collect dispersed knowledge. Finally, complex scientific projects such as mapping craters on new planets are being designed into collective endeavours whereas everyone can help NASA scientists to collect relevant information through the use of an online videogame.[3]

In parallel, the open government paradigm is challenging the traditional boundaries between public institutions and citizens, by enabling a direct access and reuse of public information and embedding new modalities for collective information-gathering and decision-making. Open government is based on a post-Weberian idea of public administrations in which they are not the exclusive controllers of knowledge in society,[4] but the facilitators of 'collective intelligence'.[5] The trend towards a reconfiguration of the information management within public institutions, as well as in the scientific domain, finds its origin in the new 'peer' production model of the Internet.[6]

Building upon these premises, this chapter will look at how Internet-based open and interactive platforms can help remodelling the infrastructure of technical expertise in the EU, in particular with regard to EFSA and other EU Agencies which are considered 'knowledge gatekeepers'. It is argued that the open government paradigm can transform the operational aspects of sourcing expertise in the EU. The open government paradigm provides also a very concrete proposal to reform EU technocratic bodies and move them closer to its citizens. In this context, open government might be able to provide a more accountable model for '*open, efficient and independent public administrations*' in accordance with the principles of Article 298 of the TFEU.

The chapter is subdivided into three sections. In the first, the different models used by EU agencies to collect and use technical expertise and information are described. In the second section, the features underpinning the open government as a distinct organisational model used by public administrations to obtain technical

3 See http://beamartian.jpl.nasa.gov/welcome (last accessed on 18 August 2013). For more examples of innovative civic engagement projects can be found on the website of the GovLab of the New York University: http://www.thegovlab.org/ (last accessed 28 August 2013)

4 Noveck, B.S., *Wiki-Government: How Technology Can Make Government Better, Democracy Stronger and Citizens More Powerful* (Washington: Brookings Institution Press, 2009).

5 By 'collective intelligence' is here understood the capacity of open collective platforms to act as a quality-enhancing mechanism, owing to the simultaneous and unrestricted capacity of all (the 'many eyes' to look at the problems) to have access to information, to report erroneous information and to contribute to the improvement of the information exchange systems.

6 Benkler, Y., *The Wealth of Networks: How Social Production Transforms Market and Freedom* (New Haven, CT; Yale University Press, 2006).

expertise are described. In the third section, the use of open government will be analysed in the particular context of EU agencies and in particular of EFSA.

EFSA, EU Agencies and Scientific Experts

The institutional rationale for the creation of EFSA has been the need to centralise expertise by aggregating technical and scientific knowledge in a single EU-wide body, decentralised from the Commission and independent from political influences. To accomplish this goal, the establishment of a new EU agency was the solution at hand to create an independent body able to aggregate dispersed knowledge in a technical area.[7]

A feature common to all EU agencies is that they manage an enormous quantity of regulatory and technical information that they use to advise EU institutions.[8] This feature is, in most cases, their very *raison d'être*.[9] In the provisions of the founding Regulations, they are explicitly given the tasks of collecting information, providing advices to other EU institutions, setting up interconnected databases to share information. In some other cases, the establishment of a supra-national body determines the centralisation of the epistemic community in a specific regulatory field.[10] A European agency is *de facto* a platform where technical information are collected and shared: more appropriately, a 'forum for discussion'.[11] Control of information rather than control of other instruments of governing such as coercion or wealth, has been the most visible regulatory function[12] given to EU agencies in the complex framework of EU executive power.[13]

This function is often considered either a neutral quality of expert regulatory bodies or an exemplification of their soft power. However, technical and scientific

---

7 Demortain, D., *Scientists and the Regulation of Risk: Standardising Control* (Cheltenham, UK and Northampton, MA, USA: Edward Elgar Publishing, 2011).

8 Chiti, E., 'An important part of EU's institutional machinery: Features, problems and perspectives of European agencies', (2009) 46 *Common Market Law Review*, 1395–1452.

9 Communication (EC) 'The operating framework for the European regulatory Agencies' COM (2002) 718 fin. at p. 5: 'The independence of their technical and/or scientific assessments is, in fact, their real raison d'être. The main advantage of using the agencies is that their decisions are based on purely technical evaluations of very high quality and are not influenced by political or contingent considerations.'

10 Vibert, F., 'Better Regulation and the Role of EU Agencies', in S. Weatherhill (ed.), *Better Regulation* (Oxford: Hart Publishing, 2007).

11 This description echoes the assessment made by the Court of Justice with regard to the tasks of the European Network and Information Security Agency (ENISA) in Case C-217/04 *United Kingdom v. Council and Parliament* [2006] at paras 56–7.

12 Majone, G., 'The new European agencies: Regulation by information' (1997) 4(2) *Journal of European Public Policy*, 262–75.

13 Curtin, D., *Executive Power of the European Union: Law, Practices, and the Living Constitution* (Oxford: Oxford University Press, 2009).

deliberations which entail normative judgements result in the substantial influence of administrative regulation.[14] EU agencies filter information relevant for regulatory action, they frame the public discourse around the assessment of risks and, by controlling database and expertise, they decide what information is available to the decision-makers or the public. Emerging scholarship is uncovering the power of 'gatekeeping' and framing information as regulatory strategies,[15] and this is particularly evident in sensitive policy areas such as the safety of food or medicinal products, the protection of the environment, or the supervision of financial markets.

The resulting executive power of European agencies depends heavily on their capacity to collect and manage the relative expertise. It is then paramount to ask how and where EU agencies receive the expertise needed to perform their technical and scientific advisory role.

There are essentially two models used by EU agencies to obtain their relevant expertise. They are not mutually exclusive and often overlap:

The first model is what could be termed the 'outsourcing' model: this is the case when the relevant technical information is provided to the agencies through the activities of advisory scientific committees or expert panels which are established within their institutional structure but that are independent of their bureaucratic secretariat. These committees are composed of members appointed in the light of their technical and scientific expertise and in a large majority they are academic experts. This is a model generally used by public administrations in areas where it is inefficient or inappropriate to self-generate the technical expertise or it would nonetheless be insufficient to deal with complex multidisciplinary issues that require a broad range of technical expertise. This model is used in the case of EFSA, but is also dominant in other science-based regulatory EU agencies such as the European Medicines Agency (EMA) or the European Chemicals Agency (ECHA).

The second model is the 'networking' of national expert bodies. In this case, technical information enters the system of an agency through a network of national administrations in which the EU agency acts as sort of central 'hub' of widely dispersed knowledge which is accredited through the selection made at the national level.[16] In this model, the technical expertise is channelled through a multiplicity of other institutional actors which either have internal capacity to generate this knowledge or replicate at a national level the 'outsourcing' model above. This is more evident in the case of the newly established regulatory bodies

14 Fisher, E., 'Drowning by numbers: Standard setting in risk regulation and the pursuit of accountable public administration', (2000) 20 *Oxford Journal of Legal Studies*, 109.

15 Carpenter, D., *Reputation and Power: Organizational Image and Pharmaceutical Regulation at the FDA* (Princeton: Princeton University Press, 2010).

16 Ammannati, L. (ed.) *Networks. In search of a model of European and Global regulation* (Torino: Giappichelli Editore, 2013).

in the field of energy and telecommunications (respectively ACER, BEREC) and in some aspects also for the activities of EFSA. In a more extended declination of the networking model, the collection of information is accomplished through not only the information flow from other similar national expert bodies agencies but through other interested parties such as research centres and universities (as it is the case of the European Environment Agency (EEA) and its 'focal' points). In some cases, legislation mandates European agencies to set up network infrastructures in order to collect information and data. This feature provides EU agencies with the possibility to master an autonomous system of information collection. This can be seen with the case of EU-wide electronic information-exchange systems in which regulatory data are processed. We refer here to many electronic information-exchange systems operated by various agencies such as the *Eudravigilance* of EMA or the *Information Exchange Platform (IEP)* of EFSA. However, also in this latter case, the data collected are assessed only by (and within) the network of selected and accredited experts of EFSA and no access is provided to external experts or the scientific community.

It is then clear that although the organisational models of information within European agencies may vary according to the different sectors in which they operate, they share a similar informational model which is based on a self-contained and insulated capacity to generate technical and scientific expertise. This expertise is hence subject to a political bottleneck represented by the selection procedures to choose and appoint the network of *elite experts* who are supposed to provide the best scientific opinion on any matter for which they have been selected.

This underlining model can be seen in various aspects of the legal and administrative measures adopted to govern the information flows of agencies. For example, formal procedures are adopted in cases where a scientific opinion of EFSA could create a potential source of conflict with other scientific opinions of other EU agencies or bodies and to contact the concerned organisation '*in order to ensure that any relevant scientific information is shared*' and take action in order to solve the scientific issue. EFSA has also adopted standing framework rules for the communication of information in certain matters of common interests with other EU agencies.[17] These aspects confirm that agencies are, from a pure cognitive point of view, closed and self-contained at least with regard to the information flow concerning the scientific and technical matters for which they are competent.

17 A reference here is made to 'Memorandum of Understandings' (MoUs) or 'working arrangements' signed between EFSA and other agencies in order to share technical information and expertise see as an example the MoU between EFSA and ECDC of September 2010 available at: http://www.efsa.europa.eu/en/cooperationagreements/docs/mouecdcrenewed.pdf or the working arrangement between EFSA and EMA http://www.efsa.europa.eu/en/cooperationagreements/docs/mouema.pdf (last accessed on 11 December 2012).

The Emergence of Open Government as a Governance Model of Scientific and Regulatory Information

'False friends' are words belonging to different languages that look or sound similar but that have a different meaning. The concept of open government is also subject to a similar risk of being misunderstood. Open government is not about creating openness and transparency of public institutions.[18] Transparency provides the conceptual argument to empower citizens and stakeholders with direct access to information held by public institutions.[19] It operates mainly as an accountability mechanism and is considered as a tool to create effective deterrence of malpractice, corruption and regulatory capture.[20] The open government paradigm rests on a different idea of governance of regulatory information which is directed not at opening to public scrutiny governmental activities, but at transforming public administrations into digital platforms and lifting the barriers that hinder the participation of external actors in the processing of data held by public institutions. Open government presupposes a capacity of these institutions not only to provide and receive information but also to engage actively the public with the crowdsourcing of some regulatory functions, including the collective gathering of relevant information. They are supposed to act as catalyst of dispersed knowledge and expertise in society and not only through a closed group of experts. Fast and pervasive ICT tools render accessible to everyone, with minimal or even without any restriction, data and information held by public administration and they enable the participation of citizens and interested parties in the collection and elaboration of regulatory information. The release of public data in open government is often considered a means to an end; the ultimate end being the creation of collaborative regulatory regimes.[21]

It is true that the open government implies a certain necessary degree of administrative transparency because granting access to data and information enables everyone to have a better understanding of how public administrations operate. However, whilst transparency has been associated historically with public accountability and the strengthening of trust in government, open government

18 Yu, H. and Robinson, D.G., 'The new ambiguity of open government', (2012) 59 *UCLA Law Review Discourse*, 178; Shkabatur, J., 'Transparency with(out) accountability: Open government in the United States', (2013) 31 (1) *Yale Law and Policy Review*.

19 Curtin, D., *Executive Power of the European Union: Law, Practices, and the Living Constitution* (Oxford: Oxford University Press, 2009).

20 Stiglitz, J., 'On Liberty, the Right to Know, and Public Discourse: The Role of Transparency in Public Life', Oxford Amnesty Lecture (1999), in Gibney, M.J., (ed.), *Globalizing Rights: The Oxford Amnesty Lectures* (Oxford: Oxford University Press, 1999).

21 O'Reilly, T., 'Government as Platform', in D. Lathrop and L. Ruma (eds), *Open Government: Collaboration, Transparency and Participation in Practice* (Sebastopol: O'Reilly Media, 2010).

aims at a more ambitious goal: it is directed at creating the conditions for engaging citizens in the government activities and at increasing the efficiency of the administrative action.

To better understand this concept, openness here invites action rather than passive observation. Openness in this case does not equal access to a tightly controlled environment – like having access to a 'museum' – but it is instrumental in the possibility of using and manipulating a valuable informational asset: the bulk of data and technical information held by public institutions. In this latter concept, the idea of openness reflects a permissive and unrestricted use of a resource as in the 'open source software' or the collectivisation of editorial power in the case of Wikipedia.

It would be difficult to define what is the significance of open government for public administrations without understanding the values and the social practices resulting from its technological inspiration and in particular the 'peer' production model of the Internet. The digital innovations epitomised by social networks such as Facebook and Twitter or search engines like Google have transformed not only the way we are exposed to or have access to information but also the nature and function of knowledge.[22]

Digital technologies and products enhance the interoperability of data, the possibility to hyper-link and aggregate data and finally the use of visualisation techniques to increase the significance of data. It is the emergence of new values and practices to characterise a new system of information production which is based on collaboration and collective sharing of data, expertise, resources. This can be either an intentional process built into the technical platform – for example, Wikipedia or the open source software – whereas users voluntarily contribute information and expertise to an existing project which is capable to internalise added value from users' information or a hidden functionality of a platform which exploit the users' data – for example, the mechanism by which Google refines the relevance of the indexed web pages as a result of a search query by understanding users' data. With the aggregation of data, there comes also a tendency for enabling the incorporation of the feedback of users for the purpose of quality improvement. This is what is referred to by technology experts as the '*perpetual beta*', the intrinsic functionality which enables a continuous upgrade of the system. It is interesting to note that one of the justifications for keeping systems 'open' is that it is the 'collective intelligence' of users to increase the quality and accuracy of the information. This can also imply that the users are also able to test the products and report possible faults or inaccurate information. This is along the line of the approach that '*given enough eye-balls, all problems are shallow*' which is why the capacity of users to report technical bugs and to incorporate contributions into the code led to the success of the production model of open source software. Finally, as the platform becomes a

22 Benkler, Y., *The Penguin and the Leviathan: How Cooperation Triumphs over Self-Interest* (Random House: New York, 2011).

'collective' good, the distinction between users and producers of information is fundamentally altered. There are essentially network externalities that create incentives for users and producers to contribute information and this results in outcomes that can be qualitatively superior to 'closed', hierarchically governed projects.[23] The profound socioeconomic changes of digital technologies affect also the roles and the functions of public administrations. This is not only limited to the organisational structure of administrations that increasingly adopt digital technologies to operate and connect their resources in a network but also with regard to the possibility that digital technologies are used to communicate and interact with the public. If applied in the context of governmental activities, these digital innovations could alter the way expert public bodies accomplish their task. The network model of knowledge in the Internet is founded on the collective governance of information and expertise and in particular it operates by enabling access to data and promoting participation in the decision-making processes on the publicly accessible data.

To date, the most important experiment of digital collaborative governance in public administration is taking place in US under the Obama Administration.[24] With the *Transparency and Open Government Memorandum*, US public administrations have been invited to reflect on how to incorporate digital data-rich platforms to interact with US citizens into their processes. It is remarkable that the level of transparency and the participation of the public in the open government paradigm is not only directed at maximising the policy objective of increasing the accountability of institutions and the efficiency of administrative action, but is grounded on a more philosophical underpinning that 'knowledge is widely dispersed in society' and 'civil servants benefit from having access to that dispersed knowledge'.

US public institutions, including the FDA, the body with close affinity to EFSA, have released a number of high-value datasets, containing aggregated information about inspections or product recalls.

There are signals that the open government paradigm is influencing reforms in public administrations also in Europe as the policy plans of the Digital Agenda demonstrate.[25] However, it is also fair to note that the immediate impact of open government on the operational aspect of EU expert bodies has yet to be fully explored.

---

23 It is worth noting that much controversy surrounded the finding that Wikipedia is as accurate as the Encyclopaedia Britannica with regard to science information, rebutting one of the most popular objections as to the reliability of information of encyclopaedias everybody can edit: see Giles J., *Internet Encyclopaedias go head to head*, in 438 *Nature* 2005 at 900-901.

24 Coglianese, C., 'The transparency president? The Obama administration and open government', (2009) 22 *Governance*, 529.

25 Communication (EC), 'A Digital Agenda for Europe' COM (2010) 245.

The Case for the Open Government of EFSA (and other EU agencies)

It has been recalled that the control and management of technical expertise in the area of food safety is the core institutional mission of EFSA. And yet, the way EFSA, or, in different contexts, other EU agencies interact with the public to collect and process relevant data and technical information or provide scientific advices is still characterised by a self-contained logic of technical expertise. In this framework, the public is the passive recipient of 'accurate and objective' information or the target of educational programmes. In the traditional model of sourcing expertise common to EFSA and other EU agencies, the collection and production of scientific expertise and the interaction with the public are two entirely separate activities. In the open government model, the public is the *locum* where the 'dispersed knowledge' can be found and public administrations would act as platforms in order to aggregate this knowledge.

The ongoing debate regarding the reform of EU agencies[26] is curiously silent on this crucial aspect of their activities. This debate seems to be more focused on the traditional institutional elements of the agencies' organisation and governance such as the role and nature of relationship with the European Commission, the composition of the Management Board and the influence of Member States, or more prosaic elements such as the legal status of their staff. It seems taken almost for granted that the conventional models of sourcing expertise through an elitist filter – 'outsourcing' to the most accredited experts or 'networking' resources of national public administrations – will not be revised, notwithstanding the changes to both the practice and methodology of science and the relationship between public institutions and citizens. Bureaucratic bodies are naturally risk-averse and they have a natural tendency in carrying on traditional administrative practices, unless forced by acts of authority, legal obligations or necessity. In some circumstances, it cannot be excluded that non-experts can assist experts in delivering more responsive scientific opinions. In this sense, it seems noteworthy to highlight that recently the EMA has released a concept paper discussing the possibility to develop a framework of interaction between 'children and young people' and one of its scientific committee, the Paediatric Committee which is responsible for advice on medicinal products to be used in the paediatric population.[27]

Arguably, the open government paradigm might improve the way European agencies operate and are perceived by EU citizens. It would not only transform the

---

26 Over the summer of 2012, the three EU institutions have agreed to issue a joint statement on the reform of EU decentralised agencies: European Commission, 'Breakthrough as EU institutions agree common approach on agencies' (Press release, http://europa.eu/rapid/press-release_IP-12–604_en.htm?locale=en; European Commission 2012).

27 See http://www.ema.europa.eu/docs/en_GB/document_library/Scientific_guideline/2012/09/WC500132555.pdf (last accessed 10 December 2012).

information flows of the regulatory framework but give European agencies a new legitimacy in their institutional advisory role. It is then appropriate to consider here some of the benefits of introducing the new systems of deliberation based on open government into the activities of EFSA or other science-based EU agencies, and then to analyse the legal and political framework that could provide the basis of its implementation.

There are various reasons why the open government model could be applied to European agencies. First, it is often contended that citizens perceive European institutions as driven by a distant and technocratic rationale. It has been conventionally claimed that decisions of EU institutions respond to a non-democratic logic. This dichotomy between technocracy and democracy seems to neglect that a basic prerequisite of both democracy and science is the openness of the decision-making process. Moreover, this simplified criticism misses the point that the very models of scientific expertise are being gradually democratised due to digital technological innovations and the culture of open data.[28] The quality of technical and scientific expertise is not merely 'contaminated' by the possibility that citizens, scientific communities and interested stakeholders can participate and integrate into appropriate platforms their 'voice'. In this light, models of technical expertise relying on the open government paradigm will be a powerful response to the perceived distance between citizens and allegedly technocratic institutions such as European agencies. Open government of these bodies will also be a way to support the creation of an active European civil society that is more engaged in the activities of EU institutions through both the expansion of network and communication technologies and legal-administrative means.[29]

Second, the use of digital technologies creates substantial economic benefits in terms of expanding the availability of experts and increasing the quality of regulatory information. This could lead to a substantial reduction of the rent-seeking positions of the privileged army of professional 'experts' advising European agencies and it can create the conditions for European agencies to exploit online collaborative platforms able to 'crowdsource' expertise. This can be seen with the case of the online encyclopedia *Wikipedia*, but also more directly with public administrations in projects such as the 'Peer-to-Patent' of the US patents and trademarks offices.[30] Public administrations are starting to realise the full potential of crowdsourcing also because it represents an efficient way to use public resources. Digital innovations have unleashed great opportunities to

28 For a recent and comprehensive contribution to the debate of scientific openness see report from the Royal Society, 'Science as an open enterprise June 2012' (available at http://royalsociety.org/uploadedFiles/Royal_Society_Content/policy/projects/sape/2012–06–20-SAOE.pdf, last accessed 23 October 2012).

29 Habermas, J., *The Crisis of the European Union: A Response* (Cambridge: Polity Press, 2012), 46.

30 White House, 'Peer-to-Patent' (available at: http://www.whitehouse.gov/open/innovations/Peer-to-Patent, last accessed on 15 October 2012).

upgrade the modalities of knowledge production. In this context, the US example offers a possibility for public administrations to take advantage of dispersed collective intelligence in order to make European citizens cooperate to obtain and produce useful regulatory information.

Finally, the crowdsourcing of expertise and the reconfiguration of the information flows between European agencies and the public could represent a concrete possibility of modernising the role of agencies with a new model that has a low financial burden and an almost immediate effect on the legal governance of agencies. Even though open government cannot be seen as a way to address accountability issues but rather as a way to organise and share critical information, in the case of European agencies the opening of the regulatory system through interaction with the public and through the collection of technical and scientific information would help to remedy some long-standing problems of these organisations.[31] This is valid in particular for the real, potential or perceived 'conflict of interests' situations where agencies are bound to be locked up until the current obscure and piecemeal structure to obtain technical and scientific expertise is upheld.[32] External experts – the 'outsourcing' model – or the 'networking' of available expertise from national public administrations, seem to be prone to a discretionary filtering of relevant information into the regulatory system. In fact, it is the privileged position given to some predefined actors in the regulatory process that makes particularly sensitive what other interests these actors might be serving. Only a genuine holistic openness of these institutions and the active involvement of the public might guarantee that the content of the regulatory information managed by the agencies is free from undue influences and regulatory capture.[33]

Among EU agencies, EFSA is probably the one that has more systematically used communication tools to interact with consumers and citizens also through the use of social media. However, it is probably high time that the piecemeal interaction of EU agencies with the public is transformed into a principled system for a continuous exchange of technical information and expertise and a reconsideration of EU technical bodies as platforms for aggregating dispersed knowledge.

---

31 Hofmann, H.C.H. and Morini, A., 'The pluralisation of EU executive: Constitutional aspects of 'agencification' (2012) 37 *European Law Review*, 419–43.

32 A problematic aspect of the governance of European agencies is the management of situations of 'conflict of interests' of experts or staff members in particular with regard to the elaboration of scientific and technical advice used in the regulatory decision-making of EU institutions. For a recent analysis, limited to only 4 agencies (EMA, EFSA, ECHA and EASA) see: European Court of Auditors, 'Management of Conflict of Interest in Selected EU Agencies' (http://eca.europa.eu/portal/pls/portal/docs/1/17190743.PDF, last accessed 14 October 2012, Special Report No 15, 2012) and Gabbi, S., *Independent Scientific Advice: Comparing Policies on Conflict of Interests in the EU and US*, in *European Journal of Risk Regulation* 2011 pp. 213–226.

33 Wagner, W.E., 'Administrative law, filter failure and information capture' (2010) 59 *Duke Law Journal*, 1321–1432, in particular at p. 1419.

We have seen from the US experience that the first step to mobilise collaborative platforms and create the conditions for effective open government is to release data held by public institutions. It would then be necessary to create the technological and administrative conditions for enabling the public to analyse and make use of data. It is an implied assumption that much of the regulatory information collected by agencies is evaluated and processed exclusively within these agencies, and exploited with the use of a limited set of resources and experts. This situation is not compatible with a model of open government where institutions seek the active involvement of the public to process and analyse data. Some concrete measures to reconsider the governance model of technical and scientific expertise of European agencies are also at hand. First, it is necessary to extend the application to EU agencies of legal obligation regarding reuse of public sector data. EU agencies should be subject to obligations similar to the ones included in the Directive 2003/98/EC on the reuse of public sector information. There is no justification, at the EU level, for exempting EU agencies from the obligations to allow public access and reuse of data held by public institutions which are imposed upon the public administrations of Member States.[34] Though this will not be sufficient in itself to implement the open government of EU agencies, it is argued that access to data held by public administrations will be important in providing direct access to the sources of the information entering the regulatory system and the cognitive background of technical and scientific expertise used by scientific experts.

The second step would be to engage the public, interested communities and stakeholders in helping EU agencies to make use of released data by creating incentive-led, benefit-sharing mechanisms that result in a better, more open and more efficient accomplishment of the agencies' mission.[35] In this context, it is important that EU agencies think of alternative economic models (such as for example, prizes, grants or public competitions)[36] in order to procure knowledge and other immaterial assets which could be more efficient and also increase civic

34 It is important to note that the Commission has adopted a Decision on the reuse of Commission documents; Commission Decision (EC) of 12 December 2011 on the reuse of Commission documents [2011] OJ L 330/39; however, this does not impose any legal obligation on EU agencies.

35 With appropriate incentives there would be a more balanced representation of interests before a regulatory body and private parties such as regulated entities could be set to compete against each other in order to help the regulatory body in taking regulatory actions.

36 A commendable and neglected example of the clever use of reputation-based incentives that EU agencies can use in order to obtain resources from EU citizens has been the project of a small EU agency, the European Institute for Gender Equality (EIGE) which has effectively 'crowdsourced' the creation of its logo by setting up a 'logo competition'. Rather than using public resources in order to purchase traditional commercial services, the EIGE has launched a public context for logo ideas. More details about the initiative can be found here: http://www.eige.europa.eu/content/logo-competition (last accessed 11 December 2012).

engagement in their activities. The crowdsourcing of complex regulatory activities can be the beginning of a new participatory model by which the EFSA could achieve to reach the involvement not only of stakeholders and interested parties but of all EU citizens.

Conclusion

It is becoming evident that in order to guarantee that the best scientific expertise is provided to EU institutions and citizens, EFSA should strive to use the best organisational models to source science and expertise.

The standard of 'the best possible scientific expertise' has a clear and profound significance. It is the counterpart of the trust and independence entrusted to scientific bodies such as EFSA to be the holder of a cognitive monopoly in certain technical areas such as food safety. Moreover, it carries with it an obligation to keep rules and procedures under constant review and update. This imperative cannot disregard in the era of the Internet the possibility of using digital collaborative platforms in order to engage actively the public in aggregating 'dispersed knowledge'.

This chapter has made a case for reconsidering the traditional model of sourcing expertise in EU agencies in the light of the open government paradigm. As EFSA and other EU agencies have a crucial informational role in the respective regulatory frameworks, it is surprising that little attention is devoted to reforming and modernising the modalities by which agencies source their technical expertise. The case for a different model of collaboration between accredited experts, scientific communities and EU citizens is justified by the changing environment and practices in science.

Furthermore, open government might have a special significance for EFSA and other EU agencies as it would represent a way to engage the public in the deliberations and decisions which have a direct and often important consequence in their lives. It is a way to legitimise science as a basis to take decisions in a democratic society and also it is a way to implement *in concreto* the principle laid down in Article 298 of the TFEU that EU institutions should be supported by open, efficient and independent public administration.[37]

It has been a mistake in the past to dismiss too often superficially the scientific quality of the crowdsourced online encyclopedia – and the result – Wikipedia – is

37 Article 298 (1) of the TFEU states '*In carrying out their mission, the institutions, bodies, and agencies of the Union shall have the support of an open, efficient and independent public administration*'. This article has been generally held to provide the legal basis for legislating on an EU general administrative procedure. It appears indeed that a common administrative procedure is only one of the tools that can be used in order to implement Article 298 TFEU, see Nieto-Garrido E., *Possible Developments of Article 298 TFEU: Towards an Open, Efficient and Independent European Administration*, in *European Public Law* Vol. 18, 2 2012.

undoubtedly the landmark achievement of the digital era. EFSA and other EU agencies might have much to learn from all these digital models for the collective crowdsourcing of expertise.

Chapter 13
EFSA the Respondent: A View from the Court of Justice of the European Union

Caoimhin MacMaoláin

Introduction

The original draft of the General Food Law Regulation accorded the European Food Safety Authority (EFSA or 'the Authority') an anomalous position.[1] It was set up to provide specialist advice to the EU legislative institutions on food safety. However, the Regulation provided that there was no obligation on these institutions to follow such advice. Instead, the institutions were required to pay regard to them. This chapter examines the consequences of this position and the cases which explain it.

The most significant case law involving EFSA relates to actions seeking the annulment of influential EFSA opinions, and possibly the payment of compensation for any consequent damage suffered. Crucially, it is the fact that EFSA opinions do not have to be followed, and therefore only form a part of the decision-making process, that results in much of what EFSA does being beyond direct Court scrutiny.

EFSA Accountability

It is important to state at the outset that the EFSA can be held to account for its actions, albeit in quite limited and well-defined circumstances. The General Food Law Regulation provides that EFSA may incur liability in two situations. First, it states that:

> [t]he contractual liability of the Authority shall be governed by the law applicable to the contract in question [and the] Court of Justice ... shall have jurisdiction to give judgement pursuant to any arbitration clause contained in a contract concluded by the Authority.[2]

---

1 Regulation (EC) 178/2002 of the European Parliament and of the Council of 28 January 2002 laying down the general principles and requirements of food law, establishing the European Food Safety Authority and laying down procedures in matters of food safety. [2002] OJ L 31/1.

2 Article 47(1) of Regulation 178/2002, note 1 above.

This is obviously limited to the contractual liability of EFSA, which exists by virtue of the creation of legal personality for the Authority.[3] This status also provides EFSA with the possibility of instituting legal proceedings itself, including the taking of action against those who owe contractual duties to it. However, the General Food Law Regulation further provides that:

> [i]n the case of non-contractual liability, the Authority shall, in accordance with the general principles common to the laws of the Member States, make good any damage caused by it or its servants in the performance of their duties [and the] Court of Justice shall have jurisdiction in any dispute relating to compensation for such damage.[4]

This, coupled with the more general provision on damages set out in Article 340 TFEU, has given rise to a series of cases, testing the extent to which EFSA can be held liable in its role as a primary point of reference for EU decision-makers on matters of food safety. EFSA's status is such that where it advises a course of action, this will or may be followed, with serious and lasting consequences. A recommendation to refuse the authorisation of a particular foodstuff or ingredient could, for example, have large financial ramifications for its producers or developers. In such circumstances, they are likely to seek redress from somewhere, particularly where there is a view that the opinion issued was flawed in some way.

As stated in the introduction to this chapter, two main legal remedies exist for those who seek to have the activities of EFSA scrutinised before the Court – action for damages and applications for annulment. The two most significant decisions in this regard both address both of these issues. These two cases, *Dow* and *FMC*, will therefore form the main focus for this discussion on the relationship between EFSA and the Court. They will first be used to assess the extent to which EFSA opinions can be annulled in the usual manner, before turning to examine the position of the Court on awarding damages to compensate for the consequences of EFSA decisions.

Annulling EFSA Opinions

The orders delivered in *Dow* and *FMC*, by what is now the General Court, appeared on the same day in June 2008. In *Dow*,[5] the applicant, who was a manufacturer and distributor of plant protection products, notified the Commission that it would like to have an active substance (haloxyfop-R) authorised for use in agriculture.[6]

3 Article 46(1) of Regulation 178/2002, note 1 above.

4 Article 47(2) of Regulation 178/2002, note 1 above.

5 Case T-397/2005 *Dow AgroSciences Ltd v EFSA* [2008] ECR II-90.

6 Authorisation would result in the inclusion of the substance into the list set out in Annex I to Council Directive (EC) 1991/414 of 15 July 1991 concerning the placing of

It submitted a dossier in support of this application to the Danish authorities, who in turn recommended to the EFSA that they should not allow this herbicide to be registered as an authorised plant protection substance. EFSA advised the Commission that it concurred with the opinion of the Danish Government and in June 2007 a Decision was made, confirming that the application for authorisation would not be granted.[7] The EFSA scientific report on the matter expressed concerns about the potential for the substance at issue to cause groundwater contamination and the poisoning of fish. The applicant brought an action for the annulment of this EFSA opinion and the award of compensation for damage sustained.

Under Article 263 TFEU, the Court of Justice can review the legality of legislative acts and of acts of the institutions which are intended to have a legal effect on third parties. Post-Lisbon, it further provides that:

> [i]t shall also review the legality of acts of bodies, offices or agencies of the Union intended to produce legal effects *vis-à-vis* third parties.

Due to the rules on legal standing, set out in Article 263(4) TFEU, it has been notoriously difficult for private individuals (non-privileged applicants) to have their application for the annulment of such acts admitted in the first place.[8] Traditionally, the act in question must have been addressed to the applicant specifically, or it must have been 'of direct and individual concern to them'. The test of 'direct and individual concern', originally established by the Court of Justice in *Plaumann*,[9] has been of such a nature that it has only been in the most limited of circumstances that applications for the annulment of Union acts would be heard at all. EFSA contended in *Dow* that there was no reference to it as a body whose acts were open to judicial review in, what was at the time, Article 230 EC, now Article 263 TFEU. This was, apparently, the case, as it is only since the Treaty of Lisbon amendments were made that the reference to 'bodies, offices or agencies

---

plant protection products on the market. [1991] OJ L 230/1. Directive 1991/414 has since been replaced by Regulation 1107/2009, note 30 below.

7 Commission Decision (EC) 2007/437 of 19 June 2007 concerning the non-inclusion of haloxyfop-R in Annex I to Council Directive 1991/414/EEC and the withdrawal of authorisations for plant protection products containing that substance. [2007] OJ L 163/22.

8 For further discussion on this historical interpretation, see Usher, J., 2003, 'Direct and individual concern: An effective remedy or a conventional solution?', *European Law Review* 28(5) 575–600. As will be discussed below, the situation has changed to a degree since the amendments were made to Article 263 TFEU, in particular by opening up the possibility of natural or legal persons instituting proceedings against a regulatory act which is of direct concern to them. For further discussion on this, see Buchanan, C., 2012, 'Long awaited guidance on the meaning of 'regulatory act' for locus standi under the Lisbon Treaty', *European Journal of Risk Regulation* 3(1) 115–22; and Balthasar, S., 2010, 'Locus standi rules for challenges to regulatory acts by private applicants: The new Article 263(4) TFEU', *European Law Review* 35(4), 542–50.

9 Case 25/1962 *Plaumann and Company v Commission* [1963] ECR 95.

of the Union' was added. However, even if the application made here were deemed admissible, it was also EFSA's contention that the measure at issue was not open to any such legal challenge before the Court of Justice, as the decision it delivered was merely 'a procedural step in an ongoing decision-making process' and that it 'does not entail any change in the applicant's legal position'. Essentially, EFSA was claiming that they issued an opinion, but that it was the role of the Commission to adopt any binding decision that might follow this.

The Court's deliberations in *Dow* present us with a clear example of the extent to which opinions delivered by EFSA can traditionally be judicially reviewed. The Court commenced with a reaffirmation of the well-established principle that only measures with binding legal, damaging and distinct effects are open to challenge. More specifically, an act that is part of a procedure can only be examined by the Court where it is the definitive decision, setting out the position of the institution concerned at the conclusion of that procedure. Therefore, preliminary or preparatory measures cannot be subjected to actions for annulment under Article 263 TFEU.[10] The opinion delivered by EFSA here was part of a process set out in a Commission Regulation.[11] This involved three defined stages: the drafting of an assessment report by a rapporteur Member State; the adoption of an EFSA opinion on the safety of the active substance for which authorisation is being sought; and the preparation of a final report and draft directive or decision by the Commission. The Court in *Dow* makes it clear that it is only the final part of this process, the production of a directive or decision, can produce any legal effects for third parties. The contested measure here, the EFSA opinion, was therefore deemed to be a mere 'preliminary step in the procedure'. It could not be the subject of an action for annulment before the Court of Justice.

It could of course be argued that the delivery of an EFSA opinion is such a vital part of the decision-making process that it is, at the very least indirectly, a key factor in shaping the legal effects that are ultimately produced. This argument was made in *Dow*. It was, however, rejected. The Court accepted that an EFSA opinion can be very persuasive in any Commission decision, but also that there was no obligation whatsoever on that institution to follow the opinion passed to it by EFSA. The opinion created no binding legal effects on anyone and, as such, fell outside the parameters of any Article 263 TFEU examination.

A similar application was also dismissed by the Court in *FMC*.[12] Here, the applicants were the manufacturers and distributors of carbofuran, commonly

10 Case 60/1981 *IBM v Commission* [1981] ECR 2639.

11 Article 8 of Commission Regulation (EC) No 451/2000 of 28 February 2000 laying down the detailed rules for the implementation of the second and third stages of the work programme referred to in Article 8(2) of Council Directive 1991/414/EEC. [2000] OJ L 55/25.

12 Case T-311/2006 *FMC Chemical SPRL and Arysta Lifesciences SAS v EFSA* [2008] ECR II-88.

used as a pesticide and widely recognised as having a high toxicity level. Following an application for the authorisation of the use this substance, EFSA delivered an opinion to the Commission which concluded that it should not be included on the permitted list. Belgium, the rapporteur Member State in this application, was also of the opinion that carbofuran should not be authorised for use as a pesticide. The Commission followed their advice.[13] Evaluations undertaken on the safety of carbofuran identified a number of concerns about the effect of this substance on birds, in particular, but also on mammals, sea life, bees and earthworms. The applicants sought the annulment of this decision to ban their product.

Again, the Court in *FMC* was being asked to annul the EFSA conclusion that the substance was not safe for use for its intended purpose. EFSA and the Commission were both of the view that this application was inadmissible. EFSA submitted that the nature of the decisions that it makes, and their role in the legislative process, mean that it was not possible for it to be the subject of Article 263 TFEU proceedings. The first point was that this provision of the Treaty made no reference at the time to agencies or bodies not specifically listed, such as the Commission, Council and Parliament. This has, as stated, now changed and EU agencies and bodies are listed in Article 263 TFEU, but EFSA also claimed that its decisions were a mere procedural step in an ongoing process, and did not alter the legal position of the applicant in any way. Again, the Court agreed. The conclusions delivered by EFSA on the appropriateness of using carbofuran as a pesticide was not, therefore, the type of measure that could be the subject of annulment proceedings.

While *FMC* and *Dow* both ultimately reach the same conclusions about the nature of EFSA's role in the legislative process, some of the arguments put forward by the applicants in these cases go some way to explain the legal status of the Authority's decisions. In *FMC*, for example, the Court addressed the claim that EFSA opinions are actually the conclusion of the administrative stage of the evaluation of pesticides, or other plant protection products, and may, therefore, be the subject of annulment actions. Given that the Commission tends to follow EFSA's advice, it is certainly arguable that this presents more than a mere 'procedural step in an on-going process'. The real, and in many ways final, decision is being made by EFSA. The Commission's role is, far more often than not, to formally 'rubber-stamp' a decision on the basis of what it has been advised. It has been suggested elsewhere that the Commission is de facto obliged to follow the EFSA opinion, as it is (a) not equipped to depart from the outcome of the scientific advice presented; and (b) could well feel the wrath of public opinion should it authorise the use of substances in food production which it

13 Resulting in the publication of Commission Decision 2007/416/EC of 13 June 2007 concerning the non-inclusion of carbofuran in Annex I to Council Directive 1991/414/EEC and the withdrawal of authorisations for plant protection products containing that substance. [2007] OJ L 156/30.

has been warned are unsafe.[14] The applicants in *FMC* made a similar argument, relying on what the Court had previously held in *Alliance for Natural Health*.[15] Here, the Court of Justice stated that certain considerations put forward in the case could:

> depending on the circumstances, be advanced in support of an action for annulment of a final decision refusing an application for modification of the positive lists [of vitamins and minerals which may be used in the manufacture of food supplements] or an action for damages against the European Food Safety Authority under Article 47(2) of Regulation 178/2002.[16]

The applicants in *FMC* therefore advanced the argument that this was recognition by the Court that the possibility of bringing an action against a final decision of EFSA refusing an application for authorisation existed. However, this was also rejected. The Court in *FMC* was of the view that this did not refer to EFSA opinions, but instead it was a reference to the possibility on an action against a 'final decision … without specifying that the decision is actually adopted by EFSA'.[17] This was deemed to 'in no way [confirm] that an action for annulment may be brought against a final decision of EFSA'. This view was supported by the fact that Regulation 451/2000, as amended, did not empower EFSA to adopt any 'final decision'.[18] It provides that:

> EFSA shall evaluate the rapporteur's draft assessment report and deliver its opinion on whether the active substance can be expected to meet the safety requirements of the Directive to the Commission.[19]

---

14 Alemanno, A. and Mahieu, S., 2008, 'The European Food Safety Authority before European Courts: Some reflections on the judicial review of EFSA scientific opinions and administrative acts', *European Food and Feed Law Review* 3(5), 320–33, at p. 325. It has, of course, been held elsewhere that the political institutions of the Union are not bound to follow expert advice, as was most famously held in Case T-13/1999, *Pfizer* [2002] ECR II-3305 and, more recently, in case C-77/2009, *Gowen* [2010] ECR I-13533. For further discussion see, respectively, MacMaoláin, C., 2003, 'Using the precautionary principle to protect human health', *European Law Review* 28(5), 723–34; and Alemanno, A., 2011, 'Case C-77/09, Gowan', *Common Market Law Review* 48(4), 1329–1348.

15 Joined cases C-154/2004 and C-155/2004 *Alliance for Natural Health and National Association of Health Stores v Secretary of State for Health* [2005] ECR I-6451.

16 Joined cases C-154/2004 and C-155/2004, note 15 above, at paragraph 88.

17 Case T-311/2006, note 12 above, at paragraph 58.

18 Articles 8(7) and (8) of Regulation 451/2000, note 11 above, as amended by Commission Regulation (EC) No 1490/2002 of 14 August 2002 laying down further detailed rules for the implementation of the third stage of the programme of work referred to in Article 8(2) of Council Directive 1991/414/EEC and amending Regulation (EC) No 451/2000. [2002] OJ L 224/23.

19 Article 8(7) of Regulation 451/2000, note 11 above.

It then further states that:

> [a]t least six months after receipt of the EFSA opinion ... the Commission shall submit the draft review report [and] a draft directive to include the active substance [on the permitted list] or a draft decision addressed to the Member States to withdraw the authorisations of plant protection products containing the active substance.[20]

A combination of these factors led the Court in *FMC* to the opinion that the EFSA report did not, and could not, conclude the administrative stage of the safety evaluation. Only a Commission directive or decision could be regarded as the final stage in the procedure.

It was also argued in *FMC* that EFSA had been delegated the power to adopt decisions that have binding legal effects on third parties, and could therefore be the subject of judicial review. However, the Court, noting its famous decision in *Meroni*,[21] found that these powers only exist where the delegating authority, in this case the Commission, makes an express decision to delegate. Looking at the wording of Regulation (EC) No 451/2000, the Court found that the Commission has to draw up a review report on the basis of the EFSA opinion, as outlined above. It is the Commission, and not EFSA, which then issues the draft directive or decision. The Regulation, as amended, is quite clear on this. No such power has been delegated to EFSA, expressly or otherwise, as was the contention here. Similar arguments were made, and rejected, by the Court in *Dow*.

Regulatory Acts

One potentially significant alteration to the position of the individual applicant who seeks the annulment of an EFSA opinion is that which is now set out in Article 263(4) TFEU. This provides that:

> [a]ny natural or legal person may, under the conditions laid down in [Article 263 TFEU] institute proceedings against an act addressed to that person or which is of direct and individual concern to them, and against a regulatory act which is of direct concern to them and does not entail implementing measures.

Defining what constitutes a 'regulatory act' is key to ascertaining the possibilities that this may present to the previously inhibited non-privileged applicant.

20 Article 8(8) of Regulation 451/2000, note 11 above.

21 Case 9/1956 *Meroni v High Authority* [1957–58] ECR 133.

Decisions of the General Court in *Inuit*[22] and *Microban*[23] suggest that 'all acts of general application' are covered by Article 263(4) TFEU and are, therefore, open to legal challenge by those who are directly concerned by them, provided they do not entail implementing measures.[24] In the latter case, the applicants were not the subject of the contested decision, which excluded specific substances (triclosan) from the permitted list of additives that could be used in the manufacture of materials intended to come into contact with foodstuffs.[25] They could therefore only bring an action for annulment in the circumstances if the decision was either a regulatory act of direct concern to them and not requiring any implementing measures, or if it was a decision of direct and individual concern to them. In establishing whether this decision was a 'regulatory act', the Court, noting its earlier order in *Inuit*, stated that this would be so if it was an '[act] of general application apart from [a] legislative act'. Further to this, it would be of 'general application' if it applied to 'objectively determined situations [producing] legal effects with respect to categories of persons envisaged in general and in the abstract'. Given that the Decision did not include triclosan in the permitted list, its use would be prohibited in the Union after 1 November 2011. The contested decision was thus deemed to apply to 'all natural and legal persons who are engaged in the production and/or marketing of triclosan and materials and articles containing that substance'. The decision was, therefore, a regulatory act – examinable under the terms of Article 263(4) TFEU.

The Decision in *Microban* did not concern an application against an EFSA opinion, as such, either. EFSA was involved in the regulatory process, having confirmed an earlier Scientific Committee on Food evaluation which had found that the use of triclosan as a contact material was acceptable. This substance was ultimately not included on the permitted list, however, because an application to have it authorised had been withdrawn by a third party. The applicants in *Microban* were the manufacturers and sellers of these products. Their business was thus adversely affected by the exclusion of triclosan from the permitted list. The importance of this is that, following the determinations in both *Inuit* and *Microban*, a new type of EU act is more readily open to judicial review and the possibility of challenging this act is opened up to more non-privileged applicants. 'Regulatory acts', as they have been qualified by the Court, could therefore be capable of challenge before the EU Courts, once they are of direct concern to the applicant and do not require Member States to take further implementing measures,

22 Order of the General Court in Case T-18/2010 *Inuit Tapiriit Kanatamiand others v Parliament and Council*, 6 September 2011.

23 Case T-262/2010 *Microban International v Commission*, 25 October 2011.

24 Paragraph 18 of the Judgement in *Microban*, note 23 above.

25 Commission Decision (EC) 2010/169 of 19 March 2010 concerning the non-inclusion of 2,4,4 '-trichloro-2'-hydroxydiphenyl ether in the Union list of additives which may be used in the manufacture of plastic materials and articles intended to come into contact with foodstuffs under Directive 2002/72/EC. [2010] OJ L 75/25.

provided they produce legal effects. If applied, the approach of the Court in earlier case law, such as *Dow*, may still place limits on this new possibility that has been created by the inclusion of Article 263(4) TFEU in the Treaty. 'Producing legal effects' may still have to be proven, meaning that a demonstration must be made that the EFSA opinion delivered was highly persuasive and an integral part of the regulatory procedure.

Seeking Redress for the Consequences of EFSA Opinions

It has become clear that unless a specific power to make legally binding decisions is delegated to EFSA, then the decisions that it makes cannot readily be the subject of judicial review. It has here been contended that this situation mostly persists, despite the changes made to Article 263 TFEU, in particular the inclusion of agencies and bodies as being amongst those organs of the Union which may have the validity of their actions tested before the Court, and the inclusion of regulatory acts in this important Treaty provision. Part of the reason for this is the failure to set any clear decision-making powers for EFSA in the General Food Law Regulation. However, as stated, that same legislation does provide that EFSA can be held liable where it causes damage by its acts or omissions.[26]

Separate to the annulment actions, the applicants in both *Dow* and *FMC* sought damages for the losses that they suffered as a result of the respective EFSA opinions on the safety of their products. In addition to the provision in Regulation 178/2002 for EFSA to incur non-contractual liability for damage caused by it, Article 340 TFEU also stipulates that:

> [i]n the case of non-contractual liability, the Union shall … make good any damage caused by its institutions or by its servants in the performance of their duties.

However, it has become well established through the case law that this liability will only be realised where a set of conditions are satisfied. First, the conduct of the Union body must have been 'unlawful', involving some 'sufficiently serious' breach of the law.[27] Second, there must have been some measurable damage caused to the applicant. Third, there must be a 'causal link' between the alleged conduct and the damage suffered.[28] In *Dow*, the applicants brought their claim for damages on three grounds: the loss of profit suffered as a result

---

26 Article 47(2) thereof.

27 See, for example, Joined Cases C-46/1993 and 48/1993, *Brasserie du pêcheur* and *Factortame*, [1996] ECR I-1029.

28 See, for example, Case 26/1981 *Oleifici Mediterranei v EEC* [1982] ECR 3057; and Case T-175/1994, *International Procurement Services v Commission* [1996] ECR II-729.

of reduced sales of their products which contained the unauthorised substance; the consequent damage to their reputation; and the additional costs incurred in supplying EFSA with data which was requested during the evaluation procedure. In order to satisfy the conditions that must be met before a claim for damages can be assessed by the Court, any applicant must be able to quantify in monetary terms the damage that they have suffered. The Court in *Dow* found that all that had been submitted to it was a series of abstract and general assertions, such as that arising from 'damages resulting from the bad reputation that the contested measure has brought to the image of the company' and 'lost profits deriving from its customers' and distributors' stated intention to stop purchasing [its] products'. This sort of claim led the Court to the finding that the applicant had failed to provide sufficient evidence which verified the reality or quantity of any damage suffered. The claim for damages was also, therefore, deemed inadmissible.

Testing EFSA Opinions in Other Types of Action

While the main case law involving EFSA has dealt with applications for the annulment of its decisions and its non-contractual liability for its actions, other cases and applications have made different claims against the Authority. There have been claims made, for example, that EFSA has withheld information that should be made available. It has also been contended that the Authority has failed to operate proper tendering procedures for the supply of services. Outside the Court, there have also been calls for independent inquiries into the scientific methods that EFSA employs in its assessments.

Applications have been made to the General Court for the annulment of decisions made by EFSA, which resulted in a partial refusal to grant requests for access to documents. In *ClientEarth*,[29] which at the time of writing was a pending case, the applicants alleged that the Authority had withheld intermediate drafts and the scientific advice provided by EFSA's Pesticides Steering Committee and Plant Protection Products and their Residues Panel, which relate to the approval procedure for pesticide substances under the terms of Regulation 1107/2009.[30] This application has been made on the basis of four contentions. First, it is alleged that the refusal to disclose the documents is contrary to Regulation 1049/2001.[31] This Regulation provides that:

29 Pending case T-214/2011 *ClientEarth and PAN Europe v EFSA*.

30 Regulation (EC) No 1107/2009 of the European Parliament and of the Council of 21 October 2009 concerning the placing of plant protection products on the market and repealing Council Directives 1979/117/EEC and 1991/414/EEC. [2009] OJ L 309/1.

31 Regulation (EC) No 1049/2001 of the European Parliament and of the Council of 30 May 2001 regarding public access to European Parliament, Council and Commission documents. [2001] OJ L 145/43.

> [a] confirmatory application [for access to documents] shall be handled promptly [and] in the event of a total or partial refusal, the institution shall inform the applicant of the remedies open to him or her, namely instituting court proceedings against the institution.[32]

The Regulation extends to the operations of agencies established by the institutions, including EFSA.[33] This claim relates to an allegation that EFSA failed to reply within the time limits prescribed by the Regulation. Second, it was claimed that the contested decision violates the Aarhus Convention on Access to Information, Public Participation in Decision-making and Access to Justice in Environmental Matters,[34] by failing to provide the applicants with access to the requested drafts and scientific advice provided by EFSA. Third, it was contended that the decision to refuse disclosure was not based on any of the permitted exceptions to the duty to disclose, such as that which allows EFSA to keep information confidential where to do otherwise would seriously undermine its own decision-making procedures.[35] Finally, it was claimed that the decision was not shown to be necessary for some public interest purpose, nor were sufficient reasons given for the refusal to provide the applicants with the documents and draft reports. Whatever the outcome in *ClientEarth*, it is vital that access to EFSA deliberations and documentation is maintained where feasible. Although this may be restricted in certain circumstances, in particular out of the necessity of protecting the confidentiality of EFSA and/or those affected by its decisions, this must be limited to those circumstances where this is absolutely necessary if confidence in the transparency and accountability of the Authority's operations is to be maintained.[36]

On an administrative level, aspects of the way in which EFSA runs tendering processes for the supply of services have been tested before the Court on several occasions. In *Dynamiki*, the applicant claimed that EFSA had erred in its award of contracts for the supply of information technology services.[37] The dispute arose when, following a protracted series of communications between the applicants

32 Article 8 of Regulation 1049/2001, note 31 above.

33 The Preamble to Regulation 1049/2001 provides, in recital 8, that '[i]n order to ensure the full application of this Regulation to all activities of the Union, all agencies established by the institutions should apply the principles laid down in this Regulation'.

34 Article 4 thereof.

35 As set out in Article 4 of Regulation 1049/2001, note 31 above.

36 Article 4 of Regulation 1049/2001, note 31 above, provides that '[t]he institutions shall refuse access to a document where disclosure would undermine the protection of the public interest; [the] privacy and the integrity of the individual; [the] commercial interests of a natural or legal person, including intellectual property; court proceedings and legal advice; the purpose of inspections, investigations and audits, unless there is an overriding public interest in disclosure'.

37 Case T-69/2005 *Evropaïki Dynamiki v EFSA*, Order of the Court of First Instance, 19 October 2007, not reported.

and EFSA, it was claimed by the former that the Authority had been wrong to exclude its bid in the tendering process for the provision of IT services. This followed, in particular, the fact that EFSA had later cancelled the call for tenders but still awarded part of the contract at issue to one of the parties who had applied for the overall award. It was alleged by the applicants that this was a misuse of power and contrary to the law relating to public procurement. It was also claimed that EFSA had not provided sufficient reasons for its decision to cancel its original call. The Court found that the contentions made by the applicants were inadmissible, primarily because the call for tenders had already been cancelled, so no claim related to that original call could now form the subject of legal proceedings. While it ultimately refused to adjudicate on the case the Court did make two important declarations here. It found that the applicant could potentially bring an application for compensation for damage suffered as a result of the allegedly unlawful conduct of EFSA throughout the contested tendering procedure. It also instructed EFSA to pay all of the legal costs, as this would '[constitute] a fair reflection on the circumstances in the [case]'.

Finally, EFSA has been the subject of calls for independent inquiries into its work. The Alliance for Natural Health, for example, claims that EFSA's scientific methods are flawed, and must therefore be reviewed.[38] The concern relates, in particular, to EFSA's decision to issue a positive assessment on the use of sodium monofluorophosphate as a food supplement. As the chemical in question is normally used in toothpaste and mouthwash products to prevent or treat tooth decay and dental disease, the Alliance for Natural Health has suggested that any assessment of its use as a supplement should be for the European Medicines Agency to make, and not EFSA. Their concerns relate, in particular, to the fact that allowing the addition of fluoride to supplements, in addition to their existing inclusion in toothpaste, mouthwash and, in some Member States, the public drinking water supply, means that consumers could become over-exposed to the consumption of the chemical, and suffer detrimental health consequences as a result. They were also highly critical of the perceived lack of transparency in EFSA decision-making processes. Referring back to the decision of the Court of Justice in *Alliance for Natural Health*,[39] it was claimed that an inquiry into EFSA's main operations is now required as there has been a failure to comply with the instructions set out in the case that assessment procedures must be accessible, quick and, most importantly, based on a full assessment of the risk posed to public health, established on the basis of the most reliable scientific data available and the most recent results of international research.[40]

38 For further detail see the statements issued at: www.anh-europe.org.

39 Joined cases C-154/2004 and C-155/2004, note 15 above.

40 Ibid., paragraph 73.

Concluding Remarks

Article 263 TFEU is now more relevant for bodies, such as EFSA, post the amendments made by the Lisbon Treaty. Offices and agencies of the Union were excluded from those organs which could have the legality of their acts challenged before the Court of Justice under the previous Article 230 EC. This has now changed. The Lisbon Treaty explicitly includes EU bodies, offices and agencies as being among those organs of the Union whose actions are subject to judicial review. Agencies had already become the scope of Court examination prior to this.[41] Lisbon cemented this position into EU law. However, the nature of EFSA's role in the decision-making process means that any opinion it delivers cannot be annulled by the Court unless it produces legal effects for third parties. 'Opinions' are not 'decisions', and cannot therefore be subject to ECJ scrutiny in the same way. EFSA opinions may, however, be subject to Court examination should the Commission choose to follow their advice and the opinion delivered forms the foundations for EU institutional action.

Many regulations and directives make specific reference to the need to take EFSA opinions into consideration when making science-based decisions and, where they do not, to explain why not.[42] This remains crucial to ensuring that EFSA retains its position as a primary point of reference in the development and application of food law. Subjecting these decisions to the interrogation of judicial review, albeit after they have been realised in the form of an institutional decision, is the safest way of ensuring that the Authority is secure against claims that its procedures are not transparent and that it lacks accountability for its actions. It is vital for the maintenance of a system that seeks to ensure that the supply of food is safe, and that it is scientifically verified as being so.

41 Case T-411/2006 *Sogelma-Societá generale lavori manutenzioni appalti Srl v European Agency for Reconstruction (AER)* [2008] ECR II-2771.

42 For example, Article 17(1) of Regulation (EC) No 1924/2006 of the European Parliament and of the Council of 20 December 2006 on nutrition and health claims made on foods, [2006] OJ L 404/9, provides that: '[w]here the draft decision is not in accordance with the opinion of the Authority, the Commission shall provide an explanation for the differences'.

Chapter 14
A View of EFSA from the European Parliament

Dagmar Roth-Behrendt

Introduction

Food lies in the heart of all Europeans. It is strongly embedded as one constitutive aspect of each national tradition and utterly linked to the various European cultures. The level of public attention to food safety issues has been very high in Europe, particularly over the last 15 years. Europeans expect from their public institutions that they carefully control risks related to food. Confidence therefore plays a huger role in this public policy area than in many others. Since the mid 1990s, a series of crises have affected this trust between the Europeans and their public authorities, and the former have started demanding food safety standards of a higher level to prevent them from experiencing fear over the products they consume every day. The European Parliament has played an important role in this constant demand for safe food.

The decision to separate risk assessment from risk management was a major lesson learnt from one of the most concerning incidents in food safety over the last decades, the BSE crisis. It gave birth to the European Food Safety Authority. In only 10 years, EFSA has managed to become the landmark agency in Europe for scientific advice in the areas of pesticides, animal health and welfare, chemicals in food, nutrition, and the fight against zoonoses. One must surely appreciate the limited time it took EFSA to be recognised for the seriousness of its scientific assessments. Despite the success of this young European agency, some critics have also arisen, for instance on transparency or on the independence of scientific advice in food-related risks from commercial or political interests – they must also be heard to make sure EFSA continues to progress.

Over the last years, EFSA has striven to learn from its experience. After 10 years of existence, the Authority can consider the great amount of accomplished work. The European Parliament appreciates the quality of EFSA's scientific assessments which has enabled even more enlightened decision-takings at EU level in the field of food and feed. Europeans must be proud to have such an agency dedicated to their safety.

As a Member of the European Parliament, I will continue to carefully scrutinise EFSA's work and speak truly but in trust with EFSA.

The Establishment of the Food Safety Authority in Times of the BSE Crisis

Over the EU's history, there had been repeated calls for the creation of a European food regulatory agency much before the outbreak of the so-called 'mad-cow' disease (or bovine spongiform encephalopathy, BSE) 16 years ago in Europe. This BSE crisis was one of the main drivers for the creation of EFSA. It has revealed to the public some wrong agricultural practices, such as the feeding of ruminants with animal proteins. It has also put in evidence the importance of safe food in our daily lives and the need to ensure that consumers have confidence in the decision-making processes underpinning food law.

This BSE outbreak in the mid 1990s made it clear for the European Parliament that alongside a new specific legislation on prevention, control and eradication of transmissible spongiform encephalopathies (TSE), a food authority was needed. EFSA was thus created in 2002 and notably tasked to provide the best scientific opinions in view of the preparation and discussion of EU legislation and policies that have an impact on food and feed safety.

The following year, EFSA became formally in charge of providing independent scientific advice to decision-makers in the EU and the EU's response to the BSE crisis was indeed influenced by EFSA's scientific advice. The replacement of the ad hoc Group of the European Commission Scientific Steering Committee by a permanent scientific body like EFSA has contributed to the success of the EU's response to the crisis in the following years. EFSA must be proud of its contribution to the coordinated response it provided all along the last 10 years.

As for the European Parliament, it has repeatedly highlighted that consumer protection, animal health and the eradication of TSEs must always remain a crucial objective of the Member States and the European Commission. No matter how the downward trend in TSE cases can be, it must not lead to less stringent control and surveillance. Since the complete eradication of BSE can probably still take years (given its long incubation period), the Member States and the European Commission have to remain steadily attentive and they must cautiously monitor the development of TSEs in case of a re-emergence of the disease.

This is the reason why my report on the implementation and outlook of the EU legislation on TSE and on related feed and food controls (adopted by the European Parliament in July last year) 'underlines the importance of ensuring that the significant decline in BSE cases in the European Union does not lead to less stringent TSE measures or to a reduction in the strict control and surveillance mechanisms in the EU'. Fighting zoonoses can only be successful if the most robust legal framework exists and if Member States implement these provisions properly by supplying sufficient staff and financial means to ensure the necessary controlling measures.

I am convinced that one of the most important lessons from the BSE crisis has been the need to apply the highest of quality standards to the raising and feeding of animals. In view of this objective, high standard scientific assessments will continue to be expected from EFSA. However, at that time of the BSE crisis, Member

States were much more prone than now to take all the necessary measures to make sure their legislation was as safe as possible. As the shadow of a food safety crisis seems to vanish and as we have the perception that we are smoothly going back to a more 'normal situation', Member States are quickly losing their enthusiasm. They are becoming too timid and we are for instance missing the opportunity to make the electronic identification of bovines progressively mandatory. It is as if we were waiting for future crisis to be then forced to take decisions.

Has EFSA Delivered Over the Last 10 Years?

When looking at EFSA's achievements, Members of the European Parliament would certainly mention its joint role with the European Centre for Disease Prevention and Control (ECDC) in advice provision for the control of salmonellosis. Between 2006 and 2010 the EU has experienced a decrease by nearly one-half of human salmonella. EFSA's advice on risks, evaluation of the impacts of adopted measures, analysis of EU-wide survey and data from Member States are recognised in this field. EFSA has so far fulfilled its risk assessment role in a satisfactory way but communicating on these positive outcomes is uneasy as the public attention is often more easily attracted by new food crisis than successes. The European Parliament has supported EFSA's work in this field and some of its Members have urged to increase investment in tackling animal-to-human diseases.

In the recent (May to July 2011) outbreak of Escherichia coli in Germany and then France, EFSA has also shown its ability to perform in times of crisis and to provide the expertise asked by European regulators and the European Parliament. In order to provide immediate scientific assistance, the Authority set up and participated in a task force in June 2011 together with experts from the European Commission, some EU Member States, ECDC, the World Health Organisation (WHO) and the Food and Agriculture Organisation (FAO). The positive aspect of EFSA's risk assessment lies in the effective cooperation between the Authority and the Member States or other European agencies such as ECDC. We should build on this success in other areas and make sure this quality is maintained in future possible outbreak.

Another very controversial area is nutrition where EFSA's assessments work on thousands of health claims have led to some critics. The number of nutrition and health claims which argue that a food product holds some positive nutritional properties has soared in Europe over the last years. In May 2012, 222 of the 3,000 claims received were finally admitted, without the European Parliament contesting this list of permitted health claims. For the other claims (mainly botanicals and food supplements) that were put 'on hold' by the Commission already in September 2010, EFSA indicated that the evidence of 'traditional use' alone does not constitute sufficient evidence to prove the substantiation of a claim and I cannot agree more.

A deeply controversial issue is the assessment of Genetically Modified Organisms (GMOs) and more precisely those related to plants. Public opinions and Governments are very much divided on the thorny issue of the authorisation of GMO cultivation, as well as of their placing on the EU market and of the use of their derived products in the food and feed chain.[1] Indeed, GMOs themselves but also the regulatory approach to them is looked at differently in each Member State, as well as in the different parts of the society. While those different standpoints are reflected in the European Parliament, a significant amount of its Members have repeatedly called for some caution in this area where thorough and scientific evidence of high quality, as well as the precautionary principle should guide the consideration of any new authorisation. EFSA's role consists in assessing potential risks of GMOs to human and animal health and to the environment. These case-by-case assessments are all the more crucial that they will constitute the scientific basis of discussion for EU risk managers and the European Parliament. This is why EFSA must ensure it provides them with the best quality scientific assessments in the field of feed and food products. The youngest diverging scientific opinions on GMO maize or potato and uproars in many different Member States have proved that EFSA and the Commission still have some way to go to guarantee the best state of science and consumer trust.

The Way Forward

EFSA has grown and developed over the last 10 years. It has become an agency well-recognised for its rigorous work and it must continue to ensure that it provides the best scientific evidence and advice at all times. In case of doubts concerning the safety of food or ingredients, EFSA has to use the precautionary principle in its daily work and it has to appear in its risk assessments. EU citizens must be able to enjoy the same level of protection everywhere in the European Union. The best European food legislation assessed by EFSA is the best guarantee in this respect and the European Parliament relies on EFSA's expertise for deciding on what food safety legislation should apply in the EU. In order to get the most suitable scientific advice, EFSA needs the best scientists in Europe; it should make sure it continues to attract them.

EFSA must also ensure that it provides information to the European legislators and risk managers in a clear and intelligible way. In this respect, communication is key. It is true that communicating risk assessments and scientific information more generally, in a clear and timely manner constitutes a real challenge. Scientific assessments conducted at the EU level should be transferred in a non-scientific language while remaining accurate. In this respect also the European Parliament

1 On EFSA's contribution to the risk analysis of GMO products, see in this volume Poli, S., 'Scientific Advice in the GMO Area', Chapter 7.

will remain vigilant so that these scientific assessments at EU level remain of high quality and enable thoughtful decision-making.

Lastly, EFSA has to be transparent about its risk assessments and the scientists taking part in them. This is crucial if we want to ensure EFSA's reputation remains at the highest possible standard. As EFSA's experts give determining advice on the safety of our food in the EU, all scientists and members of EFSA's bodies must provide all information on any past or actual positions or activities related to the topics they are responsible for in EFSA – only then trust will exist in scientific advice or opinions.

Conclusion

Consumer confidence in food or drink is now higher than in the decade following the BSE crisis. By bringing serious scientific assessments, EFSA has played an important role in increasing general trust in the EU food safety system. However, public confidence in food safety management is fragile and EFSA should continue to invest in strong and clear communication for its assessment of new technologies notably. Expectations from European consumers as regards food information are very high. Food products should bear clear and understandable information, including on the production process. Enhanced transparency on the products and empowered consumers should be our constant aim at EU level. Transparency from public authorities in their communication on risks in the area of food and feed will also help in ensuring confidence in the area of food and feed.

Also, the European Parliament will always remain particularly demanding as regards EFSA's policy to ensure that its experts do not have vested interests in some food and feed industries. This is crucial if we want to ensure that the solid scientific reputation it took time to build is not suddenly put into question by the discovery of potential conflicts of interest. EFSA should therefore learn from its recent difficulties and remember that it is acting in a sensitive field. To gain and maintain trust in EFSA's recommendations, the European Parliament expects the agency to ensure that it constantly provides the highest sound scientific evidence and transparency. EFSA can be assured of our appreciation of its work in the provision of scientific opinions in relation to food safety. It enables the co-legislators in Europe to take actions to protect the Europeans where needed.

More importantly, EFSA must continue to aim for the best scientific advice for decision-makers. The European Parliament will continue to expect clear messages and the best scientific evidence from the agency. It should invest in attracting the best scientists, in issuing quality assessments at the quickest pace possible and in communicating clearly its findings notably to the general audience. At the same time, EFSA must also now become a landmark agency at the international level. Europeans must ensure that their expertise in the food safety assessment is also recognised outside the European Union. They should be proud of their values and aim at the constant attempt to provide the highest and safest quality of food and feed within their territory. EFSA is well prepared to support this aim and should continue to do so.

Chapter 15
A View of EFSA from the Member States

Isidora Maletić[1]

Introduction

This chapter explores the use of scientific expertise in EU harmonisation and, more particularly, the role played by the European Food Safety Authority (EFSA) within that context from the perspective of the Member States. The founding EFSA regulation, Regulation 178/2002, conferred on this agency risk assessment and risk communication powers but not a risk regulation function, the latter deemed to be more appropriately left outside EFSA's remit, within the domain of the Commission and the Member States. Various reasons were cited in the White Paper on Food Safety for the exclusion of risk management from EFSA's mandate.[2] It has been suggested, however, that a significant underlying motive for the rejection of this transfer has been the reluctance of the Member States to relinquish their control in favour of an extraneous food agency.[3] Indeed, whilst 'EFSA has not been conceived as a pan-European scientific body aimed at imposing its scientific voice over national opinions in food matters', but rather could be seen as intended at 'providing an independent European view which

1 The opinions expressed are wholly personal.

2 '*Firstly, there is a serious concern that a transfer of regulatory powers to an independent Authority could lead to an unwarranted dilution of democratic accountability. The current decision-making process provides a high degree of accountability and transparency, which could be difficult to replicate in a decentralised structure. Secondly, the control function must be at the heart of the Commission's risk management process if it is to act effectively on behalf of the consumer, notably in ensuring that recommendations for action arising from control are properly followed up. The Commission must retain both regulation and control if it is to discharge the responsibilities placed upon it under the Treaties. Thirdly, an Authority with regulatory power could not be created under the current institutional arrangements of the European Union, and would require modification of the existing provisions of the EC Treaty. For these reasons, it is not proposed to transfer risk management competencies to the Authority*', European Commission, White Paper on Food Safety (COM 719 final, 1999): para. 33.

3 Alemanno, A., 'The Evolution of European Food Regulation: Why the European Food Safety Authority Is Not a EU-Style FDA?', in C. Ansell and D. Vogel (eds), *What's The Beef? The Contested Governance of European Food Safety* (MIT Press; Bocconi Legal Studies Research Paper No. 1007451; 2006). Available at SSRN: http://ssrn.com/abstract=1007451, p. 19.

ideally complements Member States' studies',[4] contested scientific issues may in fact readily create friction between EFSA and the national authorities.[5]

This chapter aims to explore the dynamics of this interaction by scrutinising several instances where EFSA's involvement has been of considerable import from the perspective of national authorities in the context of EU harmonisation. The analysis is divided into three main sections: firstly, an examination of the scope for conflict and possible implications of EFSA's scientific evaluation for risk assessments executed by national authorities; secondly, an examination of EFSA's influence in the light of the ambitious mandate conferred on it and evolving practice emanating from the EU legislative framework; and thirdly, a prospective analysis of the possible reconciliation between divergent risk perceptions within the context of EU integration.

Establishing the Potential for Conflict: Different Risk Perceptions in EU Integration

The potential for conflict between EFSA's risk assessment and national scientific conclusions can be perceptibly deduced from the *Austrian GMOs* case. Austria notified the Commission of a draft Austrian act banning the use of genetically modified organisms (GMOs) in the region of Upper Austria in derogation of Directive 2001/18/EC, which was aimed at approximating legislation in the Member States for the authorisation of GMOs intended for deliberate release into the environment. Directive 2001/18/EC had been adopted on the basis of what is now Article 114 TFEU (formerly Article 95 EC and, before that, Article 100a of the EC Treaty),[6] which enables the EU legislature to pass legislation having as its

4 Alemanno, A., *Trade in Food, Regulatory and Judicial Approaches in the EC and the WTO* (Cameron May 2007), p. 170.

5 The potential for such conflict is implicit in the founding EFSA legislation, Regulation 178/2002, which referring to the agency stipulates that the latter 'should cooperate closely with competent bodies in the Member States if it is to operate effectively. An Advisory Forum should be created in order to advise the Executive Director, to constitute a mechanism of exchange of information, and to ensure close cooperation in particular with regard to the networking system. Cooperation and appropriate exchange of information should also minimise the potential for diverging scientific opinions'; Regulation 178/2002 of the European Parliament and of the Council of 28 January 2002 laying down the general principles and requirements of food law, establishing the European Food Safety Authority and laying down procedures in matters of food safety [2002] OJ L 31/1: Preamble, para. 44.

6 Directive 2001/18/EC of the European Parliament and of the Council of 12 March 2001 on the deliberate release into the environment of genetically modified organisms and repealing Council Directive 90/220/EEC [2001] OJ 2001 L 106/1. The Treaty of Lisbon [2007] OJ C 306/1 has amended the Treaty on European Union and the Treaty establishing the European Community. See, for a table of equivalences setting out the new numbering

object the establishment and functioning of the internal market, whilst permitting Member States, on the grounds of protection of specific interests and subject to the fulfilment of strict legal requirements, to maintain existing or introduce new national measures derogating from a harmonisation measure enacted pursuant to this internal market legal basis.[7] The Austrian notification was made under what is now Article 114(5) TFEU (formerly Article 95(5) EC) requiring the introduction of national provisions derogating from an approximation norm to be based on new scientific evidence relating to the protection of the environment or the working environment on grounds of a problem specific to the Member State concerned arising after the adoption of the harmonisation measure.[8] The draft act sought to ban the use of all GMOs in the region of Upper Austria, whereas Directive 2001/18/EC envisaged a step-by-step approval process on a case-by-case risk assessment to human health and the environment prior to the authorisation of a GMO. Furthermore, unlike Directive 2001/18/EC, the draft act foresaw a prohibition of all genetically modified seeds, irrespective of whether they had been approved or not. Austria relied as a justification for the draft act on a study on coexistence, the Müller Study, commissioned by the province of Upper Austria and the Federal Ministry of Social Security and Generations. It was submitted that the Müller Study had brought to light new scientific evidence showing a danger for the Upper Austrian environment, as well as that it had demonstrated that the Upper Austrian agricultural structure was specific (primarily because based on small-scale farms, with a substantial proportion of organic farming)[9] within the meaning of the relevant notification procedure.

Upon request from the Commission for a scientific opinion[10] on the notified derogation and following investigation of the evidence presented in the Austrian submission, EFSA's Scientific Panel on GMOs concluded that there was no new scientific evidence, in terms of risk to human health and the environment, to

---

following the Lisbon reforms, the Consolidated Versions of the Treaty on European Union and the Treaty on the Functioning of the European Union [2010] OJ C 83/361. See for discussion, Maletić, I., 'The boundaries of the Internal Market after the Lisbon Treaty' (paper presented at the Jean Monnet Seminar, Dubrovnik, Croatia, 2009) in 5 *Croatian Yearbook of European Law and Policy* (2009): 19.

7 For an in-depth analysis of the Article 114 TFEU derogation mechanism and its implications for the European internal market harmonisation paradigm, see Maletić, I., *The Law and Policy of Harmonisation in Europe's Internal Market* (Edward Elgar Publishing, 2013).

8 The conditions in Article 114(5) are cumulative, so they must all be satisfied for a Member State derogation request to be granted by the Commission (Case C-512/99 *Germany v Commission* [2003] ECR I-845: paras 80–81).

9 Furthermore, as the Müller study had been published after the adoption of Directive 2001/18/EC, Austria argued that the issue of coexistence had not been adequately covered by the approximation norm.

10 Under Article 29(1) and in accordance with Article 22(5)(c) of Regulation 178/2002.

justify the proposed national prohibition.[11] Relying largely on EFSA's reasoning,[12] the Commission was persuaded that the scientific information presented in the report commissioned by the national authorities provided no new data that would invalidate the provisions for the environmental risk assessment established under Directive 2001/18/EC. Referring extensively to EFSA's opinion,[13] the Commission determined that no new scientific evidence relating to the protection of the environment or the working environment, and no specific problem within the territory of Upper Austria arising following the adoption of Directive 2001/18/EC had been proved by the notifying Member State. It is noteworthy that EFSA's opinion seems not only to have influenced the Commission's assessment with respect to the verification of compliance with the requirements in the internal market notification procedure, but also with regard to the plausibility of invoking the precautionary principle.[14]

Whilst Regulation 178/2002, in establishing EFSA and laying down procedures in matters of food safety, has not endowed the agency with 'scientific supremacy over national scientific studies',[15] it is clear from the Commission's reliance on EFSA's analysis that its risk assessment advice can have far-reaching effects for national authorities seeking to adjust their regulatory frameworks in the light of particular scientific concerns. The relevance of EFSA's opinion is perhaps accentuated even more by the fact that it has been held that, in the context of the process of EU harmonisation, given that the notification procedure in what is now Article 114 TFEU is initiated by notifying Member States and must be capable of being concluded rapidly (the Commission has to approve or reject the relevant national provisions within six months of any given notification, with the possibility of a single extension in exceptional circumstances of complexity), the right to be heard does not apply to it.[16] Thus, in the *Austrian GMOs* case, it

11 Opinion of the Scientific Panel on Genetically Modified Organisms on a question from the Commission related to the Austrian notification of national legislation governing GMOs under Article 95(5) of the Treaty, EFSA Journal 2003: 1.

12 It is noteworthy that the judgment of the Court of Justice, referring to EFSA's contribution, states 'Those were the circumstances in which the Commission adopted the contested decision' (Cases C-439/05 and C-454/05 *Land Oberösterreich and Republic of Austria v Commission* [2007]: para. 8).

13 Commission Decision 2003/653/EC of 2 September 2003 relating to national provisions on banning the use of genetically modified organisms in the region of Upper Austria notified by the Republic of Austria pursuant to Article 95(5) of the EC Treaty [2003] OJ L 230/34: particularly at paras 64–71.

14 The Commission considered that the allegations made for recourse to the precautionary principle were 'too general and lack substance', noting that EFSA had not identified a risk capable of justifying 'taking action on the basis of the precautionary principle at Community or national level' (Commission Decision 2003/653/EC: para. 73).

15 Alemanno 2007: 192.

16 Case C-3/00 *Denmark v Commission* [2003] ECR I-2643; Cases C-439/05 and C-454/05 *Land Oberösterreich and Republic of Austria v Commission* [2007]: especially

was submitted by the applicants that their right to be heard had been breached by the Commission not giving them the opportunity to state their views on the EFSA opinion before adopting the contested decision.[17] However, this argument was rejected on the basis that 'the Commission must be able, within the prescribed period, to obtain the information which proves to be necessary without being required once more to hear the applicant Member State'.[18] The concomitant implication is that an opinion by EFSA may seemingly acquire a quasi-conclusive character.[19] The distinction between risk assessment and risk management underlying EFSA's founding institutional configuration entails of course a responsibility for the Commission, within the context of adapting the harmonisation of the internal market in the light of scientific progress, to reach a conclusion on the basis of all available evidence. Nevertheless, functional constraints may well result in an enhanced role for EFSA: indeed, in the *Austrian GMOs* case, it was held that the 'requirement that new scientific evidence must be adduced in support of the request may, in this respect, lead the Commission,

---

at paras 37, 41 and 43. See further, Maletić, I., 'The Relevance of Scientific Evidence in European Law' (paper presented at the ISUFI conference in Italy, 2007), in M. C. Malaguti, C. Dordi, S. Di Benedetto and A. Alemanno (eds) *Scientific Evidence in International and European Law. Proceedings of the Young Researcher Workshop on Science and Law* (Argo Editore, Italy; 2010); Maletić, I. 'Theory and Practice of Harmonisation in the European Internal Market' (paper presented at W G Hart Legal Workshop, London, 2008) in C. Andersen and M. Andenas (eds) *Theory and Practice of Harmonisation* (Edward Elgar Publishing; 2012).

17 See Cases T-366/03 and T-235/04 *Land Oberösterreich and Austria v Commission* [2005] ECR II-4005: para. 35. The General Court (formerly the Court of First Instance) dismissed the actions by the Land Oberösterreich and Republic of Austria seeking the annulment of Commission Decision 2003/653/EC relating to the national provisions on banning the use of genetically modified organisms notified by Austria.

18 See Cases T-366/03 and T-235/04 *Land Oberösterreich and Austria v Commission* [2005]: para. 46.

19 Though in the case at hand it was noted (Cases C-439/05 and C-454/05 *Land Oberösterreich and Republic of Austria v Commission* [2007], Opinion of Advocate General Sharpston: footnote 45) that: 'the Commission states (see point 8 of the defence in Case T-366/03 and footnote 13 to the response in Case C-439/05) that Land Oberösterreich did in fact have and use an opportunity to respond to the EFSA opinion. That statement does not appear to have been contested.' In the view of the Advocate General, 'if an expert body were to give an opinion after hearing evidence or argument contradicting that put forward by the Member State but to which the Member State had not been given an opportunity to respond, it might be necessary to consider whether that was not an essential procedural defect in the formulation of the opinion (Technische Universität München). In the absence of any such difficulty, the Member State's right to respond to any opinion on which the Commission bases its decision is satisfied by its right to challenge that decision before the Court of First Instance. At that stage, it may put forward any evidence or argument liable to refute any element on which the Commission's decision is based' (para. 137).

as part of its assessment of the merits of that request, to have recourse to outside experts in order to obtain their views on that evidence, and those views will serve as a basis for the final decision'.[20] With particular regard to the specific case at hand, it was observed that 'the Commission itself acknowledged that it was not in a position, in the present case, to assess alone the scientific evidence in the Müller report and stated that, as a consequence, it had to request an opinion from EFSA before taking a decision'.[21]

Some doubt has been cast regarding EFSA's sphere of competence, it having been observed, particularly with reference to the agency's involvement in the assessment of GMOs, that 'EFSA's expanded role has not gone uncontested'.[22] Meanwhile, however, in the light of the Austrian GMOs proceedings, it would certainly seem that from the point of view of the Member States, EFSA clearly has an onerous duty. The Commission itself indicated in the Austrian GMOs case that, despite being 'fully aware' of the safeguard options available to it pursuant to Directive 2001/18/EC, Austria considered these potential avenues inadequate for meeting its objectives and accordingly resolved to resort to the notification procedure within what is now Article 114 TFEU.[23] This procedure places the onus of proving that the conditions for derogation are satisfied on the applicant Member State, entailing that the primary responsibility for demonstrating that there is new scientific information in support of the measures notified is with the national authorities.[24] It has been held that the 'lawfulness' of the proposed domestic measures 'is closely linked to the assessment of the scientific evidence put forward by the notifying Member State':[25] in this respect, the success of

20 Cases C-439/05 and C-454/05 *Land Oberösterreich and Republic of Austria v Commission* [2007]: para. 32. On appeal, the Land Oberösterreich and the Republic of Austria sought to have set aside the judgment in Cases T-366/03 and T-235/04 *Land Oberösterreich and Austria v Commission* [2005], by which the General Court had dismissed their actions seeking the annulment of Commission Decision 2003/653/EC relating to national provisions on banning the use of genetically modified organisms notified by Austria.

21 Cases C-439/05 and C-454/05 *Land Oberösterreich and Republic of Austria v Commission* [2007]: para. 33.

22 Groenleer, M.L.P., 'The Actual Practice of Agency Autonomy: Tracing the Developmental Trajectories of the European Medicines Agency and the European Food Safety Authority' (2011) Open Forum CES Paper, 5. Available at SSRN: http://ssrn.com/abstract=1904462 or http://dx.doi.org/10.2139/ssrn.1904462: p. 13.

23 Commission Decision 2003/653/EC: para. 56.

24 The Commission recognised that, in line 'with the Court's case law, any exception to the principle of the uniform application of Community law and of the unity of the internal market must be strictly interpreted' (Commission Decision 2003/653/EC: para. 57). For a detailed analysis of the practice in this area, see Maletić 2013.

25 Cases C-439/05 and C-454/05 *Land Oberösterreich and Republic of Austria v Commission* [2007]: para. 56.

Member State applications is likely to be highly affected by an EFSA opinion testing the resilience of the data presented by the national authorities.

EFSA's Ambitious Mandate and Concomitant Responsibility within the EU Legislative Harmonisation Framework

EFSA's onerous function carries an extensive degree of responsibility. A strict prerequisite of the ambitious mandate envisaged for EFSA of becoming 'the scientific point of reference for the whole Union'[26] is the immaculate execution of its role. In this regard, it is particularly noteworthy that in the *Austrian GMOs* case, the Advocate General thought that the review of the General Court was 'open to doubt in that it may not have realised that EFSA possibly applied a more demanding standard than "specific", namely "unique"' in assessing the relevant evidence'.[27] This was significant particularly as the pertinent passages from EFSA's opinion were quoted 'verbatim' in the Commission's contested decision where they appeared 'clearly as having some importance in its reasoning'.[28] Accordingly, it did not seem 'safe to conclude' that the General Court 'would have reached the same view if it had been evaluating the evidence against EFSA's references to uniqueness or had considered the Commission's assessment to be based on such references'.[29]

An unassailable system of risk assessment is mandated in particular by the increasing reliance on EFSA's advice. Thus, for example, in the context of a Portuguese notification regarding a draft decree declaring the Autonomous Region of Madeira to be an Area Free of GMOs, the Commission, reasoning that 'the adoption of the EFSA Opinion is necessary before the adoption of a decision',[30] extended the period to rule on the Portuguese notification, relying on the possibility in what is now Article 114(6) TFEU (formerly Article 95(6) EC), to another six months. The selected course of action was deemed to be necessary in order to prevent the adoption of a decision that 'would lack the essential scientific

26 European Commission, White Paper on Food Safety (COM 719 final, 1999): para 2.

27 Cases C-439/05 and C-454/05 *Land Oberösterreich and Republic of Austria v Commission* [2007], Opinion of Advocate General Sharpston: para. 141. The Advocate General noted the use of the words 'uniquely' and 'unique' in EFSA's opinion as possibly suggesting that 'EFSA's conclusion may have been based on an understanding that, in order to justify a derogation from Directive 2001/18, it is necessary to establish that there is a problem in the Member State or region in question which is found nowhere else' (para. 103).

28 Cases C-439/05 and C-454/05 *Land Oberösterreich and Republic of Austria v Commission* [2007], Opinion of Advocate General Sharpston: para. 105.

29 Ibid.: para. 112.

30 Commission Decision 2009/828/EC of 3 November 2009 relating to the draft Regional Legislative Decree declaring the Autonomous Region of Madeira to be an Area Free of Genetically Modified Organisms, notified by the Republic of Portugal pursuant to Article 95(5) of the EC Treaty [2009] OJ L 294/16: para. 24.

support on such a complex matter'.[31] Accordingly, in the view of the Commission, 'a thorough scientific risk assessment' would be required to verify whether the submitted data was indeed related to the protection of the environment or the working environment on grounds of a problem specific to the Autonomous Region of Madeira arising after the adoption of the relevant EU measures within the meaning of the Article 114 TFEU procedure invoked for an authorisation request. This assessment was to be carried out by EFSA.[32]

A similar reliance on EFSA's assessment is visible in a Commission Decision concerning the presence of potentially dangerous elements in the context of toy safety. On 20 January 2011, Germany notified the Commission, pursuant to Article 114(4) TFEU, of its intention to retain existing domestic provisions on lead, arsenic, mercury, barium and antimony, as well as for nitrosamines and nitrosatable substances released from toy material, in derogation from Directive 2009/48/EC on the safety of toys. With respect to arsenic, the Commission held that the measures notified by Germany with regard to this toxic element could not be considered as justified on grounds of protection of human health. In doing so, however, the Commission suggested that a 2009 EFSA study assessing the effects of arsenic on health casting doubt on previously accepted tolerable daily intake levels could in principle be viewed as new scientific evidence capable of triggering the revision of the arsenic limit values in the relevant approximation norm.[33]

That the Commission has acknowledged that EFSA's advisory role may have a significant impact in updating EU legislation and the formulation of EU policy can also be inferred from a notification of national provisions on the addition of nitrites to certain meat products made by Denmark pursuant to what is now Article 114(4) TFEU (formerly Article 95(4) EC). The Commission indicated[34] that, in the scientifically complex regulatory area at hand, necessitating a balance

31 Commission Decision 2009/828/EC: para. 26.

32 Ibid.: para. 22.

33 Commission Decision 2012/160/EU of 1 March 2012 concerning the national provisions notified by the German Federal Government maintaining the limit values for lead, barium, arsenic, antimony, mercury and nitrosamines and nitrosatable substances in toys beyond the entry into application of Directive 2009/48/EC of the European Parliament and of the Council on the safety of toys [2012] OJ L 80/19: para. 31; Directive 2009/48/EC of the European Parliament and of the Council of 18 June 2009 on the safety of toys [2009] OJ L 170/1. An action has been brought on 14 May 2012 for the annulment of this Commission Decision: firstly, in so far as the national provisions notified for maintenance of the limit values for antimony, arsenic and mercury are not approved; and, secondly, in so far as the national provisions notified for maintenance of the limit values for lead and barium are approved only until 21 July 2013 (Case T-198/12 *Germany v Commission* [2012] OJ C 200/19).

34 Commission Decision 2010/561/EU of 25 May 2010 concerning national provisions notified by Denmark on the addition of nitrite to certain meat products [2010] OJ L 247/55: para. 10.

to be struck between, on the one hand, the protective effects of nitrites (enabling the microbiological safety of meat products) against the multiplication of bacteria, in particular those responsible for botulism, and, on the other, the risk of the formation of nitrosamines (found to be carcinogenic) through the presence of nitrites in meat products,[35] the relevant legislation had been transformed in line with the influential opinions provided by the Scientific Committee for Food[36] and EFSA.[37] Furthermore, according to the Commission, appropriate consultations with EFSA would continue to be required in the monitoring of the implementation of the relevant EU measures.[38]

Reconciling Risk Perceptions within the EU Integration Framework

The duty to take into consideration[39] scientific evidence available within the context of the harmonisation of the internal market suggests that it would be difficult to depart from a risk assessment carried out by EFSA. Indeed, EFSA's opinion may act as 'a source of constraint'[40] on both EU institutions and the Member States. It is thus not surprising to find that its scientific findings have been referred to also by national authorities in their applications pursuant to the safeguard procedure in the context of the harmonisation of the internal market. Thus, for example, on 17 October 2011, Sweden notified the Commission, pursuant to Article 114(5) TFEU and by way of derogation from the relevant EU legislation in the field, of its intention to introduce national provisions to

35 Commission Decision 2010/561/EU: para. 7.

36 Opinion on nitrates and nitrites expressed on 19 October 1990, European Commission – Reports of the Scientific Committee for Food (twenty-sixth series): 21 and Opinion on nitrates and nitrite expressed on 22 September 1995, European Commission – Reports of the Scientific Committee for Food (thirty-eighth series): 1.

37 Opinion of the Scientific Panel on Biological Hazards on a request from the Commission related to the effects of Nitrites/Nitrates on the Microbiological Safety of Meat Products (2003/14: 1 2003: 1).

38 Commission Decision 2010/561/EU: para. 66.

39 See Case C-3/00 *Denmark v Commission* [2003], relating to a previous Danish notification under what is now Article 114(4) TFEU in which the Court of Justice had held that, when rejecting the Danish request concerning the use of nitrites in meat products, the Commission had not taken sufficient account of scientific opinions casting doubt on the appropriateness of the amounts of nitrite authorised by the relevant directive in the field (Directive No 95/2/EC of the European Parliament and the Council on food additives other than colours and sweeteners [1995 OJ C 200/19]). For an examination of this case and its implications within the broader context of the harmonisation paradigm under Article 114 TFEU, see Maletić 2013.

40 Alemanno 2007: 193.

lower the content of cadmium allowed in phosphorous fertilisers.[41] In support of its request, the Swedish authorities submitted a national risk assessment, taking into account data relating to the assessment of the risks to human health and the environment from cadmium in fertilisers in Sweden, as well as a scientific opinion from the EFSA on cadmium in food.[42]

Similarly, in the context of the abovementioned notification made by Germany to retain, in derogation from Directive 2009/48/EC on the safety of toys, its existing provisions on lead, arsenic, mercury, barium and antimony, as well as for nitrosamines and nitrosatable substances released from toy material, Germany argued, with specific respect to lead, that the migration limits established in the EU approximation norm for this toxic metal were no longer scientifically based. In support of this contention, the German authorities referred to a 2010 EFSA study carrying out a comprehensive assessment and suggesting that there is no scientifically justified threshold dose for the adverse effects of lead on human health. The Commission deemed the measures notified as justified on grounds of the major need of protection of human health: in particular, the Commission accepted that the migration limits for lead as established in the EU harmonisation measure 'no longer offer an appropriate level of protection for children',[43] noting that, in line with the assertion of the applicant Member State, the tolerable daily intake used for calculating the limits had been questioned by EFSA. Indeed, taking EFSA's views into account, the Commission had already undertaken the revision of the relevant limits. Accordingly, the German measures related to lead notified pursuant to Article 114(4) TFEU could be approved.[44]

---

41 The national measures, purporting to lower the content of cadmium allowed in phosphorous fertilisers to a maximum level of 46 grams of cadmium per tonne of phosphorous, were in contravention of Regulation 2003/2003 of the European Parliament and of the Council of 13 October 2003 relating to fertilisers [2003] OJ L 304/1 and were intended to decrease the maximum level of 100 grams of cadmium per tonne of phosphorous for which a derogation had already been granted to Sweden.

42 Opinion of the Scientific Panel on contaminants in the Food Chain on a request from the European Commission on cadmium in food, EFSA Journal 2009/980: 1; Commission Decision 2012/230/EU of 18 April 2012 extending the period referred to in Article 114(6) of the Treaty on the Functioning of the European Union in relation to national provisions concerning the maximum admissible content of cadmium in fertilisers notified by the Kingdom of Sweden pursuant to Article 114(5) of the TFEU [2012] OJ L 116/29.

43 Commission Decision 2012/160/EU of 1 March 2012 concerning the national provisions notified by the German Federal Government maintaining the limit values for lead, barium, arsenic, antimony, mercury and nitrosamines and nitrosatable substances in toys beyond the entry into application of Directive 2009/48/EC of the European Parliament and of the Council on the safety of toys [2012] OJ 2012 L 80/19: para 54.

44 The measures were approved until the date of entry into force of EU provisions setting new limits for lead in toys or 21 July 2013, whichever came first.

The latter set of proceedings suggests that the interaction dynamics between national authorities and EFSA need not necessarily assume an 'adversarial' character. Perhaps an indication of how different risk perceptions may be accommodated and how scientific findings by EFSA and national authorities may be reconciled can be found in the Commission Decision concerning the abovementioned notification by Denmark on the addition of nitrite to certain meat products. Pursuant to what is now Article 114(4) TFEU, Denmark notified to the Commission national provisions on the addition of nitrites, which it considered necessary to maintain in contravention to its obligation to transpose into national law Directive 2006/52/EC on food additives. In accepting the Danish measure, the Commission observed that the national legislation was 'compatible with the relevant scientific opinions of the Union's scientific bodies'.[45] Accordingly a margin of discretion could be afforded to the Danish regulator, which had achieved 'satisfactory results with its legislation': the request to maintain the domestic measures could be temporarily accepted on grounds of protection of health in Denmark, even though the relevant EU legislation from which derogation had been sought could generally be regarded as an 'adequate response' to the need to cater for two conflicting health risks in meat products.[46]

Concluding Observations

EFSA was conceived as an independent authority, entrusted with tasks mainly confined to risk assessment and communication.[47] Nevertheless, the challenge of separating risk management and risk assessment should not obscure the extent of EFSA's decisive role. Indeed, it has been observed that 'as food law is heavily based on science, the delegation for scientific assessment of risk to the authority could also be said to provide EFSA with a quasi-regulatory power'.[48] It is precisely because of this substantial responsibility that EFSA's actions are susceptible to strict scrutiny. Indeed, as has been seen above, EFSA was conceived as eventually becoming 'the scientific point of reference for the whole Union'.[49] It is in the light of this ambitious mandate and the evolving practice of increasing reliance on EFSA's assessments that concerns[50] over EFSA's independence, accountability,

---

45 Commission Decision 2010/561/EU of 25 May 2010 concerning national provisions notified by Denmark on the addition of nitrite to certain meat products [2010] OJ L 247/55: para. 52.

46 Commission Decision 2010/561/EU: paras 50–54.

47 See the European Commission, White Paper on Food Safety (COM 719 final, 1999).

48 Alemanno, 2007: 161.

49 European Commission, White Paper on Food Safety (COM 719 final, 1999), p. 2.

50 Vos, E. and Permanand, G., 2008. 'Between Health and the Market: The Roles of the European Medicines Agency and European Food Safety Authority' in *Health*

transparency, financial dependence, with continued reservations regarding the scope of legal review of EFSA's opinions,[51] acquire accentuated significance.

A decade anniversary may present an opportune chance to address some of these enduring preoccupations, most prominently perhaps, as vividly illustrated by the *Austrian GMOs* case, the continued need to find effective ways of reconciling risk assessment and risk management within the EU regulatory system whilst 'maintaining appropriate functional separation'.[52] Undoubtedly, 'the elaboration of harmonised transparent approaches to risk assessment is not only a prerequisite for a proper functioning of the authority but will also be a decisive factor for EFSA's success'.[53] Furthermore, the limited structural involvement of Member State representatives within EFSA's organisational structure may induce EFSA to endeavour reinforcing its cooperation with the national authorities.[54] However, EFSA is not alone in the fundamental attempt to accommodate scientific expertise within the context of EU harmonisation.[55] Indeed, as exemplified by the Danish notification concerning the addition of nitrite to meat products, a critical role in the administration of different risk perceptions is to be performed by the Commission,[56]

Systems Governance in Europe: The Role of EU Law and Policy, edited by E. Mossialos, G. Permanand, R. Baeten, and T. Hervey (Cambridge University Press; Maastricht Faculty of Law Working Paper, 4). Available at SSRN: http://ssrn.com/abstract=1337111, p. 11.

51 Alemanno, A. and Mahieu, S., 'The European Food Safety Authority before the European Courts', 5(3) *EFFL* (2008), 320, suggesting that clarifications in this area could helpfully take into account the procedural regime applicable to other agencies performing roles in closely related fields, in particular considering the possibility of introducing greater homogeneity in the minimum standards of judicial review and remedies for challenging the measures of such agencies.

52 Alemanno, A., 'The European Food Safety Authority at Five', 1(3) *EFFL* (2008), 2.

53 Alemanno 2007: 178.

54 Vos and Permanand 2008. See in this respect EFSA, 2006, 'Strategy for Cooperation and Networking between the EU Member States and EFSA'; EFSA, 2011, 'Technical Report on Scientific Cooperation between EFSA and Member States: Taking Stock and Looking Ahead'. It has been argued that 'The introduction of a mere duty of cooperation does seem to fall short in providing an effective answer to the fundamental question of the relationships between the EFSA and the national authorities responsible for food safety issues. The institution of an Advisory Body, as a mechanism of exchange of information between the national authorities and the EFSA, is unlikely to prove decisive in overcoming the difficulties arising from diverging scientific opinions' (Alemanno 2006).

55 EFSA's founding regulation provides that it 'shall contribute to a high level of protection of human life and health, and in this respect take account of animal health and welfare, plant health and the environment, in the context of the operation of the internal market' (Regulation 178/2002: Article 22(3)).

56 Within the specific context of the Article 114 TFEU procedure, the Commission has a fundamental role in evaluating the evidence presented by EFSA and the national authorities. In this respect, it is noteworthy that the Commission increasingly notifies and consults other Member States too prior to taking a decision. For an extensive analysis of the practice in this area, see Maletić 2013.

required to act in a manner conducive both to economic integration and concomitant with scientific advancement, and the European Courts, increasingly called upon, within the remit of their judicial review, to reconcile conflicting scientific opinions within the scope of EU integration.

Section 2: The Stakeholders' Perspective

Chapter 16

Ten Years of EU Food Law: An Industry Perspective

Roberto Ciati

Introduction

The birth of the European Food Safety Authority (EFSA) was an important moment in the European Union's development. The decision to plan and set up an Agency whose role is to be a scientific reference for European institutions and all EU Member States on extremely important and complex matters such as food safety, guidelines for correct nutrition as well as improvements in animal and plant health, represents a key step for Europe.

The fundamental goal of creating a single reference framework for the whole continent was, and surely still is, a most complex task. At the same time, it must be viewed as one of the EU's unifying aspects, both with regard to the internal market as well as the strengthening of the EU's role towards other non-member countries. To pursue and achieve this goal over time, EFSA has adopted a model as a fundamental basis for its work. This model, which has progressively evolved over time, aims at assessing risks by defining independent and transparent scientific opinions and at issuing useful and reliable documents and recommendations to the European Commission, Parliament and Member States.

This model is key for supplying European institutions with reliable scientific positions regarding scientific advancements that have been coming about at an increasing speed. It is also an important tool to reach the clear and necessary objective of offering consistent and uniform interpretations of existing legislation. Indeed, leveraging the best scientific knowledge gleaned from experts in various fields and including it in official opinions and guidelines can equip legislators with the most advanced assessments to better protect all European citizens. It also helps and to define the consistent references which are important for manufacturers and all the players in the food supply chain. In light of its role, objectives and operating methods, the industrial world reacted positively to EFSA's creation: for the agro-food industry being able to plan, research, design and develop new products and manage entire supply and distribution chains within a clear and simple reference framework is without any doubt an improvement. Moreover, the ability to offer products on the market that are increasingly in line with the necessary safety guarantees and healthy nutritional requirements certainly constitutes a further stimulus for the agro-food sector to improve the products already on the market and to invest on the research and development of new and innovative ones. Last but not least, by implementing internal governance mechanisms based on the exchange of information on potential risks and pooling different knowledge and expertise through strict cooperation between EFSA and the competent Authorities (for example, the Advisory Forum), avoids the duplication of projects and studies and situations where the various Authorities must cooperate are better defined leading, once again, towards a more rational and uniform assessment of matters within their competence.

This chapter does not seek to analyse in detail the 10 years of EFSA's history or the evolution over time of its relations with the industrial sector. Rather, it wishes to offer a more pragmatic approach by focusing on two key topics and conducting case studies of relevant aspects of EFSA's functioning, in order to identify positive developments and possible areas for improvement.

In this perspective, and starting from the basic assumption that only open and constructive dialogue can lead to real improvement of the system, we will go through the following topics.

Independence and Transparency

EFSA founding Regulation (EC) No 178/2002 states that EFSA must 'provide the Community institutions and the Member States with *the best possible scientific opinions* in all cases provided for by Community legislation and on any question within its mission'.[1] This very clear and ambitious statement implies a continuous access to top quality science, thanks to a fruitful interaction and involvement with the best scientists. Now, the principle of independence, a basic pre-requisite for EFSA's role, has very complex implications and identifying a structure that can give all stakeholders a wide and complete guarantee can become an infinite path and a continuous source of observations and criticisms. In fact, in itself the concept of independence is tied to multiple, and sometimes contradictory, economic, political, social, philosophical and ethical interests as well as other various types of considerations. Basing a structure or a policy on these multiple visions could result in the impossibility of reaching a universally shared and satisfying solution, and would prevent the very cooperation that is necessary to the current scientific process. Indeed, on the other hand if it is important to pursue impartiality and objectivity, which are key components of independence, we must also be careful not to lose the expertise of professionals with industry ties which could create an information asymmetry. In this respect, the preferred approach for consolidating EFSA's independence may be to define independence as autonomy;

1 Regulation (EC) No 178/2002 of the European Parliament and of the Council of 28 January 2002 _Art. 23 (a) – *Official Journal of the European Communities* 12.2002 – L31.

in other words through a drastic and innovative increase in the transparency of EFSA's assessment and decision-making processes. Various initiatives undertaken over the last 10 years have represented an improvement in that direction. We can highlight, in particular, the Rolling Work Plan of EFSA's activities with its stakeholders, where many initiatives are listed, such as the Consultative Platform and Technical meetings / Working Groups or the last pilot project, launched in 2012, of open scientific meetings which allow observers to attend some meetings of the Scientific Committee and a number of Scientific Panels.[2]

Yet, we believe that even more effective methods should be introduced to prevent the Authority's independence from being challenged. Increasing the circulation of discussion documents during the assessment process, technical consultations with a wider panel of stakeholders, publishing discussions (e.g. live streaming on the Internet); and clarifying better the criteria used to increase contribution from public and private experts, are but a few suggestions of what could be done to dramatically increase independence at the basis of EFSA's opinions.

To sum up, dogmatic independence and total non-permeability to any external interference could become an abstract and philosophical concept while transparency in the thinking, discussion and decision-making processes is an action that can be concretely activated. This would ensure that no expertise or knowledge is lost, avoiding – at least – or drastically reducing any potential information asymmetry. A transparent path and open interaction with all the best experts are the most important principles to reach clear and science-based opinions, and provide consumers with a precise reference frame and the industry with a well-defined and level playing field.

The Relation with Third Parties

The relation with stakeholders is a key topic for EFSA's role and its mission, defined as an organisation committed to openness, transparency and dialogue. Overall, we can identify two different types of stakeholders: on the one hand, Civil Society, which includes consumer organisations, NGOs and market operators such as farmers, food manufacturers, distributors and science professionals, and on the others Institutional stakeholders, which include the European Commission, the European Parliament and the Member States. Over the past 10 years, EFSA has steadily improved its interactions with these third parties.

Without going through all the initiatives put in place by EFSA in the course of its 10 years of existence, this section will underline a few relevant examples and two specific topics related to civil society.

One such initiative is the Scientific Colloquia: started in 2004, it aims to engage scientists from across Europe and beyond in scientific discussions and debates, specifically on the issues of food and feed safety. Another positive initiative is the

2 See www.efsa.europa.eu.

Consultative Platform: created in 2005 and composed of EU-wide stakeholder organisations working in areas related to the food chain. In particular, plenary meetings of the Stakeholders Platform are relevant event where horizontal and scientific issues are discussed with all members through an engaging two ways communication process. Finally, as already mentioned in the previous chapter, the pilot project allowing observers to attend some meetings of EFSA's Scientific Committee and some Scientific Panels, is a crucial improvement. These actions have brought about useful and fruitful cooperation with the industry and other relevant players, like for example in the field of nanotechnology or the re-appraisal of the additives list. Therefore, EFSA should continue and move forward in this direction as stated in the 'EFSA's Communications Strategy: 2010–13 perspective' where coherence and dialogue are key words to increase audience interactivity.[3] In addition, we would point out a specific requirement related to a very important topic as the health claims approval: the need to offer pre-submission meetings with the applicants as a key step for the full appraisal process that, at the moment of writing, was not extremely clear, as is described in the specific chapter.

Communicating with Civil Society: The Food Safety Case

The first topic considered is the area of food safety where EFSA has doubtless produced work of excellent quality and quantity, updating historical assessments through the acquisition and processing of recent scientific works, comparing new areas linked to scientific advancements. This work was impressive considering the fact that the scientific progress has been (and will be) really complex because of the incredible speed of analytical techniques and technology. Such advancements open very articulated scenarios that are hard to assess in terms of risk and danger to the population. Even in such positive assessment, two points are deemed fundamental: the response times and the topic of real risk compared to perceived risk. Response times are crucial in food safety matters in our highly connected and open computerised world. That's always true and not only during the management of full-blown emergencies, which have the added complication of needing to be prepared to respond immediately to perceptions that are in the public domain. In fact, as food safety is a necessary and fundamental requirement for each food item and any service connected to it, rapid assessment of a situation, and its subsequent communication, is a condition for the authoritative and correct information to European citizens. Meanwhile, it also allows all players of the production and distribution chains to operate correctly and resolutely through effective and efficient actions. We should aim at reducing, or avoiding, large-scale operations that could become very complex and, in specific cases, counter-productive, leading to excessive alarms which only later could prove to be unfounded.

3 EFSA's Communications Strategy: 2010–2013 perspective.

The reliability and speed by which news is transmitted via the Internet and its subsequent amplification raises the urgent need for a new EFSA approach on how to manage its new scientific opinions. As EFSA is responsible for offering scientific recommendations and interpretations to various parties it should gear its communications keeping in mind that all citizens are listening, thus illustrating clearly and carefully what the real possible risks are, and which of the most widely spread perceptions are less substantial or actually non-existent. Whether they relate to contaminants or the safety of specific ingredients used, EFSA communications must be even more clearly interpreted to reduce any potential distortion or alarm to a minimum and, where necessary, use rapid and simple documents which illustrate the scientific position in an easily accessible manner. We realize that these, and the speed required, imply different, and probably additional, resources. But it is also true that a review of computerised means and methods of communication could significantly increase the perception that the utmost, and the best, is being done.

We must not underestimate how crucial and, in many cases, decisive perception is in forming public opinion in its widest sense including stakeholders and citizens alike. This situation then becomes critical when we look at how risk and potential dangers arising from these topics are assessed most widely spread sentiments and perceptions in the population are certainly not based on scientific knowledge, especially in an era when the authority and seriousness of sources is growing ever more difficult to evaluate. We know that this road is long and difficult but we believe that it is one that the European scientific authority must follow: the meaning of hazard and risk linked to the probability approach are not clear and intuitive concept for most people.

Communication with Industry: The Health Claims Case

The second and last topic chosen as a test case for EFSA's value to the food and feed industry is the assessment of nutrition and health claims.

The need for this major EFSA task grew from a real situation where several thousand claims were put forward and supported in various ways by industry, deriving from different approval routes and probably resulting from equally unstandardised assessment criteria.[4] It therefore consisted of a very wide-ranging and complicated scientific revision which, right from the start, was applauded by the manufacturing sector. To clearly define which claims were recognised as valid and to have a clear and transparent approval process was, and still is, a very important aspect in the management of retail products and the development of new offers. The path followed by EFSA was very complex and difficult given the high number of assessments to be carried out and the study of a vast range of scientific literature available and/or produced specifically to support each individual claim.

4 See Official Member States claim existing on the market list.

A few crucial points emerged from this laborious task that should be further examined and possibly improved in the future to make the process even more efficient and reliable.

The starting point is the consideration that we are talking about food and not pharmaceutical products. Medical and nutritional science has for a long time focused its efforts on changing eating habits to implement the international guidelines defining daily nutritional or dietary models aimed at preventing many incorrect metabolic aspects. These overlapping guidelines have long shown an extraordinary power to prevent the main non-transmissible diseases.

All the studies behind these guidelines, from the randomised case-control trial to epidemiological surveys, are not easily considered as sufficient to support specific health claims borne by products, leading also to a very difficult positive acceptance for many ad hoc supporting evidences given by the industrial sector. This gives rise to conflicting positions between the food industry and EFSA. On the one hand, the claims are generally seen as too promising and not well supported. On the other, EFSA's approach is seen as too restrictive for food products from a nutritional-medical point of view. Attempts have been made to mitigate these divergent assessments by progressively opening up to specific sectors. Though this initiative is going in the right direction, it came too late for assessing the different claims and should probably be made more efficient and more proactive. Given the assessment methods, we believe that a multi-step approach should be considered, whereby the proposer presents the scope and hypothesis at the basis of the project and how these are to be demonstrated. Opinions, indications and suggestions to support and validate these proposals would be put forward by EFSA panels without any advance promise of approval. This new approach could be a step forward in the transparency and open discussion on the food industry's forthcoming application. We do not need to underline how the path followed up to now has undoubtedly impaired the research and development vision of entire industrial sectors. All agri-food players clearly cannot accept in the same way the risk of undertaking a long and costly development process when faced with such a complex assessment system where interpretation and interaction during the assessment process is also difficult. It is much easier to use what has already been approved as a basis and add new product offers, de facto restricting both the field of execution and, above all, potential new horizons.

There is wide scope for improvement in the approval process. Focusing on systematic interaction and discussion is at times a simple way of preventing and resolving a series of questions at their source thereby avoiding or reducing criticisms.

Conclusions

In summarising the various points touched upon in this chapter and considering the important decisions contained in the strategic guidelines prepared or being prepared by EFSA (see 'Preliminary Management Plan 2013' and 'Policy on Independence and Scientific Decision-making Process'), we believe that improvements will come from focusing on the following areas.

The opinions issued by EFSA are very relevant, not only for European and national institutions but also for the media at large. This implies a constant and progressively increasing harmonisation of risk assessment methodologies both in the various areas of responsibility and in the ability to communicate via the mass media which systematically report EFSA opinions.

Response times and clarity of interpretation of scientific opinions are crucial both in taking the correct and incisive operational decisions as well as the management of communications that derive thereof, not only in the event of emergencies but also in specific applications in the area of health and/or nutrition. In the latter case, the possibility of the correct decision by industry, in its method and timescale, on whether to proceed or not in the request, has important consequences in the management of innovation, development and research processes – all strategic aspects for the development of the EU agri-food sector.

The continuous and necessary improvement of every scientific opinion must arise from the collection of information and a more open and constructive discussion with all the stakeholders involved. These meetings, continuously carried out in a spirit of transparency, should not be seen as compromising EFSA's independence but rather as acquiring further expertise and useful information which is strictly 'science-based'.

The use of the most advanced computer technologies is also encouraged as provided for in the Preliminary Management Plan 2013,[5] not only for the various procedures for submission of applications but also to make the assessment route useable and transparent and allowing real interaction between the requesting party and the panel of experts.

In our opinion, this series of suggestions would consolidate and strengthen scientific discussion and exchange, enriching it with further contributions and leading to heightened achievement and better definition of the various results expected without invalidating the roles and responsibilities of the parties involved.

It would mean being able to guide a real and open discussion in a transparent manner, which in itself is already a fundamental step towards encouraging the necessary development of the largest European industrial sector within clear rules and guidelines.

---

5 Preliminary Management Plan of the European Food Safety Authority for 2013.

Chapter 17
The Consumers' Perspective of EFSA

Sue Davies

Introduction

Ten years on since the establishment of the European Food Safety Authority (EFSA), there are many new challenges facing the Authority and the food supply chain. But many of the issues that led to its establishment and the fundamental issues of independence, openness and transparency that lie at the heart of why and how it was set up at arms' length from the EU institutions remain just as relevant today.

Looking back over the past 10 years, a great deal has been achieved in terms of greater coordination between Member States, scientific robustness and independence, transparency of decision-making and ultimately consumer protection.[1] It is essential that EFSA builds on this in the years to come and that it continues to have the support of wider EU stakeholders, particularly in a time of economic crisis and an increasingly deregulatory culture.

The Way We Were

In the years leading up to the establishment of EFSA, our food system was in crisis. Consumers received scant attention when it came to decision-making. Food policy was in the domain of the Directorates-General for Agriculture and Industry promotion and DG Health and Consumers was weak in comparison.

While there was already an extensive body of food legislation in place, there were significant gaps and a lack of coherence to scientific advice. Much of the responsibility lay with committees across Member States and the EU's scientific committees, such as the Scientific Committee for Food, had a large burden and were limited in their scope.

Coordination across Member States on issues such as foodborne disease was limited and ad hoc with no integrated approach in place. Salmonella food poisoning was at unacceptable levels, the Belgian dioxins crisis had highlighted weaknesses in the way that food scares were handled across Member States and there was no meaningful attention being given to nutrition policy at EU level.

---

1 External Evaluation of the European Food Safety Authority, Final Report, Ernst & Young, September 2012.

The food supply chain was becoming more integrated and more complex as reflected by debate around issues such as growth hormones and genetically modified foods, but developments in the supply chain were not being anticipated and addressed with sufficient urgency. These raised important trade questions, but also highlighted a disconnect between consumer perceptions of how food was produced and what was often the reality. Consumer confidence was therefore low.

Weaknesses That Had to Be Addressed

In 2000, Which? gave evidence to a UK House of Lords Select Committee Inquiry into EU food policy.[2] We summarised the key weaknesses of EU food policy that needed to be addressed as follows:

Box 17.1 EU food policy: problems to be tackled

- a fragmented approach to food policy;
- an inability to anticipate new developments and practices in the food chain;
- a lack of clear objectives for food policy;
- conflicting priorities of industry and trade promotion and consumer protection to the detriment of public health;
- inadequate consumer involvement reflected in the emphasis of EU food policies;
- a reactive rather than proactive approach;
- an inability to respond swiftly to food safety problems as highlighted by the dioxins scandal;
- a lack of coordination across the EU's food-related policies and also between Member States when a food safety problem emerges;
- problems with enforcement;
- inefficient communication and inadequate information about food-related risks;
- a lack of confidence in EU scientific advice;
- a lack of openness and transparency over decision-making;
- a failure to adequately represent – and defend – consumer interests at the World Trade Organization;
- a lack of clarity over the EU's role in nutrition policy.

It took a crisis, however, to ensure that these issues were finally taken seriously. The announcement of the likelihood of a link between Bovine Spongiform Encephalopathy (BSE) and 10 cases of a new form of Creutzfeld Jakob Disease

2 House of Lords European Union Committee Seventh Report: A European Food Safety Authority, 16 May 2000.

(vCJD) was finally made by the UK Secretary of State for Health on 20 March 1996.[3] It had taken around 10 years since BSE had first been identified for the potential health implications to be acknowledged and as a result the UK's food policy framework was in turmoil. BSE had highlighted the need for a more proactive and consumer-focused approach to food policy and a removal of conflicts of interest where conflicting responsibilities meant that trade interests were being weighed against public health issues, delaying essential protection methods and open communication with the public.

Which? renewed its call for an independent food agency[4] in order to de-politicise food policy and ensure that scientific advice was kept distinct from political decision-making. This, along with pressure from other organisations and a stakeholder-wide acknowledgement that the existing approach was unsustainable, led to the creation of the Food Standards Agency in 2000[5] with an unambiguous remit to put consumers first, be evidence-based, independent and operate openly and transparently.

Similar re-examinations of responsibilities for food policy were taking place in other Member States. In France, for example, the Agence Française de Sécurité Sanitaire des Aliments (AFSSA) or French Food Safety Agency was created in order to create a clearer distinction between risk assessment and risk management decisions. Whereas the UK made this separation within the same agency, in France these responsibilities were split between different institutions.

It took slightly longer for the full repercussions of the BSE crisis to be realised by the EU institutions. In February 1997, the results of a Temporary Committee of Inquiry were adopted by the European Parliament. This was very critical of the handling of BSE at a national as well as European Council and Commission level and highlighted the extent to which scientific advice had been influenced by national and trade interests.

A Communication on Consumer Health and Food Safety[6] was published in April 1997 establishing three principles: first, that responsibility for legislation should be separate from that for scientific consultation; second, that responsibility for legislation should be separate from that for inspection; and third, that there should be greater transparency and more widely available information throughout the decision-making process and inspection measures. Scientific advice was to be based on the principles of excellence, independence and transparency. A new Scientific Steering Committee was established and scientific advice as well as the Food and Veterinary Office put under the responsibility of DG Health and Consumers.

---

3 Lord Philips of Worth Matravers, 'The BSE Inquiry, Volume 1, Findings and Conclusions' (October 2000).

4 A National Food Agency, Which? policy report (1997).

5 UK Food Standards Act (1999).

6 Communication of the European Commission – Consumer Health and Food Safety, April 1997. http://ec.europa.eu/food/fs/sc/comec1en.pdf.

The White Paper on Food Safety[7] in 2000 took a fundamental look across all food policy and set out plans to create a European Food Authority, the principle objective of which was to contribute to a high level of consumer health protection in the area of food safety, through which consumer confidence could be restored and maintained. Through the White Paper and the programme of legislation it also envisaged, the need to ensure a robust regulatory framework with an emphasis on consumer and public health protection was finally recognised.

Guiding Principles

At the time that EFSA was set up a key issue was, therefore, the need to separate risk assessment from risk management. BSE had brought to a head the inherent problem of having scientific advice within the same institution, i.e. the European Commission, that also had responsibility for dealing with political aspects of food policy. The perception was that politics and science had become too inter-twined and so the integrity of scientific opinions had lost credibility. This was compounded by a lack of transparency over the way that scientific opinions were reached. There were concerns that the selection of experts and how they reached their decisions was not transparent enough. More generally, consumer groups raised concerns that there was insufficient involvement of consumers and their representatives within decision-making and that they had limited input relative to the resources of the private sector.

The entire EU approach to risk analysis was therefore in question. Risk assessment needed to be opened up. A clearer distinction between risk management was needed and the different factors taken into account by policy makers needed to be open and clearly distinguished. Risk communication also needed to be given much greater weight so that there was much wider engagement and consultation with stakeholders throughout the process, leading ultimately to a more socially acceptable level of risk. It had to be changed from a top down process to an ongoing dialogue.

Openness of processes was needed as well as greater openness about what was and what wasn't known. There had been too many unnecessary delays in communicating with the public about potential risks and this seemed to stem largely from an anxiousness to limit any impact on trade interests. The lack of transparency also meant that dissent or minority views among scientific committee members had not been made clear enough.

Another central theme that helped to guide the approach at this time was the need to acknowledge and deal more effectively with uncertainty. BSE had highlighted a too frequent tendency to confuse 'absence of evidence' with 'evidence of absence' and therefore the need to ensure that a precautionary approach was inherent within the EU's approach to risk governance.

7 European Commission, White Paper on Food Safety (COM 719 final, 1999).

When the founding regulation was finally adopted in 2002,[8] EFSA was set up at arms' length from the Commission, Member States and Parliament. It was given responsibility for providing scientific advice and technical support in all fields which have a direct or indirect impact on food and feed safety, including communicating on risks.[9] It has to take account of animal health and welfare, plant health and the environment. It has to act in close cooperation with the relevant competent bodies in the Member States and promote coherence between risk assessment, risk management and risk communication functions with the Commission and Member States. As well as developing common risk assessment methodologies, EFSA has to do work to identify emerging risks.

Political and Wider Independence

The Authority is required to ensure that it carries out its functions independently and with a high degree of transparency. This means independent of any food industry interests, as well as political interference. Its management board, advisory forum made up of member state representatives and Executive Director are all required in the founding regulation to act independently in the public interest and make an annual declaration of interest.[10]

Crucially, its scientific work is carried out mainly through its Scientific Committee and Scientific Panels. Unlike the United States Food and Drug Administration model, for example, most opinions from the Authority will be issued by the Committee or one of EFSA's eight scientific panels, which are made up of experts from across Europe who are appointed to take on this work, but apart from the reimbursement of expenses, are unpaid. The rationale for this is that committees made up of different experts from around the EU (generally 21 per Panel) ensure greater independence and a multidisciplinary approach.

The other unique aspect of EFSA that was put in place in order to ensure that it is a truly arms' length body is its management board. Whereas other EU agencies have governing bodies made up of representatives of Member States, EFSA's board is independent of the Member States. Its members apply by open competition and are appointed by the Council in consultation with the European Parliament based on a list of candidates selected by the Commission. They are required to be 'appointed in such a way as to secure the highest standards of competence, a broad range of relevant expertise and, consistent with these, the broadest possible geographic distribution within the Union'.[11] This measure was

8 Council Regulation (EC) 178/2002 of 28 January 2002 laying down the general principles and requirements of food law, establishing the European Food Safety Authority and laying down procedures in matters of food safety [2002] OJ L31/1.

9 Regulation (EC) No 178/2002, Article 25.

10 Ibid., Article 37.

11 Ibid., Article 25.

also intended to de-politicise scientific advice and ensure that it was not unduly skewed by national interests which may differ from wider EU interests.

Learning from the UK FSA's approach, the regulation also specifies that management board meetings must be held in public, unless dealing with administrative issues that are too confidential – a measure to help establish trust in its work from the outset. Consumer representatives and other interested parties can also observe the proceedings of some of the activities of the Authority.

Challenges Facing EFSA

Ten years on, the challenges facing EFSA have changed significantly since it was first established in 2002. In the early years, the focus was on establishing the core principles that would guide the Agency and building its capacity. As well as meeting in public, for example, a decision was made to web-stream management board meetings so that stakeholders across the EU could see how decisions were being made. Mechanisms for engaging stakeholders were put in place through stakeholder colloquia, leading to a more formal arrangement through a Stakeholder Consultative Platform.[12] The Advisory Forum was constituted as a means of ensuring effective networking with Member States, whilst also ensuring that their influence was kept separate.

A fundamental aspect was the creation of the Scientific Committee and Scientific Panels that would do much of EFSA's work – and how to ensure that EFSA could function effectively and still rely on these experts from its new base in Parma. Inevitably much of the initial focus was on food safety aspects.

EFSA's responsibilities and its organisation steadily increased in line with the development of a more comprehensive regulatory framework for food. Many responsibilities that were previously shared among national risk assessment bodies became the responsibility of EFSA – including for example assessment of food additives and genetically modified organisms (GMOs).

As the public health impact of obesity and diet-related disease finally began to be seen as an area where the EU needed to take a greater role, EFSA's work in areas relating to dietary advice expanded. This included advice on nutrient profiling, dietary reference values and nutrition and health claims. Food safety assessments also expanded to environmental risk assessments in the case of GMOs and some pieces of legislation required EFSA to look at issues of efficacy (for example in relation to pesticides legislation). EFSA's work also encompasses a large body of work relating to animal health and welfare.

EFSA also conducts work on common approaches to risk assessment and has developed more comprehensive networks for sharing of information between

12 EFSA Stakeholder Consultative Platform Terms of Reference, EFSA Management Board meeting, 10 March 2005.

Member States – from work on folic acid fortification to general risk communication. The work around emerging risks also evolved with a specific unit created.

From a consumer organisation perspective, the transparent approach and ready engagement with consumer organisations across the EU was a welcome change of approach. The location in Parma was a challenge for accessibility, but the establishment of the Stakeholder Consultative Platform with a mix of stakeholders from different backgrounds, including four spaces and chairing role for the European Consumer Organisation (BEUC) was positive. The distinction between risk assessment and risk communication versus risk management with the European Commission and Member States was supported as it meant that it was much clearer where the science stopped and the politics or economic interests started.

This distinction also meant that new challenges were presented, including for example, how to ensure sufficient cooperation with the EU institutions while maintaining independence and how to ensure that EFSA could communicate effectively. It has an explicit responsibility for risk communication, but many aspects of risk communication also require information about the risk management approach.

European consumer organisations also highlighted the crucial issue of the way that questions are framed or the 'risk assessment policy' determined. If you do not ask the right questions, you will not get the right answers and many issues put to or addressed by EFSA will have many dimensions beyond food safety – including ethical aspects and in the case of nutrition issues, how individual risk assessments fit within a wider public health context.

Changing Political and Economic Context

Since the establishment of EFSA, there has been a shift in the issues that preoccupy food policy, compared to those that guided it at the end of the 1990s.

In contrast to the focus given to health and consumer issues after the realisation of food safety failings, food safety is no longer the headline issue that it once was. This is, in many ways, a mark of the success that has been achieved in this area – responding to gaps in food regulation and changing the institutional structures. Greater openness about food risks has also meant that there is less suspicion among the public that information is being hidden.

At the time EFSA was created, the need to put consumer interests first was seen as a priority. There was a recognition that failure to do so and the resulting lack of consumer trust and confidence would also be damaging in the longer term to economic and trade interests. Political priorities are, however, different. The growth agenda, for example, through the Europe 2020 Strategy,[13] means

13 Europe 2020: A Strategy for Sustainable Growth and Jobs, 2010. http://ec.europa.eu/europe2020/index_en.htm.

that economic interests are being given much greater priority. There is also an increased focus on the burden of regulation.[14]

While not yet undermined, many of the watch words that guided food policy a decade ago such as consumer involvement, precaution, independence and transparency can no longer be taken for granted. Whereas lessons from the UK helped to shape the nature of EFSA, they should also act as a warning in the current climate. The UK Food Standards Agency so strongly supported as the extent of the BSE crisis emerged is gradually being weakened. Its responsibilities have shrunk to pure food safety policy in England, with issues such as food labelling and food authenticity now back with the Department for Environment, Food and Rural Affairs (Defra) which also has a responsibility to promote the UK food industry.[15] Nutrition policy has returned to the politicised environment of the Department of Health, meaning that many of the positive initiatives that had been underway have now stalled.[16] The Agency still has wider responsibilities in Northern Ireland, Scotland and to a lesser extent Wales but a new Scottish food agency is planned to take over its responsibilities in the coming years.

Recent handling of food issues, such as a failure to agree a regulation on novel foods, including an approach to control the use of animal cloning for food production; plans to relax controls over processed animal proteins (PAPs) in animal feed; and proposals to permit carcass treatments in abattoirs are indications of how consumer issues seem to be being sidelined.

The recent E coli outbreaks in Germany and France[17] which led to many deaths and long-term health problems illustrated how devastating food safety issues can be. But 10 years on, it is just as important that the primacy of consumer and public health protection is recognised.

New Demands on Independence

Recent years have also seen a different focus to debates around independence. When EFSA was set up, the make-up of its management board and its Scientific Panels were seen as a key way to ensuring its independence. Political independence as much as independence of economic interests was seen as crucial. A requirement to declare interests and appointment of people from a range of backgrounds, were important mechanisms for ensuring independence.

---

14 Communication on EU Regulatory Fitness (2012) 746 COM Final, 12.12.12.

15 Business Plan 2012–15, Department for the Environment, Food and Rural Affairs, 31 May 2012.

16 'Taste for Change?' (Policy Report, Which? 2012).

17 'Tracing seeds, in particular fenugreek (Trigonella foenum-graecum) seeds, in relation to the shiga-toxin producing E. coli (STEC) O104:H4 2011 outbreaks in Germany and France' (Technical Report of the European Food Safety Authority EFSA 2011).

In recent years, there has been criticism from some non-governmental organisations and the European Parliament that EFSA's scientific committees and management board are not sufficiently independent. The requirement in the founding regulation that four members of the board shall have their background in organisations representing consumers and other interests in the food chain has, for example, come under much greater scrutiny than when the legislation was adopted. Strong consumer representation on the board is essential, as is ensuring that board members are able to fulfil the requirement that they act independently in the consumer interest. It is also important that this criticism does not prompt a re-examination of whether the board should be made up of individuals rather than Member States – returning to a system where national interests will have much more influence over the agenda rather than collective EU needs.

The nature of the Scientific Committee and Panels has also received a lot of attention. It is no longer enough to declare interests, EFSA is expected to be free of potential interests. This scrutiny of EFSA's independence at all levels has led to the publication of a clearer EFSA policy on independence,[18] setting out the measures in place covering the board, staff and experts – as well as EFSA's overall approach. This also strengthened the criteria for selection of experts and set out clear criteria for selection of chairs of the Scientific Committee and Scientific Panels and Working Groups.

Another difficult area is the need for EFSA to ensure that it is able to take into account the totality of the evidence when developing an opinion. EFSA's Science Strategy[19] adopted at the end of 2011 recognises that EFSA needs to further boost its capacity and efficiency to support EFSA's Scientific Committee and Scientific Panels to monitor and screen new scientific information and provide systematic literature review. This includes developing a system to regularly identify new data which points to the need to reconsider existing opinions.

A lot of EFSA's work is, however, assessing company dossiers submitted as part of the EU's product or health claim approval process. The requirement is therefore on the company to provide this, rather than for EU tax payers to fund research to help them take their product to market. The multi-member, multidisciplinary Scientific Panel approach should help to ensure that these dossiers are given sufficient scrutiny, but it is also essential that the risk assessment considers other relevant data, in the field in order to ensure that all relevant information, is taking into account when a decision is reached. Close links with DG Research are also needed in order to ensure that the European Commission research priorities can help to address EFSA's data requirements.

18 'Policy on Independence and Scientific Decision-making Processes of the European Food Safety Authority' (2011).

19 European Food Safety Authority, 'EFSA Science Strategy 2012–16' (2012).

Guidance vs Interference

Related to this is the issue of how much EFSA should interact with the private sector whose products it is assessing. On the one hand, it is important that food industry applicants understand what is required of them through clear guidance. But, on the other, EFSA needs to maintain a distance from the companies whose products it assesses in order to ensure that it is not unduly influenced and its independence brought into question.

An applications desk has been created to help with queries from all stakeholders on the process which is a welcome step. But it is important that this maintains a careful balance. It is not EFSA's role to help companies market their products. Its responsibilities have to stay firmly focused on the consumer interest.

The potential for EFSA to charge fees for applications submitted to it for assessment has been on the agenda – and subject to much dispute for a while. This could be a way of ensuring that tax payers are not funding company product approvals. The number of dossiers submitted to EFSA under the regulation on nutrition and health claims[20] illustrated the problem. There were initially around 40,000 submissions which were whittled down to 4,000 but still placed enormous demands on EFSA's Panel on Dietetic Products, Nutrition and Allergies (NDA). But the introduction of fees, if paid to EFSA rather than the European Commission, also risks undermining the perception of EFSA's independence. The perception can be as important as the reality and so the mechanism for the collection of fees, if they are ever introduced, would therefore be very important.

Proactive vs Reactive Work

As the nutrition and health claims regulation illustrates, the applications for products under EU regulations requiring approval take up a large proportion of EFSA's work. It is important that EFSA is able to do this. Independent assessment and pre-market authorisation are the cornerstone of EU food legislation that helps to protect EU consumers.

It is, however, also important that EFSA is able to focus on new and emerging risks and use its self-tasking function as effectively as possible to ensure that it is keeping abreast of more general risks that may impact on consumers. Its work on data collection is a fundamental aspect of this. Networks also need to continue to be developed globally in order to identify risks that may have implications for the EU and also respond effectively when a crisis erupts and scientific advice is needed rapidly – as happened with the Fukushima nuclear power plant incident in 2011, for example. A balance needs to be struck between providing timely advice to enable a precautionary and rapid approach and also ensuring that it is as robust as possible.

20 Regulation 1924/2006 of 20 December 2006 on nutrition and health claims on food.

To a large extent, EFSA's workload can be anticipated as it can take years for new EU regulations that will impact on it to be debated and adopted by the European Parliament and Member States. It is essential that the legislative process takes account of the potential implications for EFSA, including requirements for additional expertise, when drafting and implementing the legislation.

Transparency and Austerity

With an increasing focus on economic aspects and many cuts in spending taking place across the board, measures once taken for granted to ensure transparency of the process and stakeholder engagement are also at risk of being less stringent. Live web-streaming of EFSA's management board meetings have shifted over to on-demand audio recordings which cost considerably less. The meetings do still take place in public. A balance, therefore, needs to be struck between transparency and inclusiveness and responsible use of scarce resources. Effective consumer engagement, however, remains essential in order to help ensure that EFSA's work tackles the issues that matter most to consumers.

EFSA has recently initiated a pilot project where stakeholders can register to observe the work of the Scientific Committee or Panels. Despite some initial concern that this could be disruptive, it appears to have worked well, as it does in the UK. It is important that there are more routine open meetings of the Scientific Committee and Panels so that it is clear how they approach risk assessment, that they work independently and how they ultimately reach their opinion.

The other Legitimate Factors

A central issue to risk analysis has always been the extent to which risk management should be guided by science and the extent to which 'other legitimate factors' should be taken into account. This issue preoccupied the Codex Alimentarius Commission, the United Nations body that sets international food standards for many years[21] which recognises the role of other factors besides science in its guidance on risk analysis[22] and is embedded in the EU's general food law regulation which established EFSA. This states that '*risk management shall take into account the results of risk assessment, and in particular, the opinions of the Authority, other factors legitimate to the matter under consideration and the precautionary principle* ...'.

---

21 Codex Alimentarius Commission, 'Statements of principle concerning the role of science in the Codex decision-making process and the extent to which other factors are taken into account' (Codex Alimentarius Commission Procedural Manual, 20th Edition, Joint FAO/WHO Food Standards Programme 2011).

22 Codex Alimentarius Commission, 'Working Principles for Risk Analysis for Food Safety for Application by Governments' (CAC/GL 62–2007, 2007).

These 'other factors' are therefore clearly a risk management responsibility. However, it can be difficult to disentangle wider social and ethical issues from some of the work that EFSA does – and public perception of EFSA's opinions may not make this distinction. Similarly the way that people balance the potential risks and benefits will determine what level of risk they find acceptable. In practice, the stark separation between risk assessment and management may not fit with how people assess the relative risk. This has been the case for example with the assessment of new technologies. The assessment of GMOs and animal cloning have, for example, been particularly controversial.

This issue is also made more complicated because, although set out in the general food law regulation, other legitimate factors are still not explicitly set out by risk managers and many decisions will still be presented as based on 'the science'.

Consumer Engagement

Consumer and wider stakeholder engagement is essential in order to ensure that EFSA is taking into account and addressing the issues of most concern to consumers. As already highlighted, this should start with the framing of the question in order to ensure that the context is the right one. Consumer organisations have been critical of EFSA's work where a scientific risk assessment may be too narrowly framed and fail to take account of wider risks that may have a bearing. This is crucial in order to ensure that risk managers are able to make effective use of EFSA opinions and that issues do not 'fall through the cracks'. Examples could include risk assessments on nutrition issues, where a narrow focus on the available evidence (as seen with EFSA's initial work on sugar for example) could suggest that there is not a public health issue. Cross-panel working is also essential in order to ensure that all aspects of an issue are looked at. This has been seen in the way that a request for advice on meat inspection has been shared between EFSA panels dealing with human health, contaminants and animal welfare aspects.

Strong consumer representation is also essential on the management board in order to ensure that the overall direction of EFSA's work is in the consumer interest. Consumer representatives should also be appointed to the Scientific Panels as is the case in the UK where the value of a challenging lay representative is valued and helps to ensure greater transparency.

But on a more general basis, it is essential that EFSA's risk communication work is accessible to consumers and that it seeks the views of consumers. Consumer and other public interest organisations also need to be involved in EFSA's work on a regular basis. The Stakeholder Consultative Forum is a valuable way of ensuring this, but consumer organisations also need to be involved in wider consultations and colloquia in order to ensure that stakeholder input is balanced, regardless of relative resources to enable participation.

Sustainability of the EU Risk Assessment Model

The increasing demands placed on EFSA have prompted some questioning of whether the EU risk assessment model – that is, the Scientific Panel approach – can be used for a more limited number of assessments.[23] This approach is, however, enshrined in the founding regulation and was the model used by the European Commission – and within Member States – prior to the creation of EFSA.

As EFSA's workload has increased, the demands placed on the scientists who give their time to help EFSA with its work have increased. As well as the time demands of the work, a lot of travel is also required, although more meetings now take place by teleconferencing. EFSA's Science Strategy therefore places greater emphasis on the supporting role of EFSA staff in order to manage the workload and make the best use of the external experts.[24]

This is necessary, but it is important that it does not go too far. Moving the risk assessment work 'in house' would be a backward step as it would place much greater responsibility on individual employees, however expert they are, rather than ensuring a consensus-based approach to reaching opinions with a wide range of input. While company dossiers may appear a straightforward candidate for a more streamlined approach, they are also likely to be the most controversial, and therefore need to be subject to a diverse range of independent scrutiny. The Scientific Panel model must therefore be sustained.

Future Challenges

The issues highlighted above also need to be considered in light of new challenges that the food supply chain is likely to present for EFSA in the coming years. It is essential that EFSA is able to keep abreast of new technologies and processes that may present a risk to consumers. This includes further work on nanotechnologies and understanding the implications of synthetic biology for the food chain.

Understanding the interactions and cocktail effects of different chemicals in the supply chain continues to be an issue, including ongoing work around low dose effects. Efforts to streamline and simplify work in this area, such as the concept of threshold of toxicological concern, must not result in a lower level of protection for consumers.

As Europe continues to tackle obesity and diet-related disease, nutrition and public health must continue to be an important part of EFSA's work – whether through continuing to provide consumers with information about health and nutrition claims that they can trust or providing clearer guidance on nutritional requirements to inform policy.

---

23 External Evaluation of the European Food Safety Authority, Final Report, Ernst & Young, September 2012.

24 European Food Safety Authority, 'EFSA Science Strategy 2012–16' (2012).

Other aspects of EFSA's work will be more mundane, but are just as important – including work to further reduce the incidence of food poisoning such as salmonella and campylobacter and the threat of antibiotic resistance. There is still a lot that is poorly understood about Transmissible Spongiform Encephalopathies (TSE) such as atypical BSE and these must be closely watched.

While EFSA's work takes into account environmental issues to some extent, for example, in relation to GMOs and animal cloning, this is likely to become a greater focus in the coming years. The challenges of producing more food in a way that is sustainable is likely to require robust scientific advice on what consumers should be eating to be both healthy and sustainable. EFSA may, therefore, have a role in taking this forward as the EU develops a clearer approach to sustainable food. The environmental impact of food may also be increasingly relevant to EFSA as the effects of climate change may present different hazards, such as new pathogens, for the food supply chain.

The complexity and globalisation of the supply chain means that it is difficult to anticipate the issues that will impact on EFSA in the future. The E coli outbreaks in Germany and France in 2011, which EFSA eventually tracked back to Egyptian fenugreek seeds highlighted how interconnected the EU food chain can be and how a threat in one part of the world can rapidly impact on consumers in another. It also demonstrated the important role that EFSA needs to play in dealing with outbreaks that cross national borders and require multidisciplinary scientific input along with a rapid reaction. The widespread contamination of beef products with horsemeat, while not a safety issue, also highlighted the complexity of the supply chain, as well as the risk from fraud in the current economic climate.

The Next 10 Years

Looking back at the role of EFSA and what it has achieved over the past 10 years against the weaknesses of EU food policy set out by Which? back in 2000, a lot has been achieved.

While trade and food industry interests inevitably have a lot of influence, the establishment of EFSA has helped to ensure that there is an independent approach to risk assessment and communication and previous conflicts in the way that scientific advice was provided have been removed. The focus on emerging risks and EFSA's self-tasking role means that there is a more proactive approach to dealing with food risks, although this needs to go further and feed through into the regulatory framework which still lags behind market developments. EFSA has ensured greater consumer involvement in its work and has a clear consumer focus. Recent handling of food scares such as the Irish dioxins incident where feed became contaminated and the E. coli outbreaks in Germany and France have seen a more coordinated response to food safety problems. EFSA has also played an important role in the handling of these incidents, ensuring one clear EU-wide risk assessment, rather than potentially conflicting national perspectives. Its approach to risk communication has also meant that the information about food-related risks is now far more accessible and understandable and provides the basis for wider communication to the public through Member States.

Further action is still needed, building on this, to ensure a more proactive approach and make most use of EFSA's self-tasking role as well as responding to European Commission and Parliament requests. Further steps are also needed to ensure transparency of the risk assessment process and therefore establish greater trust.

But overall, the EU food system and EU consumers are in a much better place since the creation of EFSA. The challenge is to keep it that way and continue to build on the progress that has been made so far. It is essential that 10 years on since it was created, the fundamental principles of independence, transparency, scientific excellence and a high level of consumer protection that formed the basis of EFSA are recognised as being just as important in today's turbulent climate.

Chapter 18
A Yankee in King Arthur's Court: A Lawyer's Perspective of EFSA

Luis González Vaqué and Sebastián Romero Melchor

Introduction

When we, as legal professionals, are asked to write about the European Food Safety Authority's 10 years of tireless work, we feel tempted to read the preamble and articles of Regulation 178/2002 anew.[1] It is indeed essential to take the legal basis of EFSA's very existence as a starting point, as well as to identify the original terms of reference that are at the root of EFSA's tasks and competencies.

Union food law is based on sound scientific knowledge.[2] In this context, EFSA has taken over the role of the Scientific Committees attached to the Commission by issuing scientific opinions in its field of competence (see paragraph 45 of the Regulation's preamble, where, in addition, it is stated that 'it is necessary to reorganise these Committees to ensure greater scientific consistency in relation to the food supply chain and to enable them to work more effectively').

On the other hand, the doubts, perplexities and difficulties that arise when a legal professional is interpreting not only EFSA's opinions, but also all of its abundant activity, are nothing new. It has been said, and it is true, that a Scientific Committee and Permanent Scientific Panels should therefore be set up within the Authority to provide these opinions. It is necessary to reorganise these committees, in order to ensure a more coherent scientific approach in relation to the food chain, as well as to allow them to carry out their work more efficiently. Consequently, a Scientific Committee and several technical scientific commissions in charge of issuing these opinions should be created within EFSA.

At the tenth anniversary of its existence, EFSA delivered its, arguably, most controversial work, which resulted in the approval of Regulation 432/2012 establishing a list of permitted health claims made on foods (hereinafter, the

---

1 Regulation (EC) 178/2002 of the European Parliament and of the Council of 28 January 2002 laying down the general principles and requirements of food law, establishing the European Food Safety Authority and laying down procedures in matters of food safety [2002] OJ L 31/1, pp. 1–24.

2 Commission of the European Communities, 'White Paper on Food Safety', COM (1999) 719 final, 12 January 2000, Brussels, available at http://ec.europa.eu/dgs/health_consumer/library/pub/pub06_en.pdf (last visited on 12/13/2012).

'Permitted List').[3] Beside the theoretical questions and challenges around the Permitted List,[4] its practical consequences on the industry and other stakeholders are hard even to summarise; applicability of the *flexibility principle*,[5] food sold with rejected health claims that have been legally sold in national markets for years, product withdrawals as of 14 December 2012, the impact of diverging enforcement activities to farther reaching impacts, like hampering innovation.[6]

As an example of the relevance of this piece of legislation, the French Association for Food Supplements Industry (Synadiet) has estimated the impact of the Permitted List on the French food supplement market. In particular, they have estimated that more than 80 per cent of products will be affected; an estimated cost of over €80M (linked to withdrawal and destruction of products); a threat to the jobs of around 6,000 employees and a time frame of about 15 months to enact changes in labelling and in supplying distribution channels.[7] Another

---

3 Regulation (EU) 432/2012 of 16 May 2012 establishing a list of permitted health claims made on foods, other than those referring to the reduction of disease risk and to children's development and health. [2012] OJ L 136, p. 1.

4 Cf. e.g. M. Hagenmeyer, A. Hahn, 'Surprisingly "Cheap" Health Claims for Food Supplements – By Courtesy of EFSA' (2010) 6 EFFL, P., Coppens, 'Regulation (EU) No. 432/2012 Establishing a List of Permitted Health Claims' (2012) 4 EFFL, pp. 162–9; etc.

5 Pursuant to the so-called '*flexibility principle*', applicants should be able to use not only the permitted claims but also any claim '*considered to have the same meaning for consumers*' provided it fulfils the same conditions of use, provided that the average consumer – who is reasonably well-informed and reasonably observant and circumspect, taking into account social, cultural and linguistic factors – can be expected to understand the beneficial effects as expressed in the claim, this test is met [see Recital 9 of Regulation 432/2012, Article 5(2) and Recital 16 of Regulation (EC) 1924/2006 of the European Parliament and of the Council of 20 December 2006 on nutrition and health claims made on foods (OJ L 404/9 of 30.12.2006) (hereinafter, the 'Claims Regulation') and Case 210/96 *Gut Springenheide and Tusky* [1998] ECR I-4657, paragraph 31]. This margin of flexibility has the following limits (i) consumers should not be misled by the modified wording of the claim [Article 2 of Directive 2000/13/EC of the European Parliament and of the Council of 20 March 2000 on the approximation of the laws of the Member States relating to the labelling, presentation and advertising of foodstuffs (OJ L 109, 6.5.2000, pp. 29–42)]; (ii) the modified wording of the claim should demonstrate the same relationship that exists between a food category, a food or one of its constituents and health; and (iii) consumers must be expected to understand the beneficial effect as expressed in the claim [Article 5(2) of the Claims Regulation]; in other words, the degree of simplification of the wording cannot conceal the health benefit expressed in the approved claim.

6 M. Hagenmeyer and A. Hahn, 'Surprisingly "Cheap" Health Claims for Food Supplements – By Courtesy of EFSA' (2010) 6 EFFL, cited at 4, p. 339.

7 Presentation by *Kergosien*, 'Impact of the EU Regulation on the Plant Food Supplements Industry', 15/3/2012, held by PlantLIBRA in Strasbourg, 4/07/2012, available at http://www.plantlibra.eu/web/sites/default/files/u3/Files/KERGOSIEN-%20Strasbourg%20–2012.pdf (last visited on 13/12/2012).

study[8] states that the majority of the food supplement sector expects the economic impact to be substantial and largely negative.[9]

In light of the above, we wish to explore the functioning of this 'bureaucratic monster',[10] which has been accused of generating huge costs to the taxpayer. By trying to identify the different actors involved in the process: EFSA, the European Commission (hereinafter, the 'Commission'), Member States, and the industry on one side; and scientists and legal professionals on the other, more pragmatic side, we question the separation of roles and responsibilities between the different actors. We do this with a specific emphasis on the claims' wording, as well as by analysing their interaction. We then move on to conclude that their conversation is rather a dialogue of the deaf, instead of cooperation.

Scientists and Legal Professionals – A Dialogue of the Deaf?

In the field of Food Law, although it seems otherwise, legal professionals and scientists are in the same trench. Both groups of professionals have to deal with a complex system, which is organised as a regulation at various levels, affecting production in all its phases. This *system* requires legislators and administrators to simultaneously reconcile competition, globalisation of markets and safety, and imposes that food companies must face a regulation that is characterised both by the diversity of sources, and by the fact that it has been adopted under different criteria, organisation and responsibilities.

Within this complex situation, both legal and institutional innovation has been the central and controversial topic in recent years, not only nationally but also at EU level.

These dynamics have led to EU Food Law incorporating a specific content seen from different perspectives, but they should aim at the same goal. The element that catches our attention, after a quick analysis of what happened since 1992, is Food

8 G. Brookes, 'Economic Impact assessment of the European Union (EU)s Nutrition & health Claims Regulation on the EU food supplement sector and market', commissioned for the European Health Claims Alliance, available at www.pgeconomics.co.uk/pdf/Impact-Assessment-health-claims.pdf (last visited on 13/12/2012).

9 Viability of a number of SMEs, market share of products originating outside EU expected to increase, expectation that the 'other substances' part of the EU market for food supplements may decrease in size by about 25% (€645 million at the ex-production facility level or €1,031 million at retail level) and result in a 30% loss of gross profitability (€242 million); additional costs associated with, for example, stock and packaging write offs and changes, would likely add €291 million resulting in total short-term losses equal to two-thirds of annual gross profits in the 'other substances' market and 41% of total gross profits in the broader market, including vitamins and minerals; etc. in Brookes, cited at 8, p. 5.

10 M. Hagenmeyer and A. Hahn, 'Surprisingly 'Cheap' Health Claims for Food Supplements – By Courtesy of EFSA', (2010) 6 EFFL, cited at 4, p. 339, naming the Claims Regulation and EFSA's opinions a bureaucratic monster.

Law's tendency to invade other areas introducing innovations (very often, the result of new technical and scientific awareness). New scientific knowledge and new rules that in principle had been established to meet the demands of innovative regulations that have emerged in the field of food safety, consumer information, nutrition, etc. Even concerning problems related to physical activity, overweight and obesity.

In recent years there have been many issues that have animated the debate on Food Law: traditional products, trademarks and service marks, GMOs in agriculture and food as well as the liability regimes, the precautionary principle and the new rules regarding marketing communications, claims of territorial identity of products and productive activities.

The result has been reflected in a number of application areas that are within the framework of the relationship between law and science and currents that characterise the 'Law in the knowledge society'. The solution of the problem is to accept conscientiously the complex relationship between legal and technological innovation, combining within this relationship the interpretation of each of its elements, whether or not newly introduced.

As regards the technological innovation, it is well known that it has influenced Law in establishing a relationship with diverse food, both in relation to the amount of supply, as in the qualitative aspect of handling, storage and logistics of food products, especially since the nineteenth century.

However, legal innovations were also important: traceability to the precautionary principle, the origin of a large area to the new system of controls trusting public powers under private agencies. Indeed, the element that characterises the Food Law of the last two decades is precisely its continuous innovation, i.e. the *Rechtsreform in Permanenz*.[11]

We must therefore take into account innovations, trying not to get lost among so many changes that continue to occur. One wonders whether the innovation in itself has a meaning for legal professionals: it constitutes a legal category or, in any case, is a component that somehow affects the legislation, especially if we refer to Food Law.

The elements on turning this process can be summarised as follows:

- innovation
- globalisation
- regulation
- market.

In this context it is clear that scientists and lawyers are condemned to understand each other.

11 U. Noack and D.A. Zetzsche, 'Corporate Governance Reform in Germany: The Second Decade' (2005) 10 Centre for Business & Corporate Law Research Paper Series, Düsseldorf.

Of course, this collaboration and mutual recognition is not always easy. A good example of the complexities surrounding the interaction between scientists and lawmakers can be found in the analysis of the roles of EFSA and the Commission in the approval of health claims under the Claims Regulation.

It is common ground that, in order to achieve a high level of protection of human life and health and the protection of consumers' interests, EU food law is based on the separation of risk analysis. Thus, risk assessment is entrusted to EFSA, which should undertake its task in an independent, objective and transparent manner, based on the available scientific information and data.

On the other hand, risk management decisions are the responsibility of the EU and national legislators, which should take into account the results of risk assessments, and in particular, the opinions of the EFSA as well as other factors legitimate to the matter under consideration to the circumstances or the nature of the measure.[12]

This framework determines the allocation of responsibilities between EFSA and the Commission within the authorisation procedure of health claims under the Claims Regulation. Indeed, whilst EFSA performs the scientific risk assessment on health claims, within the remit of its mission as defined in Article 22 of the Regulation, the Commission, together with the Member States, is in charge of adopting the risk management decisions on their authorisation.

In so doing, EFSA should ensure that any health claim authorised under this procedure complies with the core principle of scientific substantiation referred to in Article 6 of the Claims Regulation by performing a scientific assessment of the highest possible standard.[13]

The Commission, on its part, takes other legitimate factors into consideration when deciding on the final authorisation of health claims, and notably, the requirement for consumer understanding provided under Article 5(2) of the Claims Regulation, according to which the use of health claims shall only be permitted 'if the average consumer can be expected to understand the beneficial effects as expressed in the claim'.[14] This requirement takes into account the

---

12 Cited *supra* note 1.

13 Ibid., Recital (23): '[h]*ealth claims should only be authorized for use in the Community after a scientific assessment of the highest possible standard. In order to ensure harmonised scientific assessment of these claims the European Food Safety Authority should carry out such assessments*'.

14 Ibid., Recital (19): '[i]*t is recognized that scientific risk assessment alone cannot, in some cases, provide all the information on which a risk management decision should be based, and that other factors relevant to the matter under consideration should legitimately be taken into account including societal, economic, traditional, ethical and environmental factors and the feasibility of control*'. Along the same lines, Recital (30) of the Claims Regulation provides: '[i]*n some cases, scientific risk assessment alone cannot, in some cases, provide all the information on which a risk management decision should be based. Other legitimate factors relevant to the matter under consideration should therefore be taken into account*'.

different commercial practices, consumer perceptions and cultural differences across the EU.

Any application for authorisation of a health claim needs to include 'a proposal for the wording of the health claim for which authorisation is sought including, as the case may be, specific conditions for use' irrespective of whether the health claim is classified under Article 13(5) or 14 of the Claims Regulation.[15]

To ensure that health claims are truthful, clear, reliable and useful to the consumer in choosing a healthy diet, the wording proposed by the applicant is taken into account in EFSA's opinion and in subsequent procedures,[16] i.e. during the discussions leading to the authorisation of the claim by the Commission, notably the 30-day period of comments envisaged by Article 16(6) of the Claims Regulation.

However, the proposed wording needs to comply with the requirement of consumer understanding provided for under Article 5(2) of the Claims Regulation.

Experience has shown that a literal application of this requirement is likely to result in the claim being rejected by EFSA, as, in most cases, it will consider that the 'consumer-oriented' claim does not allow for the rigorous scientific assessment of the claimed benefit.[17]

For that reason, it will be necessary in practice to couple wording that satisfies the consumer understanding test, with another which enables EFSA to perform a

---

15 Article 15(3)(f) of the Claims Regulation, referred to under Articles 14(1) and 18(2) of the Claims Regulation.

16 Ibid., Recital (29).

17 For instance, in an opinion on Gum Periobalance™ tablets and chewing gum oral health, EFSA stated that '*rebalancing the oral microflora is a term which cannot be used for a scientific evaluation since the 'normal' balance is not defined. Oral health is also a wide term, and as such does not allow a scientific evaluation*' (Cf. Scientific Opinion of the Panel on Dietetic Products, Nutrition and Allergies on a request from the Sunstar Suisse, S.A. on the scientific substantiation of a health claim related to Gum Periobalance™ tablets and chewing gum oral health [(2009) 1178 *EFSA Journal*, 1–8]. Further, with regard to the claim '*Lactoral is recommended in order to improve the general immunity by maintaining the microbiological balance*', EFSA found that the claimed effect of improving the general immunity and the proposed biological mechanism of maintaining the microbiological balance have not been sufficiently defined by the applicant to allow an adequate evaluation of the effect and its impact on health (Cf. Scientific Opinion of the Panel on Dietetic Products, Nutrition and Allergies on a request from the Institute of Biotechnology, Sera and Vaccines BIOMED S.A. on the scientific substantiation of a health claim related to LACTORAL and improvement of the general immunity [(2008) 860 *EFSA Journal*, 1–8]). The same comment was made with regard to the words '*natural intestinal microflora*' in the claim '*Lactoral helps to maintain natural intestinal microflora during travel, changing the climatic zone or a diet, especially in poor hygiene conditions*' (Cf. Scientific Opinion of the Panel on Dietetic Products, Nutrition and Allergies on a request from the Institute of Biotechnology, Sera and Vaccines BIOMED S.A. on the scientific substantiation of a health claim related to LACTORAL and maintenance of natural intestinal microflora during travel [(2008) 863 *EFSA Journal*, 1–8]).

scientific assessment of an objective, specific, measurable function. Both sets of wording should be presented together.[18]

EFSA's Role in the Assessment of the Wording of the Health Claim

According to Article 16(3) (b) of the Claims Regulation, EFSA has to verify 'that the wording of the health claim complies with the criteria laid down in [the Claims Regulation]'.[19] This requirement applies both for health claims referred to in Articles 13(5) and 14 of the Claims Regulation.[20]

Article 16(3)(b) seems to require EFSA to assess the wording proposed by the applicant against any criteria contained in the Claims Regulation, without making a distinction between those that are relevant to EFSA's competences – which are essentially of scientific and technical nature[21] – from those which are not.

This interpretation cannot be maintained, as it would result in EFSA encroaching on the risk management powers conferred on the EU and national legislators. Indeed, the fact that consumer understanding remains outside the scope of EFSA's assessment emerges clearly from the soft law, regulatory developments, and practical experience gained following the entry into force of the Claims Regulation.

In the event of a favourable opinion, authorising a health claim, EFSA is obliged to include a proposal for the wording of the health claim, in accordance with Article 16(4) of the Claims Regulation. In doing so, it must be remembered that EFSA's scientific experts are specialised in the field of applied science, and their core competence involves reviewing scientific data and studies on risks associated with certain hazards.

When starting an evaluation, EFSA scientific panels may decide to meet with other stakeholders to form a better view, and share the planned approach for the risk assessment.[22] However, these types of meetings have been rather exceptional,[23] and EFSA has issued its opinions without much consultation with stakeholders or academic peers.[24]

18 For example, '*Helps maintain normal platelet aggregation* [directed at EFSA]. *Helps to maintain a healthy bloodflow and benefits circulation* [directed at the Commission]'.

19 Cf. Article 16(3)(b) of the Claims Regulation.

20 Cf. Article 16(3)(b) of the Claims Regulation, referred to under Articles 14(1) and 18(3) of the Claims Regulation. The latter provision expressly states that '[t]*he procedure laid down in Article 16(3)(a) and (b), (5) and (6) shall apply mutatis mutandis*'.

21 Cf. Article 22 of the Regulation.

22 A. Smith, S. Terry and D. Detken, '10 years of the European Food Safety Authority (EFSA) and the EU Food Safety Authority' (2012) 3 EFFL, pp. 111, 113–14.

23 EFSA Conference on Nutrition and Health Claims, 8–10 November 2006 held in Bologna, Italy.

24 Coppens (n 4) 168.

In this respect, EFSA is a paradigm of an agency that actively, and often decisively, intervenes in the approval procedure of community laws. Despite this important role, it is often unapproachable. We will likely be able to confirm this view when judgments in the cases mentioned below[25] are delivered.

Commission's Role in the Assessment of the Wording of the Health Claim

Compliance with the principle of consumer understanding referred to in Article 5(2) of the Claims Regulation (as well as other legal requirements arising from the Claims Regulation) is considered at a later stage of the authorisation procedure. In particular, once the claim has been assessed by EFSA, it will be dealt with at the level of the Standing Committee on the Food Chain and Animal Health, Summary Records (hereinafter, 'SCFCAH') and the informal Commission's Working Group on Health and Nutrition Claims.

In other words, EFSA's obligation to evaluate the wording of the health claims proposed by the applicant against the criterion of consumer understanding enshrined in Article 5(2) of the Claims Regulation was abandoned. Instead, the assessment of the wording proposed by the applicant would be limited to a scientific and public health perspective.

The above is corroborated by the recently published Frequently Asked Questions intended to complement EFSA's Technical Guidance. It expressly acknowledges that consumer understanding will only be dealt with by the Commission, i.e. at a later stage of the authorisation procedure.[26] This was confirmed at the Technical meeting organised by EFSA on 15 June 2009 to inform food business operators of the recent developments concerning the assessment of health claims.[27]

A similar change occurred with regard to the scientific assessment of the list of health claims referred to in Article 13(3) of the Claims Regulation. Although the Commission's formal request required EFSA to assess the wording of health claims to ensure compliance with the criteria laid down in the Claims Regulation,[28]

25 Cited in notes 42, 43, 46 and 48 *infra*.

26 EFSA Panel on Dietetic Products, Nutrition and Allergies (NDA), 'Frequently Asked Questions (FAQ) related to the assessment of Article 14 and 13.5 health claims applications on request of EFSA' (2009) 7(9)*EFSA Journal* 1339 [8 pp.]. doi:10.2903/j.efsa.2009.1339, p. 6.

27 According to the press, Professor Albert Flynn, chair of the NDA Panel, stated that EFSA suggested a wording that *'reflects the scientific evidence – we don't ask whether consumers understand the word'* and that the European Commission may consider other aspects – *such as consumer understanding*. Whereas EFSA needs to communicate the scientific aspects, the Commission should have more flexibility and should not feel constrained by the words scientists use (Cf. 'Flynn tells industry to go to the Commission on wording' (2009) 396 EU Food Law; and 'EFSA opens up on EU health claims' published on <NutraIngredients.com> on June 16, 2009).

28 European Commission request to the European Food Safety Authority for scientific advice on the Community list of permitted health claims pursuant to Article 13 of Regulation 1924/206 on nutrition and health claims made on foods, p. 3 and 5.

the Panel on Dietetic Products, Nutrition and Allergies (hereinafter, the 'NDA Panel') commented at its 21st plenary meeting that 'EFSA can evaluate whether the wordings used to express the claimed effect reflect the scientific evidence, but would not go any further, e.g. to take into account consumer understanding'.[29]

Consequently, it emerges from the soft law and regulatory developments which followed the entry into force of the Claims Regulation that EFSA's responsibility in the assessment of health claims is kept to a scientific and technical level, leaving the duty to assess consumer understanding to the risk managers.

Practical Experience

As mentioned, EFSA is required to propose a wording for the health claim only if it favours its authorisation. In so doing, EFSA takes primarily into account the need to reflect the scientific evidence validated in the assessment, without considering the need for consumer understanding.

This has been corroborated in the application for the authorisation of the health claim 'helps to maintain a healthy blood flow and benefits circulation'. The applicant justified the wording proposed for the health claim in light of the need for consumer understanding: '[t]he claimed health benefit is a reduction in platelet aggregation, which contributes to overall vascular and cardiovascular health. The proposed health claim resulting from that health benefit represents a concept of the significance of platelet function in vascular health which is understood by the consumer'. Nevertheless, EFSA considered that the wording proposed by the applicant did not reflect the scientific evidence, since only measures of platelet aggregation had been used in the studies presented whereas 'blood flow' and particularly 'circulation' depend on many other factors that had not been addressed in the studies provided. Therefore, EFSA proposed the following wording: '*helps maintain normal platelet aggregation*'.[30, 31]

29 NDA Panel, 'Minutes of the 21st Plenary Meeting of the Scientific Panel on Dietetic Products, Nutrition and Allergies held on July 9–11' (published on August 18, 2008, p. 3).

30 Scientific Opinion of the Panel on Dietetic Products, Nutrition and Allergies on a request from the PROVEXIS NATURAL PRODUCTS LIMITED on the scientific substantiation of a health claim related to Water-soluble tomato concentrate (WSTC I and II) and platelet aggregation (2009) 1101 *EFSA Journal*, 1–15.

31 Similarly, McNeil Nutritionals supported the health claim '[b]*y actively lowering/reducing LDL-cholesterol (by up to 14% within 2 weeks, by blocking cholesterol absorption), plant stanol esters reduce the risk of (coronary) heart disease*' with data on consumer understanding. However, and although EFSA proposed a different wording to better reflect the scientific evidence, the Panel did not comment on the data related to consumer understanding (Scientific Opinion of the Panel on Dietetic Products, Nutrition and Allergies on a request from McNeil Nutritionals Ltd related to the scientific substantiation of a health claim on plant stanol esters and lower/reduced blood cholesterol and reduced risk of (coronary) heart disease. [(2008) 825 *EFSA Journal*, 1–13].

Other criteria provided in the Claims Regulation – such as the need to comply with the authorised legal categories of health claims – also remain ancillary to the pivotal requirement of scientific substantiation. An example is provided in the opinion on Xylitol chewing gum/pastilles and reduce the risk of tooth decay: by referring directly to this risk reduction, EFSA proposed a wording which did not comply with the definition of reduction of disease risk claim referred in Article 2(2)(6) of the Claims Regulation. EFSA justified this proposal by the lack of identification of a clear specific risk factor for tooth decay affected by xylitol chewing gum in the scientific data presented in the application.[32]

Furthermore, the Commission and Member States have on several occasions given precedence to the principle of consumer understanding over the need to reflect the scientific evidence validated by EFSA:

1. Further to the publication of EFSA's opinion on Xylitol chewing gum/pastilles and reduce the risk of tooth decay, EFSA identified two possible risk factors upon request of the Commission: 'Streptococcus mutans bacteria reduced in plaque' and 'reduces plaque'. Although the former was supported by the strongest scientific evidence, it was acknowledged that the latter would be better understood by consumers.[33] Consequently, Member States approved the wording referring to dental plaque as the risk factor at the SCFCAH meeting of 27 April 2009.[34]
2. Along the same lines, whereas EFSA proposed the wording 'essential fatty acids are needed for proper growth and development of children' on the basis of the scientific evidence presented to support the claim 'regular consumption of essential fatty acids is important for proper growth and development of children',[35] Member States expressed concerns about the risk of misleading consumers when the term 'needed' is included in a health claim for an essential nutrient, as it could give the impression that the food bearing the claim is considered to be necessary. Although in strict scientific terms the term 'needed' could be justified, they considered that terms such as 'important' – i.e. the wording proposed by the applicant – could be more appropriate for consumer's perception.[36]

32 Scientific Opinion of the Panel on Dietetic Products, Nutrition and Allergies on a request from LEAF Int, Leaf Holland and Leaf Suomi Oy on the scientific substantiation of a health claim related to xylitol chewing gum/pastilles and reduce the risk of tooth decay. [(2008) 852 *EFSA Journal*, 1–16].

33 European Food Safety Authority, 'Summary of the meeting of the Commission Working Group on Nutrition and Health Claims of January 12, 2009'.

34 Cf. SCoFCAH, Summary Record of Meeting of April 27, 2009, p. 2.

35 Cf. Scientific Opinion of the Panel on Dietetic Products, Nutrition and Allergies on a request from Unilever PLC/NV on α-linolenic acid and linoleic acid and growth and development of children. [(2008) 783 *EFSA Journal*, 1–10].

36 Cf. SCoFCAH, Summary Record of Meeting of December 18, 2008, p. 4.

Legal Professionals: The Final Link in the Chain

By legal professionals, we refer not only to lawyers and judges who are ultimately in charge of applying food law, but also to those involved in the legislative process, and who have to give a legal shape to the scientific data they are provided.

In this chain, we cannot and should not assess whether scientists prevail over legal professionals, or vice versa. It is obvious that it would be difficult for the legal professional to draft effective rules that will achieve the envisaged purpose, if the scientific foundations it is based on are not sufficiently sound.

Similarly, bad legislative techniques used in formulating a sound and reliable scientific principle can undermine all previous investigation, data gathering and coordination amongst interested parties. We do not at all intend to suggest that the legal professional is more important than the scientist. What we want to emphasise is that the legal professional lies at the end of a decision-making chain, with respect to the approval of food law.

The same holds true for the implementation phase: it will finally be up to lawyers and especially judges, through a more or less pertinent interpretation, to achieve the law's purpose and the beneficial effect it was meant to have in practice.

Day-to-Day Challenges when Applying the Permitted List

The industry now has to comply with the applicable Permitted List. Non-compliance can trigger private as well as public enforcement actions. As from 14 December 2012, the question on whether and how far businesses can deviate from the wording of the claims contained in the Permitted List lies at the end of the supply chain.

Even health claims on vitamins and minerals, despite being considered to be widely known to consumers, can sometimes raise difficulties. Reference to 'vitamin C contributes to normal collagen formation for the normal function of cartilage' or 'vitamin C contributes to normal energy-yielding metabolism' have been included in the EU list and, thus, can be validly used, but are definitely not 'consumer-oriented'.

The more challenging questions are in relation to the flexibility principle. Claims like 'enhances performance' could be of interest to many food supplement producers, most of them containing vitamins and minerals. This claim has, however, not been included in the Permitted List.[37]

However, making reference to the flexibility principle, one could argue that the authorised claims 'reduction of tiredness and fatigue' and 'contribution to normal

37 Reference to '*physical performance*' or '*endurance performance*' are authorised in two claims: '*carbohydrate-electrolyte solutions contribute to the maintenance of endurance performance during prolonged endurance exercise*' and '*creatine increases physical performance in successive bursts of short-term, high intensity exercise*', both of these claims with specific conditions of use.

energy-yielding metabolism' in connection with vitamin C, are wide enough to cover the supposed claim, since the wording would demonstrate the same health relationship.

Additionally, one should also bear in mind that Claims not present in the Annex to the Permitted List are an exception. So-called 'on hold' claims, i.e. claims for which the EFSA has yet to complete a scientific evaluation (e.g. 'botanical claims'), or whose consideration by the Commission has not yet been completed, may continue to be used[38] provided that they (i) are scientifically substantiated, and (ii) comply with existing national provisions applicable to them.[39]

In the absence of implementing rules or guidance at EU or national level, the enforcement authorities of the Member States enjoy a wide margin of manoeuvre for the application of the 'flexibility principle'. This, in turn, may entail diverging interpretations among Member States' regulators and judiciary.

The Role of the CJEU

The ultimate interpreter of EU law, the Court of Justice of the European Union (hereinafter, the 'CJEU'), will be the one to provide more clarity on the above. In its only Judgment[40] on the Claims Regulation issued so far, the CJEU interpreted the definition of 'health claim' broadly, by ruling that claims for merely temporary or fleeting effects of a food on human health, such as in the claim 'easily digestible', are indeed health claims. The Court stressed that since this definition does not provide information on whether that relationship must be direct or indirect, or on its intensity or duration, the term relationship 'must be understood in a broad sense'.[41]

We might find new and interesting elements in the light of which to interpret the much questioned Claims Regulation in the Judgments to be delivered in the following pending cases. In case T-17/12,[42] the applicants claim the defendant

38 Recitals 10 and 11 of the Permitted List.

39 On the basis of Article 28(5) and (6) of Regulation 1924/2006, according to which: '*Health claims as referred to in Article 13(1)(a) may be made from the date of entry into force of this Regulation until the adoption of the list referred to in Article 13(3), under the responsibility of food business operators provided that they comply with this Regulation and with existing national provisions applicable to them, and without prejudice to the adoption of safeguard measures as referred to in Article 24.*'

40 Case C-544/10 Deutsches Weintor [2012] ECR I-0000, not yet published.

41 S. Romero Melchor and V.C. Edwards, '"Health Claim" Definition to Be Interpreted Widely, EU Court Rules', European Regulatory / UK Regulatory Alert 10 September 2012, available at http://www.klgates.com/eu_food_alert_12–09–10/ (last visited on 14/12/2012).

42 Action brought on 16 January 2012. The parties Moritz Hagenmeyer (Hamburg, Germany) and Andreas Hahn (Hanover, Germany) claim that the General Court should annul the part of Commission Regulation (EU) No 1170/2011 of 16 November 2011 refusing to authorise certain health claims made on foods and referring to the reduction of disease risk concerning the applicant's claim 'Regular consumption of significant amounts

declared it mandatory that a 'risk factor' be named in the application, although no such obligation results from the Claims Regulation. The fact that the applicants actually named a 'risk factor' in the wording of the health claim which they made was overlooked by the defendant.

There are four legal challenges lodged against the Commission over the Permitted List. We note that EFSA's assessment of health claims is the ultimate objective of these challenges. In case T-296/12[43] the applicants mainly argue that the non-inclusion of many health claims in the permitted list infringes the Claims Regulation by applying improper assessment criteria. For instance, it infringes the principle of good administration, legal certainty and the duty of collaboration with national food authorities, the obligation to provide adequate reasons, in addition to procedural flaws[44] and general principles of law.[45]

In case T-334/12,[46] the legal challenge is against both the Commission and EFSA and seeks the annulment of the prohibitions set out by the Claims Regulation. The applicants submit that the Claims Regulation and the Permitted List, together with the Union Register of nutrition and health claims made on

---

of water can reduce the risk of development of dehydration and of concomitant decrease of performance' [2012] OJ C 89, p. 26.

43 Action brought on 2 July 2012. The parties The Health Food Manufacturer's Association (East Molesey, United Kingdom); Quest Vitamins Ltd (Birmingham, United Kingdom); Natures Aid Ltd (Kirkham, United Kingdom); Natuur- & gezonheids Producten Nederland (Ermelo, Netherlands); and New Care Supplements BV (Oisterwijk, Netherlands) claim that the General Court should annul the Permitted List, other than those referring to the reduction of disease risk and to children's development and health (OJ L 136, p. 1); and annul Commission Decision of 16 May 2012 adopting a list of permitted health claims and creating a list of so-called on-hold health claims that are neither rejected nor authorised by the Commission [2012] OJ C 250, p. 19.

44 '[t]*he adoption of a permitted list of general function health claims while keeping certain claims under the transitional measures of Article 28 of Regulation (EC) No 1924/2006 (i.e. splitting the assessment process and adopting a partial list of claims under article 13(1)) lacks any legal basis. It further infringes the principles of good administration, legal certainty and non-discrimination for a number of reasons, including: there was no justification for the splitting of the process; the split lacked transparency; there was no consultation or adequate reasons given for the split; some claims are put "on-hold" and continue to benefit from the existing transitional periods under Regulation (EC) No 1924/2006 (despite the legal uncertainty of those transitional periods).*'

45 Breach of the right to be heard and breach of legal certainty.

46 Action brought on 25 July 2012. The parties Plantavis GmbH (Berlin, Germany) and NEM, Verband mittelständischer europäischer Hersteller und Distributoren von Nahrungsergänzungsmitteln & Gesundheitsprodukten e.V. (Laudert, Germany) claim that the General Court should annul Commission prohibitions laid down by the Claims Regulation in conjunction with the Permitted List and the European Commission's Union Register in respect of permitted and prohibited health claims [2012] OJ C 311, p. 9.

foods,[47] unlawfully interfere with the food industry's legal positions, and infringe several fundamental rights, because the prohibitions are disproportionate.

The Spanish food association, Afepadi and others in case T-354/12[48] argue that the principle of legal certainty has been infringed. The last legal challenge has not yet been published in the EU's Official Journal,[49] but it is reported that the claim is that the Permitted List, on the basis that Article 13 of the Claims Regulation is unclear, that the scientific criteria applied by EFSA are not suitable, and that EFSA's evaluation process lacks transparency.[50]

Overall, we can conclude that every link in the chain is important, and if one of the links fails, the final piece of legislation will necessarily be flawed. This conclusion will help us evaluate EFSA's reach and influence when adopting legal provisions.

On the Sunny Side of the Street

Evidently, the assessment of activities carried out by EFSA in these past 10 years is, in general terms, positive. Bearing in mind the need to act as an independent scientific body of reference, EFSA has conducted its tasks efficiently. It has evaluated risk, without losing sight of the need to ensure the proper functioning of the internal market.

Indeed, a report recently presented by international auditors,[51] has noted the high quality of EFSA's scientific outputs and risk communication activities, and

47 Available at http://ec.europa.eu/nuhclaims/?event=search&CFID=3005979&CFTOKEN=a826cfc7585498e6–202BB084-EBB1–9B60–1723C800F8C14E79&jsessionid=92128aa435079cf42b2e6547f286d22102c1TR.

48 Action brought on 3 August 2012. The parties Asociación Española de Fabricantes de Preparados alimenticios especiales, dietéticos y plantas medicinales (Afepadi) (Barcelona, Spain), Elaboradores Dietéticos, SA (Spain), Nova Diet, SA (Burgos, Spain), Laboratorios Vendrell, SA (Spain), Ynsadiet, SA (Madrid, Spain) claim that the General Court should annul recitals 11, 14 and 17 in the preamble to Commission Regulation (EU) 432/2012 as they are seriously detrimental to the applicants' interests; and in the interest of legal certainty, declare that the rejection of the health claims listed in Article 13 of Regulation (EC) 1924/2006 of the Parliament and of the Council must result from a legislative act, [2012] OJ C 29, p. 30.

49 Action brought by the Italian National Association of Health Products Manufacturers, Feder Salus on 20 September 2012.

50 GAP – Global Alliance for Probiotics, available at http://www.gap-probiotics.org/legal-challenges-lodged-european-commission-health-claims-regulation/ (last visited on 14/12/2012).

51 EFSA is obliged to commission an external evaluation of its achievements every six years under Article 61 of its Founding Regulation. This independent review assesses working practices and the overall impact of the Authority. It takes into account the views of stakeholders at European and national level. EFSA's Management Board subsequently

highlighted the Authority's culture of transparency and robust systems to ensure the impartiality of its scientific advice.[52]

However, greater clarity of messages and availability in more languages would facilitate outreach to a broader public. EFSA should further enhance efforts to make its risk assessment and decision-making activities more open to public scrutiny to meet increasing stakeholder expectations. The impact of the pilot programme to open panels to observers needs to be evaluated and the possibility of widening access to documentation connected to screening procedures and conflicts of interests should also be considered.

EFSA, in complying with its mission, has issued a significant number of scientific opinions on controversial matters. As legal professionals, we must admit that these opinions have allowed the European lawmakers and the Member States to take more knowledgeable risk management decisions, which ensure food and feed safety.

On the contrary, we are not sure EFSA has actually helped assure or improve the public's general confidence in food related matters (Recital 40 of Regulation 178/2002). This is not due to reasons of inefficiency, or to a lack of 'scientific accuracy', but rather to other reasons, such as no visibility with the public opinion, inefficient communication and collaboration with the stakeholders and scientific peers, the Commission being primarily responsible of communicating risk management measures, lack of clear guidance from lawmakers and others. Consequently, there should be an appropriate information exchange between EFSA and the Commission.

It is worth questioning whether increasing EFSA's visibility would serve the purpose of increasing the consumer's confidence anyway, given the difficulties in communicating scientific information to consumers.

---

makes recommendations to the European Commission regarding changes to the Authority and its working practices. The first evaluation was made in 2005. This second evaluation was carried out by Ernst & Young in 2011. The review covers EFSA's performance from January 2006 to December 2010 – and was extended to include the adoption of the agency's Policy on Independence and Scientific Decision-Making Processes in December 2011. The methodology used was that deemed most appropriate by the consultants based on their experience, as described in detail in the report. The qualitative research included face-to-face interviews with key stakeholders, telephone interviews and questionnaires, benchmarking with similar organisations, direct observation of key meetings and analysis of key operating documents. The consultants sought the opinions of the most relevant stakeholders, including NGOs, with varying response rates. All these observations were considered before the authors reached their overall conclusions.

52 See Press Release, '*EFSA 10 years on – Independent report says Authority delivering on all fronts, outlines recommendations for further progress*', of 5 September 2012, available at http://www.efsa.europa.eu/en/keydocs/docs/efsafinalreport.pdf.

Conclusion: More Openness?

As the Regulation has envisaged collaboration between EFSA and the Member States (who, in line with their obsessive bureaucratic habit to expand inefficiently, have created not only national 'clones', but even regional 'clones'), EFSA would need to find ways to collaborate with other interested parties. We are not yet in a position to propose how or in which way this collaboration could materialise (for instance, through an institutionalised collaboration, or an informal one; through a permanent collaboration or an ad-hoc one, etc.).

We partially agree with the critics[53] questioning EFSA's commitment to openness and transparency. Although the evaluation provides independent confirmation that EFSA is meeting its obligations and in some cases is exceeding its mandate, and whilst acknowledging the work EFSA has carried out to engage all stakeholders, and recognising the instruments it has put in place to guarantee this commitment to dialogue, we believe this cannot be fully sustained in the specific field of our study. The industry's reaction to the Permitted List, which translated in several challenges being lodged before the CJEU, as well as the difficulties interpreting the Regulation and the Permitted List in the day to day of providing legal advice on the use of health claims, are clear indications that something has gone wrong in the legislative process, with EFSA at the very heart of it.

53 EFSA's response to criticisms of its external evaluation, available at http://www.efsa.europa.eu/en/faqs/faqresponsecriticismextev.htm (last visited on 14/12/2012).

Chapter 19
Rule of Science: A Food Law Professor's Perspective

Bernd van der Meulen and Rozita Spirovska Vaskoska[1]

> … the king required three things of him. He was to provide for the neteté, sureté and bon marché in the city. The two former of these are of too mean a nature, tho no doubt of considerable importance, to be the subject of a lecture.
>
> Adam Smith. Monday, March 28, 1763

Too Mean to be Treated?

Introduction

The quote above, taken from a lecture on legal science, connects three things: hygiene, safety and market. To clarify its meaning a little, let us add a further quote:[2]

> The neteté of a country regards the regulations made in order to … prevent the bad effects of corrupting and putrefying substances. This could never be treated in this place. The security of the people … the best means of bringing about this desirable end is the rigourous, severe, and exemplary execution of laws properly formed …[3]

Apparently, in the view of Adam Smith a part of law can be of 'considerable importance', yet unworthy of discussion. In his opinion this applies to the prevention against corrupting and putrefying substances, i.e. to hygiene.

There can be little doubt that the Law and Governance Group at Wageningen University owes much of the position it holds today to opinions such as this one

1 The case study in section 3 is a product of Rozita Spirovska Vaskoska's MSc thesis research within the Law and Governance Group. The thesis is available at: http://edepot.wur.nl/206868.

2 A. Smith, 'Lectures on Jurisprudence' in R.L. Meek, D.D. Raphael and P.G. Stein (eds), *Liberty Classics* (Indianapolis 1982); The quote above is from p. 331 (Report of 1762–3), this one from p. 203 (Report dated 1766).

3 Admittedly, we have manipulated the quote a little to better suit our purposes: we have deleted the words that make visible that it's the hygiene of the streets Smith had in mind, rather than the hygiene of food.

voiced by Adam Smith that hygiene and security, also with regard to food are not topics worthy of academic debate among lawyers. When the Law and Governance Group at Wageningen University, a university of life sciences in the Netherlands, started to expand its scope from the primary sector to encompass the entire food chain, food law was virtually non-existant in the Netherlands and rare anywhere in the world.[4] The group set out to chart and organise this wasteland and claim it as ours. In other countries, other people had already done or did likewise. Ten years down the line, it is fair to conclude that 'food law' has established itself as an academic discipline in its own right.[5]

So what is important to discuss in jurisprudence and what is not? And why should lawyers pay attention to safety and security in food after all? It is interesting that the position quoted above has been taken by Adam Smith, the founding father of economic science as we know it today.

It is Adam Smith himself who introduced the concept of an 'invisible hand' that will bring about the best in societies through the workings of market mechanisms. Other approaches to the same end – bringing about the best in societies – are the majority vote and the leadership of experts. In thinking on food law these three approaches compete for prevalence. It is argued that both of the former two are democratic in certain ways. In politics every citizen has one vote. In the economy consumers vote through the way they spend their money. So the possibility they have to influence the way the market shapes society is congruent with their buying power. In the technocracy, decision is ultimately entrusted to 'other' people. It is obvious that in so far as we look to experts for leadership in European food law, these experts are found within EFSA and have been over the last 10 years.

Overview

This contribution, addresses science in food law at three levels of abstraction: macro, meso and micro. At the macro level we want to share some thoughts of a more philosophical nature on the three major models of regulation. At the meso level we want to focus on the role and the rule of science within the structure of EU food law. Finally, at the micro level, we will look at the practical interplay between EFSA and risk managers in a case study on emergency measures. This contribution is concluded with a short reflection.

---

4 Leading centres were – and still are – Reading in the UK and Bayreuth in Germany. The European Food Law Association (EFLA) existed since the 1970s and in the United States food enjoyed attention in the slipstream of medicines to which it is intimately connected through the competence of the Food and Drug Administration (FDA) and the derived scope of the Food and Drug Law Journal.

5 A memorable date is 26 September 2012 when the University of Pretoria in South Africa celebrated its inaugural seminar positioning itself as the first university on the African continent to take up food law. For details on food law in (South) Africa see: http://web.up.ac.za/default.asp?ipkCategoryID=17837.

Macro

Democracy, Economy and Science

EU food law is evolving at the crossroads between the three main approaches to regulation. One could label these approaches 'political-democratic', 'economic' and 'scientific'.

In a 'political-democratic' approach, the content of legislation is determined by the support a majority is willing to lend to certain policy opinions. In the economic approach, it is not left to the wisdom of people to decide what is best for society, but to economic automatisms. If the laws of economics, like the one on supply and demand, can function freely, it is expected that the outcomes automatically will be optimal. Economists still like to refer to Adam Smith's 'invisible hand'. The legislature should do no more than create and protect the conditions for a free market. In the scientific approach, finally, it is entrusted to the experts to decide what is best for all of us.

These three approaches do not mutually exclude each other. On the contrary they touch and overlap. The political-democratic approach functions under the rule of law. The law has the responsibility to protect citizens' freedoms from the power of government and to protect minorities from the whims of the majority. To this end, the law puts government in chains. It provides governments with well-defined and limited powers (or competences), it binds them to obeying the law and it provides citizens (people as well as businesses) procedures and instruments to ensure the government's compliance.[6] This is in particular true in the European Union where powers are not only enumerated and limited to protect the liberty of the *people*, but also to ensure that the Member States do not lose more of their sovereignty than they have transferred deliberately. Vice versa, powers of the Member States are limited to protect the internal market. Both the rule of law and the economic approach to regulation require governments to restrain themselves. Actions need justification and need to be proportionate. Justification can be found in necessity. Necessity can be established by science. Here the three approaches meet.

In the Treaty on the Functioning of the European Union (TFEU) this notion surfaces in the Articles 34 and 36. Member States should exercise restraint in limiting businesses' liberties in trade (Article 34 TFEU) unless a specific justification exists (Article 36 TFEU). The most important interest recognised as justification is, from the food law point of view, the protection of health.

In this line, the Court of Justice of the European Union (CJEU) established case law deriving from the principle of proportionality a requirement of scientific

6 The amount of publications on the rule of law concept, and the related concept 'Rechtsstaat' is without number. One of the better summaries is, B. M. Hager, 'The Rule of Law: A Lexicon for Policy Makers' (Mansfield Center for Pacific Affairs, 2nd edn 2000), available at: http://www.mansfieldfdn.org/backup/programs/program_pdfs/lexicon.pdf.

proof of the necessity of measures creating trade barriers. An example of a measure judged disproportionate is the administrative practice of the Danish authorities, consisting of systematic prohibition, because of unknown effects on human health, of the marketing of all foodstuffs to which vitamins or minerals have been added, unless such enrichment in nutrients would meet a need in the Danish population.[7] According to the CJEU, exceptions justified on the grounds set out in Article 36 TFEU (at that time Article 30 EC Treaty), as they must be interpreted strictly, require a 'detailed assessment, case-by-case', of the effects of a given product. Such an evaluation must prove that prohibition of that product is necessary for the protection of the interests referred to in this provision.[8] In this light, the mere absence of a nutritional need in the population is not sufficient to justify an import ban.[9]

Rule of the Market

In the first half of the 1990s, developments in law in general and also in food law tended towards the economic approach. Simplification and deregulation was called for. After 9/11 (2001), this approach collapsed on a grandiose scale. In matters bearing any relevance to security, reliance on market forces was replaced by command and control; centralisation of powers, tightening of obligations, increased harshness of measures and a close-knit web of legislation. The world of food underwent a similar transformation ahead of time. The food safety scares of the 1990s meant for food law what 9/11 meant for law in general.

The ground breaking disasters in the world of food were not intentionally and maliciously made by people (like 9/11), but resulted from the autonomous activity of biological and chemical agents, in some cases helped by ignorance and carelessness or even reckless disregards of people's well-being, but generally not by intent to hurt. This reflects in the legislator's responses. While we have certainly witnessed centralisation, resort to command and control, tightening of requirements and inspections, these are usually not geared to prevent damaging actions by people, but to prevent accidents resulting from biological and chemical (even physical) agents.[10] There are some indications that currently a trend towards food fraud is emerging.[11] If this trend continues, further adaptations of food law may be called for to enable dealing with actual malice.

---

7 Case 192/01, *Commission* v. *Denmark*, [2003] ECR I-9693.

8 Case 192/01, *Commission* v. *Denmark*, paras. 46 and 56, see also Case E-3/00, *EFTA Surveillance Authority* v. *Norway*, EFTA Court Report 2000/01, p. 73. See: http://www.eftacourt.int/images/uploads/E-3–00_Judgment.pdf.

9 Case E-3/00, *EFTA Surveillance Authority* v. *Norway*, para. 28.

10 This may have contributed to the scale the Melamine crisis acquired. The regulatory system was not prepared for health hazards intentionally hidden in food products.

11 See for example: Grocery Manufacturers Association (GMA) and A.T. Kearney, 'Consumer Product Fraud. Deterrence and Detection' (2010), http://www.gmaonline.

Rule of Law

The example of 9/11 has clearly shown that, when fear rules, the rule of law is sacrificed. Public authorities escape the limits set on their powers and people are limited in their means to hold authorities accountable. This is well documented outside the world of food. It is our impression that also in the world of food the rule of law has suffered. The focus on the protection of consumers from food-borne risks shifts attention away from protection from power born risks. Crucial responsibilities have been entrusted to people who are knowledgeable about food safety, but seem to be less aware that they function on the basis of powers provided by law which can only be exercised if and when the legal conditions have been met and in compliance with the requirements connected to it.[12] At this moment in time this is no more than a hunch. So far no evidence has been collected. But who can, for example, point us out a decision by the European Commission on the approval of a novel food where the Commission establishes its competence to decide by showing that the food at issue indeed meets the definition of a novel food instead of immediately jumping to the safety issue?[13] Or, how much truth is there in the complaints heard from businesses at conferences that in the process of risk analysis as applied in the interplay between the Commission and EFSA, the risk communication requirement is applied with less than full rigour?[14] At the very least, some stakeholders feel

org/downloads/research-and-reports/consumerproductfraud.pdf. See also: http://www.foodfraud.org/.

12 In particular the formal (SCFCAH) and informal (CAFAB) systems of comitology give a political form to administrative decision-making giving participants the impression they are empowered to create law rather than (only) to *implement* it.

13 If a food is not a novel food, the conditions for application of the Novel Foods Regulation are not fulfilled therefore the Commission is not competent to approve it as a novel food or to refuse such approval, regardless of the risks involved (which would then be either under another approval scheme such as that for food additives, or under Article 14 of Regulation 178/2002). On this issue see: B. van der Meulen, 'Reconciling food law to competitiveness' (2009), www.WageningenAcademic.com/reconciling.

14 According to Article 3(13) of Regulation (EC) 178/2002 of 28 January 2002 laying down the general principles and requirements of food law, establishing the European Food Safety Authority and laying down procedures in matters of food safety [2002] OJ L31/1, 'risk communication' means the interactive exchange of information and opinions throughout the risk analysis process as regards hazards and risks, risk-related factors and risk perceptions, among risk assessors, risk managers, consumers, feed and food businesses, the academic community and other interested parties, including the explanation of risk assessment findings and the basis of risk management decisions. If complaints by businesses are to be believed for example regarding the way the health claims files are processed 'the interactive exchange of information and opinions *throughout* the risk analysis process ... among *risk assessors*, risk managers, consumers, feed and food *businesses*, the academic community and *other interested parties*' (emphasis added) remains hypothetical. By contrast procedures are perceived as black boxes. In practice, risk communication does

excluded from rather than included in the risk assessment process. This is not a place to elaborate but we think it to be of considerable importance and urge our colleagues to consider it for empirical research.

Meso

The Rule of Science

In food law, the third road has been chosen. Answering the question what in terms of food safety is best for all is entrusted not to majorities, nor to the market but to science.

To this end the 'constitutional regulation' of food law, Regulation 178/2002 'the General Food Law' provides the following:

> Article 6
>
> **Risk analysis**
>
> 1. In order to achieve the general objective of a high level of protection of human health and life, food law shall be based on risk analysis except where this is not appropriate to the circumstances or the nature of the measure.
>
> 2. Risk assessment shall be based on the available scientific evidence and undertaken in an independent, objective and transparent manner.
>
> 3. Risk management shall take into account the results of risk assessment, and in particular, the opinions of the Authority referred to in Article 22, other factors legitimate to the matter under consideration and the precautionary principle where the conditions laid down in Article 7(1) are relevant, in order to achieve the general objectives of food law established in Article 5.

Food law shall be based on risk analysis! Food law shall be science based. Except where this is not appropriate to the circumstances or the nature of the measure, all rules and requirements, measures and decisions regarding food[15] start from science. And science is EFSA.[16]

---

not seem to be understood in terms of Article 3(13) of Regulation 178/2002 as an element of the risk analysis methodology of decision-making, but only in terms of Article 10 of Regulation 178/2002 as a risk management tool to inform the consumers.

15 i.e. all food law as defined in Article 3(1) of Regulation 178/2002.

16 In food law, science comes from different sides. In many cases the private sector takes a science based position on the safety or functionality of a product, deriving the science from publications or from proprietary research. The scientific underpinning of

Elsewhere we have labelled Article 6 of Regulation 178/2002 the most infringed upon provision in all of food law.[17] We have not seen one single piece of general food legislation on which DG Sanco actually asked prior advice from EFSA.[18] The European Court of Justice has ruled that – at least with regard to *national* legislation – the requirement of prior risk assessment does indeed apply to general rules (as well).[19] The Court ruled that a prior authorisation scheme for processing aids in France was incompatible with EU law (including Article 6 of Regulation 178/2002) if no risk assessment showed evidence of (potential) problems with processing aids. Also on this issue we will not dwell here, though it is definitely worthy of further legal and empirical research.

In the way the institutions in Brussels and Parma mutually give meaning to the phrase that food law is based on risk analysis, the role of science is firmly placed behind the phase of legislation and only in the phase of execution of the law. Thus the risk analysis framework is framed as an administrative law procedure, not a legislative procedure. In this view EFSA's main responsibility seems to be to provide scientific advice in the preparation of *decisions*[20] with regard to individual foods and substances (and claims made with regard to these).

The General Food Law is vague on the scope of application of the risk analysis methodology. Article 6 of Regulation 178/2002 states that food law should be based on risk analysis, but does not provide for a specific trigger to the procedure. Nor does it answer the question of who bears the burden to produce the scientific data needed for the risk assessment. In some specific contexts specific legislation provides for procedures including scientific advice by EFSA. Examples are the market authorisation schemes for food additives, genetically modified foods, novel foods and health claims. In all these cases the burden to produce the science is on the private sector. In this contribution we will bypass these examples and focus our attention on a case that is evidently about risk management but where the legislator does not specifically impose an obligation to ask for EFSA's opinion. Does the mere fact that risk management is at stake trigger risk analysis? In other words, what is EFSA's role in such risk analysis 'pur sang'?

---

such position is then reviewed by risk assessors at national level or by EFSA. In its third section Article 6 of Regulation 178/2002 places EFSA at the summit of the pyramid of risk assessment as primus inter pares.

17 B. M.J. van der Meulen, 'Science based Food Law' (2009) *European Food and Feed Law Review*, pp. 58–71.

18 See: M. Hugas, E. Tsigarida, T. Robinson and P. Calistri, 'The EFSA Scientific Panel on Biological Hazards first mandate: May 2003 – May 2006. Insight into foodborne zoonoses' (2009) 20 *Trends in Food Science & Technology*, 188–93.

19 Case C-333/08 European Commission v. French Republic [2010] OJ C 91.

20 In some situations the legislator has chosen the *form* of legislation for such decisions (such as including a substance in a positive list) but that does not mean the measure is not of a specific rather than a general nature.

For the remainder of this contribution, it is proposed to address the role EFSA has played with regard to a specific type of measures: emergency measures on the basis of Article 53 of Regulation 178/2002.

Micro

Science in Emergency

So to what extent does science come to bear in the areas that are undisputedly within the context of the risk analysis principle and thus within the sphere of competence of EFSA, but where involvement of EFSA is not specifically set up as a procedural requirement? One of the most telling examples of risk management takes place in the face of acute food safety concerns, i.e. in the context of emergencies.

The General Food Law, in Article 53 empowers the European Commission to take emergency measures:

> Article 53
>
> **Emergency measures for food and feed of Community origin or imported from a third country**
>
> 1. Where it is evident that food or feed originating in the Community or imported from a third country is likely to constitute a serious risk to human health, animal health or the environment, and that such risk cannot be contained satisfactorily by means of measures taken by the Member State(s) concerned, the Commission, acting in accordance with the procedure provided for in Article 58(2) on its own initiative or at the request of a Member State, shall immediately adopt one or more of the following measures, depending on the gravity of the situation: (a) in the case of food or feed of Community origin:
> (i) suspension of the placing on the market or use of the food in question;
> (ii) suspension of the placing on the market or use of the feed in question;
> (iii) laying down special conditions for the food or feed in question;
> (iv) any other appropriate interim measure.

Science Base of a Decade of Emergency Measures

Emergency measures introduced in Articles 53 (and 54) of Regulation 178/2002 are on the Commission's (and conditionally on Member State's) disposal to manage serious risks to human health. Under the risk analysis methodology of Article 6 of Regulation 178/2002, risk management measures should be based on risk assessment, except when that is not appropriate to the circumstances or the nature of the measure. The decision-making through risk analysis translates into managing risks by using science input. EFSA is the independent scientific point of reference in risk assessment, whose opinions should enable the EU institutions and Member States to take informed risk management decisions necessary to ensure food and feed safety.[21]

An inventory of emergency measures from the 10 year period 2003–12 since EFSA's Scientific Committee and Panels became operational shows that EFSA's support is scarcely sought in the preparation of emergency measures. Measures are approved by the Standing Committee for the Food Chain and Animal Health (SCFCAH) most often without engaging EFSA. Out of 67 cases,[22] EFSA's opinion was requested only 6 times.[23] These cases are discussed below. When requested, EFSA's scientific input to the Commission has been delivered under the following provisions:

- scientific opinion, under Article 29 of Regulation 178/2002;[24]
- scientific and technical assistance, under Article 31 of Regulation 178/2002;[25]
- any information for purpose of risk analysis as outcome of RASFF notification analysis, under Article 35 of Regulation 178/2002.[26]

---

21 Recital 34 Regulation 178/2002.

22 As of 21 October 2012.

23 Further empirical research is needed into the question to what extent all these other cases can be considered based on existing scientific knowledge, thus on *prior* risk assessment. Such as would be the case in enforcement against infringements on specific science based legal limits.

24 Article 29(1) Regulation 178/2002:

1. The Authority shall issue a scientific opinion:

(a) at the request of the Commission, in respect of any matter within its mission, and in all cases where Community legislation makes provision for the Authority to be consulted;

(b) on its own initiative, on matters falling within its mission.

25 Article 31 Regulation 178/2002:

Scientific and technical assistance

1. The Authority may be requested by the Commission to provide scientific or technical assistance in any field within its mission. The tasks of providing scientific and technical assistance shall consist of scientific or technical work involving the application of well-established scientific or technical principles which does not require scientific evaluation by the Scientific Committee or a Scientific Panel. Such tasks may include in particular assistance to the Commission for the establishment or evaluation of technical criteria and also assistance to the Commission in the development of technical guidelines.

2. Where the Commission refers a request for scientific or technical assistance to the Authority, it shall specify, in agreement with the Authority, the time limit within which the task must be completed.

26 Article 35 Regulation 178/2002:

Rapid alert system

To enable it to perform its task of monitoring the health and nutritional risks of foods as effectively as possible, the Authority shall be the recipient of any

Commission Regulation 1304/2003 specifies the procedure to be applied by EFSA to requests for scientific opinions referred to it under Article 29(a) of Regulation 178/2002. It emphasises that the EU legislative process depends on the receipt of scientific opinions[27] and that priority should be consistent with the Union interest.[28] Priority is overriding when it comes to requests from the Commission in urgent situations[29] and all necessary measures must be taken to ensure that the opinion is delivered as soon as possible.

According to Article 8(2) of Commission Regulation 1304/2003:

> An urgent need shall be deemed to exist in case of:
> - an emerging risk likely to constitute a serious risk to human or animal health or the environment and likely to have a Community dimension;
> - an urgent need on the part of the Commission for a more detailed scientific basis for managing a serious risk to human or animal health or the environment.

Six emergency measures from the inventory have used scientific input. Next to the extent of engaging EFSA, it is interesting to observe if its scientific opinion is followed.

Cases

Jelly mini-cups Commission Decision 2004/374/EC on jelly mini-cups banned the use of a group of gelling additives in jelly cups based on life-threatening risk emerging both from the shape and size of the products, and from their chemical and physical properties. Meanwhile, several Member States (the United Kingdom, France and Austria) had already taken measures to temporarily prohibit the placing on the market or the import of jelly cups.[30] The SCFCAH during the adoption of the measure on Konjac additive took this view:[31]

---

messages forwarded via the rapid alert system. It shall analyse the content of such messages with a view to providing the Commission and the Member States with any information required for the purposes of risk analysis.

27 Recital 4 of Commission Regulation (EC) No 1304/2003 of 11 July 2003 on the procedure applied by the European Food Safety Authority to requests for scientific opinions referred to it (Text with EEA relevance) [2003] OJ L 185.

28 Recital 11 Commission Regulation 1304/2003.

29 Article 6(2) Commission Regulation 1304/2003.

30 European Food and Safety Authority, 'Opinion of the scientific panel on food additives, flavourings, processing aids and materials in contact with food on a request from the Commission related to the use of certain food additives in jelly mini cups' (2004) 82(1) *EFSA Journal*, 1–11.

31 SCFCAH, Summary record of the meeting of 19th March 2002. Section on toxicological safety. Brussels.

> It is considered that in the present case warning through labelling is not sufficient to protect human health, especially with regard to children and that due to the disparity of measures taken by some Member States and no measures taken by others, Community-wide measures are necessary to provide adequate protection to human health.

The Commission decided to request a scientific opinion from EFSA with the substantiation that it is of public health relevance.[32] The question was submitted under Article 29 of Regulation 178/2002. The Commission planned to review the decision in view of the opinion and examine whether there is a need to propose to the European Parliament and to the Council an amendment to Directive 95/2/EC. EFSA's Scientific Panel on Food Additives, Flavourings, Processing Aids and Materials in Contact with Foods issued the opinion that any gel-forming additive from seaweed and non-seaweed origin that gives rise to a confectionary product with similar size, physical/or physicochemical properties and could be ingested the same way as jelly mini-cups, would give rise to a risk of choking. According to EFSA, this risk was not restricted to children only.[33]

The review of Commission Decision 2004/374/EC resulted in suspension of the placing on the market and import of jelly mini-cups containing gel-forming food additives derived from seaweed and certain gums.[34] EFSA's scientific opinion was followed in decision-making. The negligible economic implications with the small market share of jelly mini-cups, seems to have added weight to the scientific opinion, in favour of the ban.

Genetically modified (GM) rice from the United States On 18 August 2006, the United States informed the EU of the inadvertent release of GM LL Rice 601 on their market and the potential export into the EU of this rice.[35] The rice was not authorised or commercialised in the United States, but it ended up in the rice supply chain to an unknown extent. The Commission took an emergency measure through Commission Decision 2006/578/EC. The measure was based on the presumed risk of an unauthorised GM product and the precautionary principle. This decision

32 Recital 9 of Commission Decision (EC) of 13 April 2004 suspending the placing on the market and import of jelly mini-cups containing the food additives E 400, E 401, E 402, E 403, E 404, E 405, E 406, E 407, E 407a, E 410, E 412, E 413, E 414, E 415, E 417 and/or E 418 [2004] OJ L 118/70.

33 EFSA (2004). 'Opinion of the scientific panel on food additives, flavourings, processing aids and materials in contact with food on a request from the Commission related to the use of certain food additives in jelly mini cups' (82) *EFSA Journal*, 1–11.

34 Annex I Directive 2006/52/EC of the European Parliament and of the Council of 5 July 2006 amending Directive 95/2/EC on food additives other than colours and sweeteners and Directive 94/35/EC on sweeteners for use in foodstuffs [2006] OJ L 204.

35 Recital 2 Commission Decision (EC) of 23 August 2006 on emergency measures regarding the non-authorised genetically modified organism LL RICE 601 in rice products [2006] OJ L 230/8.

required, among other things, an analytical report with every consignment proving the absence of the GM rice. The decision was extended by Commission Decision 2006/601/EC.

On 25 August 2006 the Commission asked EFSA[36] under Article 35 of Regulation 178/2002 for an opinion. Meanwhile, both the United Kingdom's Food Standards Agency and the Netherlands' Food and Consumer Product Safety Authority (NVWA), in their expert advice[37] and risk assessment[38] respectively, concluded that LL RICE 601 is not of health concern. A month later, EFSA issued a statement:

> The available data are not sufficient to allow the safety of LLRICE601 to be assessed in accordance with the EFSA guidance for risk assessment. However, on the basis of the available molecular and compositional data and on the toxicological profile of PAT[39] proteins, EFSA considers that the consumption of imported long grain rice containing trace levels of LLRICE601 is not likely to pose an imminent safety concern to humans or animals.[40]

Taking up EFSA's opinion and the contamination discovered in products declared free of the LL Rice 601, the Commission extended and strengthened the import conditions in Commission Decision 2006/754/EC. However, the Commission inverted the order in the conclusion of EFSA highlighting the uncertainty and the insufficiency of data, despite EFSA's conclusion that it is not likely to pose an imminent safety concern:

> Recital 5 Commission Decision 2006/754/EC
>
> The European Food Safety Authority, requested for scientific support on the issue, issued a statement on 14 September 2006 concluding that although it can be considered that the consumption of imported long grain rice containing trace levels of 'LL RICE 601' is not likely to pose an imminent safety concern to humans or animals the available data are insufficient to enable a full safety assessment of the genetically modified rice 'LL RICE 601' in accordance with the EFSA guidance.

Two years later, the United States Grain Inspection, Packers and Stockyards Administration came out with plan of elimination of the GM rice from the

36 EFSA question number EFSA-Q-2006–00328.

37 Available at: http://www.food.gov.uk/news/newsarchive/2006/sep/gmricetest.

38 Available at: www.vwa.nl/txmpub/files/?p_file_id=12446.

39 PAT proteins stands for Perilipin, Adipophilin and TIP47 proteins.

40 EFSA, 'Statement of the Scientific Panel on Genetically Modified Organisms in response to the request of the European Commission on inadvertent presence of genetically modified rice LL RICE601' (2006) *EFSA Journal*.

market. The Commission responded with softer measures, ending with only random testing on the market in its last decision on LL Rice 601 in 2010.[41] The strict import conditions lasted almost four years, under the umbrella of the precautionary principle.[42]

Red 2G colour Regulation 1333/2008 on food additives took into account that the authorisation of some food additives dated 30 years back and prescribed a re-evaluation to be performed taking into account new data and studies. The process of reassessment of food colours and similar substances takes into account the dynamic nature of science bringing new knowledge in the world that certainly should affect the regulative framework of the subjected matters of research. The first colour that was re-evaluated was Red 2G. EFSA's risk assessment[43] revealed that it is metabolised in the body to aniline, whose genotoxicity cannot be excluded.[44]

Endorsing EFSA`s opinion, the Commission took an emergency measure in response, banning the use of Red 2G, which previously was used only in breakfast sausages and burger meat. This is the only emergency measure directly induced by risk assessment results of EFSA.

Milk and milk products from China When China's milk and milk products were found to be adulterated with melamine, at first sight there seemed to be no reason for concern as Chinese milk and milk products were prohibited on the EU market. But, composite products containing milk or milk products were not. Therefore, the Commission asked EFSA for scientific and technical assistance under Article 31 of Regulation 178/2002 concerning melamine in infant milk and other milk products in China.[45] Five days later, EFSA issued its opinion on the topic[46] and expressed the view that there is no concern of exceeding the Tolerable Daily Intake for adults. However, in a worst-case scenario when a child consumes biscuits, chocolate and

41 Commission Decision (EC) of 8 June 2010 repealing Decision 2006/601/EC on emergency measures regarding the non-authorised genetically modified organism 'LL RICE 601' in rice products, and providing for random testing for the absence of that organism in rice products [2010] OJ L 141/10.

42 On discussion of the application of the precautionary principle in this case see: A. Szajkowska, (2000). 'The impact of the definition of the precautionary principle in EU food law' (2010) 47 *Common Market Law Review*, 173–96.

43 EFSA question number EFSA-Q-2007–126.

44 EFSA (2007). EFSA re-evaluates safety of food colours and adopts first opinion: Food colour Red 2G raises potential safety concerns.

45 EFSA question number EFSA-Q-2008–695.

46 EFSA, 'Statement of EFSA on risks for public health due to the presences of melamine in infant milk and other milk products in China' (2008) 807 *EFSA Journal*, 1–10.

milk toffee containing the highest contamination of melamine ever found, the Tolerable Daily Intake can be exceeded three times.

Two days after the launch of the scientific opinion, the Commission adopted Decision 2008/757/EC requiring checks of all consignments that contain more than 15 per cent milk content. Hence, the stringent import conditions relied on the worst-case scenario of EFSA. Considering the fact that 15 per cent milk content was difficult to measure, all upcoming consignments[47] had to be checked until later good compliance decreased the frequency to 20 per cent.[48]

Sunflower oil from Ukraine A RASFF notification on 23 April 2008 spotted sunflower oil from Ukraine that was contaminated with mineral oil. The Commission asked EFSA under Article 35 of Regulation 178/2002[49] to assess the risk posed by the contamination. The opinion of EFSA based on the Joint Expert Committee on Food Additives' toxicity levels that depend on the type (viscosity) of the mineral oil, showed that the current estimated exposure represented only one-tenth of the Acceptable Daily Intake and therefore was not of public health concern.[50]

Next to EFSA's statement, the Commission considered also the uncertainty of the contamination source and presumed a risk. The presumed risk overruled the estimation of EFSA of no public concern. The sunflower oil containing high levels of mineral oil was counted as unfit for human consumption and thereby unsafe. The emergency measure brought by Commission Decision 2008/433/EC prohibited import of sunflower oil from Ukraine unless accompanied with a certificate witnessing the absence of mineral oil. Next to the certificate, sampling and testing was requested to be performed by the Member States.

Milk and milk products from holdings with confirmed scrapie The previous examples of emergency measures give an insight into the Commission taking emergency measures in response to scientific opinion. The case of the milk and milk products from holdings with confirmed scrapie, distinguishes itself, as the scientific findings were interpreted in an opposite manner by a Member State – France – on one side, and the Commission on the other.

On 6 November 2008, EFSA published an opinion of its Scientific Panel on Biological Hazards on the exposure risk from Transmissible Spongiform

47 Article 2(2) of Commission Decision (EC) of 26 September 2008 imposing special conditions governing the import of products containing milk or milk products originating in or consigned from China [2008] OJ L 259/10.

48 Article 4(1) of Commission Regulation No 1135/2009 of 25 November 2009 imposing special conditions governing the import of certain products originating in or consigned from China, and repealing Commission Decision 2008/798/EC [2009] OJ L 311/3.

49 EFSA question number EFSA-Q-2008–780.

50 EFSA, 'EFSA statement on the contamination of sunflower oil with mineral oil exported from Ukraine' (2008) *EFSA Journal*.

Encephalopaties'[51] through milk and milk products derived from small ruminants. The Panel concluded that the use of milk and milk products from a flock with classical scrapie may carry an exposure risk of Transmissible Spongiform Encephalopathy for humans and animals.[52] Two days later, the French food safety agency AFSSA reached the same conclusion as EFSA and went further recommending that the marketing of milk and milk products from affected herds should be prohibited. Following the instruction, France adopted an emergency measure under Article 54 of Regulation 178/2002. The Commission in this case took into account EFSA's acknowledgements, but also criticised some foundations of the conclusions that were brought. Moreover, doubts were raised regarding the human species barrier in using animal models and the mimicking of the natural route through the exposure routes used in the experiments.[53] In addition the Commission enlightened its position of an actor determining the acceptable level of risk and keeping the balance of costs and benefits.[54] The risk was judged to be low and acceptable by the Commission and a claim was made that France goes beyond what is necessary to avoid serious risk to human health, even taking into account the precautionary principle.[55]

In response to the emergency measure, the SCFCAH, under Article 54(2) of Regulation 178/2002, supported the Commission's intention to suspend the French emergency measure. To that end, the Commission launched Commission Decision 726/2009/EC concerning suspension of interim protection measures taken by France on the introduction into its territory of milk and milk products coming from a holding where a classical scrapie case was confirmed. France brought an action for annulment of that decision[56] that ended with rejection. In a response, France initiated (a new) case[57] as an appeal to the General Court. By the ruling of 11 July 2013, the Court dismissed the appeal.

Harvest

From the above follows that in emergency risk management measures, the Commission only rarely seeks EFSA's opinion, and when it does uses it only as

51 Scrapie is one form of Transmissible Spongiform Encephalopathy.

52 EFSA, 'Opinion of the Scientific Panel on Biological Hazards on the human and animal exposure risk related to Transmissible Spongiform Encephalopathies (TSEs) from milk and milk products derived from small ruminants' (2008) *EFSA Journal*.

53 Recital 22 Commission Decision 726/2009/EC.

54 Recital 24 Commission Decision 726/2009/EC.

55 Recital 25 Commission Decision 726/2009/EC.

56 Case T-485/09 France v. Commission [2010] OJ C 37/41.

57 Case C-601/11 Appeal brought on 28 November 2011 by the French Republic against the judgment of the General Court (Third Chamber, Extended Composition) delivered on 9 September 2011 in Case T-257/07 France v Commission [2012] OJ C 80/5.

one consideration among many that is sometimes followed (fully or selectively) and sometimes overruled.

These findings place the picture of a rule of science into perspective. Emergency management in EU food law turns out to be classically political in essence after all and only exceptionally to be science based.

Discussion

In the twenty-first century the neteté and sureté can by no means be considered too mean to be treated in legal scholarship. Quite on the contrary, they raise important issues regarding the form legal interventions should take and the content they should have. They are at the heart of one of three prevalent models of regulation.

The rule of science by no means is a settled matter in food law. On a philosophical level, it has to find its position towards democracy, the rule of law and the market. On a systems level, it has to find its place among the principles of European food law.

Key player within science based EU food law is the EFSA. It seems, however, that EFSA has not yet been fully granted its core position within the system. EFSA is excluded from general legislation. But also within the undisputed domain of its core competence, scientific advice for risk management decisions in individual cases, the impact of the rule of science remains limited.

Section 3: The International Perspective

Chapter 20

The European Food Safety Authority: A Look from the United States

Stephanie Tai[1]

Introduction

When governments address food safety, they use scientific information to identify causes, remedy problems, and manage risks. Scientific advisory bodies represent one way governments gather this information. This Chapter compares how US Food and Drug Administration (FDA), Food Advisory Committee (which provides advice to FDA) and EFSA (which provides advice to the European Commission Directorate General for Health and Consumer Affairs) structure their advisory processes, and aims to enhance discussions of structural reform through greater understanding of these bodies.[2]

Theoretical Accounts of Expertise

Philosophers are only recently developing deeper theoretical accounts of the use of experts in democratic societies.[3] Tensions arise from the discord between democratic and anti-elite values[4] and concerns of 'ideology and partisanship sneaking in under the guise of value-neutral expertise',[5] and have engendered several intense philosophical debates. The most contested area concerns the

---

1 An earlier version was published in the *Wisconsin Law Review*.

2 For an initial comparison between EFSA and the US FDA, see A. Alemanno, 'The Evolution of European Food Regulation – Why the European Food Safety Authority Is Not a EU-Style FDA?', in *What's the Beef? The Contested Governance of European Food Safety* (C. Ansell and D. Vogel (eds), 2006).

3 E. Selinger and R. P. Crease, 'Introduction to The Philosophy of Expertise 1', in *The Philosophy of Expertise* (E. Selinger and R. P. Crease (eds), 2006) [hereinafter *The Philosophy of Expertise*].

4 See, e.g., S. Turner, 'What is the Problem with Expertise?', in *The Philosophy of Expertise*, 164.

5 Selinger and Crease, *supra* note 3.

nature of expertise – whether ultimately reduced to power and trust, or warranted by possession of knowledge uniquely accessible to the expert.[6] Other disputes revolve around the relationships between lay people and experts[7] and the source of expert legitimacy.[8]

Comparing scientific advisory committees in different jurisdictions cannot resolve these underlying problems about the metaphysical nature of expertise and concerns with its use.[9] It can, however, reveal how different governments attempt to resolve these tensions by encoding their conceptions of expertise into institutional designs. Such insights may be helpful for more deliberately reconciling the use of advisory bodies with actual preferences and beliefs regarding expertise. Accordingly, we can pose certain questions of advisory committees.

What is the Composition of the Scientific Advisory Committee?

This question illuminates how different governments accord trust and legitimacy to experts – for example, whether members are deemed experts due to credentials or track records. A requirement that advisory committees comprise individuals from a range of stakeholder spheres might entail an approach that trust should be accorded based on experts' critical and supportive arguments; alternatively, if committees may vary in composition so long as members disclose certain interests, this could represent a position that trust should be accorded by weight of experts' biases regarding the matter being evaluated.[10]

To What Extent is the Scientific Advisory Committee Governed to Incorporate Lay Viewpoints?

The use of layperson viewpoints can reflect varying visions of expertise. One concern with relying on specialised experts is that putative experts can have intellectual blind spots.[11] Introduction of lay viewpoints into an 'expert' deliberation could be an attempt to open the door to such self-criticism. Alternatively, it could be a way to enhance the credibility of decisions by extending authority

6 S. Fuller, 'The Constitutively Social Character of Expertise', in *The Philosophy of Expertise*, 342–55.

7 J. Harding, 'Epistemic Difference', in *The Philosophy of Expertise*, 328–9; A. I. Goldman, 'Experts: Which Ones Should You Trust?', in *The Philosophy of Expertise*, 21.

8 H.M. Collins and R. Evans, 'The Problem of Legitimacy and the Problem of Extension', in *The Philosophy of Expertise*, 59; Turner, *supra* note 4, at 165–77.

9 See, e.g., E. Said, 'Opponents, Audiences, Constituencies, and Community', in *The Philosophy of Expertise*, 377.

10 Goldman, *supra* note 7, at 21, 30.

11 Said, *supra* note 9, at 384.

and responsibility to the citizenry, or incorporating a sort of experience-based expertise into the process of risk assessment.[12]

To What Extent is the Scientific Advisory Committee Required to be Transparent?

Such a requirement is consistent with a vision that trust could be based on the lay evaluation of expert arguments, either through review of their statements, or in conjunction with external support. Transparency mechanisms may also allow for opportunities to contest expert advice through external critiques of advisory committee reports.[13]

How Frequently are the Views of the Scientific Advisory Committee Sought or Provided?

This question highlights whether experts are used as actual bases for decisions or for rhetorical support.[14] Lack of consistency in consultation could suggest a number of possibilities, ranging from the recognition that experts are only required in certain circumstances or are used only when expected to support a predetermined decision.[15]

How is Decisional Authority Distributed between the Scientific Advisory Committee and Government Decision-Makers?

This question explores the relationship between democratic governance and expertise. An evaluation of the distributional power requires an inquiry into certain structural variables. One variable is whether experts must present advice in the form of 'neutral' scientific assessments about risks, or may also provide risk management judgments.[16] Another is the degree to which the decision-maker must defer to expert recommendations, and whether that entails ceding authority to experts even when lacking expertise or accountability.[17]

---

12 H.M. Collins and R. Evans, 'The Third Wave of Science Studies: Studies of Expertise and Experience', in *The Philosophy of Expertise*, 83–5, 94.

13 Ibid., at 94; see also D. Ihde, 'Why Not Science Critics?', in *The Philosophy of Expertise*, 393–403.

14 H. Doremus, 'Precaution, Science, and Learning While Doing in Natural Resource Management', 82 *Wash. L. Rev.*, 547, 560–61 (2007).

15 Turner, *supra* note 4, at 169–77.

16 C. Coglianese and G. E. Marchant, 'Shifting Sands: The Limits of Science in Setting Risk Standards', 152 *U. Pa. L. Rev.* 1255, 1275 (2004); see also R. A. Pereira, 'Why Would International Administrative Activity Be Any Less Legitimate? – A Study of the Codex Alimentarius Commission', 9 *German L.J.*, 1693, 1701 (2008).

17 Collins and Evans, *supra* note 8, at 48–50.

Food Safety Expertise in the United States and the European Union

United States: The FDA Food Advisory Committee

Composition The main advisory committees used by FDA to obtain food safety information are the Food Advisory Committee and the Science Board.[18] (For this chapter, the Food Advisory Committee is more relevant, given its specific focus on food safety.) Members of these committees are required to be drawn from areas including scientific societies, industry, and consumer groups, but non-scientists may be present as non-voting members to provide perspectives from consumer and industry groups.[19]

FDA currently has three types of advisory committee membership positions with respect to food safety,[20] described as 'Academician/Practitioner', 'Consumer', and 'Industry'.[21] FDA regulations set forth different nominations processes, responsibilities, and restrictions for these positions.[22]

Academic/practitioner members are the only voting members of committees.[23] Members are drawn from a nominations process published in the Federal Register and must be experts on the subject matter for which they are being consulted.[24] In soliciting academic/practitioner members, FDA requests nominations of 'technically qualified' individuals with 'experience interpreting complex data' 'able to analyze detailed scientific data and understand its public health significance'.[25] From these nominations and other sources, the Commissioner selects individuals for membership.[26]

Unlike academicians/practitioners, consumer and industry members may not vote.[27] The FDA website describes such members as having 'specialised … points

18 21 C.F.R. § 14.100(a)(2) (2009).

19 Questions and Answers Regarding Advisory Committee Membership, http://www.fda.gov/AdvisoryCommittees/AboutAdvisoryCommittees/CommitteeMembership/ucm117646.htm (last visited 1 Nov. 2012).

20 21 C.F.R. §§ 14.84 (c) and (d) (2009).

21 FDA, Membership Types, http://www.fda.gov/AdvisoryCommittees/AboutAdvisoryCommittees/CommitteeMembership/MembershipTypes/default.htm (last visited 1 Nov. 2012).

22 See, e.g., 21 C.F.R. §§ 14.84(c) and (d), 14.86(a) and (c) (2009).

23 Ibid., § 14.80(b)(1)(i). Nonvoting members are described as those representing consumer and industry interests. Ibid., § 14.84(c)–(d).

24 Ibid., §§ 14.80(b)(1)(i); 14.82.

25 FDA, Applying for Membership, http://www.fda.gov/AdvisoryCommittees/AboutAdvisoryCommittees/CommitteeMembership/ApplyingforMembership/default.htm (last visited 1 Nov. 2012).

26 21 C.F.R. § 14.80(d) (2009).

27 Ibid., § 14.84(c)–(d).

of view',[28] suggesting a treatment of academicians/practitioners as lacking specialised points of view.

The FDA website describes three roles for consumer members: representing consumer perspectives, serving as liaisons with consumers and consumer organisations, and aiding discussions on scientific matters affecting consumers.[29] Though their roles are described as different from academicians/practitioners, consumer members must be able to engage with scientific knowledge and evaluate benefits and risk.[30] Under FDA regulations, consumer members are selected through a nominations process published in the Federal Register, and various consumer groups are encouraged to nominate and vote on candidates.[31]

Industry members are required to address issues from the perspective of the affected industry as a whole.[32] Rather than voting, industry organisations are encouraged to jointly select an industry member; FDA selects an industry member only when industry organisations are unable to choose an individual.[33]

Current Food Safety Advisory Committee members include scientists from a range of sectors, but predominately from universities. The 2010 Food Advisory Committee had voting members from one non-profit, one private hospital, one state government, one private consultant group, and six universities, along with one non-voting consumer and two non-voting industry representatives.[34] The same committee, in 2012, had voting members from one private hospital, one federal agency, and nine universities along with two non-voting consumer and two non-voting industry representatives.[35]

Scientific independence Several FDA requirements govern potential bias of voting members. Members must be selected such that they 'have diverse professional education, training, and experience so that the committee will reflect a balanced composition of sufficient scientific expertise to handle' the problems before it and may be removed for 'demonstrated bias that interferes with the ability to render objective advice'.[36] Voting members are governed by federal conflicts-of-interest law, and are generally restricted from participating in matters that have

28 FDA, Membership Types, *supra* note 21.

29 Ibid.; see also 21 C.F.R. § 14.86(a) and (c)(1).

30 FDA, Membership Types, *supra* note 21.

31 21 C.F.R. § 14.84(c)(1), (3)-(4) (2009).

32 Ibid., § 14.86(c)(4).

33 Ibid., § 14.84(d).

34 FDA, Roster of the Food Advisory Committee, http://www.fda.gov/AdvisoryCommittees/CommitteesMeetingMaterials/FoodAdvisoryCommittee/ucm120672.htm (last visited 1 Nov. 2012).

35 FDA, Roster of the Food Advisory Committee, http://www.fda.gov/AdvisoryCommittees/CommitteesMeetingMaterials/FoodAdvisoryCommittee/ucm120672.htm (last visited 1 Nov. 2012).

36 21 C.F.R. § 14.80(b)(i) and (f) (2009).

a direct and predictable impact on their financial interests.[37] (Non-voting members are not subject to conflict-of-interest laws on grounds that financial interests are irrelevant their representation.)[38]

Nevertheless, individuals may remain members if the appointing FDA official certifies that their need outweighs their conflict.[39] Publicised incidents involving conflicts in the pharmaceutical advisory process have engendered criticisms of FDA's conflict-of-interest procedures.[40] Concerns raised include the widespread industry support of academic research and lack of universal guidelines.[41]

Meeting structure and transparency FDA does not govern the substance of the committee deliberations, except to require relationship with the issue on which FDA is seeking advice. But non-binding guidance prescribes the manner in which members engage in the voting process.[42] This guidance, addressing 'momentum' concerns in sequential voting, urges committee members to vote simultaneously to enhance the integrity of voting results, but also recognises that the voting process simply helps 'gauge a committee's collective view on complex, multifaceted issues' and considers the overall discussion relevant to the decision-making process.[43]

Statutes and regulations, specific to FDA as well as applicable to all federal agencies, also create transparency through an open-meeting requirement.[44] All committee meetings must include an open portion for which transcripts must be made public, and in which any interested party may present information either in person or writing.[45] Notice must be published in the Federal Register, and

37 18 U.S.C. § 208(a) (2006).

38 21 C.F.R. § 14.80(a)(2) (2009).

39 18 U.S.C. § 208(b)(3) (2006).

40 See, e.g., E. R. Glodé, 'Advising Under the Influence?: Conflicts of Interest Among FDA Advisory Committee Members', 57 *Food & Drug L.J.*, 293, 294, 304–15 (2002); S. P. Croley and W. F. Funk, 'The Federal Advisory Committee Act and Good Government', 14 *Yale J. on Reg.*, 451, 498–9 (1997); W. Steineker, 'Who's Guarding the Henhouse?: Conflicts of Interest and the FDA Advisory Committee Regime', 20 *Geo. J. Legal Ethics*, 935 (2007); but see E. Leitzan, 'Advisory Committees at FDA: The Hinchey Amendment and "Conflict of Interest" Waivers', 39 *J. Health L.*, 415 (2006).

41 Glodé 2002: 318–22.

42 FDA, Guidance for FDA Advisory Committee Members and FDA Staff: Voting Procedures for Advisory Committee Meetings (2008), available at http://www.fda.gov/downloads/RegulatoryInformation/Guidances/UCM125641.pdf.

43 Ibid., at 4–5.

44 21 C.F.R. §§ 14.25, 14.29 (2009); 5 U.S.C. app. §§ 2(b)(5) and 10(b) (2006).

45 21 C.F.R. § 14.65(c) (2009); 21 C.F.R. §§ 14.25(a)-(b), 14.27(a), 14.29(b), §14.70 (2009); see also FDA, Draft Guidance, The Open Public Hearing: FDA Advisory Committee Meetings 3–4 (2005), available at http://www.fda.gov/downloads/RegulatoryInformation/Guidances/UCM125734.pdf.

meetings must be held in publicly accessible areas.[46] FDA non-binding guidance also recommends that committees make meeting briefing materials available unless certain privacy exemptions apply.[47]

Portions of the meeting, however, may be closed if the FDA Commissioner approves a request containing supporting rationales.[48] Appropriate reasons include discussion of trade secrets, private personal information, investigatory methods, and drafts of proposals where 'premature disclosure would significantly impede proposed agency action'.[49] One scholar has observed that in practice, closure is mostly limited to instances of preserving trade information and committee member privacy.[50]

The reasons for closure must be published in the Federal Register, and closed meeting portions must be limited in scope.[51] Moreover, during closed portions, only voting committee members and a limited number of other types of individuals may attend.[52]

Subject matter and form of advice FDA is in certain areas legally required to consult with advisory committees; otherwise, it draws on advisory committees to conduct public hearings on important issues, to review those issues, and to provide advice and recommendations.[53] To clarify its discretionary use of advisory committees, FDA promulgated a non-binding guidance describing its consideration of several factors: whether the issue of such public interest or so controversial that consultation would be highly beneficial, and whether the advisory committee could have such special expertise that consultation is necessary to fully consider an issue.[54]

In practice, FDA has focused using its Food Advisory Committees to assess technical reports and preliminary regulatory proposals; such charges include evaluating a report on establishing major food allergen thresholds,[55] a proposed

---

46 Ibid., §§ 14.20, 14.22(b).

47 FDA, Guidance for Industry: Advisory Committee Meetings – Preparation and Public Availability of Information Given to Advisory Committee Members 4–15 (2008), available at http://www.fda.gov/downloads/RegulatoryInformation/Guidances/UCM125650.pdf.

48 21 C.F.R. § 14.27(b) (2009).

49 5 U.S.C. § 552b(c)(4),(6)-(7); 21 C.F.R. § 14.27(b)(3).

50 J. T. O'Reilly, 'Advisers and Secrets: The Role of Agency Confidentiality in the Federal Advisory Committee Act', 13 *N. Ky. L. Rev.*, 27, 48–9 (1986).

51 21 C.F.R. §§ 14.25(c) and 14.27(b) (2009).

52 Ibid., § 14.27(c)(1)-(2).

53 Ibid., §§ 14.1(a)(2)(ii)-(iv) and 14.5(a).

54 FDA, Draft Guidance for the Public and FDA Staff on Convening Advisory Committee Meetings at 4 (2008), available at http://www.fda.gov/downloads/Regulatory Information/Guidances/UCM125651.pdf (last visited 1 Nov. 2012).

55 Food Advisory Committee Meeting, Approaches to Establish Thresholds for Major Food Allergens and for Gluten in Food 2005, http://www.fda.gov/ohrms/dockets/ac/05/questions/2005–4160q1_Charge%20%20Questions.htm (last visited 1 Nov. 2012).

FDA action plan to address the issue of acrylamide in food,[56] and changes in infant formulas that should be accompanied with clinical studies to support assurances of normal physical growth.[57]

FDA retains a significant degree of discretion regarding the extent to which it uses Committee advice.[58] Judicial review, however, may limit this discretion by requiring FDA to provide a reasoned basis for declining to follow an advisory committee's recommendation, at least for federal actions subject to judicial review.[59]

European Union: The European Food Safety Authority

Composition The General Food Law (GFL)[60] structures EFSA to contain a Management Board, an Executive Director, a Secretariat, an Advisory Forum, a Scientific Committee, and Scientific Panels.[61] Membership selection of the primary advice-giving bodies – the Scientific Committee and Panels[62] – is conducted through a managerial process. The Management Board is charged with appointing members for three-year terms.[63] Publication of the selection process is required in the Official Journal of the European Union, as well as 'relevant leading scientific publications and on the Authority's website'.[64]

Management Board members are appointed by the Council of the European Union from a list compiled by the EC.[65] Members should 'secure the highest standards of competence, a broad range of relevant expertise and, consistent with these, the broadest possible geographic distribution with the Union', and four members must have backgrounds in consumer advocacy or other food chain interests.[66]

---

56 FDA, Introduction, available at http://www.fda.gov/ohrms/dockets/ac/03/briefing/3925b1_Introduction.pdf (last visited 1 Nov. 2012).

57 FDA, Background and Questions: FDA Food Advisory Committee Infant Formula Task Force (2002), available at http://www.fda.gov/ohrms/dockets/ac/02/questions/3903q1_Questions%20final.pdf (last visited 1 Nov. 2012).

58 21 C.F.R. § 14.5(b) (2009); see also Steineker, *supra* note 40, at 941–2, n.52.

59 *Tummino v. Von Eschenbach*, 427 F. Supp. 2d 212, 232–3 (E.D.N.Y. 2006).

60 Regulation (EC) No. 178/2002 of the European Parliament and of the Council of 28 January 2002 art. 1(2) [hereinafter EC General Principles].

61 E. Vos and F. Wendler, 'Food Safety Regulation at the EU Level', in *Food Safety Regulation in Europe: A Comparative Institutional Analysis* 65, 76 (Ellen Vos and Frank Wendler (eds), 2006).

62 Ibid., at 79–81.

63 EC General Principles, *supra* note 60, art. 28(5).

64 Ibid.; see also EFSA, Decision of the Executive Director Concerning the Selection of Members of the Scientific Committee, Scientific Panels and External Experts (14 Mar. 2011), http://www.efsa.europa.eu/en/keydocs/docs/expertselection.pdf [hereinafter EFSA Scientific Selection Decision].

65 EC General Principles, *supra* note 60, art. 25(1).

66 Ibid.

Potential Scientific Panel members are subject to validity and eligibility checks, external review, and inquiry into their technical, managerial, and communications expertise.[67] Unlike FDA, Panel members are also selected using a national representational focus, under the EFSA requirement that 'every effort is made to secure a proper geographical … balance' and prioritise members from 'underrepresented Member States'.[68]

The Scientific Panels are predominately composed of members from domestic food safety agencies. For example, the 2010 Panel on Contaminants in the Food Chain comprised 13 food-safety-related agency, 4 university, and two non-profit members.[69] This contrasts with the FDA Food Advisory Committee, where members are primarily from universities and with few from private industry.

Scientific independence Scientific independence has been described as 'of primary importance to [EFSA's reputation for] … provid[ing] objective and credible scientific advice to more political institutions'.[70] EFSA governs bias somewhat differently from FDA. Rather than excluding those with conflicts and allowing participation only if need for those individuals outweighs the conflict, EFSA applies a balancing test at the screening stage and additional measures during the advisory process.

At the screening stage, EFSA evaluates '[t]he extent of any potential conflict of interests' in determining member selection,[71] similar to FDA. Afterwards, EFSA relies on a combined disclosure/re-evaluation mechanism. Committee and Panel members may participate so long as they 'act independently of any external influence' and annually disclose any direct or indirect interests considered prejudicial to their independence[72] – a requirement that extends beyond the FDA's financial-bias focus. This declaration includes those of a 'scientific nature when the individual has been involved in research relating to the subject that is being scrutinised'.[73] Experts must also submit specific declarations of interest before every meeting, which may then be the basis for further remedial measures.[74]

Some scholars have questioned the independence requirement, citing ambiguity regarding whether independence 'applies to the relation of EFSA to the

---

67 EFSA Scientific Selection Decision, *supra* note 64, art. 4–6.

68 Ibid., art. 8, 17(1)(b).

69 EFSA, CONTAM Panel 2009–2012, https://doi.efsa.europa.eu/doi/doiweb/panel/CONTAM/wg/75463; see also Vos and Wendler, *supra* note 61, at 80–81.

70 S. Gabbi, 'Independent Scientific Advice: Comparing Policies on Conflicts of Interest in the EU and the US', 2011 *Eur. J. Risk. Reg.*, 213, 216 (2011).

71 EFSA Scientific Selection Decision, *supra* note 64, art. 7.

72 EC General Principles, *supra* note 60, art. 37(2).

73 EFSA, Implementing Act to the Policy on Declaration of Interests Procedure for Identifying and Handling Potential Conflicts of Interest 5, located at http://www.efsa.europa.eu/en/keydocs/docs/doiconflicts.pdf (last visited 11 Nov. 2012).

74 Ibid., at 4–6.

Commission and Member States …, to industry, or the stakeholder organisations' and raise critiques regarding actual EFSA independence from the Commission, Member States, and stakeholder groups.[75] Others suggest that disclosure may be insufficient to protect independence, either due to the weight of certain financial interests, or because disclosure itself entails implicit acceptance of certain biases.[76]

The 2011/2012 controversy over the EFSA Panel on Genetically Modified Organisms's approval of the use of potato antibiotic marker genes may further these debates. Critics of this decision focused on conflicts created by panel members' funding from the biotechnology industry and association with pro-biotechnology organisations.[77] Yet, these critics do not suggest that any members failed to fully disclose their interests; indeed, these criticisms appear drawn from the disclosure forms.[78] This suggests a growing dissatisfaction towards the conflicts process as insufficiently exclusionary, the disclosure process as insufficiently motivating motivate members to reach independent conclusions, or the substantive decisions themselves.

Meeting structure and transparency The governance structure of EFSA Scientific Panel meetings is more formalised than for FDA. The Scientific Committee and Panels are required to reach decisions through a majority vote of their members.[79] Moreover, internal guidelines govern planning and conduct of meetings, addressing minority opinions, adopting scientific opinions, creating additional working groups,[80] and resolving divergences between its own opinions and other EC or EC Member State advisory bodies.[81]

But EFSA Scientific Committee and Panels are subject to less governance than the FDA advisory committees with respect to public attendance. While the GFL leaves optional public hearings,[82] EFSA has promulgated internal guidelines to allow for public attendance of Management Board meetings.[83] The Panels, however, are not required to allow for public participation or meet in accessible

75 Vos and Wendler, *supra* note 61, at 100–101.

76 Gabbi, *supra* note 70, at 217–18.

77 See, e.g., Corporate Europe Observatory, *Approving the GM potato: conflicts of interest, flawed science and fierce lobbying*, at 9, located at http://www.corporateeurope.org/sites/default/files/publications/Amflora_COI_report_2011.pdf (last visited 1 Nov. 2012).

78 EFSA, Declaration of Interest GMO Panel 2012–2015, located at https://ess.efsa.europa.eu/doi/doiweb/wg/638172.

79 EC General Principles, *supra* note 60, art. 28(7).

80 EFSA, Scientific Committee Operations Decision, *supra* note 68, art. 12–19.

81 EC General Principles, *supra* note 60, art. 30; 30(2); 30(3)-(4).

82 Ibid., art. 28(1).

83 EFSA, Decision of the Management Board of the European Food Safety Authority Concerning Implementing Measures of Transparency and Confidentiality Requirements, art. 2 (10 Mar. 2005), http://www.efsa.europa.eu/en/keydocs/docs/transparencyimplementation.pdf [hereinafter EFSA Transparency Decision].

locations.[84] Instead, the only attendance requirements are that representatives of EC departments be able to attend,[85] and observers 'interested in EFSA's works, meetings and events' be allowed to attend upon '[a]cceptance by EFSA' so long as they do 'not in any way interact, participate or intervene in the discussions, drafting, voting or in other activities carried out there'.[86]

Transparency requirements also apply to the Scientific Panels. The Panels must make public their agendas, minutes, opinions, and information upon which their opinions are based.[87] EFSA must also make available upon request scientific opinions, including those refused or modified.[88] Transcripts of the actual meetings, however, are not required.

EFSA has also adopted internal guidelines regarding the need for and structure of public consultations, citing concerns of transparency and Article 42 of the GFL,[89] which urges EFSA to develop effective contacts with various stakeholders.[90] These guidelines treat public consultation as the 'creation of an effective exchange on a draft scientific output based on a decision of EFSA to seek comments from the public'.[91]

Subject matter and form of advice The scientific assessment of food safety risks primarily takes place within the Scientific Committee and Panels. The Scientific Committee is focused more on oversight,[92] so the Scientific Panels are those analogous to the FDA advisory committees as the bodies that directly provide food-safety related advice.[93]

Scientific Panels retain greater independent authority to direct their attentions than the FDA advisory committees, which are limited to addressing questions posed by FDA.[94] A Panel can issue scientific opinions at the request of the Commission or Member States,[95] as well as on its own initiative.[96] A Panel may

---

84 Vos and Wendler, *supra* note 61, at 104–05.

85 EC General Principles, *supra* note 60, art. 28(8).

86 EFSA Scientific Selection Decision, *supra* note 64, at 2 n.5.

87 Ibid., art. 38(1).

88 Ibid., art. 6(1)-(2).

89 EFSA, EFSA's Approach on Public Consultations on Scientific Outputs at 3, available at http://www.efsa.europa.eu/en/keydocs/docs/consultationpolicy.pdf [hereinafter EFSA Public Consultation Approach] (last visited 1 Nov. 2012).

90 EC General Principles, *supra* note 60, art. 42.

91 EFSA Public Consultation Approach, *supra* note 89, at 3.

92 EC General Principles, *supra* note 60, art. 28(2).

93 Ibid., art. 28(4).

94 21 C.F.R. § 14.1(a) (2009).

95 EC General Principles, *supra* note 60, art. 29(1)(1). Such requests, in turn, may be either at the discretion of the Commission or Member States, or required under the General Principles of Food Law. *See* Vos and Wendler, *supra* note 61, at 88–9.

96 Ibid., art. 29(1)(b).

even reject requests by the Commission to re-examine previously addressed issues if it determines that no new scientific information justifies re-examination.[97]

Unlike FDA advisory committees, EFSA and its Scientific Panels are formally restricted to issues of risk assessment,[98] rather than including risk management (choosing policy instruments to address risks).[99] Decisions regarding risk management are left to the decision-making body that consults with EFSA.[100] EFSA's recommendations, for the most part, are more assessment-based than that of the FDA advisory committees. Nevertheless, EFSA's recommendations also contain management components, such continuing to reduce the level of dietary exposure to arsenic,[101] highlighting the practical difficulty of separating scientific assessments from management decisions.

The FDA advisory committees are less formally governed by distinctions between risk assessment and management, as FDA advisory committees are sometimes charged with advising on 'broad and general matters' or 'on specific technical or scientific issues, which may relate to regulatory decisions before FDA'.[102] The former category expressly covers matters of policy, while the latter may still blur the lines between risk assessment, evaluation and management.

Case Study: Acrylamide

FDA and EFSA's treatment of acrylamide, a potential carcinogen associated with carbohydrate-rich foods cooked at high temperatures, provides a helpful comparison between the two agencies.

FDA FDA began developing an acrylamide action plan after various studies raised concerns regarding its carcinogenicity. FDA initially developed its plan in conjunction with a subsection of the Food Advisory Committee.[103] During this meeting, the Subcommittee, composed of scientists primarily from academia though inclusive of industry and state government,[104] heard from the director of the FDA's Center for Food Safety and Applied Nutrition (CFSAN) regarding FDA's preliminary plans. These plans included developing rapid screening

97 Ibid., art. 29(5).

98 Ibid., art. 23.

99 Vos and Wendler, *supra* note 61, at 87 n.155.

100 See, e.g., EC General Principles, *supra* note 60, pmbl. 53.

101 EFSA Panel on Contaminants in the Food Chain [CONTAM], 'Scientific Opinion on Arsenic in Food', 7(10), 1351, *EFSA J.* (2009), available at http://www.efsa.europa.eu/en/efsajournal/doc/1351.pdf.

102 21 C.F.R. § 14.1(b)(2) (2009).

103 67 Fed. Reg. 69,225 (15 Nov. 2002).

104 Transcript of the Meeting of the Food Advisory Committee, Contaminants and Natural Toxicants Subcommittee at 5–7 (Dec. 4, 2002) [hereinafter FAC Dec. 4, 2002 Transcript] (on file with author). Three of these members had been granted conflict-of-interest waivers to allow them to participate. Ibid., at 9.

methods, assessing dietary exposure, identifying mechanisms for acrylamide formation, assessing risks, informing and educating consumers about developing understandings of risks, and creating public–private partnerships for information gathering.[105] The committee heard mostly from CFSAN speakers,[106] but also from the director of a joint FDA/University of Maryland partnership.[107]

At the end of the meeting, the Subcommittee suggested further actions, including determining acrylamide sources, identifying high acrylamide-level foods, developing safe limits, and examining potential cumulative interactions between acrylamide and other biological processes.[108] The Subcommittee also recommended FDA move forward quickly on toxicology and risk assessment research, given their time-intensive nature.[109]

FDA adopted these recommendations in an amended plan,[110] which it presented to the entire Food Advisory Committee.[111] The Food Advisory Committee heard from guest speakers from the Georgetown University School of Medicine, Proctor and Gamble, Frito Lay, RTI International, and ILSI Risk Science Institute.[112] The Committee heard from no members of the public, as none registered to provide public comment.[113]

After these hearings, the Committee developed recommendations regarding scientific development and public communication. One member urged FDA to research the relationship between consumption patterns and acrylamide exposure of different subpopulations; another suggested FDA coordinate with the National Institutes of Health to leverage additional funding; yet another suggested that allowing industry to 'share without jeopardizing their own brand[s]' would enhance information exchange.[114]

The Committee also urged FDA to develop its approach towards communicating complicated messages about uncertain risks by drafting a consumer-oriented explanation of FDA's current actions and investigations into the risks posed by acrylamide.[115] Committee members recommended FDA develop an interpretive document for its website to explain the strengths

105 Ibid., at 19–21.

106 See, e.g., ibid., at 53–257; Transcript of the Food Advisory Committee, Contaminants and Natural Toxicants Subcommittee at 2–8 (Dec. 5, 2002) [hereinafter FAC Dec. 5, 2002 Transcript] (on file with author).

107 FAC Dec. 4, 2002 Transcript, *supra* note 104, at 258–311.

108 FAC Dec. 5, 2002 Transcript, *supra* note 106, at 127–9.

109 Ibid., at 125.

110 Food Advisory Committee, Transcripts at 25 (Feb. 24, 2003), http://www.fda.gov/ohrms/dockets/ac/03/transcripts/3925t1.doc.

111 68 Fed. Reg. 5297 (Feb. 3, 2003).

112 Food Advisory Committee on Acrylamide, Guest Speakers (2003), http://www.fda.gov/ohrms/dockets/ac/03/roster/3925r1_guest%20speakers%20roster.htm.

113 Transcript of the Food Advisory Committee, Contaminants and Natural Toxicants Subcommittee at 93 (25 Feb. 2003) (on file with author).

114 Ibid., at 129, 133, 138.

115 Ibid., at 144–5, 150.

and weaknesses of its data and to recruit relevant organisations to aid in communication.[116]

FDA followed most of the Committee's recommendations. It agreed to examine differing consumption patterns by age and ethnic groups and 'pursue contacts with the National Institutes of Health about the potential for research or funding interactions related to acrylamide toxicology.'[117] It also sought information from manufacturers on acrylamides in foods; however, rather than shielding the manufacturers from brand jeopardy, the notice instead states that manufacturers need not identify particular product lines by brand.[118]

The FDA website on acrylamides in food[119] now contains a consumer-oriented explanation of its activities on acrylamide, albeit shorter than recommended by the Committee.[120] FDA also agreed to recruit the aid of agricultural extension and consumer organisations to enhance consumer outreach.[121]

EFSA The EC also began to address acrylamide after scientific studies suggested potential risks. At this time, EFSA was not yet established, and the relevant advisory body, the EC Scientific Committee on Food, was consulted. The Committee issued an opinion in 2002, making some general suggestions, including limiting the food levels of acrylamide to 'as low as reasonably achievable',[122] and endorsing the interim advice of the joint Food and Agriculture Organisation of the United Nations (FAO)/World Health Organization (WHO) Expert Committee on Food Additives on minimising potential risks.[123]

---

116 Ibid., at 146, 152.

117 FDA, FDA Action Plan for Acrylamide in Food, Mar. 2004, http://www.fda.gov/Food/FoodSafety/FoodContaminantsAdulteration/ChemicalContaminants/Acrylamide/ucm053519.htm.

118 FDA, Acrylamide in Food: Request for Comments and for Scientific Data and Information, 74 Fed. Reg. 43,134, 43,136 (Aug. 26, 2009).

119 FDA, Acrylamide in Food, Aug. 2009, http://www.fda.gov/food/foodsafety/foodcontaminantsadulteration/chemicalcontaminants/acrylamide/default.htm (last visited 1 Nov. 2012).

120 FDA, Acrylamide Questions and Answers, May 2009, http://www.fda.gov/Food/FoodSafety/FoodContaminantsAdulteration/ChemicalContaminants/Acrylamide/ucm053569.htm (last visited 1 Nov. 2012).

121 FDA Action Plan for Acrylamide in Food, *supra* note 117.

122 EC, Scientific Committee on Food, *Opinion of the Scientific Committee on Food on New Findings Regarding the Presence of Acrylamide in Food*, SCF/CS/CNTM/CONT/4 Final 13–14 (July, 3 2002), available at http://ec.europa.eu/ food/fs/sc/scf/out131_en.pdf.

123 FAO/WHO Consultation on the Health Implications of Acrylamide in Food, 25–7 June 2002, *Final Report of a Meeting Held in Geneva*, available at http://www.who.int/foodsafety/publications/chem/en/acrylamide_full.pdf.

After EFSA was formed, its Scientific Panel on Contaminants in the Food Chain returned to acrylamide[124] when the joint FAO/WHO Expert Committee published another report in 2005 that contained various risk assessment recommendations, such re-evaluating approaches based on the 'results of ongoing carcinogenicity and long-term neurotoxicity studies,' and developing 'occurrence data on acrylamide in foods as consumed in developing countries'.[125] The Joint Report also made an apparent risk-management recommendation: that 'appropriate efforts to reduce acrylamide concentrations in food should continue'.[126]

The Panel (eight university, seven government agency, three non-profit institute, and two joint government/university members),[127] issued an evaluation of this Joint Report.[128] The Panel generally endorsed the Report but left open whether it specifically adopted the recommendation to continue to reduce acrylamide concentrations in food. The bulk of the Panel statement focused on addressing risk assessment-related issues such as exposure approaches and database uncertainties. The Panel also concluded that it need not independently evaluate acrylamide risks and could rely upon the joint FAO/WHO Expert Committee assessment.

After the Panel statement, EFSA gathered more occurrence data on food acrylamide levels pursuant to an EC recommendation that acrylamide-food-level data be gathered over a three-year period to better understand exposure risks.[129] This request led to a 2009 report concluding that acrylamide levels in food was generally decreasing except for food groups such as biscuits, breakfast cereals, French fries, and other potato products.[130]

EFSA also held a colloquium to encourage further information exchange.[131] This colloquium drew together scientists from food safety agencies, professional

---

124 EFSA, *Statement of the Scientific Panel on Contaminants in the Food Chain to a Summary Report on Acrylamide in Food of the 64th Meeting of the Joint FAO/WHO Expert Committee On Food Additives* 1 (19 Apr. 2005), available at http://www.efsa.europa.eu/en/efsajournal/doc/619.pdf [hereinafter EFSA, *Statement on 2005 FAO/WHO Report*] (last visited 1 Nov. 2012).

125 Joint FAO/WHO Expert Committee on Food Additives Sixty-Fourth Meeting, *Summary and Conclusions* at 17, JECFA/64/SC (Feb. 8–17, 2005), available at ftp://ftp.fao.org/es/esn/jecfa/jecfa64_summary.pdf (last visited 1 Nov. 2012).

126 Ibid.

127 This data was collected from various websites and is on file with the author.

128 EFSA, *Statement on 2005 FAO/WHO Report*, *supra* note 124.

129 Commission Recommendation of 3 May 2007 on the Monitoring of Acrylamide Levels in Food, C(2007) 1873, ¶3, 2007 O.J. (L 123/33).

130 EFSA, 'Results on the Monitoring of Acrylamide Levels in Food', 285, 1–26, 4, *EFSA Sci. Rep.* (2009), http://www.efsa.europa.eu/en/efsajournal/pub/285r.htm.

131 EFSA, Scientific Colloquium Series, May 22–3, 2008, *Acrylamide Carcinogenicity – New Evidence in Relation to Dietary Exposure* [hereinafter EFSA Acrylamide Symposium] (Briefing Notes for Discussion Groups, 2) available at http://www.efsa.europa.eu/en/supporting/doc/colloquiaacrylamide.pdf (last visited 1 Nov. 2012).

organisations and trade associations[132] to discuss epidemiological studies, carcinogenicity mechanisms and dietary exposure data.[133] EFSA published a summary report describing the consensus that scientific research had not yet improved upon previous risk assessments, but that ongoing studies were anticipated to enhance existing risk assessments and reduce uncertainties.[134] In 2011, the EC recommended that 'Member States carry out investigations in cases where the levels of acrylamide in food exceed the prescribed indicative values'.[135]

Implications for Understanding Expertise

The structures of FDA and EFSA expert bodies illustrate the varied approaches of governments towards expertise.

What is the composition of the Scientific Advisory Committee? Comparing selection requirements illustrates differing approaches towards trust and legitimacy. While the FDA Commissioner retains discretion for selecting panel members, she must do so based on nominees' credentials, which emphasises educational and employment background. Other FDA considerations, however, highlight the experiential demonstration of ability that at least one theorist suggests is sounder than sole reliance on credentials.[136] In contrast, EFSA's approach, where members of expert panels are appointed by a management body mandated to be geographically diverse, suggests a focus that extends beyond technical criteria and into political considerations of representational diversity.

The composition of these bodies also reflects varying approaches towards expert trust. Members of the FDA advisory committees are primarily drawn from universities, suggesting that FDA treats academics as either more scientifically expert or legitimate advisers. However, the occasional presence of members from industry and consumer organisations suggests that stakeholder affiliation alone is not a barrier towards trust.

In contrast, the predominance of scientists from national government agencies on the EFSA Scientific Panels highlights an emphasis on political balance and interest-group avoidance. Indeed, the focus on interest-group avoidance may be

132 EFSA Acrylamide Symposium (Series Participants), available at http://www.efsa.europa.eu/en/events/documents/colloque080522-ax3.pdf (last visited 1 Nov. 2012).

133 EFSA Acrylamide Symposium (Series Program), available at http://www.efsa.europa.eu/en/events/event/colloque080522-a.pdf (last visited 1 Nov. 2012).

134 EFSA Acrylamide Symposium (Summary Report, 26–7), available at http://www.efsa.europa.eu/en/events/event/colloque080522-m.pdf (last visited 1 Nov. 2012).

135 EC, *Commission Investigation on Investigations into the Levels of Acrylamide in Food* (Jan. 10, 2011), available at http://ec.europa.eu/food/food/chemicalsafety/contaminants/recommendation_10012011_acrylamide_food_en.pdf (last visited Nov. 10, 2012).

136 Goldman, *supra* note 7, at 24, 33–4.

even stronger in practice, given the dearth of members from the commercial food industry. Such exclusion suggests a treatment of expertise as normatively shaped by private employment.

Both approaches are directed toward similar ends: the reduction of bias. But the means are different; FDA addresses bias through the removal of (some) financially biased experts, while EFSA uses a combined screening/transparency/re-evaluation requirement. While both couple their participation requirements with additional legal requirements for interest disclosure, recent controversies over an EFSA panels' approval of the use of genetically modified markers suggests that critics either consider the joint screening/disclosure/re-evaluation requirement insufficient to guarantee the legitimacy of their advice or use process-based critiques as proxies for substantive opposition.

To what extent is the Scientific Advisory Committee Governed to incorporate lay viewpoints? Facially, the FDA system provides more direct avenues for lay participation than the EFSA Scientific Panels. Lay representatives from consumer and industry groups can and do serve as non-voting committee members, highlighting the relevance of experience-based knowledge.[137] Yet the requirement that consumer and industry members be able to engage with scientific knowledge may indicate that such representatives participate not as entirely lay individuals, but informed amateurs with useful roles in scientific deliberations.

The public participation aspect of the FDA advisory structure may be more formal than substantive. Although a few members of the public have attended other meetings, none attended the FDA Food Advisory Committee acrylamide meeting.[138] Thus the question is open as to whether these opportunities actually incorporate lay participation or merely serve to enhance the credibility of the FDA advisory committees' decisions.

The situation is reversed in the EFSA Scientific Panel context. While fewer formal requirements mandate the introduction of lay viewpoints, the GFL's normative aspirations may influence EFSA to pay greater attention to lay individuals,[139] and the EFSA Management Board structure may lead it to further engage with public perspectives.[140]

EFSA's public consultation guidance provides additional evidence of aspirations towards active public engagement. This guidance defines public

137 See generally J. Annas, 'Moral Knowledge as Practical Knowledge', in *The Philosophy of Expertise*, 280–301.

138 In the 24 FDA Food Advisory Committee meetings listed on the FDA website held 1997–2005, 4 meetings had no public comments, 18 had one to ten public comments, and only 2 had ten or more public comments. See U.S. FDA, Food Advisory Committee, http://www.fda.gov/AdvisoryCommittees/CommitteesMeetingMaterials/FoodAdvisoryCommittee/default.htm (last visited 13 Mar. 2010) (data compiled by author).

139 EC General Principles, *supra* note 60, pmbl. § 56.

140 Ibid., art. 28, para. 9.

consultation 'an effective exchange on a draft scientific output based on a decision of EFSA to seek comments from the public, namely the non-institutional stakeholders, which include academics, NGOs, industry and all other potentially interested and affected parties'.[141] While this guidance places stakeholder input within the discretion of EFSA, the additional emphasis on effectiveness can push such consultation processes beyond formal opportunity.

To what extent is the Scientific Advisory Committee required to be transparent? Both the FDA and EFSA expert bodies must publish their meeting agendas, results, and background materials. Their differences, however, highlight concerns regarding formal versus substantive transparency. The FDA advisory committees must publish transcripts of the open portion of their meetings and allow attendance, but need not make their output substantively accessible. In contrast, the EFSA Scientific Panels, which lack requirements for deliberative transparency, must 'develop and disseminate information material for the general public' in the form of 'objective, reliable and easily accessible information'.[142]

Thus FDA and EFSA end up placing the responsibility of translation into two different areas. FDA shifts the burden of translation onto public sphere actors such as NGOs and trade groups. EFSA Scientific Panels, however, must engage with the translation process themselves. This is perhaps related to EFSA's charge – broader than that of the FDA advisory committees – of engaging in risk communication as well as scientific analysis.[143]

How frequently are the views of the Scientific Advisory Committee sought or provided? For both the FDA and EFSA advisory bodies, consultation is sometimes legally mandated, suggesting experts are considered necessary to reach a legitimate decision in these circumstances. Apart from mandated areas, the EFSA Scientific Panels retain greater authority than the FDA advisory committees to initiate studies and reject requests to re-examine previous determinations, suggesting a greater degree of normative authority than the FDA advisory committees, despite the formal confinement of the EFSA Scientific Panels to areas of risk assessment. Priority-setting decisions for studying risk includes normative factors, such as the types of populations exposed to a risk and the types of potential harms involved. Thus the discretion to initiate studies and reject requests to re-examine previous studies puts at least those normative decisions within the authority of the EFSA Scientific Panels.

How is decisional authority distributed between the Scientific Advisory Committee and government decision-makers? Both governments adopted the recommendations of their respective acrylamide advisory bodies – recommendations that contained both scientific and management components.

141 EFSA Public Consultation Approach, *supra* note 89, at 3.
142 EC General Principles, *supra* note 60, art. 40(2).
143 Ibid., pmbl.(35).

The presence of both components suggests that categories of 'neutral' or scientific phases of risk assessment and policy-based phases of risk management may be blurred in practice, even when legally distinct. These practical difficulties in separation should caution those who propose legal methods of separation.

Moreover, the case study contrasts the confined discussions of the FDA Food Advisory Committee and the outreach-based actions of the EFSA Scientific Panel. The former body focused on gathering information from other experts, while the latter collected information through more extended means – working with industry to gather primary data and conducting colloquia to encourage additional information exchange. EFSA's authority to seek a greater range of inputs may reflect its own institutional function not only as a body of scientific experts for consultation, but also as a liaison with the greater scientific community.

Conclusion

This chapter has attempted to provide an account of the governance of scientific advisers through the lens of theoretical questions regarding expertise. By comparing the institutional structures and experiences of the FDA Food Advisory Committee and the EFSA Scientific Panel, the chapter highlights how both bodies, considered 'expert', are structured and constrained in manners consistent with different theoretical conceptions of expertise.

Chapter 21

EFSA in the International Arena: Caught in a Legal Straightjacket – or Performing an Autonomous Role?

Martijn Groenleer and Simone Gabbi[1]

Introduction: International Relations and Agency Autonomy

Most agencies of the European Union (EU) are established in environments that are replete with other organisations, not only other European bodies and member state agencies, but also international organisations and third country agencies. In order for EU agencies to execute their tasks and to realise their objectives, they usually engage in exchanges with such organisations. In fact, they often do not have much choice, as isolation from their environments is not a real option.[2]

The European Food Safety Authority (EFSA) is not an exception to this practice, as it operates in a field – that of the assessment of risks related to food and feed – that has for an important part been developed by international organisations, such as the Food and Agriculture Organization (FAO) and the World Health Organization (WHO), and third country agencies, such as the US Environmental Protection Agency (US EPA) and the US Food and Drug Administration (US FDA). Delivering high-level scientific advice requires EFSA to interact with such fellow bodies worldwide, in order to take stock of their findings and results. Indeed, the very concept of independent scientific advice, on which EFSA has been built, draws its legitimacy from the level of excellence of the outputs delivered by the pre-existing counterparts that are active in its environment.[3]

---

1 The views expressed here are those of the author and do not necessarily represent, and should not be attributed to EFSA or any other institution, body or agency of the European Union.

2 Groenleer, M.L.P. 2012. 'Linking up Levels of Governance: Agencies of the European Union and their Interaction with International Institutions'. In *The Influence of International Institutions on the European Union*, ed. O. Costa and K.-E. Joergensen. Basingstoke: Palgrave Macmillan.

3 Gabbi, S. 2011. 'Independent Scientific Advice: Comparing Policies on Conflicts of Interest in the EU and the US'. *European Journal of Risk Regulation* 2: 213–17; Shamoo, A.E. and Resnik, D.B. 2009. *Responsible Conduct of Research*. Oxford: Oxford University Press.

Clearly, EU agencies cannot act as they please in the international arena. The EU institutions may involve them in the EU's relations with international institutions working in their particular fields of action, but they often do not have to do so, at least not formally. In accordance with the Meroni doctrine,[4] agencies can only engage in exchanges with institutions in the international scene if an international legal personality, or rather international role, is explicitly foreseen in their statutes. In any case, it is usually not EU agencies but the Commission and the Council of the EU, and increasingly the European Parliament (EP), that decide on formal agreements between third countries and European or international bodies.[5] The opportunities for agencies to engage in international relations are thus constrained by formal mandates and legal powers.

There are various reasons why the EU institutions do not allow agencies to develop a fully autonomous international role. The key argument, particularly used by the Commission to substantiate its central position, is the need to ensure the unity of the EU's actions in its relations with its partners. The Commission claims that, if it has to answer to the Parliament on the achievement of policy objectives for which EU agencies in practice are the responsible actors, it also needs to exert some kind of control over the operations of agencies.[6] This holds especially for establishing and maintaining international relations, where there is said to be a clear need for the EU to speak with one voice. Along the same line of reasoning, it is fundamental for EU institutions that EU agencies do not appear to be committing the EU to international obligations.[7]

Yet, agencies often enjoy some room for manoeuvre with regard to the exchanges in which they engage on a daily basis. As found by an evaluation of EU agencies published in December 2010: 'Many [EU agencies] have signed multiple MoUs with key international organisations, and contacts are maintained through meetings, and sometimes concrete cooperation at the operational level.'[8]

4 European Court of Justice, Joined cases C-9/56 and 10/56 *Meroni & Co. vs. High Authority*, [1958] *ECR* 133, pp. 152–4. In a narrow reading, also extended to the food safety domain, this doctrine implies that EU agencies may only perform tasks that have been explicitly attributed to them and do so within the legal boundaries prescribed in the delegating provisions. See e.g. Joined cases C-154/04 and 155/04, Alliance for Natural Health, [2005] ECR I-6451, §90. The doctrine has been constitutionalised by Article 290 TFUE.

5 Chapter I of Title V of the Treaty of the European Union and Article 218 of Treaty of the Functioning of the European Union.

6 Groenleer, M. 2006. 'The Commission and Agencies'. In *The European Commission*, ed. D. Spence. London: John Harper Publishing.

7 Point 25 of the Joint Statement of the European Parliament, Council of the EU and European Commission on decentralised agencies, 18 July 2012, available at http://ec.europa.eu/commission_2010–2014/sefcovic/documents/120719_agencies_joint_statement_en.pdf (last accessed on 27 August 2012).

8 Ramboll, Eureval, Matrix insight. Evaluation of the EU decentralised agencies Conclusions at System Level. Final Report. Volume II. December 2009. Evaluation for

In addition, while agencies generally cannot themselves enter into formal international agreements with other institutions, they can, for instance, make use of more practical working arrangements.[9] The growth of these – often informal – exchanges in the international arena, according to the Common Approach on EU agencies the Council and published in July 2012, has made it necessary to 'streamline' the international relations of agencies, in order to 'ensure that agencies operate within their mandate and the existing institutional framework'.[10]

Indeed, EU agencies do not necessarily serve as passive channels for the interaction between international organisations and third country agencies, on the one hand, and the EU institutions, on the other hand. They often seem to play an active role as policy entrepreneurs, making use of the opportunities offered by the policies and policymaking processes of these organisations to influence institutions and behaviour in the EU and its member states. Through their interaction with international organisations and third country agencies, EU agencies may even increase the autonomy vis-à-vis their political overseers, namely the EU institutions and member states.[11]

Here, EFSA seems to be an exception. Whereas it, for instance, cooperates with the FAO and the WHO – its experts participating in the meetings of these bodies – it usually does so at the request and in support of the European Commission, in line with the relatively limited scope of action allowed by its legal framework. This is slightly different for some of its sister EU agencies, such as the European Medicines Agency (EMA). Even though international relations are the prerogative of the Commission, in practice EMA has often represented the EU in international meetings, such as those of the International Conference on Harmonisation, which includes authorities and industries of the three most important regulatory regions of the world with regard to the development of innovative medicines (the USA, the EU and Japan). At first glance, EFSA's international role thus seems to be limited, or at least more limited than that of other EU agencies.[12]

The above raises the question of what international role EFSA *actually* has performed so far – has it indeed been constrained by the formal-legal controls put

---

the European Commission ABAC Contracts No. 30-CE-0230814/00 Specific contract No 003, at 77, available online at http://www.statewatch.org/news/2012/apr/evaluation-eu-agencies-vol-II.pdf (last accessed on 30 September 2012).

9 Ott, A. 2008. 'EU Regulatory Agencies in EU External Relations: Trapped in a Legal Minefield between European and International Law'. *European Foreign Affairs Review* 13 (4): 515–40.

10 Point 25 of the Joint Statement of the European Parliament, Council of the EU and European Commission on decentralised agencies, 18 July 2012, available at http://ec.europa.eu/commission_2010–2014/sefcovic/documents/120719_agencies_joint_statement_en.pdf (last accessed on 27 August 2012).

11 Groenleer, M.L.P. 2012. 'Linking up Levels of Governance', *supra*, footnote n. 2.

12 This contribution focuses on EFSA's international role; it does not compare EFSA's role to that of other EU (regulatory) agencies, such as EMA or the European Chemicals Agency.

in place by the legislator and the concerned EU institutions or has it even so been able to act relatively autonomously at the international level? In order to address this question, this chapter examines EFSA's international relations, notably those with international organisations and third country agencies in its field of action. It adopts a dynamic perspective, describing these relations throughout the agency's development. The chapter demonstrates that EFSA has developed a considerable international role, despite the relatively limited scope of action allowed by its legal framework. It concludes with identifying the practical implications of our findings as well as avenues for further research on the international relations of EU agencies.

The Legal Framework for EFSA's International Relations

In order to analyse EFSA's international relations,[13] it is necessary to first briefly examine the legal framework in which the Authority operates vis-à-vis the outside world. In general, the point of reference is Regulation (EC) No 178/2002, hereinafter the General Food Law (GFL). The GFL recognises the legal personality of EFSA for all dealings with the EU and its member states, with specific reference to the need to buy its premises and interact with the host member state.[14] But the GFL also makes clear that the Parma-based agency is working for the risk managers of the EU, and that only the Commission, the EP and the member states may request an EFSA opinion.[15]

Yet, the GFL assigns the Authority a number of tasks that are relevant to its international relations. First of all, it requires EFSA to provide scientific and technical assistance, underlining that this may be done only when requested by the Commission, with a view to improving cooperation between the EU and applicant countries, international organisations and third countries.[16] It is considered fundamental that the Commission's positions are underpinned by strong scientific and technical arguments developed on the basis of internationally available and recognised information, evidence, data and risk assessment practices. Hence, EFSA supports the Commission with regard to scientific and technical issues in its work at the World Organisation for Animal Health (OIE), the International Plant Protection Convention (IPPC), the European and Mediterranean Plant Protection Organisation (EPPO), the Codex Alimentarius Commission (CAC), the Joint FAO/WHO Expert Committee on Food Additives (JECFA), the WHO, and the FAO.

13 The analysis builds on the framework as developed in Groenleer, M.L.P. 2012. 'Linking up Levels of Governance', *supra*, footnote n. 2.

14 Article 46(1) of Regulation (EC) No 178/2002.

15 See Article 29 of Regulation (EC) No 178/2002. Exceptionally, EFSA also has the possibility of undertaking a self-task.

16 Article 23 of Regulation (EC) No 178/2002.

Furthermore, the GFL requires EFSA to work with applicant countries, third countries or international bodies to search for, collect, collate, analyse and summarise relevant scientific and technical data in the fields within its mission.[17] In that respect, it could be concluded that reference to data collection with international organisations and third countries should be interpreted as also implying data exchange with these bodies. In fact, it is extremely unlikely that data collection is only one-way and that international and third country risk assessment bodies submit their data to EFSA without agreements on the mutual exchange of data. The GFL also specifically requires the Authority to work with countries that have concluded agreements with the EU by virtue of which they adopt and apply EU legislation, such as the rules and procedures laid down in the GFL.[18]

Finally, the GFL foresees an obligation for the Authority to identify emerging risks that are of relevance to the EU.[19] Although this provision does not explicitly mention an attribution of powers allowing EFSA to engage in international activities, one could argue that such powers, in line with the doctrine of implied powers, are 'implied' by the powers expressly stated in the GFL.[20] In a world characterised by such phenomena as global trade, mass migration and climate change, EFSA has an obligation to attend to scientific signals from international bodies and third countries' agencies, and thus enable the EU risk managers to be avant-garde. In order to be aware, and possibly ahead of emerging trends in the development of new risks or of risks that are expected to become of relevance to the EU, it seems that the Authority must be allowed to interact at the international level.

In addition to the GFL, other EU legal acts may establish a framework for EFSA's cooperation with third countries or international bodies – for example the EU Pre-accession Programme or certain international agreements between the EU and third countries or international organisations in which EFSA is attributed an operational role.[21] Yet, it is apparent from the brief analysis above that the main areas of action where EFSA enjoys some margin of manoeuvre and the

17 Article 33(2) of Regulation (EC) No 178/2002. In the period until 2007 the Authority also contributed to strengthening the food safety systems in accession or candidate countries, through involving these future EU member states in its work. This contribution, however, concentrates on EFSA's relations with international organisations and non-EU countries not being accession or candidate countries.

18 Article 49 of Regulation (EC) No 178/2002.

19 Article 34 of Regulation (EC) No 178/2002. See also Chapter 6, 'EFSA under Pressure: Emerging Risks, Emergencies and Crisis'.

20 On the doctrine of implied powers in case of the European Community and European Union, see Eeckhout, P. 2004. *External Relations of the European Union: Legal and Constitutional Foundations*. Oxford: Oxford University Press.

21 For more details on EU agencies' contributions to the EU Pre-accession Programme, see Coman-Kund, F. 2012. 'Assessing the Role of EU Agencies in the Enlargement Process: The Case of the European Aviation Safety Agency'. *Croatian Yearbook of European Law* 8: 335–68.

possibility to undertake a more proactive approach are those of data collection and emerging risks.

Development over Time: Increased International Strength and Profile

2003–2005: Forging International Links in an Ad Hoc Manner

Having outlined the legal framework and the formal restrictions it imposes on EFSA's role at the international level, it is time to look at how the agency has implemented this structure in its daily activities. Between 2003, when EFSA started operating, and 2006, EFSA's institutional interactions with international or third country bodies developed in an ad hoc manner. The Authority engaged in relations with international organisations, including visits to identify future areas of cooperation, exchanges of information about significant reports or opinions prior to publication, and the organisation of conferences on topics of common interest, such as harmonised approaches.

At the request of the Commission, EFSA experts also participated in meetings of international bodies such as the Codex Alimentarius – a joint FAO/WHO body that develops international food standards on, for instance, principles of risk analysis and biotechnology.[22] Furthermore, links were forged, for instance through visits, with food safety authorities in non-EU countries both in Europe (e.g. Norway and Switzerland) and outside Europe (e.g. the USA, Japan, China, Canada and Australia/New Zealand), and initiatives were undertaken to cooperate in particular areas of risk assessment, such as pesticides.[23]

2006–2008: Investing in Closer Contacts with Key International Partners

While EFSA established and maintained a variety of international contacts in the period preceding 2006, this seemed not a result of a deliberate strategy or systematic approach. In 2006, EFSA's Management Board identified the further development of EFSA's international activities as one of the key recommendations arising from the report of the External Evaluation.[24] As a result, from 2007

22 See further Chapter 7, Scientific Advice in the GMO Area.

23 See European Food Safety Authority, Annual Reports 2004–2006 available online at http://www.efsa.europa.eu/cs/Satellite (last accessed on 15 September 2012). The 2003 Annual Report does not include any information on EFSA's international relations.

24 Article 60 of Regulation (EC) No 178/2002. The first evaluation was undertaken in 2005 by Bureau Van Dijk Ingenieurs Conseils (with Arcadia international EEIG), EFSA/FIN-0105 – *Final Report* – 5 December 2005; online see also European Food Safety Authority, Management Board conclusions of the external evaluation of EFSA and recommendations arising from the report, available online at http://www.efsa.europa.eu/en/keydocs/docs/extevaluation2006.pdf (last accessed on 18 July 2012). In the literature:

onwards, the Authority invested in closer contacts with key international partners. It collaborated more closely with international organisations on projects such as with regard to data collection and the assessment of global scientific issues within its remit, the organisation of seminars on issues of common concern, and played a more important role in the meetings of the Codex Alimentarius.

Moreover, EFSA and the US FDA signed a statement on confidentiality arrangements to facilitate the sharing of non-public information, and held a technical meeting during which they discussed scientific subjects common to both agencies, such as approaches to the risk assessment of nanoscience and nanotechnologies, animal cloning and aspartame.[25] In 2008, EFSA hosted several delegations of international partners in order to initiate and foster technical cooperation. These delegations included New Zealand's minister of Food Safety, the director general of the Beijing Food Safety Administration, representatives of the Mercosur Countries (Brazil, Argentina, Uruguay and Paraguay) and representatives of the Japanese Food Safety Commission. The Authority also hosted a Technical Assistance and Information Exchange study and was part of the Commission delegation to the CODEX Task Force on Biotechnology in Japan.[26]

2009–Present: Towards a more Strategic International Relations Approach

However, it was felt that a more well-thought-out approach to international activities was necessary. In 2009, EFSA published a policy paper titled 'International Activities – A Strategic Approach',[27] which outlined the framework in which it operates and put forward four strategic objectives to be pursued in its international activities, namely: to support the EU in its international commitments; to ensure access to international scientific data and information in order to provide a strong basis for risk assessment and the identification of emerging risks; to participate in risk assessment at the international level; and to promote coherence in risk communications and build awareness of EFSA's activities at the international level.

Alemanno, A. 2007. 'L'Autorité européenne de sécurité des aliments souffle ses cinq premières bougies – Un bilan d'activité'. *Revue du droit de l'Union européenne* 3: 610–29; Gabbi, S. 2009. *L'autorità europea per la sicurezza alimentare*. Milan: Giuffrè.

25 European Food Safety Authority. 2007. Annual Activity Report, at 34, available online at http://www.efsa.europa.eu/en/corporate/doc/aar07.pdf (last accessed on 15 September 2012).

26 European Food Safety Authority. 2008. Annual Activity Report, at 24, available online at http://www.efsa.europa.eu/en/corporate/doc/aar08.pdf (last accessed on 15 September 2012).

27 European Food Safety Authority. 2009. International Activities – A Strategic Approach. Document Describing EFSA's strategic approach to its international activities, mb 29 01 09 item 8 doc 5 – International Activities – adopted, available online at http://www.efsa.europa.eu/en/corporate/pub/intstrategic.htm (last accessed on 27 August 2012).

As a start, the Authority mapped the variety of existing relations, both informal and formal, and at various levels in the organisation. On that basis, it prioritised organisations and countries with whom closer collaboration and an alignment of positions were considered of relevance to EFSA, and with whom longer term relations would thus have to be developed.[28] In 2009, the strategic approach was implemented through operational follow-up actions. Priority was given to actions in support of EU policy, indicating the Authority's dependence on the Commission to back up its choice in international relations.[29]

In terms of practical achievements, the strategic approach has been translated into a Memorandum of Cooperation (MoC) with the Japanese Food Safety Commission (FSC) on the collection and sharing of the data required for the assessment of current and emerging risks. As such, the memorandum goes beyond the agreement between EFSA and the FDA, negotiated in 2007, which is limited to confidentiality arrangements that are applicable only to data exchanges.[30] In addition, visits and meetings have been held with US counterparts, the OIE, the WHO and the FAO.[31] EFSA has provided a higher volume of scientific and technical support for the Commission delegation to the Codex Alimentarius, which appears to reflect the Commission's enhanced trust in the scientific competences of the Parma-based agency.

International collaboration, consultation and joint opinions, all 'implemented in line with the framework agreed with the European Commission', characterise EFSA's activities in 2010. The Scientific Panel on food additives and nutrient sources added to food (ANS) adopted an opinion on lycopene which was linked to a JECFA opinion, while the opinions on lead (CONTAM) and bisphenol A (CEF) received inputs from the WHO.[32] EFSA also exchanged letters of cooperation with several counterparts including Health Canada and the WHO, received international delegations from South Korea, Norway, China, Algeria and Japan, and, among others, co-organised with the WHO a seminar on seafood safety.[33] In 2011, EFSA's international activities grew exponentially. In addition to receiving a great number of international delegations, EFSA regularly invited FAO and OIE experts to participate in plenary meetings in the field of animal health, and

28 European Food Safety Authority. 2009. Annual Activity Report, available online at http://www.efsa.europa.eu/en/corporate/doc/aar09.pdf (last accessed on 15 September 2012).

29 See European Food Safety Authority, International Activities – above, Annex II, Key Initiatives, Actions and Indicators of Success relating to 'EFSA's International Activities – A Strategic Approach.

30 The agreements are available online on EFSA's corporate website at http://www.efsa.europa.eu/en/networks/international.htm (last accessed on 27 August 2012).

31 European Food Safety Authority. 2009. Annual Activity Report, *supra*, footnote n. 28, at 22.

32 European Food Safety Authority. 2010. Annual Activity Report, available online at http://www.efsa.europa.eu/en/corporate/doc/aar10.pdf (last accessed on 15 January 2013), at 5.

33 Ibid., at 25.

strengthened relationships with the EPPO. Notably, the Authority provided a significant amount of scientific support to the Commission in the framework of the Codex Alimentarius.[34]

Here, two cases are examined that are illustrative of EFSA's increased contribution in the international arena, in particular its scientific support work: for the meetings of the Codex Committees on Pesticides Residues (CCPR), and for the EU position on ractopamine, a growth promoter used in animal feed.

EFSA and the Codex Committees on Pesticides Residues Pursuant to the Regulation on Maximum Residue Levels (MRLs) of Pesticides, EFSA is required to assess the safety of the MRLs put forward by the concerned business operators.[35] Since EFSA is the competent body in the EU for delivering scientific advice on this particular matter, the Commission systematically asks the Authority for comments on the recommendations of the relevant Joint FAO/WHO Meeting on Pesticide Residues (JMPR) and pesticide MRLs at steps 3 and 6 of the Codex procedure.

In 2011, for example, the JMPR evaluated 12 active substances regarding the setting of toxicological reference values to be used in consumer risk assessment. EFSA compared the acceptable daily intake (ADI) and acute reference dose (ARfD) values derived by the JMPR with the values derived at EU level, and, where differences were identified, provided further explanations for the reasons for those differences. EFSA expressed a reservation about the proposed toxicological reference values for 5 of the 12 substances,[36] a reservation that was duly reflected in the Commission's position at the JPMR.

EFSA and ractopamine Another high-profile example of EFSA's contribution to the EU stance in the international standard setting (or regulatory) arena is the case of ractopamine hydrochloride.[37] The use of ractopamine as a feed additive is authorised in various countries, including the USA, Canada, Japan and Mexico, for growth promotion in pigs, cattle and, to a limited extent, turkeys.[38] However,

34 European Food Safety Authority. 2011. Annual Activity Report, available online at http://www.efsa.europa.eu/en/corporate/doc/aar11.pdf (last accessed on 15 September 2012), at 17.

35 Regulation (EC) No 396/2005 of the European Parliament and of the Council of 23 February 2005 on maximum residue levels of pesticides in or on food and feed of plant and animal origin and amending Council Directive 91/414/EEC (Text with EEA relevance), OJ L 70, 16.3.2005, p. 1, as last amended.

36 European Food Safety Authority. 2012. Scientific support for preparing an EU position in the 44th Session of the Codex Committee on Pesticide Residues (CCPR). *EFSA Journal* 10 (7): 2859. doi:10.2903/j.efsa.2012.2859. Available online at: www.efsa.europa.eu/efsajournal.

37 Pharmacologically classified as a phenethanolamine β-adrenoceptor agonist.

38 For an overview of the ractopamine dispute, see Alemanno, A. and Capodieci, G. 2012. 'Testing the Limits of Global Food Governance: The Case of Ractopamine'. *European Journal of Risk Regulation* 3: 400–407.

the use of this substance is banned in several other regulatory countries and regions, such as China and, notably, the EU. As a result, measures preventing the import of meat from animals that were fed ractopamine have been put in place in these legal systems. The adoption of a standard foreseeing the possibility of establishing an acceptable daily intake and MRLs is therefore of great importance for the USA, Canada, Japan and Mexico, as it would demonstrate the possibility of the safe use of ractopamine under certain conditions and allow trade between these countries and the EU. According to the JECFA, the establishment of such as standard was scientifically justified and possible.[39]

EFSA was asked by the Commission to provide an opinion on the evaluation of ractopamine hydrochloride performed by the JECFA, in consultation and cooperation with other organisations such as the EMA and the German Federal Office of Consumer Protection and Food Safety (BVL), acting as EU Reference Laboratory for substances such as ractopamine. EFSA's Scientific Panel on Feed Additives (FEEDAP) concluded that the human study used by the JECFA could not be taken as a basis to derive an ADI and, consequently, no proposal for MRLs could be made. EMA's Committee on Veterinary Medicinal Products (CVMP) and countries such as China and India supported EFSA's conclusions with regard to the safety evaluation of ractopamine.[40] On the basis of the science expressed by its agencies, the Commission not only claimed that ractopamine poses risks to human health, but also that it has negative effects on animal health and welfare.

Nevertheless, the EU was not successful in convincing other countries such as the USA, Canada and Mexico. On 5 July 2012, after years of political deadlock, the CAC narrowly adopted (69 votes in favour, 67 against) the first MRLs for ractopamine hydrochloride, irrespective of the scientific position put forward by the EU on the basis of EFSA's and EMA's advice.[41] It remains to be seen whether the World Trade Organization (WTO) will accept the scientific arguments as delivered by EFSA and EMA to justify the restrictive measures adopted by the EU if it is confronted with a challenge related to their compatibility with the recently adopted standard.

In spite of the mixed outcomes so far, the above examples show the increased strength and profile of the Authority's international relations, and the efforts EFSA put into streamlining its interactions at the international level, especially when it

---

39 Ractopamine has been evaluated at the 40th, 62nd, 66th, JECFA meetings, and by a special review in 2010.

40 European Food Safety Authority. 2009. Scientific Opinion of the Panel on Additives and Products or Substances used in Animal Feed (FEEDAP) on a request from the European Commission on the safety evaluation of ractopamine. *EFSA Journal* 1041, 1–52.

41 As duly highlighted by the Commission in a press release available online at http://europa.eu/rapid/middayExpressAction.do?date=06/07/2012&guiLanguage=en (last accessed on 3 September 2012).

comes to supporting the EU's position in the international arena. The Authority now engages in operational cooperation with international organisations that undertake similar work, and maintains close contacts with other food safety authorities that have collected data or carried out studies that are of relevance to food and feed safety in the EU.

Beyond Functional Needs for International Relations: Strategic Motives

It seems that until 2007, engaging in interactions with international organisations and third country bodies was primarily seen as a functional necessity ensuing from the agency's objectives and tasks. Establishing relations with food safety agencies in countries outside the EU and with international organisations was regarded as essential for sharing data and information, as well as for developing common methodologies and underlying principles. By building collaborative partnerships, EFSA sought to secure a larger pool of scientific data and information; it also allowed the Authority to take part in international harmonisation efforts on data collection and risk assessment. Finally, international relations were seen as necessary to promote coherent communication, based on shared perceptions of the risks in the food and feed chain.

It also appears that international cooperation has been considered of importance in view of the changes in EFSA's institutional environment and the risks that may emerge from such changes. In 2008, the EFSA Strategic Plan for 2009–13 identified the most important drivers for change, including globalisation, increased innovation, matters linked to sustainability and climate change, and the societal and policy changes that have a potential impact on EFSA's future work.[42] In order to identify emerging food and feed risks as early as possible, it was proposed to strengthen the Authority's international relations. As stated in EFSA's 2009 Annual Report: 'Crops, animals, and food and feed products are transported around the world in an increasingly global world – as are the associated risks. Therefore, being involved internationally – in support of EU policy – is paramount for EFSA's ability to keep Europe's food supply safe and to protect consumers.'

Yet, it seems that, over time, the Authority realised that establishing and maintaining international relations can also serve other purposes, notably the 'ultimate aim' of becoming a scientific point of reference not only for the EU but also outside the EU. Through international relations, EFSA can assert itself vis-à-vis agencies in the member states and the EU institutions. In its 2007 Annual Report, EFSA mentions two reasons for stepping up its activities in the area of

42 European Food Safety Authority. 2008. Strategic Plan for 2009–2013, adopted by the Management Board on 18th December 2008, available online at http://www.efsa.europa.eu/en/corporate/pub/strategicplan.htm (last accessed on 27 August 2012).

international relations.[43] The first reason is primarily functional: to ensure 'that EFSA has access to the best information and science worldwide for conducting its risk assessments'. The second reason is more of a strategic nature: to ensure 'that recognition of EFSA's support to European food and feed laws, through its risk assessments, is increasingly global'.

The 2009 Annual Report is even clearer on this point, as it acknowledges that 'the Authority is also building awareness of its activities internationally to build its reputation as an organisation that is globally recognised and trusted as the European reference body for risk assessment'.[44] In this respect, it should not be forgotten that one of the reasons why the EU created a European food agency was the need to regain the confidence of the EU's international partners[45] by establishing food safety and animal and plant health measures in line with basic rules set in the international arena, notably those in the framework of the WTO (also referred to as sanitary and phytosanitary, or SPS, measures).

Another, related development is the 'mainstreaming' of international relations in the Authority's day-to-day activities: international relations are now an integral part of other activities, not a separate activity (under a separate heading in the annual report). Of course, the agency still receives international delegations and meets to discuss cooperation with its counterparts, but such visits and discussions have become part of EFSA's scientific and technical work, which thus encompasses authorities in the member states and the EU institutions, as well as international organisations and agencies in non-EU countries. International cooperation is also no longer an activity undertaken only at the managerial level, by the director or by a separate unit in the Authority; contacts have become more operational and are increasingly established and maintained by EFSA experts.

In other words, EFSA's international relations have developed both quantitatively – in terms of its volume – and qualitatively, in terms of the way they are established and maintained, the reasons underlying such relations and the variety of actors that are involved in them.

Implications of the Authority's Changed International Role

The quantitative and qualitative change in EFSA's international relations may have implications for the place of the Authority in the EU food and feed regulation landscape and, more broadly, for the EU's institutional system. We begin,

43 European Food Safety Authority. 2007. Annual Activity Report, *supra*, footnote n. 25, at 40.

44 European Food Safety Authority. 2009. Annual Activity Report, *supra*, footnote n. 28, at 25.

45 See e.g. recital n. 22 of Regulation (EC) No 178/2002.

however, with an assessment of the effects on the Authority's performance – of great importance for its international reputation.

To what extent has international cooperation led to improved scientific advice, in the sense that scientific outputs are of higher quality? Whether EFSA's international relations contribute to the delivery of outputs that are of a higher quality than in the past, is of course difficult to determine. From the discussion about the way EFSA's strategic approach to international relations is implemented, it appears that cooperation enhances the agency's risk assessment work. The interactions currently taking place between EFSA and its international counterparts, notably data sharing and collection, enable the Authority to be increasingly complete and accurate in carrying out its support tasks. However, this does not mean that EFSA's assessment work, through its international role, is necessarily more accepted (in the EU and globally), or that disagreements over science have disappeared, as the ractopamine case clearly shows.

Yet, EFSA – through its international relations – contributes to the creation of a single European regulatory space, building epistemic communities of supranational and national specialised civil servants and scientific or technical experts. Although we have not dealt with this aspect here in depth, EFSA has for instance supported accession and candidate countries in their efforts to adapt to EU rules and guidelines and to learn from established practice. As the network's hub, the Authority has linked up international organisations and agencies in third countries with the EU institutions and agencies in the member states in an often informal way, through mutual visits, coordination meetings, joint conferences, etc.[46] Indeed, one of EFSA's strengths is its enhanced role in network governance: it remains independent, but cooperates with fellow risk assessment bodies and includes their expertise in its work more than it did previously.

Apart from more accurate and complete scientific advice in support of the EU's position and a level of sectoral integration through functional cooperation in its area of competence, EFSA's increased international role may lead to a de facto power shift from EFSA's political overseers, particularly the Commission's Directorate-General SANCO, to the Authority itself (or at least a power struggle between these actors). When a new regulatory body is created, and especially when independence is such a hallmark as in the case of EFSA, it can be expected that the new body will endeavour to fight with established actors for at least some 'breathing space', as indeed also happened in the case of the Authority.[47]

46 Eberlein, B. and Grande, E. 2005. 'Beyond Delegation: Transnational Regulatory Regimes and the EU Regulatory State'. *Journal of European Public Policy* 12 (1): 89–112; but see Randall, E. 2006. 'Not that Soft or Informal: A Response to Eberlein and Grande's Account of Regulatory Governance in the EU with Special Reference to the European Food Safety Authority (EFSA)'. *Journal of European Public Policy* 13 (3): 402 – 19. See further Sabel, C.F. and Zeitlin J. (eds). 2010. *Experimentalist Governance in the European Union: Towards a New Architecture*. Oxford: Oxford University Press.

47 Gabbi, S. 2007. 'The Interaction between Risk Assessors and Risk Managers: The Case of the European Commission and the European Food Safety Authority'.

Whereas EFSA's early years were characterised by an antagonistic relation with the Commission, for instance over its role in risk communication, this does not seem to be the case for EFSA's international activities. The absence of a power struggle over international relations could at least partly be explained by the fact that EFSA's international activities have gained strength only in recent years and cooperative institutional relations had developed in the meantime. It also appears that in conducting its international activities, the Authority has respected the pre-existing institutional balance and operated within the legal framework set out in the GFL and in line with EU objectives and priorities. Although EFSA's creation as such may have contributed to the fragmentation of the EU's institutional system in terms of the multiplication of actors involved in food and feed regulation, it appears that its technical contributions to the scientific discussions at the international level have not caused incoherence or inconsistency with the position of the EU, as represented by the Commission and the member states.

The likelihood of EFSA speaking with a different voice than the Commission or the member states is reduced not only as a result of the legal framework applicable to EFSA's international activities, but also through the explicit and prior approval of key documents in which EFSA's international approach is outlined.[48] Until now, this explicit and prior approval has, on the one hand, proven an adequate control mechanism preventing any action or reaction not considered in line with or supportive of the policies pursued by the Commission and the member states; it has, on the other hand, also limited the agency's autonomy in international operations.

Furthermore, if we benchmark EFSA's international activities against the Common Approach on EU agencies recently agreed upon by the Commission, the Parliament and the Council, we find that these appear to be complying with the requirements laid down in this document. In line with the Common Approach, agencies should have a clear strategy for international activities; the strategy should be approved by agencies' management boards; an early exchange of information should be ensured between agencies, the partner DGs and if appropriate EU delegations; and agencies should not represent the EU or commit it to an outside audience.[49] These are all features that can be found in EFSA's strategic approach to international activities. Indeed, EFSA's international strategy has been adopted by the Management Board, on which the Commission is represented, and entails

European Food and Feed Law Review 3: 126–35; Groenleer, M. 2009. *The Autonomy of European Union Agencies: A Comparative Study of Institutional Development*. Delft: Eburon; Groenleer, M.L.P. 2011. 'The Actual Practice of Agency Autonomy: Tracing the Developmental Trajectories of the European Medicines Agency and the European Food Safety Agency'. In *CES Open Forum*. Cambridge: The Minda de Gunzburg Center for European Studies at Harvard University.

48 E.g. EFSA's Annual Management Plans and Annual Activity Reports, *supra*.

49 Point n. 25 of the Common Approach annexed to the Joint Statement of the European Parliament, the Council of the EU and the European Commission on decentralised agencies of 19 July 2012.

full and prior coordination with the partner DGs for endorsement of international initiatives that go beyond the tasks explicitly mandated by the GFL.[50]

One aspect that deserves closer scrutiny and a deeper analysis is the role of national agencies vis-à-vis their ministries as a result of their relations with EFSA, and in turn, the positions of national agencies and ministries together vis-à-vis the international scientific committees and bodies with which EFSA is also liaising. EFSA's networking capabilities may have contradictory effects. On the one hand, they may empower national agencies vis-à-vis their ministries because national agencies are the ones directly liaising with the Authority in transnational networks. This bypassing is a more frequently described phenomenon in multilevel settings.[51] On the other hand, EFSA's networking capabilities might also lead to a gradual attenuation of the residual role played by national agencies in international scientific committees and bodies, because their role is slowly but surely being taken over by the Authority in view of reinforcing the EU's position in multilateral negotiations and international organisations.

Conclusions: Linking Up Levels of Governance

This chapter discussed the importance of international relations for assessing the input an EU agency can offer to the broader EU legal and political system, by examining the international role of EFSA. The analysis showed that the agency's international relations, despite being embedded in a rather stringent legal framework, have gained strength throughout its 10-year existence and in recent years have been streamlined. The agency now contributes on a regular basis to the EU's position in the international arena. In view of the budgetary constraints that many risk assessment bodies in the EU member states face, it is not unlikely that EFSA's role as a networking hub for data collection and sharing in the international arena will only further increase.

Furthermore, whereas the establishment and maintenance of international relations was initially mainly seen as a functional necessity, EFSA came to realise that such relations could also serve to further develop its international reputation. International relations have now been mainstreamed into the agency's day-to-day activities. Establishing and maintaining such relations is no longer only a managerial task: it is now also an operational one. In future research, these (preliminary) findings should be compared with the development over time of other regulatory agencies' international relations, in order to shed light on differences and similarities, both legal and political.

50 See European Food Safety Authority. 2010. Annual Activity Report, *supra*, footnote n. 32, at 18.

51 Egeberg, M. (ed.). 2006. *Multilevel Administration: The Transformation of Executive Politics in Europe*. Basingstoke: Palgrave Macmillan; Slaughter, A.-M. 2004. *A New World Order*. Princeton: Princeton University Press.

EFSA's international relations and the quantitative and qualitative growth thereof seem to have contributed, in a functional way, to improved (or at least more complete and accurate) scientific advice. More broadly, they have also added to increased administrative (or regulatory) integration in the EU, among individual member states, especially those that have recently become EU members, particularly in the field of food and feed risk assessment. The increased role of the agency in the international arena does raise questions about the division of labour between the risk managers and the risk assessor, and a possible power shift from the former to the latter. The analysis demonstrated that EFSA's operations until now have been consistent with the legal framework in which it operates and with the recently adopted Common Approach on EU agencies.

Thus, although EFSA is another European actor at the international level and therefore furthers the fragmentation of the EU politico-administrative system, it at the same time contributes to linking up different levels of governance, both 'upwards' to international bodies and 'sideways' to third country agencies. Further research needs to be conducted on what this means for 'downward' relations with agencies at the national level, and their role and influence in the field of food and feed risk assessment.

Chapter 22
The European Food Safety Authority in Global Food Safety Governance: A Participant, a Benchmark, and a Model

Ching-Fu Lin

Introduction

The past decades have witnessed an exponential increase in food scares of various sources, ranging from bovine spongiform encephalopathy (BSE) in beef, dioxin in pork, and melamine dairy products, to E. coli cucumbers and radioactive residues. Moreover, globalisation of economic activities, advancement of food science, development of transportation technology, and multi-nationalisation of food industries, together with the advent of the World Trade Organization (WTO), have significantly transformed the production, transportation and consumption of food,[1] and therefore have further intensified the scale, severity, frequency and impact of food safety outbreaks as such.

All these food safety incidents have driven equally mushrooming regulatory responses that, at domestic, international and transnational levels, have aimed at addressing existing and emerging risks in many fields closely linked to public health and world trade. A variety of actors – governments, international organisations, industry, nongovernmental organisations (NGOs), scientific expert groups and transnational business associations – have also participated in the regulatory activities. National governments, through a multifaceted process with scientific, social and political features, have been adopting internal and border measures to mitigate foodborne hazards. In addition, international organisations have more recently been establishing multilateral health and trade rules as well as sanitary and phytosanitary (SPS) standards that transcend national boundaries and enter terrain traditionally associated with sovereign authority. Other actors, such as multinational corporations dominating global food supply chains, consumer NGOs and private standard-setting associations (such as GlobalGAP), have been actively engaging in global food safety governance through innovative approaches.

1 Motarjemi, Y. et al., 'Future challenges in global harmonization of food safety legislation' (2001) 12(6) *Food Control*, 340–41.

However, there is arguably no meta-framework existing or emerging that dictates, coordinates or pioneers the making of such diverse norms.[2] These active spheres of global food safety norm-making constitute an *evolving governance complex* being formed and transformed, configured and reconfigured by different actors at different levels with different experimental approaches.[3] Where two or more spheres interact, for example between national governments' regulatory autonomy and international organisations' authority, many stimulating issues emerge, such as those of horizontal and vertical allocation of authority, accountability of national and international regulatory bodies, transparency of global lawmaking processes, and legitimacy of regulatory outcomes.

As the work of the Codex Alimentarius Commission (CAC) stands at the centre of global food safety lawmaking, the Codex regime faces problems involving the soundness of science, the legitimacy of rules, the accountability of rule-makers, and the transparency of decision-making processes. The elaboration of international food standards inevitably intertwines with science, risks and politics, and has important economic, social and cultural implications. Therefore, states, international organisations, scientists, industry and NGOs engage in Codex food safety norm-making activities via different channels and in different manners in order to materialise their respective interests.[4] Their participation is able to promote or undermine the legitimacy, transparency and accountability of Codex. Indeed, many scholars and practitioners have criticised the Codex platform's inability to produce good-governance regulatory results.[5] Here, for clarity and simplicity, I refer to the Codex Alimentarius Commission as CAC. When the term 'Codex' is referred to, its scope covers the risk regulation regime constituted by the CAC, Joint FAO/WHO scientific expert committees which work closely with the CAC, and CAC members.

Bearing in mind the multi-level nature of Codex's regulatory sphere, the technological complexity of food science, and its role of being an international reference point for food standards, I examine the role the European Food Safety

2 But see van der Meulen, B.'The global arena of food law: Emerging contours of a meta-framework' (2010) 3(4) *Erasmus Law Review*, 217–40.

3 Lin, C.F., 'Reassessing the Codex Alimentarius Commission: an analysis of the ractopamine hydrochloride dispute' (Paper to the Future of Transnational Law: The EU, USA, China, and the BRICS (2012 WISH Conference), Shenzhen, China, 2012).

4 Smythe, E., 'In whose interests? Transparency and accountability in the global governance of food: Agribusiness, the Codex Alimentarius, and the World Trade Organization', in J. Clapp and D. Fuchs (eds), *Corporate Power in Global Agrifood Governance* (Cambridge: MIT Press, 93–123, 2009).

5 See e.g. Hüller, T. and M.L. Maier., 'Fixing the Codex? Global food safety governance under review', in C. Joerges and E.U. Petersmann (eds), *Constitutionalism, Multilevel Trade Governance and Social Regulation* (Oxford: Hart Publishing, 267–99, 2006); Silverglade, B.A., 'The WTO Agreement on Sanitary and Phytosanitary Measures: Weakening food safety regulations to facilitate trade?' (2000) 55 F*ood and Drug Law Journal*, 518–24; Alemanno, A., *Trade in Food* (London: Cameron May 2007): 262–7.

Authority (EFSA) plays in global food safety governance. The EFSA is a relatively young international platform performing risk assessment and risk communication, and providing the European Commission (EC) as well as European Union (EU) Member States with scientific advice that they take into account when forming regulatory measures in food safety areas.[6] Albeit with some criticism, the EFSA is usually regarded as a good example of a food safety rule-maker in a broad sense.[7] The EFSA's institutional design is arguably adequate in terms of producing accountability, legitimacy and transparency, among other important outcomes. Here again, for clarity and simplicity, I refer to the EFSA as an agency of the EU. When 'EFSA regime' is referred to in this chapter, the scope of the term covers the risk regulation regime constituted by the EC, EU Member States and the EFSA.

I argue that the EFSA regime can, in addition to the current *participant* role, serve as a *benchmark* for evaluating the Codex activities, and a *model* of food safety governance for the edification of the Codex.[8] The EFSA has recently been actively participating as part of the EU delegation in the Codex scientific activities in developing food safety standards, guidelines, codes of practice, and other instruments. Apart from participating at the political and scientific levels, the EFSA regime can serve as a benchmark for assessing the Codex governance structure and processes in light of the essential similarities between the two systems. Bearing in mind the similarities discussed below between the EFSA regime and the Codex, I use the EFSA regime as a constructive model of good governance from which the Codex can learn in its future reforms if so desired.

The Codex as the Centre of Global Food Safety Governance

Global food safety governance takes place basically under the auspices of three most relevant international organisations: the WHO, the WTO and the CAC.[9]

6 Alemanno, A., 'The European Food Safety Authority at five' (2008) *European Food and Feed Law Review*, 1, 2–24.

7 For an extensive review, see EFSA, 'External Evaluation of EFSA Final Report' (Parma, EFSA 2012a); Alemanno, A., 'The European Food Safety Authority at five' (2008) 1 *European Food and Feed Law Review*, 2–24.

8 One should nevertheless be aware of the fundamental differences between the EFSA as an agency of the EU and the CAC. However, they are fully comparable when we see the EFSA and Codex as regulatory regimes. See infra discussion in Part III.2.

9 It should be noted that there exist other sorts of standard-setting or rulemaking by national governments or non-state actors. In particular, some scholars observe that private actors, especially multinational corporations (MNCs), are increasingly engaging in food safety standard setter activities by means of private regulation. See, e.g., Clapp, J. and D. Fuchs (eds), *Corporate Power in Global Agrifood Governance* (Cambridge, MIT Press 2009); Prévost, D., 'Private sector food-safety standards and the SPS Agreement: Challenges and possibilities' (2008) 33 *South African Yearbook of International Law*, 1–37; Vandenbergh, M.P., 'The new Wal-Mart effect: The role of private contracting in global

While it is intuitive to appreciate a meta-framework that coordinates existing international institutions with a comprehensive regulatory and cooperative strategy at the global level, what we learn about is that there currently exists no such overarching structure targeting food safety issues in a comprehensive and holistic manner. A review of the normative activities of the WTO and the WHO shows that the CAC is currently the most active and influential institution, insofar as the making of global food law orients Codex activities.[10]

The CAC is an international governmental body established according to the two resolutions adopted by the Eleventh Session of the Food and Agriculture Organization of the United Nations (FAO) Conference in 1961 and the Sixteenth World Health Assembly (WHA) in 1963.[11] The two international institutions also adopted the Statutes and Rules of Procedure for the Commission.[12] To date, 185 members (184 member countries and one member organisation) are represented in the CAC. Led by the 10-member Executive Committee, the CAC also consists of 24 active committees and task forces.[13] The mandate of CAC, which

governance' (2007) 54(4) *UCLA Law Review*, 913–70; Havinga, T., 'Private regulation of food safety by supermarkets' (2006) 28(4) *Law and Policy*, 515–33; Fulponi, L., 'Private voluntary standards in the food system: The perspective of major food retailers in OECD countries' (2006) 31(1) *Food Policy*, 1–13; Henson, S., 'The role of public and private standards in regulating international food markets' (Paper to the IATRC Summer Symposium: Food Regulation and Trade: Institutional Framework, Concepts of Analysis and Empirical Evidence, Bonn, Germany, May 28–30, 2006). However, it is beyond the scope of the present study to examine these topics in any kind of depth.

10 'The WHO and the WTO are two major international organizations in global food safety governance, and although they approach lawmaking differently, they operate via the same channel – the Codex. The WHO participates at the ex ante stage of Codex lawmaking; that is, preparation of scientific evaluation and risk assessment, but not the lawmaking per se. The WTO, by contrast, participates not in the Codex process, but mainly in the ex post reinforcement of Codex normative outcomes through its own effective enforcement mechanisms ... [T]he two international organizations "participate" in an indirect way that secures the position of the Codex as the core global rulemaker in the field of food safety regulation, beyond what is normally understood as a mere scientific reference point.' Lin, C.F., 'Reassessing the Codex Alimentarius Commission: an analysis of the ractopamine hydrochloride dispute' (Paper to the Future of Transnational Law: The EU, USA, China, and the BRICS (2012 WISH Conference), Shenzhen, China, 2012).

11 FAO/WHO. 'Understanding the Codex Alimentarius' (3rd Edition available at: ftp://ftp.fao.org/docrep/fao/008/y7867e/y7867e00.pdf [accessed 15 October 2012] 2005).

12 The Statutes of the Codex Alimentarius Commission (Statutes) provide the legal basis for the Commission's work and formally reflect the concepts behind and reasons for its establishment. The Rules of Procedure of the Codex Alimentarius Commission (Rules of Procedure) describe and formalise working procedures appropriate to an intergovernmental body.

13 In addition to the Committee on General Principles and six regional coordinating committees (Africa, Asia, Europe, Latin America and the Caribbean, the Near East, and

includes two goals, is to develop international food standards, guidelines, and recommendations to 'protect the health of consumers' as well as 'ensure fair practices in food trade'.[14]

The Codex standard-setting process is framed by the structured *Procedures for the Elaboration of Codex Standards and Related Texts*.[15] The same procedures apply to the elaboration of Codex guidelines, codes of practices, and other texts.[16] The eight-step standard-setting process shows important elements of a global food safety lawmaking process.

Prior to the establishment of the WTO and its explicit reference to the CAC as the international food safety standard setter, the CAC was regarded as a technical body that would work in a largely epistemic manner, unaffected by international power struggles or commercial interests.[17] The Codex Committees essentially operated as technical bodies in close cooperation with the Joint FAO/WHO scientific expert bodies.[18] Mainly because of the voluntary soft-law nature of the Codex standards, CAC Members were not in conflict when faced with disagreement in setting standards. Rather than block the standard-setting process, Members in disagreement over the substance of a food safety standard, would either simply declare that they have no intention of adhering to the standard and deviate from the standard.[19] Therefore, while the Codex Procedural Rules specify that a 'simple majority vote' is permissive and sufficient for the adoption of a standard, the customary practice has been consensual decision-making.[20]

However, with the explicit reference of the WTO Agreement on the Application of Sanitary and Phytosanitary Measures (SPS Agreement) to the CAC

North America and the Southwest Pacific), subsidiary bodies directly related to food safety include, inter alia, the Codex Committees on Contaminants in Foods, Food Additives, Food Hygiene, Pesticide Residues, Residues of Veterinary Drugs in Foods, Food Import and Export Inspection, and Certification Systems.

14 FAO/WHO 2005: 25.

15 FAO/WHO, Codex Alimentarius Commission Procedural Manual (20th Edition. Rome, FAO/WHO 2011a).

16 For a discussion of the distinction of standards, guidelines, codes of practices, and other instruments, see Gruszczynski, L., *Regulating Health and Environmental Risks under WTO Law* (Oxford: Oxford University Press 2010): 82–4.

17 Veggeland, F. and Borgen, S.O., 'Changing the Codex: The role of international institutions' (Working Paper 2002–16 of the Norwegian Agricultural Economics Research Institute, January 2002, available at: http://www.ecolomics-international.org/caa_veggeland_borgen_changing_codex_nilf_oslo_02.pdf [accessed: 15 October 2012] 2002).

18 Ibid.

19 Ibid.

20 Peel, J., *Science and Risk Regulation in International Law* (Cambridge: Cambridge University Press 2010): 287–9; Jukes, D., 'The Codex Alimentarius: Current Status' (available at: http://www.reading.ac.uk/foodlaw/codex-1.htm [accessed 15 October 2012], 1998); There are also rare instances where standards were adopted by majority voting. Yet, the customary practice remained adoption by consensus.

as the international food safety standard setter,[21] the CAC has become the quasi-legislative standard setter,[22] and its standards arguably de facto mandatory in WTO food safety disputes.[23] The CAC has experienced a paradigm shift and arguably become politicised under WTO influence,[24] as significant trade interests are usually at stake in the Codex standard-setting processes. Codex standards have a decisive impact on the market access of agricultural, animal and other food products.[25] This is evident in CAC meetings, where industry actors have been increasingly participating as the majority of observers or even as government delegates.[26] More and more frequently, the Codex is criticised as unable to safeguard global food

21 SPS Agreement Article 3.1 and Annex A.3. The SPS Agreement specifically refers to three international standard-setting bodies, now as the oft-called 'Three Sisters:' the Codex dealing with food safety, the International Plant Protection Convention (IPPC) dealing with plant health, the World Organization for Animal Health (OIE) dealing with animal health. SPS Agreement Article 3.2 provides that 'Sanitary or phytosanitary measures which conform to international standards, guidelines or recommendations shall be deemed to be necessary to protect human, animal or plant life or health, and presumed to be consistent with the relevant provisions of this Agreement and of GATT 1994.' WTO Members are encouraged to participate actively in the Three Sisters, which provide other forums for delivering technical assistance.

22 Trachtman, J.P., 'The world trading system, the international legal system and multilevel choice' (2006) 12 *European Law Journal*, 480.

23 Charnovitz, S., 'Triangulating the World Trade Organization' (2002) 96 *American Journal of International Law*, 51; Picciotto, S., 'Rights, responsibilities and regulation of international business' (2003) 42 *Columbia Journal of Transnational Law*, 146. Some may argue that after the WTO Appellate Body decision on the United States – Continued Suspension of Obligations in the EC – Hormones Dispute (WT/DS320/AB/R, 16 October, 2008), the Codex standards have become not mandatory (even de facto mandatory), as the Appellate Body has reaffirmed WTO members' right to deviate from international standard to a high extent. However, it remains unclear what impacts the US – Continued Suspension would project on the Codex standard setting process and the Codex's actual influence, considering the pre-emptive effects the Codex has, as well as the possible path dependence of CAC members.

24 Alemanno, A., *Trade in Food* (London: Cameron May 2007), 262–3; as put by Alemanno, the express reliance on the Codex standards, guidelines, and recommendations has 'an impact not only on their functioning but also on their nature'. As the Codex standards directly or indirectly play a role in the results of WTO dispute-settlement cases, 'WTO members have incentives to make sure that the new standards of the Codex, IPPC and OIE find inspiration in their current or future national SPS measures'.

25 Steward, T.P. and D.S. Johanson, 'The SPS Agreement of the World Trade Organization and international organizations: The roles of the Codex Alimentarius Commission, the International Plant Protection Convention and the International Office of Epizootics' (1998) 26 (1) *Journal of International Law and Commerce*, 27–54.

26 Smythe, E., 'In whose interests? Transparency and accountability in the global governance of food: Agribusiness, the Codex Alimentarius, and the World Trade Organization', in J. Clapp and D. Fuchs (eds), *Corporate Power in Global Agrifood Governance* (Cambridge: MIT Press, 93–123 2009), 95.

safety through an accountable, transparent and legitimate process.[27] The soundness and independence of scientific opinions as well as the level of transparency are particularly under fire but also of importance in order to secure legitimacy and accountability of the Codex decision-making process.[28] Although CAC member have endeavoured in a piecemeal manner to have more structured procedural rules for scientific and political decision-making, more effective reform projects for securing transparency, accountability and legitimacy is desired.

The EFSA and Its Roles in Global Food Safety Governance

The EFSA was established in January 2002 in accordance with Regulation (EC) No 178/2002, commonly referred to as the EU General Food Law.[29] As the keystone of the EU food safety regulatory system, the EFSA is designed to serve as an objective, independent scientific reference point and to 'provide scientific advice and scientific and technical support for the [EU] legislation and policies in all fields which have a direct or indirect impact on food and feed safety'.[30]

The EFSA operates as an independent agency separate from the EC, European Parliament, and EU Member States, and does not represent any government, organisation or sector. To bridge the EFSA and EU Member States for technical and information exchanges, its Advisory Forum serves as a platform to network national food safety authorities and to facilitate the pooling of scientific knowledge.

As a scientific reference point at the EU level, the EFSA's Scientific Committee and Panels stand at the heart of its normative sphere to provide the EC as well as EU Member States with scientific advice that they take into account when forming regulatory measures in areas such as food safety, animal health, and plant protection.[31] Through an open selection process on the basis of knowledge in risk assessment, experts with different scientific backgrounds are nominated and listed in the Scientific Panels. The EFSA's Scientific Panels operate in a

---

27 For a comprehensive analysis on the challenges and opportunities of the Codex, see Hüller and Maier 2006.

28 Pereira, R.A., 'Why would international administrative activity be any less legitimate? A study of the Codex Alimentarius Commission' (2008) 9(11) *German Law Journal*, 1693–1718; Livermore, M., 'Authority and Legitimacy in global governance: Deliberation, institutional differentiation, and the Codex Alimentarius' (2006) 81 *NYU Law Review*, 766–801.

29 European Union (EU) General Food Law, Regulation (EC) 178/2002 of 28 January 2002 laying down the general principles and requirements of food law, establishing the European Food Safety Authority and laying down procedures in matters of food safety [2002] OJ L31/1. For a comprehensive introduction to the EU General Food Law, see Alemanno 2007: 73–223, Van der Meulen, M. and B. Van der Velde., *European Food Law Handbook* (Netherlands: Wageningen Academic Publishers 2008).

30 EU General Food Law, Article 22.2.

31 Ibid., Articles 22 and 23.

horizontal fashion, that is, each Panel is responsible for risk assessment task on different areas in the food supply chain, including additives, biological hazards, contaminants, animal feed, dietetic products, genetically modified organisms (GMO), processing aids, plant protection products and many others. In all these areas of work, the EFSA Scientific Committee and Panels conduct risk assessment and deliver scientific opinions with the assistance of related working groups and networks for subsequent risk management decision-making.

Here I argue that the EFSA as a regime can engage in the structure and processes of global food safety governance not only at the political and technical levels, but also at the normative level. That is, more than the *participant* role of the EFSA regime in the Codex scientific and deliberative activities, I argue that the EFSA regime can further serve as a *benchmark* for evaluating the Codex activities, and a *model* of food safety governance for the edification of the Codex.

The EFSA as a Participant

The EFSA regime has recently been actively engaging in the greater Codex scientific activities in developing food safety standards, guidelines, codes of practice, and other instruments. For example, the EC requested the EFSA to provide opinions and comments on the methodologies used and pesticide MRLs for various substances recommended by the Joint FAO/WHO Meeting on Pesticide Residues (JMPR) for the 44th sessions of the Codex Committee on Pesticide Residues (CCPR) in 2012.[32] Moreover, in 2012 EFSA hosted a working group at the EFSA premises in Parma, Italy, and, with other CAC members and international organisations, jointly contribute to the work on the revision of the Codex principles for the establishment and application of microbiological criteria for food.[33] Since its establishment, EFSA experts have been frequently participating in Codex meetings and contributed in particular to the principles of risk analysis and on biotechnology.

In the ractopamine hydrochloride dispute, which has raised concerns over the scientific soundness and political legitimacy of the Codex decision-making process since 2008,[34] the EFSA is requested by the EC to move one step forward to challenge the risk assessment outcomes of the Joint FAO/WHO Expert Committee on Food Additives (JECFA) in the effort to influence and resolve the multi-year

---

32 EFSA, 'Scientific support for preparing an EU position in the 44th Session of the Codex Committee on Pesticide Residues (CCPR)' (2012) 10(7): 2859 *EFSA Journal*, 1–155.

33 EFSA, 'EFSA Welcomes Landmark Codex Working Group to Parma' [Online] (available at: http://www.efsa.europa.eu/en/events/event/120529.htm, accessed 15 October 2012).

34 Alemanno, A. and Capodieci G., 'Testing the limits of global food governance: The case of ractopamine' (2012) 3 *European Journal of Risk Regulation*, 400–12.

deadlock of the divided Codex. The EFSA reviewed the JECFA risk assessment findings and relevant scientific information with regard to the health risks of ractopamine.[35] This move can be seen as the EC's attempt to participate more actively not merely at the political level in CAC deliberations but also at the scientific level, where the EC might be better able to influence the JECFA's risk assessments.

More specifically, the Panel on Additives and Products or Substances used in Animal Feed (FEEDAP), one of the main scientific bodies comprising experts[36] external to the EFSA, is responsible for evaluating JECFA data and methodologies. Published in 2009, the extensive EFSA report on the scientific opinion of FEEDAP[37] found flaws and limitations in the JECFA's data and methodology regarding ractopamine's Acceptable Daily Intake (ADI) and received support from the Committee for Medicinal Products for Veterinary Use of the European Medicines Agency (EMA). In particular, the FEEDAP points out that the study cited by the JECFA on cardiovascular effects in humans does not merit the JECFA's suggested ADI of 0–1 micrograms per kilogram of body weight per day.[38] According to the report, the six-person sample size of the only human study is far from statistically sufficient to identify a clinically meaningful reaction. Insufficient scientific evidence and the resulting safety concerns, as emphasised by the EFSA report, rendered the JECFA's conclusion weak and disputable in terms of reference power. By relying on the EFSA's expert review, the EC declined to vote in favour of and adopt the international food safety standard for ractopamine.[39]

The EFSA as a Benchmark

Apart from participating at the political and scientific levels, the EFSA regime can serve as a benchmark for evaluating the greater Codex governance structure and processes. It should be noted at the outset that the CAC and the EFSA as an

35 EFSA, 'Scientific opinion of the Panel on Additives and Products or Substances Used in Animal Feed (FEEDAP) on a request from the European Commission on the safety evaluation of ractopamine' (2009) 1041 *EFSA Journal*, 1–52.

36 EFSA external experts are selected through an open call for expression of interest and an open and transparent selection procedure which involves an evaluation of candidates by an internal EFSA team with the process being ultimately reviewed by external evaluators. The experts are appointed by the Management Board based on proposals from the Executive Director. See EFSA, Expert Database [Online].

37 EFSA, 'Scientific opinion of the Panel on Additives and Products or Substances Used in Animal Feed (FEEDAP) on a request from the European Commission on the safety evaluation of ractopamine' (2009) 1041 *EFSA Journal*, 1–52.

38 Ibid.; WHO, 'Evaluation of Certain Veterinary Drug Residues in Food: 62nd Report of the JECFA' (2004) WHO Technical Report Series 925.

39 Alemanno and Capodieci, 'Testing the limits of global food governance: The case of ractopamine'.

agency of the EU are fundamentally different, as the former is a risk management body and the latter risk assessment (and communication) body. The CAC and its committees are not responsible for risk assessment at the international level. The JECFA and other scientific expert groups linked to the CAC, as international independent scientific expert bodies jointly administered by FAO and WHO,[40] review scientific data and perform risk assessments for the CAC. For JECFA, the experts are invited for individual meetings, depending on the subjects, agendas and tasks at hand. The EFSA as an agency, by contrast, is in charge of risk assessment and risk communication at the EU level. The EFSA's mandate does not cover risk management, which falls within the authority of the EC and EU Member States. However, from the perspective of global food safety lawmaking, the EFSA regime and Codex regimes seem fully comparable as risk regulation regimes. Actually, the EFSA risk regulation regime resembles the Codex risk regulation regime, insofar as the two systems undertake food safety regulation at the international level. In the following, I point out some essential similarities that are in place between the Codex and the EFSA regime, and that merit our taking the EFSA regime as a benchmark.

First, the EFSA regime operates in a multi-level structure of governance,[41] as does the Codex. Both the EFSA regime and the Codex are spheres of rulemaking in a broad sense, producing international standards that are further implemented through domestic law and regulation by their Members. In the EFSA regime, the EFSA conducts risk assessment and provides scientific advice to the Member States. In theory and, in the vast majority of the cases in practice, the EU and Member States follow the EFSA's advice to form their risk management measures.[42] The Codex regime, as well, uses its Expert Bodies (like the JECFA) to conduct risk assessment, based upon which Codex Committees would suggest risk management recommendations to be adopted by CAC Members as international standards. CAC members, WTO members, and other international entities further internalise such international standards. The relationship between the EFSA and EU Member States as well as the relationship between the Codex and WTO members are multi-level and, therefore, involve possible problems of delegation, accountability, and legitimacy.

40 The JECFA, the Joint FAO/WHO Meeting on Pesticide Residues (JMPR), and the Joint FAO/WHO Expert Meetings on Microbiological Risk Assessment (JEMRA) provide risk assessments for different areas to the Codex Alimentarius Commission. Here, as I use the JECFA often as an example in the discussion on the Codex, I refer to the JECFA in cases which also apply to the JMPR and the JEMRA for convenience.

41 See generally Abels G. and Kobusch A., 'Regulation of food safety in the EU: Changing patterns of multi-level governance' (Conference of the ECPR Standing Group on Regulatory Governance, 2010).

42 For an in-depth discussion on the legal status of the EFSA's scientific opinions and the interactions between the EFSA and the Commission, see Alemanno, A., 'The European Food Safety Authority at five' (2008) 1 *European Food and Feed Law Review*, 12–23.

Second, both the EFSA regime and the Codex are highly technical, specialised, scientific institutions in charge of generating professional knowledge and data, which receive default respect from members of their respective groups. Lacking adequate financial and technical capacities to assess various health risks on their own, the two organisations rely greatly on external technical and scientific expertise in different highly specialised fields (such as toxicology and microbiology) accessed on either a regular roster or an ad hoc basis. Consequently, scientific excellence (soundness of scientific evidence), transparency, and independence (avoidance of conflicts of interest) are of high importance to secure legitimacy.

Third, the activities of the EFSA regime and the Codex affect not only public health but also international trade. Therefore, trade interests of various actors, such as multinational food corporations and countries with strong agricultural sectors, may enter into the rulemaking processes. As such interests would translate into political influence, both the EFSA regime and the Codex can experience problems with the politicisation of science. To avoid the politicisation of science, the two organisations follow a structured decision-making process and a separation of risk assessment and risk management by means of institutional design.[43] That is, scientific advisory bodies responsible for risk assessments are organisationally or functionally separated from the decision-making (often political) body in charge of risk management. For the Codex case, the Joint FAO/WHO expert committees which provide scientific risk assessments for the Codex standard-setting process, are not formally part of the CAC.[44]

The EFSA as a Model

Albeit with some criticism, the EFSA regime is usually viewed as a good example of a quality food safety agency – the design of its structure and the execution of its processes are adequate in terms of producing accountability, legitimacy, and transparency, among other important outcomes.[45] Bearing in mind the similarities between the EFSA and the Codex regimes, I hereby use the EFSA regime as a constructive model of good governance from which the Codex can learn in its future reforms if so desired. In the following I identify two key institutional designs that are of great relevance and importance for the future Codex reforms to take into account. The two institutional design models are the EFSA regime's mechanisms for ensuring the independence of scientific advice and requirements to foster transparency and openness.

43 It should also be noted that neither of both rely on its own labs or conduct its own scientific studies, but merely work on existing data and studies.

44 EFSA Management Board, 'Comparison between the Tools Ensuring EFSA's Independent Scientific Advice and the Instruments in Use by Organisations Similar to EFSA' (Revised Final Report, EFSA January 2011).

45 EFSA, 'External Evaluation of EFSA Final Report' (Parma, EFSA 2012a).

Mechanisms for Ensuring the Independence of Scientific Advice

As mentioned, global food safety lawmaking, especially the work of the Codex and the EFSA regime, relies greatly on technical and scientific expertise from different highly specialised fields. As both the EFSA regime and the Codex do not have adequate financial and technical capacities to assess various health risks on their own, they use scientific bodies comprised of external experts for their risk assessment mandates. External scientists from various backgrounds come to investigate scientific data, deliberate on risk issues, and finally develop scientific opinions to inform regulatory decision-making, so the platform they convene must be designed to ensure the excellence and independence of scientific advice.[46]

The JECFA and other Joint FAO/WHO expert committees, while not organisationally part of the CAC, provide scientific advice as requested by the CAC. Following a call-for-experts announcement, scientist candidates are considered by a selection board and appointed as members of the joint expert committees.[47] If appointed, member experts are placed on a roster for a five-year term and are called upon to address specific subject matters related to their expertise.[48] In terms of excellence of scientific advice, the selection board is required to consider the scientific credentials of all the candidates 'with the highest level of expertise and as impartial and objective in their judgment'.[49] As for independence, experts are appointed according to their individual scientific

---

46 EFSA Management Board, 'Comparison Between the Tools Ensuring EFSA's Independent Scientific Advice and the Instruments in Use by Organisations Similar to EFSA' (Revised Final Report, EFSA January 2011), 28–9.

47 'FAO and WHO have complementary functions in selecting experts to serve on the Committee. FAO is responsible for selecting members with chemical expertise for the development of specifications for the identity and purity of food additives, for the assessment of residue levels of veterinary drugs in food, and to assess the quality of the monitoring data. WHO is responsible for selecting members for the toxicological evaluations of the substances under consideration, in order to establish acceptable daily intakes (ADIs), or other relevant guidance values, or to give a quantitative estimate of the health risk. Both FAO and WHO invite members who are responsible for assessing exposure.' WHO (World Health Organization), 'About the Joint FAO/WHO Expert Committee on Food Additives (JECFA)' (available at http://www.who.int/foodsafety/chem/jecfa/about/en/index3.html [accessed 15 October 2012]).

48 Ibid.

49 As expressed in the FAO/WHO call-for-experts announcements, '[i]n selecting experts FAO and WHO will consider, in addition to scientific and technical excellence, diversity and complementarities of scientific backgrounds, and balanced representation from geographic regions including developing and developed countries as well as gender'. See e.g. FAO/WHO. 'Joint FAO/WHO Expert Meeting on Risk Assessment Tools for Vibrio Parahaemolyticus and Vibrio Vulnificus Associated with Seafoods, Call for Data and Experts' (available at http://www.fao.org/fileadmin/templates/agns/pdf/jemra/Call-data – Experts-VibrioF9Dec2009.pdf [accessed 15 October 2012] 2010).

capacity and not as agents of a government or an institution.[50] Experts of the joint expert committees are required to submit an initial declaration of any real or potential conflicts of interest that may unjustifiably influence their position. If a conflict of interest exists, the declaring expert will not be selected. However, because the information regarding the declaration of interests is in general not disclosed, the mechanism to prevent conflicts of interest relies on the experts' voluntary affirmation.[51]

The EFSA regime's mechanism for ensuring the independence of scientific advice (through avoiding conflicts of interest in particular) can serve as a good example for the Codex. The EFSA has a much stricter and nuanced design for conflict-of-interest declarations, stemming from the organisation's adoption of the *Decision of the Executive Director implementing EFSA's Policy on Independence and Scientific Decision-Making Processes regarding Declarations of Interests*.[52] The Decision lays down general principles and detailed rules for identifying declarable interests, assessing declared interests, screening experts, reviewing decisions, handling breaches of rules, and so on. The Decision gives a broad definition of 'conflict of interest', which means 'a situation when an individual is in a position to exploit his or her own professional or official capacity in some way for personal or corporate benefit with regard to that person's function in the context of his or her cooperation with EFSA'.[53] It further categorises the declaration-of-interest requirements into annual written declarations of interest,[54] specific written declarations of interest,[55] and oral declarations of interest, which shall be declared at three different temporal points.[56] These rules cover a wide range of positions within and even outside the EFSA organisation, including Executive Director, Management Board Members, Advisory Board Members, Scientific Committee Members, Scientific Panels, working groups, other EFSA staff, and other external experts and consultants. Moreover, rather than rely on voluntary declarations, the EFSA must systematically and regularly examine individuals' compliance with declarations of interest and seek additional information if any is missing.[57] Omissions in disclosures of declarable interests result in breaches of rules, and concerned parties are dismissed from duty.[58] Most important, in breach-

50 Ibid.

51 EFSA Management Board, 'Comparison between the Tools Ensuring EFSA's Independent Scientific Advice and the Instruments in Use by Organisations Similar to EFSA' (Revised Final Report, EFSA January 2011), 14.

52 For full text of the Decision, see EFSA, 'Decision of the Executive Director implementing EFSA's Policy on Independence and Scientific Decision-Making Processes regarding Declarations of Interests' (2012/05/LRA, EFSA 2012).

53 Ibid., Article 1.3.b.

54 Ibid., Articles 1.3.c, 3, and 6.

55 Ibid., Articles 1.3.d, 4, and 7.

56 Ibid., Articles 1.3.e, 5, and 8.

57 Ibid., Articles 14.1 and 14.2.

58 Ibid., Article 15.

of-rule cases, the Executive Director of the EFSA can request a review of any scientific opinions adopted by the scientific body in which the concerned expert participated.[59]

Compared to the Codex regime's loose mechanism for ensuring the independence of scientific decision-making, the EFSA regime's new set of rules, through the avoidance of conflicts of interest, seems better able to foster technocratic legitimacy and facilitate subsequent cooperation. In technical bodies like the EFSA regime and the Codex, declaration-of-interest rules play a crucial role in expert-nominating and decision-making processes, and the EFSA regime's institutional design, though not flawless according to certain critics,[60] can certainly serve as a good example for future Codex reform.[61]

Requirements to Foster Transparency and Openness

The transparency of decision-making processes is a crucial element in promoting the accountability of decision-makers, in securing the soundness of scientific deliberation, and in informing interested parties of important facts.[62] In this regard, although stakeholders are not allowed to participate in the development of scientific advice, the CAC ensures that they have access to meeting minutes (not word-for-word records), scientific reports, risk assessments, safety evaluations and other information. As for meetings of such expert groups as the JECFA, the WHO and FAO websites publish electronic summaries of both key data used and conclusions reached. Dissenting scientific opinions are recorded in the published reports.

The EFSA regime's mechanism for facilitating transparency goes beyond the Codex practice. In line with its core principle of transparency and openness, the EFSA is required to publish details of its expert-selection processes and of expert declarations of interest. With regard to the Scientific Committee and the Scientific Panels, the EFSA shall 'make public without delay', inter alia, the following matters:[63]

---

59 Ibid., Article 15.4.

60 See e.g. Corporate Europe Observatory, 'Conflicts of Interest still Evident on New ESFA Expert Panels' (available at http://www.corporateeurope.org/pressreleases/2012/conflicts-interest-still-evident-new-esfa-expert-panels, accessed 15 October 2012).

61 A further issue associated with the discussion here concerns the implications of the use of independent/biased scientific expertise at the WTO dispute settlement system. However, this is beyond the scope of study of this chapter and cannot be addressed in any in-depth manner here.

62 Kingsbury, B., N. Krisch and R.B. Stewart, 'The emergence of global administrative law' (2005) 68 *Law and Contemporary Problems*, 15–61. See also Winickoff, D.E. and D.M. Bushey, 'Science and power in global food regulation: The rise of the codex Alimentarius' (2010) 35 *Science Technology Human Values*, 356–81.

63 EU General Food Law, Article 38.1.

(a) agendas and minutes of the Scientific Committee and the Scientific Panels;
(b) the opinions of the Scientific Committee and the Scientific Panels immediately after adoption, minority opinions always being included;
(c) without prejudice to Articles 39 and 41, the information on which its opinions are based;
(d) the annual declarations of interest made by members of the Management Board, the Executive Director, members of the Advisory Forum and members of the Scientific Committee and Scientific Panels, as well as the declarations of interest made in relation to items on the agendas of meetings;
(e) the results of its scientific studies;
(f) the annual report of its activities;
(g) requests from the European Parliament, the Commission or a Member State for scientific opinions which have been refused or modified and the justifications for the refusal or modification.

Furthermore, meetings of the Management Board shall be held in public in most cases.[64] In 2012, the EFSA regime went beyond the requirement of EU General Food Law by putting in place a programme that allows observer participation in the meetings of EFSA Scientific Committee and Scientific Panels.[65] The EFSA shall also ensure comprehensive access to the documents and information it keeps.[66] Finally, in line with its risk communication mandate, the EFSA is required to develop effective contacts with interested parties and *proactively* circulate scientific reports, risk assessment data, and other information tailored to satisfy the needs of different stakeholders, including those from consumer NGOs and industry.[67] In short, the EFSA rules seem more comprehensive and able to foster a higher level of transparency and openness in the scientific decision-making process than those of the Codex. As the Codex has been criticised for insufficient transparency and weak accountability, the EFSA example can shed some light on the design and implementation of the Codex transparency mechanism.

Conclusion: Beyond the EFSA Model

The proliferating food safety regulatory initiatives at domestic, international and transnational levels by various actors with different perspectives have raised concerns for their important public health, international trade and other implications. Standing as the hub of global food safety lawmaking, the Codex faces serious criticisms of its scientific soundness, legitimacy, transparency

64 Ibid., Article 38.2.

65 EFSA, 'Guidelines for Observers' (available at http://www.efsa.europa.eu/en/stakeholders/docs/observersguidelines.pdf, accessed 15 October 2012).

66 EU General Food Law, Article 41.

67 Ibid., Article 42.

and accountability. Although the CAC members have initiated several reform projects (such as amending the Codex Rules of Procedure and setting guidelines and principles for risk analysis) so that the Codex now has more structured procedural rules governing scientific and political decision-making, the Codex has yet to actively step out and look for models of good governance. Likewise, in link with the technical cooperation or normative dialogue with other scientific networks, the Codex channel seems rather one-way, passive and narrow. For example, in the ractopamine dispute, when the EU submitted the EFSA opinion to the JECFA, the JECFA Secretariat stated at the Codex 34th Session Assembly that the JECFA was rejecting the EFSA opinion because the 'EFSA had not undertaken a risk assessment by considering the original raw data, but had undertaken a review of the JECFA assessment based on the published JECFA evaluation'.[68]

As already noted, there seems to be no meta-framework that, either in place or under development, would dictate the crafting of diverse food safety norms in a coordinated manner. Active spheres in the evolving global food safety governance complex are *separately* in search of optimal approaches to better governance. Yet many initiatives, such the EFSA regime discussed in this chapter, indeed offer the Codex some exemplary values that it could take into account while putting together an effective and proactive platform for facilitating technical cooperation and normative dialogue.

Global food safety lawmaking is an ongoing process of experiments – both in a scientific and regulatory fashion. The limits of science and the limits of global food safety regulation should be seriously appreciated. The Codex should play the 'hub' role in actively building scientific networks that address specific issues through the coordination of activities, the exchange of information, the development and implementation of joint projects, and the exchange of expertise and best practices. When a scientific and regulatory network of cooperation comes into play, the Codex can undergo a reconfiguration into a constructive forum with mutually reinforcing participants. This forum would facilitate cross-sector collaboration, technical exchange and data sharing that strengthen global food safety governance.

68 FAO/WHO. 'Joint FAO/WHO Expert Meeting on Dietary Exposure Assessment Methodologies for Residues of Veterinary Drugs, Draft Report (including Report of Stakeholder Meeting' (FAO/WHO: Rome, available at: http://www.who.int/foodsafety/chem/jecfa/FAO-WHO_exposure_report_for_public_review_3_feb_2012.pdf [accessed 15 October 2012] 2011b).

Index

For Product Safety Concerns and Information please contact our EU representative GPSR@taylorandfrancis.com
Taylor & Francis Verlag GmbH, Kaufingerstraße 24, 80331 München, Germany

www.ingramcontent.com/pod-product-compliance
Ingram Content Group UK Ltd.
Pitfield, Milton Keynes, MK11 3LW, UK
UKHW020022200926
475702UK00014B/2018

* 9 7 8 1 1 3 8 2 7 0 0 2 2 *